Ezra Michener

A Retrospect of Early Quakerism

Being Extracts From the Records of Philadelphia Yearly Meeting and the...

Ezra Michener

A Retrospect of Early Quakerism
Being Extracts From the Records of Philadelphia Yearly Meeting and the...

ISBN/EAN: 9783337008406

Printed in Europe, USA, Canada, Australia, Japan

Cover: Foto ©ninafisch / pixelio.de

More available books at **www.hansebooks.com**

BURG HOUSE & SCHOOL

A

RETROSPECT

OF

EARLY QUAKERISM;

BEING EXTRACTS FROM THE RECORDS

OF

PHILADELPHIA YEARLY MEETING

AND THE

MEETINGS COMPOSING IT.

TO WHICH IS PREFIXED

AN ACCOUNT OF THEIR FIRST ESTABLISHMENT.

By EZRA MICHENER.

PHILADELPHIA:
PUBLISHED BY T. ELLWOOD ZELL.
1860.

PREFACE.

It is often difficult for a writer correctly to appreciate his own labors. Hence, whatever object he may have in view, in prefixing a Preface to his book, the effect often is to exhibit the vanities of authorship, by predicating a character for the work which his readers will not be able to realize. I hope to avoid doing this.

The task may be difficult and the performance rare, but a well-written autobiography is perhaps the most interesting and instructive history which we can have of a man. While it describes his actions, and delineates his character with a precision to which other pens could not attain, it correctly informs us of the motives which prompted the one, and the circumstances which formed the other. The same is true of any number of men, considered in their collective capacity. None can so certainly know their performances, none so clearly comprehend their motives, none so fully appreciate their true character, its lights and shadows, as themselves. The following work is founded upon this assumption.

The system of order and church government established by George Fox, his coadjutors and successors, is believed to be more in accordance with the principles and practices of primitive Christianity, as inculcated and practised by its Divine Author, than anything which the world has witnessed since the apostolic age. And it is due to the memory of that extraordinary man to acknowledge, that almost every feature of the system is more or less clearly foreshadowed in his writings. A writer in the *Annual Review* says of him : "There is no character in Christian history, since the days of its Divine Founder, more free from spot or stain, than that of George Fox. It is not less absurd to call him insane from his writings, than it would be to call Cromwell a fool from his speeches. No form of civil polity so unexceptionable in its means and ends, so beautiful in all its parts, so perfect as a whole, has ever been imagined in philosophical romance, or proposed in theory, as this man conceived, established, and reduced to practice."

But the pathway thus opened for the humble Christian traveller was found too narrow; the self-denial which it required too great; the cross which had to be borne was too heavy for a corrupt and mercenary priesthood, or a profligate and licentious laity to walk in. It was easier for them to revile Friends, and to vilify them by opprobrious epithets ; to denounce them as insane impostors and fanatical innovators ; to condemn their doctrines as false and heretical, and to persecute those honest men who conscientiously maintained them, than to imitate their pious and godly example. The seal of condemnation has been set upon that persecuting spirit, and a more dispassionate inquiry after Truth is leading the public mind more and more from under the dictation of those, who make merchandise of the free Gospel of Jesus Christ. It is gratifying to observe, that the fundamental doctrine of the Christian faith,—the indwelling presence of Christ, and His immediate revelation in the soul,—is now much more generally acknowledged than it was two centuries ago, and will hardly be denied by those who seriously examine the subject. The recorded wisdom and deep religious experience of George Fox will yet continue to stand a beacon-light to enlighten the path of the Zion-ward traveller long after his traducers shall have sunk into oblivion ; for it will ever remain to be a truth, that "The path of the just is as the shining light, that shineth more and more unto the perfect day."

THE OBJECT AND THE PLAN.

As the domestic management of the kitchen affords the best index to that of the entire household, so the primary arrangements and internal economy of a religious organization, furnish the most reliable data with which to construct its history; and though it may sometimes appear dressed in homespun, yet it wears the garb of simplicity and truth.

Keeping this sentiment constantly in view, I have endeavored to make such selections from the earlier advices and disciplinary regulations of the Yearly Meeting of Philadelphia, as will pretty fully illustrate the principles and discipline upon which its system of Church Government is founded, having reference to the fundamental doctrine already mentioned. In order to exhibit the practical working of this system, in an extended application to the various states and conditions of the members, I have copied largely from the records of the executive branches of the Society,—Monthly and Quarterly Meetings.

As Friends do not consider a high order of educational attainments an essential qualification for station in religious society, many of the records will be found ungrammatical, yet they are mostly plenary and significant of their intended purpose. Wherever it could be obtained, I have preserved the exact phraseology of the records with quotation marks, correcting only the orthography, and sometimes omitting irrelevant parts for the sake of brevity, where it could be done without impairing the sense. Each extract is intended to illustrate some social relation, to explain some important principle, or to establish some disciplinary rule.

Prefixed to the work will be found an historical account of the first establishment of the Yearly Meeting and its constituent branches, as far as they have been obtained. In this portion of the work I have been necessarily restricted to those meetings which are, or have been, kept up by that portion of Society to which I belong. Had it been practicable, I would gladly have embraced both.

While I have to regret that some Friends whose positions were favorable, could not be induced to lend a helping hand in collecting materials for the work, thereby leaving blanks, or allowing them to be filled with less important matter, I must acknowledge my obligations to many kind Friends, by whose care and assistance I have been greatly aided in my labors. Among these are some who are not in religious fellowship with me,—to whom I feel indebted for their urbanity and disinterested friendship.

It would be disingenuous to conceal the fact, that an unhappy division has taken place in our once united and peaceful Society, each portion claiming to be Friends. With the controversy growing out of that event I have nothing to do. The work here offered, with the exception just mentioned, has reference to the Society of Friends in its integrity. Whatever it may contain which is interesting to one portion must be equally so to the other.

Should the object be properly appreciated, I cherish the hope, humble as the book is, that it may serve as a nucleus around which the perishable and perishing materials of our social history will continue to gather, till it shall be made as perfect as the nature of the case will permit.

EZRA MICHENER.

NEW GARDEN, Chester Co., Penna.,
  Third month, 1860.

NOTE TO THE READER.

FROM the novelty of the design and the many hands necessarily employed in collecting materials for this work, it must be expected that errors, omissions, and redundancies will be found in its pages. Nor is the theme exhausted. Much valuable matter can yet be gleaned from the records of our Society which may be profitably incorporated into a future edition. Friends who have access to such records will now be able to judge of its imperfections, and better prepared to make selections for its subsequent improvement. Those so circumstanced are especially invited to collect and forward any such documents to the address of the writer, in order that they may be carefully preserved and arranged for use, as occasion may require.

EZRA MICHENER.

EXPLANATION.

To render the situation of the meetings more intelligible, I have given a diagram of the Quarterly Meetings constituting the Yearly Meeting, and also of the meetings composing each Quarterly Meeting, in which—

○ *a.* denotes a Meeting for Worship or Preparative Meeting.

◐ *b.* where a Monthly Meeting is held.

◎ *c.* where a Quarterly Meeting is held.

⊕ *d.* where a former meeting has been discontinued.

The places where a Quarterly Meeting is held are united by dotted lines. The several meetings composing each Monthly Meeting are connected by black lines.

The relative position and distances are necessarily only approximative; but they are sufficiently accurate, with the aid of the scale, to serve as a general guide to strangers.

I have followed the chronological arrangement of the meetings, that is, meetings of the same class. Thus, I begin with the oldest Quarter within the Yearly Meeting; the oldest Monthly in each Quarter, and the oldest Meeting for Worship in each Monthly. Hence, it will happen, that the dates of the constituent Meetings are generally older than that of the preceding meeting which they constitute.

The same order, according to dates, is observed in the distribution of the extracts under each particular head.

In conclusion, it is necessary to observe, that my friend, William Embree, who was united with me in the circular issued about the beginning of last year, has been, unhappily, prevented by increasing bodily infirmity, from actively engaging in the work; and has consequently been induced to withdraw his name, though still laboring as his strength permits.

CONTENTS.

SETTLEMENT OF MEETINGS.

RETROSPECT OF EARLY QUAKERISM.

APPENDIX.

LIST OF ILLUSTRATIONS.

what follows has a specific reference to a History of the Settlement of Friends' Meetings.

1752.—"That the clerk of this meeting, and those of the several monthly meetings, should send an account of the settlement of all the meetings in the county, to the clerk of the Yearly Meeting before the spring meeting."—(Bucks Quarterly Meeting.)

1753.—"William Trimble reports, he has made all the search necessary, respecting the first settlement of this meeting and the particular meetings thereunto belonging; and drawn out the same. This meeting orders it sent according to the directions of the Yearly Meeting."—(Concord Monthly Meeting.)

This is the latest notice I have seen of this concern till a minute of inquiry was forwarded to the Yearly Meeting from Bucks Quarter, in 1770, stating :—

1770.—"That as the Yearly Meeting had proposed the publishing the History of the Settlement of Friends in this Province; and, as many Friends have taken much pains in collecting materials for that purpose, whether it might not be proper to inquire of the Yearly Meeting, what is become of that matter; or, whether we are ever to see the work perfected?"—(Bucks Quarterly Meeting.)

The answer was: "The proposal concerning the first settlement of Friends, was recommended to the Friends who have the oversight of the press, and the Meeting for Sufferings ; to make inquiry into the circumstances of that matter ; and give their assistance towards forwarding the work."—(See Friends' Miscellany, vii, 98.)

1773.—"This meeting received the following minute from the Meeting for Sufferings, viz. :—

" ' As the accounts which have been handed to our friend, Samuel Smith, respecting the settlement of Meetings in this province, have not been so fully correct as is desired, the Clerk is directed to notify each Quarterly Meeting, that it is the desire of this meeting, that suitable Friends may be appointed in each Monthly Meeting, to make out as clear and exact accounts as may be, and transmit them as soon as they well can to their Quarterly Meeting, and thence to this meeting; that when the History is published, it may be as free from errors and mistakes as possible.'—Extracted by John Pemberton.

" And a copy of this minute being prepared for each Monthly Meeting, they are forwarded by the representatives, desiring that Friends in each Monthly Meeting may take the proper care therein, and if possible, send their accounts to our next Quarter.

" And this meeting, understanding that Chester Quarterly Meeting hath appointed some Friends to take this matter under consideration, and also search the records of that Quarter, or any other Meeting as they shall think proper, in order to obtain the first settlement of their Meetings; this meeting also appoints Thomas Carlton, William Swayne, John Churchman, James Moore, Thomas Buller, and Isaac Jackson, to join the said Friends in the service, on this meeting's behalf; as the settlement of most of the meetings belonging to this quarter, is in the records of Chester Quarterly Meeting."

" John Churchman, on behalf of the Committee, ... reported, that care has been taken therein, and that a list of the first settlement of meetings within the verge of this Quarter, is ready to be transcribed, and forwarded to the Meeting for Sufferings."—(Western Quarterly Meeting.)

1773.—" A copy of a minute from the Meeting for Sufferings was produced, requesting that the time of the first settlement of meetings may be collected. Therefore, Isaac Evans and John Lippincott are appointed to collect an account, as near as may be, of the first settlement of the meetings at Evesham and Chester, and report to next meeting."—(Evesham Monthly Meeting.)

1773.—" At a Monthly Meeting held at Richland, 4th month 15th, 1773,

" The Friends appointed by last meeting, to draw up an account of the first settlement of our meeting, to be transmitted to the next Quarterly Meeting, have performed the service as follows :—

"The first settlement of Friends in this place was about the year 1710, by our ancient friend, Peter Lester, from Leicestershire in England, who, with his wife and children, and other families, became members of Gwynedd Monthly Meeting, and a meeting for worship was, with the concurrence of that Monthly Meeting, held at the said Peter Lester's house for several years. Friends lived in amicable intercourse with the Indian natives, who at that time were numerous in these parts, and often helpful to the new settlers, in furnishing them with necessary provisions, which is gratefully remembered by some yet living among us. About the year 1723, a small meeting-house was built, and a preparative meeting then held, by the assent of the said Monthly Meeting. And Friends continuing to increase in number, by the youth growing up, and the accession of several families of Friends from other places, it became necessary, in the year 1730, to build a new meeting-house, which was done on a commodious lot of ground near the centre of the settlement. And our said meeting, through the blessing of Divine Providence, both spiritually and temporally bestowed, still continued to increase in strength and numbers, until the year 1742, when Friends thought it expedient to make application to the Quarterly Meeting, held at Philadelphia, the 1st of 9th month, 1742, to have a Monthly Meeting erected among themselves, which was granted them, to be held the third fifth day of the week in each month, and called Richland Monthly Meeting, which from that time has continued, and Friends here have since made considerable additions to their meeting-house, to accommodate the meeting.

"The above account being approved by the meeting, was signed by order and on behalf thereof, by

"SAMUEL FOULKE, *Clerk.*"

The result of the concern of the Yearly Meeting is embraced in the XXth Chapter of Samuel Smith's "Manuscript History of Pennsylvania," now in possession of the Pennsylvania His-

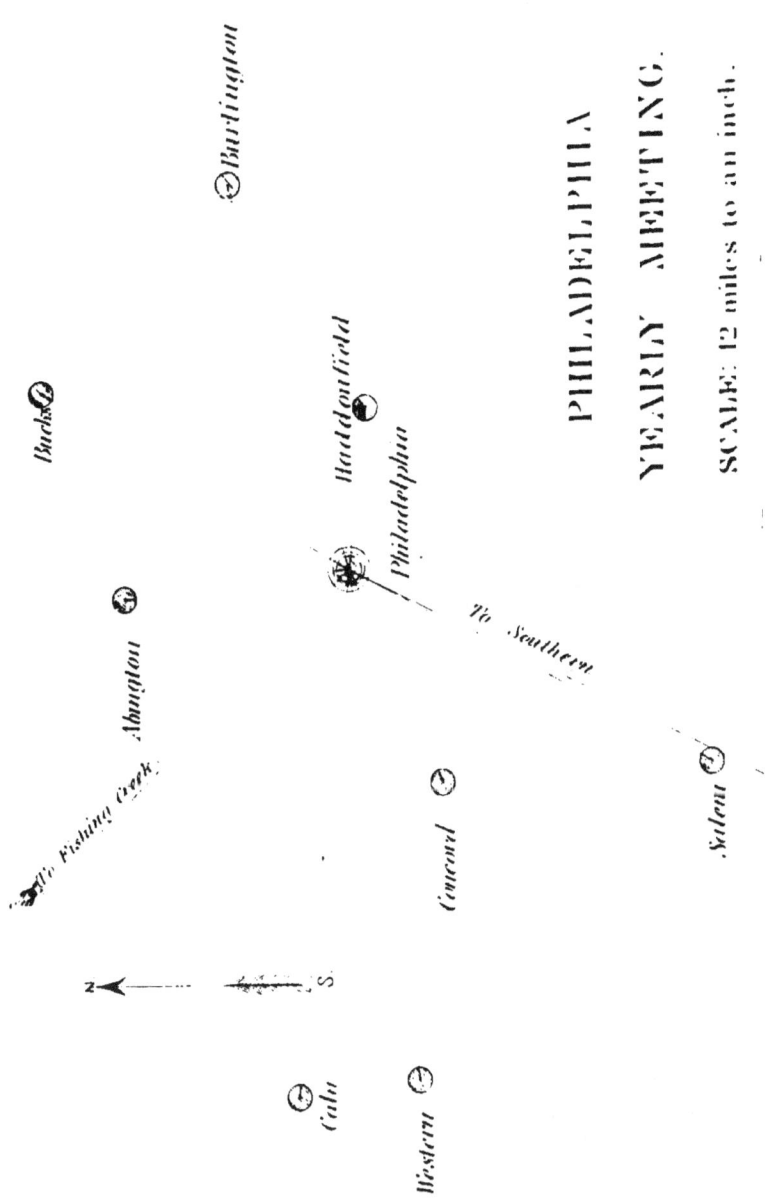

PHILADELPHIA YEARLY MEETING.

SCALE: 12 miles to an inch.

torical Society, and which may be found in the seventh volume of "Hazard's Weekly Register." The reader will perceive that I have endeavored to amplify and extend that history, by furnishing additional and more ample authentic records, where they could be obtained.

CHAPTER I.

YEARLY MEETING.

In the early settling of the American Colonies, Friends paid little regard to what would now be considered a regular order of procedure, in the establishment of meetings. They were a practical people. They soon discovered their most pressing wants, and sought the most direct means to supply them. After the establishment of meetings for worship, which were generally held at each other's houses, Monthly Meetings became their greatest need, for the right ordering of marriages, receiving and granting certificates, &c., and they were next supplied. Quarterly Meetings, as we shall see, were then less essential; every third Monthly Meeting, being called a Quarterly Meeting, without perceptibly changing either its authority, or the character of the business which it transacted. It was only as Friends became numerous, and widely diffused, that Yearly Meetings were required, to embody the principles and practices of the Society; thereby to establish a uniform order and discipline, and maintain right authority in the Church. Prior to which time, Quarterly and even Monthly Meetings, issued their advisory rules, which were deemed authoritative by the members.

1681.—"At the Monthly Meeting at Burlington, the 2d of the third month, 1681, it was unanimously agreed, that a

General Meeting be yearly held in Burlington, the first of which, to be the 28th of sixth month, 1681."—(Burlington Monthly Meeting.)

1681.—" At a General Meeting, held in Burlington, the last day of the sixth month, 1681, at the house of Thomas Gardner, it was then mutually agreed that a Women's Meeting should be established."—(Burlington Monthly Meeting.)

" But it is asked (says William Penn, in his Just Measures), why should women meet apart? We think for a very good reason. The church increaseth, which increaseth the business of the church, and women, whose bashfulness will not permit them to say or do much, as to church affairs, before the men, when by themselves, may exercise their gift of wisdom and understanding, in a discreet care of their own sex, at least, which makes up not the least part of the business of the Church; and this, while the men are upon their own proper business, also, so that, as men and women make up the Church, men and women make up the business of the Church."

The Yearly Meeting, held in Burlington, in 1683, was greatly augmented, by the attendance of William Penn, and his companions, who had recently arrived in Pennsylvania. That Meeting has left the following record :—

1683.—" Whereas, this meeting judged it requisite for the benefit and advantage of Truth, and mutual comfort of Friends, that a General Yearly Meeting might be established, for the provinces in these parts; northward, as far as New England, and southward, as far as Carolina; that by the coming of Friends together, from the several parts where Truth is professed, the affairs thereof, may be the better known and understood. And to the end, that the same may be assented to, by Friends in those parts, and places above mentioned, it is agreed that William Penn, Christopher Taylor, Samuel Jennings, James Harrison, Thomas Olive, and Mahlon Stacy, do take sure methods, by writing to Friends, or speaking, as may best fall out for their conveniency, in order to have the same established."—(Yearly Meeting.)

I think the master spirit of William Penn is visible in this transaction; and, although not expressly so recorded, it is probable that Philadelphia was the intended place for holding the General Yearly Meeting; for, only one month after the above Yearly Meeting in Burlington, another was held in Philadelphia.

In 1684, the two Yearly Meetings were again held in Burlington and Philadelphia. The latter was attended by appointments from Rhode Island, and from the Quarterly Meetings of Herring Creek and Choptank, in Maryland. In an epistle from that meeting to Friends in England they say: "We are to send an epistle to Carolina, Virginia, Maryland, and all there away; also the other way, to New England and Rhode Island, that it may be presented to them, if possible, from these remote provinces, they may send two or three from each province to our Yearly Meeting here, being as a centre or middle place, that so communion and blessed union may be preserved among all." The same epistle continues: "At the two aforementioned General Meetings, we had such a blessed harmony together that we may say that we know not that there was a jarring string among us. A great multitude came, of many hundreds, and the Gospel bell made a most glorious sound. There was the men's and women's meetings at both places, in their precious service, to inspect into Truth's matters in what related to them; and God gave them wisdom to do it, and all was unanimous."

In 1685, the two Yearly Meetings for the Provinces of New Jersey and Pennsylvania, were once more held. But the subject having been duly considered in both these meetings, it was,

1685.—"Unanimously agreed and concluded by this meeting (in Philadelphia), that there be but one Yearly and General Meeting in Pennsylvania and West Jersey—one year at Burlington, and another at Philadelphia—and to be held the next year at Burlington on the first first day in the seventh month for worship, and the fourth day to be the men's and women's meetings. The next year after to be at Philadelphia, on the same day of the same month, and to continue the same time."— (Yearly Meeting.)

It does not appear that the proposition for holding a General Yearly Meeting obtained favor in the distant provinces. Maryland alone, being a small meeting, continued to send representatives until about the year 1790, a period of more than one hundred years. The Yearly Meeting now assumed the title, "The General Yearly Meeting for Friends of Pennsylvania, East and West Jersey, and of the adjacent Provinces."

The extraordinary assumption has been made, that the meeting, up to this period, was only a General Meeting, and not, in a technical sense, a Yearly Meeting, nor endowed with the powers and privileges of such a body. There is no room for controversy on this point; but as it has been published, within the past year, that " Philadelphia Yearly Meeting was established in 1686," I simply allude to it in order that the truth of history may not be falsified thereby.

This may be an appropriate place for the following minute of advice :—

1704.—"It is the sense of this meeting, that all Quarterly Meetings give a strict charge to the members whom they appoint to attend the service of the Yearly Meeting, that none of them be absent from their duty therein, without the leave of the said meeting."—(Yearly Meeting.)

1705.—"Samuel Jennings proposed, on behalf, and at the request of women's meeting, that they may be permitted to have a Yearly Meeting stock of their own, for such services as may more properly fall under their notice; to which this meeting condescends."—(Yearly Meeting.)

After allowing women Friends to hold a Yearly Meeting, and to transact their own proper business for more than twenty years, there should not have been much condescension needed, in allowing them a little pocket-money, to aid in the service.

1712.—" As to the proposal for an alteration of the Yearly Meeting of business to Philadelphia, to be held there every year, this meeting concludes it is best, for divers considerations, to remain as it is at present established."—(Yearly Meeting.)

1755.—" Agreed to hold our Yearly Meeting, on the third first day of the week, in the 9th month."—(Yearly Meeting.)

1760.—" The consideration of the properest place for holding our Yearly Meeting for business in future, now coming under the solid notice and thought of this meeting, and much time being spent thereon, and a full opportunity given for a free expression of Friends' sentiments, and the calming influences of Gospel love being over us, it appears to be the most general sense, that Philadelphia, as it is the nearest central for the body of the Society, it is therefore the most convenient for that purpose."—(Yearly Meeting.)

The Yearly Meeting of Philadelphia had become numerically and geographically very large, reaching to Hopewell and Fairfax, in Virginia, and to the Motherkills in the State of Delaware.

The Yearly, or rather Half Year's Meeting, of Maryland, was composed of only two Quarterly Meetings, located on the opposite shores of the Chesapeake.

It was thought that a different arrangement of the Meetings, might be advantageous to both, which, after mature deliberation, was effected, in the year, 1790. The Meetings on the Eastern Shore of Maryland were united with the Monthly Meetings of Duck Creek and Motherkill, in the State of Delaware, to constitute the Southern Quarterly Meeting, as a subordinate branch of Philadelphia Yearly Meeting, and the Quarterly Meetings of Warrington and Fairfax were transferred to the Maryland Yearly Meeting, now agreed to be held annually in the city of Baltimore.

In 1819, the Monthly Meetings of Nottingham, Little Britain, and Deer Creek, were constituted a Quarterly Meeting, and at the same time, were transferred to the Yearly Meeting of Baltimore.

1793.—"This meeting convened under a humiliating sense of the Divine judgments, which have been manifested in this city, by a pestilential disorder, which has for some time prevailed, and carried off many of the inhabitants, and have to acknowledge, that, though much smaller than usual, we have been enabled to transact the weighty affairs of the Church, which have come before us, in much harmony and brotherly love, and as our confidence hath been measurably directed towards the Fountain of every blessing, strength has been derived therefrom, to conclude the business to satisfaction and comfort." —(Yearly Meeting.)

1798.—"Friends unanimously agreed that our Yearly Meeting be in future held on the third second day in the fourth month, and the meeting of ministers and elders on the seventh day preceding."—(Yearly Meeting.)

1838.—"The following report, after due consideration, was adopted, women's meeting also uniting therein, viz.: that an advantage would arise to Society if the time of holding our Yearly Meeting was changed to the second day following the second first day in the fifth month."—(Yearly Meeting.)

In the year 1829 and subsequently, the Yearly Meeting of men Friends was held at Green Street Meeting-house; and that of women Friends at Cherry Street, below Fifth. This separation of the meetings was found inconvenient. Moreover, the house did not afford women comfortable accommodations, and was no longer conveniently located for the members of the Monthly Meeting, many of whom had been driven from the commercial front of the city by the expansion of business. The Yearly Meeting held in 1855, had been looking to some means of relief, when the following minute was opportunely received from women's meeting :—

1855.—"The Yearly Meeting of women Friends, now sitting, believe it right to call the attention of men Friends to the very poor accommodations the Cherry Street house affords. Although the additional ventilation has rendered it a little more comfortable, still its crowded state, the difficulty of hearing, and our position, since the erection of the adjoining building, being by many considered unsafe, we feel it right to present the subject before you.

"Signed by

"MARY S. LIPPINCOTT, *Clerk.*

"Fifth month, 17th, 1855."

"To the Yearly Meeting.

1855.—"The committee, to whom was referred the minute from our women's Yearly Meeting, on the subject of their better accommodation, nearly all twice met, and were united in judgment that better accommodations were needed. They, therefore, propose to the Yearly Meeting to appoint a committee to carry out this view as far as way may open, provided that sufficient means can be raised by subscriptions or otherwise; which was approved, and the committee was continued to carry out the views of the report, and, if way opens, provide accommodations for both branches of the Yearly Meeting."—(Yearly Meeting.)

That committee, acting in concert with a committee of "the Monthly Meeting of Friends of Philadelphia," held at Cherry Street, proceeded to purchase two adjoining lots, situate between Cherry and Race Streets, west of Fifteenth Street. That for the Yearly Meeting having a front on Cherry Street of one hundred and sixty feet, with a depth of seventy-six feet. The Monthly Meeting's lot, lying immediately back of it, having the same width, and a depth of one hundred feet, with a central outlet ninety feet wide, extending one hundred and twelve feet, to Race Street.

Upon these premises the joint committee proceeded to erect a meeting-house for their mutual accommodation. The building is one hundred and thirty-one feet long from north to south, and eighty feet wide, with a central projection of eight feet on the east and west sides, and stands thirty feet from Cherry Street. The Yearly Meeting's apartment, where men's meeting is held, is forty-six feet by eighty, allowing the dividing line to run through the centre of its north wall. The Monthly Meeting's room, where women's Yearly Meeting is held, is sixty feet by eighty, and stands one hundred and twenty-seven feet from Race Street. Both meeting rooms have galleries on three sides. The Cherry Street house will accommodate fourteen hundred persons; the Race Street one eighteen hundred.

The two apartments are separated by a space of twenty-five feet, which is divided into three stories; each having rooms on the east and west fronts, with central stairways between them, designed to accommodate committees, and for school rooms, library, &c.

The Yearly Meeting's property is vested in McPherson Saunders, Isaac C. Parry, Barclay Knight, Clement Biddle, Abner Garret, Elias Hicks, James Dixon, George Middleton, George L. Gillingham, William E. Cooper, and George Masters, as trustees on its behalf, being one out of each Quarterly Meeting.

Friends of the three Monthly Meetings of Philadelphia subsequently purchased an adjoining lot on Race Street, of forty feet front and one hundred deep, on which they erected a house for the accommodation of "Friends' Central School."

All the funds required for those several purposes, except the proceeds of the sale of the old Cherry Street property, were raised by voluntary subscriptions; and it is gratifying to know that "the whole is paid for and clear of incumbrance, with the exception of a mortgage of five thousand dollars upon the property held by Friends as school property."

The whole expenditure may be summed up as follows:—

Cost of the Yearly Meeting's property, . .	$34,000 00
" " Monthly " " . .	52,180 70
" " Central School " . .	14,919 19
Total amount, . .	$101,099 89

The Yearly Meeting held its first session in the new house in the fifth month, 1857.

FRIEND'S MEETING HOUSE.

In the progress of the organization of our religious Society, meetings of a more transient and ephemeral character were occasionally held, under the name of "General Meetings," "Spring Meetings," &c. These were principally designed for worship; but, when an emergency required, they sometimes transacted business. Subordinate to these were the Youths' Meetings, often held quarterly, on the day following a Quarterly Meeting. All these meetings were, no doubt, useful in their day, and claimed a large share of the sympathy and concern of the Society; but, as they did not come within the scope of its regular organization, we have not thought it necessary to notice them more in detail in this work.

CHAPTER II.

MEETING FOR SUFFERINGS.

As new Yearly Meetings came to be established, they felt the want of a medium of communication with other similarly constituted bodies. During their incipient and progressive organization, they required the aid of their more experienced brethren in the work.

There was also a want of some body which could represent them during their recess, and this want was greatly increased at times, by the cruel persecutions and sufferings to which the members were exposed; often requiring the vigilant care and prompt assistance of their friends to be extended for their relief. Such was the source of the Meeting for Sufferings.

1705.—"This meeting being informed that some Friends in New England are desirous to correspond with Friends here, and it being thought necessary that there be a correspondence held, not only with them, but with other neighboring Yearly Meetings, viz., Maryland, Virginia, Carolina, Long Island,

Rhode Island, &c., Samuel Jennings, Thomas Story, Griffith Owen, Edward Shippen, and Thomas Gardner, are appointed as correspondents for this meeting, and they, or any two of them, may act in that behalf, as there may be occasion."—(Yearly Meeting.)

1709.—"It being moved at this meeting, that all Friends within the limits thereof, from their several Quarterly Meetings, bring in an account of all Friends' sufferings, that have been, or may happen among them, for their testimony to the Truth, that it may be done yearly; unto which the meeting agrees," &c.—(Yearly Meeting.)

1709.—"The care of the Press being recommended to the care of Philadelphia Monthly Meeting, [to appoint] a committee of eight Friends, any five of whom are desired to take care to peruse all writings or manuscripts that are intended to be printed, before they go to the Press, with power to correct what may not be for the service of Truth; otherwise, not to suffer anything to be printed."—(Yearly Meeting.)

The Press here mentioned is understood to have been the property of the Yearly Meeting, and held under its strict surveillance. We can hardly realize the confidence which Friends must have placed in each other in those days of primitive Quakerism, thus to allow a committee of five men, appointed in one Monthly Meeting, the absolute and unlimited power to approve, to correct or alter, or to suppress, whatever might be written for publication.

1718.—"This meeting, seeing occasion to renew to the notice of Friends, our ancient care and practice in the case of publishing books and writings, now recommend to the Monthly and Quarterly Meetings, that such be dealt with as shall write, print, or publish any books or writings tending to raise contention, or occasion breach of unity among brethren, or that have not first had the perusal and approbation of the Friends appointed by the Yearly Meeting for that purpose."—(Yearly Meeting.)

It would seem that the Yearly Meeting now appointed what are in the succeeding minute called the Overseers of the Press. We do not know when this practice was first introduced.

1722.—"Agreed, that what writings are approved of by the overseers of the Press for printing, shall be done at the charge of this meeting."—(Yearly Meeting.)

1756.—"We the committee to correspond with Friends in England, and to visit the Monthly Meetings, having had a conference with the committee appointed to adjust the Yearly Meeting's accounts; and taking into consideration the distressed state of the frontier settlements of these provinces; and that we have just grounds to apprehend that many of our friends, who are now situated in parts immediately exposed to danger, may soon stand in need of relief and assistance, and for want of a timely care and provision being made, may in the approaching winter suffer deeply. Under these considerations, we are unanimously of opinion that it will be expedient to raise such a sum of money for the stock of the Yearly Meeting, as may enable those with whom the distribution of it may be intrusted, to do more considerable service than the sums usually raised would answer. And, therefore, conclude less than one thousand pounds may not be sufficient.

"And in order that due care may be taken to distribute or employ the money to general satisfaction, we propose that the treasurers of this Yearly Meeting should observe the directions of a committee to be appointed by this meeting; and that such a committee may be constituted in the most equal manner, and that the several Quarterly Meetings be properly represented, we propose that this meeting should nominate twelve Friends, living in or near Philadelphia, for the convenience of their getting soon together; and that it be recommended to the several Quarterly Meetings to appoint four Friends to represent each quarter, and that the whole number should meet together at Philadelphia as soon as they can conveniently; and at their first meeting should regulate the manner and time of their future meetings.

"That the services proposed to be transacted by them be: To hear and consider the cases of any Friends under suffering, especially such as suffer from the Indians or other enemies, and to administer such relief as they may find necessary, or to apply to government, or persons in power, on their behalf. To correspond with the Meeting for Sufferings, or Yearly Meeting of London; and to represent the state of the affairs of Friends here; and, in general, to represent this meeting, and appear in all cases where the reputation of Truth and our religious Society are concerned; provided that they do not meddle with matters of faith or discipline not already determined in this meeting; and that at least twelve should concur on all occasions; and that, in matters of great importance, notice be given or sent to all the members of the committee."—(Yearly Meeting.)

It was unanimously agreed to raise the sum recommended; and "as the appointment of the proposed committee, and limiting their trust and authority, requires further consideration," . . . . the meeting appointed a committee of eighteen Friends to consider the same, and report to the next sitting; when

"The meeting agrees to and confirms the proposal, with this addition, that the said committee should keep fair minutes of all their proceedings, and produce the same to next Yearly Meeting. And the representatives of the several quarters are desired to meet together and nominate twelve Friends, to be returned to-morrow, for the approbation of this meeting.

"And the representatives are desired to inform Friends, in their respective quarters, that it is the mind of this meeting that they should, at their next Quarterly Meeting, nominate the four Friends to be chosen by them.

"And as this meeting (committee) when settled will be capable of discharging the services for which the committee appointed to consider the uses and manner of application of charitable legacies and donations, and to advise respecting the titles of any lands or other estate belonging to the several meetings, &c., was intended: it is the sense of this meeting that the necessary care in such matters will be a part of the proper concern of the Meeting for Sufferings."—(Yearly Meeting.)

1756.—"James Moon, Samuel Carey, Thomas Ross, and Joshua Ely (in pursuance of the direction of the Yearly Meeting), are chosen to represent this meeting as members of the Meeting for Sufferings."—(Bucks Quarterly Meeting.)

1757.—"The minutes of the Meeting for Sufferings having been read, &c., it is unanimously agreed that the said meeting should be continued, and that the Friends nominated last year be continued members of that meeting; who, in conjunction with those chosen by the several Quarterly Meetings, shall be and continue the Meeting for Sufferings, until the respective Quarterly Meetings shall nominate and appoint others in the rooms or places of those chosen by them last year."—(Yearly Meeting.)

The Meeting for Sufferings was thus continued from year to year, " as at present constituted, reserving to each Quarterly Meeting the right of changing any of the members in the places where they were respectively nominated."—(See Extracts for 1757–8–9, 1760–1–2, &c. &c.)

1764.—" When there is an apparent neglect of the members nominated by the Yearly Meeting, the said Meeting for Sufferings is authorized to appoint other Friends in the room of such, if, after seasonable admonition, they continue to neglect or decline attending ; and to acquaint the Quarterly Meetings respectively, where they observe any nominated to represent them continue neglectful of giving proper attendance, in order that such Quarterly Meetings may appoint others."—(Yearly Meeting.)

1768.—" The proceedings of the Meeting for Sufferings for the year past, being read and approved, it is agreed to continue

3

that meeting, agreeable to former minutes, until this meeting may think it necessary to order the contrary."—(Yearly Meeting.)

The Meeting for Sufferings, which had been continued from year to year, was now established as a permanent institution; but "the right of changing any of the members" was carefully reserved, and never has been surrendered by the action of any subsequent meeting.

1771.—"It is recommended to the Meeting for Sufferings, to take upon them the care and oversight of any writings which may be proposed to be printed; and in all respects to undertake the trust heretofore committed to a number of Friends appointed by this meeting, as overseers of the Press."—(Yearly Meeting.)

1775.—"As various occasions of difficulty, in this time of outward commotion, may arise, nearly affecting our religious Society; in the consideration whereof, in our Meeting for Sufferings, additional assistance and strength may be necessary, it is agreed that each of our Quarterly Meetings should nominate four judicious, experienced Friends, residing in their respective quarters, to join with the Meeting for Sufferings in their conferences on such extraordinary occasions, to whom that meeting is to give seasonable notice thereof, requesting their attendance," &c.—(Yearly Meeting.)

The increased number of Quarterly Meetings, with the occasional appointment of assistants, made the Meeting for Sufferings a large and influential body. So long as the Quarterly Meetings judiciously exercised their prerogative of changing the nominations, little danger was to be apprehended. But as the practice grew and increased, of continuing the same Friends under the appointment, they came at length to claim it as a right or privilege. This was an evidence of danger, an indication that there was an imperium in imperio, a power growing

BURLINGTON
QUARTER

To Amwell

Stony brook

N.

Trenton

Bordentown *Chesterfield*

S

Mansfield Neck *Arneytown*
Burlington *Mansfield*

Old Springfield

Rancocas *U. Springfield*

Mt Holly *Mount*

SCALE: 5 miles per inch.

Vincent town

up within the Yearly Meeting, more willing to control than to be controlled by its authority.

CHAPTER III.

BURLINGTON QUARTER.

1682.—" At a General Meeting, held at Salem, in the Province of West New Jersey, on the 11th of the second month, 1682, it was mutually agreed and ordained that a Quarterly Meeting be held at Burlington, the second second day of the fourth month next ensuing."—(Burlington Monthly Meeting.)

"Burlington Quarterly Meeting was first set up in 1682, and held at the house of William Biddle till 1711, when it was agreed to be held alternate at the meeting-houses in Burlington and Chesterfield."—(S. Smith.)

I.—BURLINGTON MONTHLY MEETING.

1678.—" Since, by the good providence of God, many Friends, with their families, have transported themselves into this Province of West New Jersey, the said Friends, in these upper parts, have found it needful, according to our practice in the place we came from, to settle Monthly Meetings for the well-ordering of the affairs of the Church.

" It was agreed that, accordingly, it should be done, and accordingly it was done this 15th of fifth month, 1678."— (Burlington Monthly Meeting.)

" Their Monthly Meetings were set up in 1678, and were held at the houses of John Woolston and Thomas Gardner, till the building of the great meeting-house in 1696."—(S. Smith.)

The general prevalence of feelings favorable to mutual

accommodation, often led early Friends to leave their meeting-houses and hold meetings at private dwellings for the convenience of individuals. Thus Burlington Monthly Meeting records the following opening minute :—

"At a Monthly Meeting, held at Upland, in the house of Robert Wade, the 15th of the 9th month, 1681."

BURLINGTON.

1677.—"Meetings for worship were first settled in Burlington in 1677. They were first held under tents made for the purpose, then successively at the houses of John Woolston, Thomas Gardner, and his widow, till the building of the great meeting-house in 1696."—(S. Smith.)

1682.—"It is ordered that a meeting-house be built, according to the draught of a six-square building, of forty feet square from out to out," &c.—(Burlington Monthly Meeting.)

1691.—"This day was ordered that Bernard Devenish should not suffer the court to be kept in our meeting-house any more."—(Burlington Monthly Meeting.)

RANCOCAS.

1681.—"Thomas Harding and John Woolman are desired to give notice to the Friends of Rancocas to confer with Friends here, next Monthly Meeting, about the meeting there, and to give the meeting an account of it."

Two months after, "It is agreed that the meeting at Rancocas be held at the house of Thomas Harding," &c.—(Burlington Monthly Meeting.)

OLD SPRINGFIELD.

1682.—"It is ordered that Friends at Esiskunk Creek have a meeting at the house of Thomas Barton on first days, for this winter season."—(Burlington Monthly Meeting.)

1687.—"A meeting for worship was set up in 1687 for

Friends at Esiskunk Creek, and held by turns at the houses of Thomas Barton, John Day, and John Curtis."—(S. Smith.)

1694.—"It is agreed that the meeting-house of Springfield is to be built of the hither side of Mattacopany bridge; that is, if the land be to be had convenient for the meeting-house."—(Burlington Monthly Meeting.)

1698.—"Old Springfield meeting-house was built in 1698, and the meeting settled there on ground given by Richard Ridgway."—(S. Smith.)

MANSFIELD NECK.

1753.—A meeting was allowed to be held near William Folwell's (supposed to be Lower Mansfield), on first days, once in three weeks, during the winter season. (See Burlington Monthly Meeting.) In 1783 it was established, with the privilege of a preparative meeting. It has since been discontinued.

II.—CHESTERFIELD MONTHLY MEETING.

1684.—"At our Monthly Meeting, at Francis Davenport's house, near Crosswick's Creek, the place now called Chesterfield, in New Jersey, the 2d of the 8th month, 1684."

"A preface to the ensuing book:—

"It hath pleased the mighty God and great Jehovah, in this last age, after the great night of darkness and apostacy which hath spread over nations, kindreds, tongues, and people, since the glorious days in which the Apostles lived, by His outstretched gathering arm, and by the word of His eternal power, to gather a people, who was weary of all dead forms and outside professions, into a waiting frame of spirit, where we durst not think our own thoughts nor speak our own words in things relating to His kingdom and way of worship. And, being thus brought down by the mighty power of God, we were the more capable to receive instruction from Him, who, through and by

His Son, Christ Jesus, the true light that lighteth every one that cometh into the world, appeared in us, and taught us His way and worship, which is in spirit and truth. This He taught us while we were in Old England, our native land, which, we may say, through the great mercy of the Lord, was, in this latter age, the first of nations where the Lord appeared in so mighty a power and bright shining glory, to the gathering of thousands into His fold, whereby his people became a body, whereof Christ is the head. And then, the Lord our God, as he did unto Paul and the elders of the churches in the Apostles' days, begat a godly care in the hearts of some of His people, whom He had gathered and brought into a living sense of His works in this day; and also of the mysterious workings of the enemy of all good, who in all ages, as the Scriptures of truth fully testify, labored, by his subtlety and transformings, to draw the Lord's people into looseness and disorder, that so the precious truth and pure way of the Lord might be dishonored, and His worthy name blasphemed.

"We say the Lord hath set some as watchmen upon the walls of Jerusalem, and hath laid a godly care, and a necessity upon some of his people, that all things in the Church of Christ may be kept sweet and clean, and that marriages, and all other things relating to the Church affairs, may be performed in the good order of the Gospel of peace. Therefore, in the wisdom and counsel of God, it was seen meet that first day and weekly meetings might be appointed, and diligently kept unto, for edification and the worshipping of God; and Monthly, Quarterly, and Yearly Meetings might be appointed, and diligently kept unto, by all such who are of an honest conversation as becomes Truth, and have the weight of the Lord's work in this, our day, and the care of the Church upon them; for the settling and ordering of the affairs thereof, and to admonish and give advice to such as stand in need thereof. And the Lord, by his providence and mighty power, hath brought some of his people out of their native country, over the great deep, into this wilderness, and remote part of the world, as West Jersey, and places adjacent, where He hath laid the same weight and care upon some of us, as he did in our native land; that all things may be well among us, to the honor of his great and worthy name; which is the ground and end of this following book.

"JOHN WILLSFORD,
"FRANCIS DAVENPORT.
"WILLIAM WATSON."
(Chesterfield Monthly Meeting.)

CHESTERFIELD.

1677.—" Chesterfield Meeting was settled about the year 1680, and their meeting-house built about the same time. But a meeting for worship on first days, was continued from the first settlement of the English in 1677, at the house of Thomas Lambert, until the building of the said meeting-house."—(S. Smith.)

STONY BROOK.

1710.—This meeting was indulged by Chesterfield Monthly Meeting, to be held once in three months.

In 1724, a committee reported that—

"A house may be built of stone, thirty-four feet long and thirty feet wide, and finished, so far as to render it useful, as they think, for about one hundred and fifty pounds, new money."—(Chesterfield Monthly Meeting.)

The house was built, and the meeting established in 1726.

AMWELL.

1727.—A meeting was allowed to be kept every first day, at the house of John Stephenson, at Amwell, by the Monthly Meeting of Chesterfield. It has since been dropped.

ALLENTOWN.

1727.—There was also a meeting held about this time at Allentown, under the direction of the Monthly Meeting of Chesterfield.

TRENT TOWN.

1734.—" Our friend, Isaac Hanam, with other Friends, requested liberty to keep a meeting for worship at Trent Town on first days, hoping it may be of good service. Therefore this meeting grants them their request for six months, and longer, as it may be found of good service."—(Chesterfield Monthly Meeting.)

" In 1740, the meeting-house at Trenton was built, and the meeting for worship settled."—(S. Smith.)

BORDENTOWN.

1740.—" The meeting at Bordentown was settled in 1740, and their meeting-house built in the same year, on ground given by Joseph Borden."—(S. Smith.)

III.—LITTLE EGG HARBOR MONTHLY MEETING.

1715.—" Having considered Edward Andrews's proposition, concerning the establishing a Monthly Meeting at Little Egg Harbor, do refer it to the Quarterly Meeting," where it was approved.—(Chesterfield Monthly Meeting.)

LITTLE EGG HARBOR.

1704.—" The meeting at Little Egg Harbor was first settled in 1704, and a meeting-house built in 1709."—(S. Smith.)

In 1714, a preparative meeting was allowed them.

IV.—MOUNT HOLLY MONTHLY MEETING.

1776.—Mount Holly Monthly Meeting was constituted in the year 1776, by a division of Burlington Monthly Meeting. It was composed of Mount Holly and Shrevesmount Meetings, and of Old Springfield and Upper Springfield Meetings.

As regards the number of members, the division was as follows. See a report, on Burlington record, signed by George Dillwyn:—

	Burlington Monthly Meeting.	Mount Holly Monthly Meeting.
Burlington, . . .	193	
Rancocas, ...	133	
Mansfield, ...	90	
Mansfield Neck, . .	60	
Old Springfield, . . .	106	50
Upper Springfield, . .	5	80
Mount, ...		104
Mount Holly, . . .		388
	587	622

MOUNT HOLLY.

It appears that Shrevesmount, on the east of the present Mount Holly, was formerly known by that name, while the latter was called Bridgton.

1687.—"The Weekly Meeting being on fourth day, that used to be kept at Thomas Olive's and John Woolman's, is now ordered to be kept at Daniel Wills's weekly."—(Burlington Monthly Meeting.)

"In 1704, a meeting was settled at Restore Lippincott's, to be held for the winter season."—(S. Smith.)

1716.—"Whereas there was one little meeting kept at two places, one at Restore Lippincott's, and one at Daniel Wills's, which hath been held for a considerable time; but now there is a meeting-house built at Mount Holly for to accommodate those two meetings, and those belonging to those meetings desire to be removed to the said meeting-house, which is approved and allowed of by the said meeting."—(Burlington Monthly Meeting.)

1742.—"The Friends of Mount Holly, alias Bridgton, requested of this meeting liberty to hold a first day evening meeting in Bridgton, for the winter season : which is allowed of by this meeting."—(Burlington Monthly Meeting.)

MOUNT. (SHREVE'S.)

1743.—"The meeting having considered the application of sundry Friends, belonging to the upper part of Mount Holly Meeting, do consent that they hold a meeting, according to their request. . . . . Michael Atkinson and Benjamin Carter are to have the oversight of said meeting."—(Burlington Monthly Meeting.)

VINCENT-TOWN.

1765.—"A written proposal from sundry Friends, for keeping an afternoon meeting during the summer, at a schoolhouse lately erected near William Bishop's, was now read and agreed to."—(Burlington Monthly Meeting.)

V.—UPPER SPRINGFIELD MONTHLY MEETING.

1783.—The new Monthly Meeting of Upper Springfield was constituted of parts of Burlington and Chesterfield Monthly Meetings, viz., of Upper Springfield, a branch of Burlington, and of Mansfield and Upper Freehold, branches of Chesterfield Monthly Meeting. It was approved by Burlington Quarterly Meeting, in the 8th month, 1782, and opened in the 5th month following.—(See Burlington and Chesterfield Monthly Meeting.)

UPPER SPRINGFIELD.

1728.—"The Meeting at Upper Springfield was settled in 1728, and their meeting-house built the same year, upon ground had of Joshua Shreve."—(S. Smith.)

MANSFIELD.

1731.—"The Meeting at Mansfield was settled in the year 1731, and the meeting-house built the same year, on ground purchased of Francis Gibbs."—(S. Smith.)

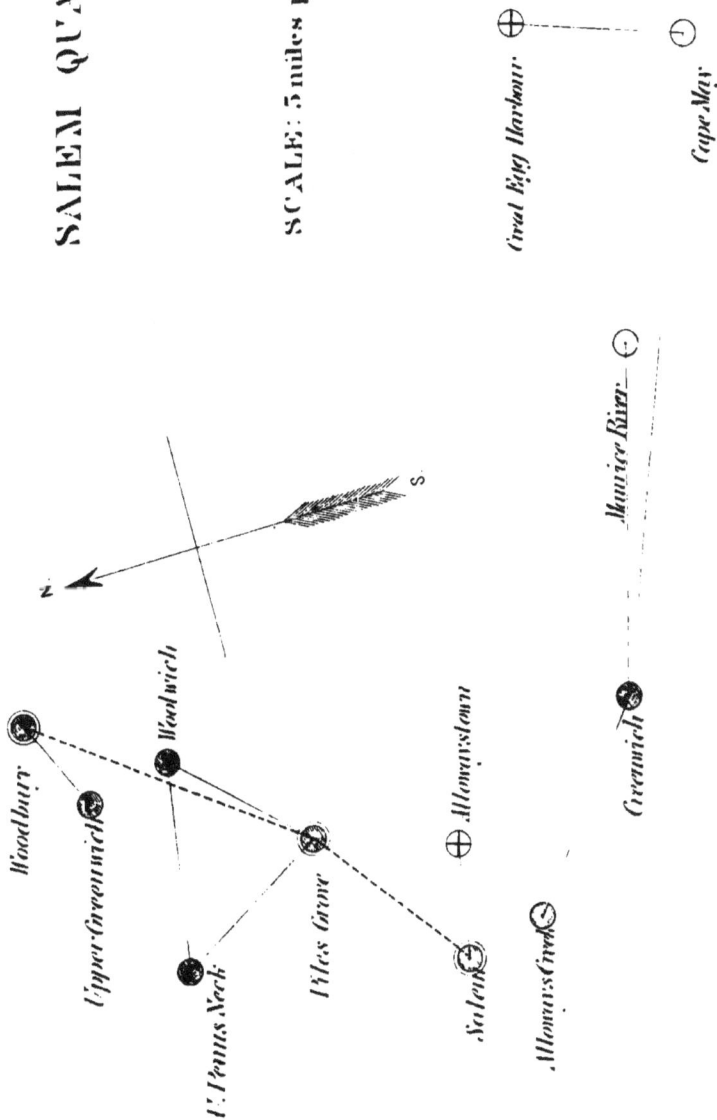

SALEM QUARTER

SCALE: 5 miles per inch.

Great Egg Harbour

Cape May

N

S

Woodbury

Upper-Greenwich

W. Penns Neck

Woolwich

W'les Grove

Allowaystown

Maurice River

Salem

Allowas Creek

Greenwich

UPPER FREEHOLD (WOODWARD'S).

1739.—"Isaac Foreman, Joseph Arney, and several inhabitants near there, requested liberty of this meeting to keep a meeting every first day, at a house of Joseph Arney's; and this meeting gave consent that they have liberty to keep a meeting for one year."—(Chesterfield Monthly Meeting.)

1740.—"This meeting gives liberty to the inhabitants near Thomas Woodward's, to make application to the Quarterly meeting for a meeting-house, according to their request."—(Chesterfield Monthly Meeting.)

1742.—"The Meeting at Woodward's was settled in 1742, and their meeting-house built the same year, on land given by Joseph Arney."—(S. Smith.)

CHAPTER IV.

SALEM QUARTER.

1682.—"At a General Meeting, held at Salem, in the Province of West New Jersey, the 11th of the 2d month, 1682,

"It was ordered, that a Quarterly Meeting be held at Salem, the third second day of the 9th month next ensuing."—(Burlington Monthly Meeting.)

1686.—"At a Yearly Meeting, held in Burlington, the 8th day of the 7th month, 1686,

"Friends of this meeting ordered, the Monthly Meeting of Salem, and the Monthly Meeting of Newton, make up one Quarterly Meeting, to be held at Salem the first second day in the 9th month; next at Newton, the first second day in the 12th month; next at Salem, the first second day in the 3d month; next at Newton, the first second day in the 6th month;—and so to continue yearly."—(Yearly Meeting.)

The Quarterly Meeting appears to have been held at Salem until the opening of Woodbury Monthly Meeting, in 1785, when it was held alternate at that place till 1837; at which time it was concluded to hold it once in the year at Salem, once at Woodbury, and twice at Woodstown, as at the present time.

I.—SALEM MONTHLY MEETING.

1676.—" At a meeting held the first day of the sixth month, 1676, it was unanimously consented thereto that the first second day of the week, in every month, the Friends within the town of New Salem in Fenwick's colony, and all Friends belonging thereunto, do monthly meet together, to consider of outward business, and of such as have been convinced, and those that walked disorderly; that they may, with all gravity and uprightness to God, and in tenderness of spirit and love to their souls, be admonished, exhorted, and also reproved, and their evil deeds and practices testified against, in the wisdom of God, and authority of Truth, as may answer the wisdom of God within them."—(Salem Monthly Meeting.)

SALEM.

1675.—" In the fall of 1675, John Fenwick arrived in this country, and landed on a neck of land, about three miles from the river Delaware, up the Asamhockin, which is now called Salem Creek. Nearly all the emigrants that came out with him were members of the Society of Friends. The most prominent among them were, Robert, Samuel, and Edward Wade, Samuel Nicholson, Nathan Smart, Edward Champney, Samuel Hedge, Richard Guy, John Thompson, John Smith, and John Adams. Friends held their meetings at the house of Samuel Nicholson."—(Thomas Shourds.)

" Friends who came with John Fenwick, in 1675, first held their meetings for worship at each other's houses; and sometimes joined with Friends who settled at Robert Wade's Landing, now called Chester."—(S. Smith.)

The brick meeting-house at the graveyard was built in 1700, at a cost of £415; which proving too small, they purchased ground and erected another house, in 1772.

THOMPSON'S BRIDGE (NOW ALLOWAYSTOWN).

"In the beginning of the last century there was a Friends' meeting established at Thompson's Bridge, now known as Allowaystown, which was attended by a number of highly respectable families,—the Thompsons, Oakfords, Hoggs, Craigs, and others; but there are only three families of Friends residing there at this time who attend Salem Meeting."—(Thomas Shourds.)

II.—GREENWICH MONTHLY MEETING.

1770?—"About the year 1770 Greenwich Monthly Meeting was established, by the preparative meetings of Greenwich and Alloway's Creek uniting, to be held alternately. Before that time, the members of both meetings belonged to Salem Monthly Meeting."—(Thomas Shourds.)

To the foregoing were afterward added those of Maurice River and Cape May.

ALLOWAY'S CREEK.

1678.—"John Denn, Christopher White, Samuel Wade, Joseph Ware, Richard Hancock, Nathaniel Chambless, James Daniel, Edward Bradway, and other Friends, settled about Alloway's Creek. They held meetings at John Denn's house till 1684, when a meeting-house was built on the north side of the creek, for the sum of forty pounds. About 1710, on account of the difficulty of crossing the creek, another house was built on the south side, near its first location, where it continued until about the year 1754, when the present house was built, in the village of Hancock's Bridge."—(Thomas Shourds.)

G R E E N W I C H.

1694.—" Greenwich Meeting was established in 1694 by Mark Reeve and others."—(Thomas Shourds.)

III.—WOODBURY MONTHLY MEETING.

1783.—"At a Quarterly Meeting, held at Salem, the 19th of fifth month, 1783, Haddonfield, in their report, sends up for the advice and approbation of this meeting, a proposal, which has taken place, and appears to be the sense of that meeting, that a division of that meeting be made, and a Monthly Meeting be made at Haddonfield for that particular meeting, and another at Woodbury for that and Upper Greenwich."

" And on the 15th of 11th month, 1784, the Quarterly Meeting acceded to the proposition, and appointed Edward Darnel, Samuel Allison, William Goodwin, Mark Miller, Mark Reeve, and Edward Bradway to attend the opening of the new Monthly Meeting."

" And it is also recommended to the said meetings when divided, to feel after each other, and to sit together at their Monthly Meetings, as they may feel their minds drawn and engaged thereto, from time to time."

1785.—" Woodbury Monthly Meeting first held, 11th of 1st month, 1785.

"This being the day fixed by the Quarterly Meeting for Gloucester and Salem, to hold the first Monthly Meeting at this place, for Woodbury and Upper Greenwich, after a solemn time of worship, in which several living testimonies were borne, Friends proceeded to business."—(Woodbury Monthly Meeting.)

The Monthly Meeting was continued at Woodbury till 1845, since when it has alternated between the two meetings.

W O O D B U R Y.

1696.—" The Meeting at Woodbury was first established to be kept at the house of John Wood, in the sixth month, 1696;

but their meeting-house being soon after built, it hath been since kept there."—(S. Smith.)

UPPER GREENWICH—FORMERLY LIPPINCOTT'S MEETING.

1740.—Among the early settlers at this place, the names of Lippincott, Fisher, Hooten, Cozens, Zane, Mickle, Wood, Bates, &c., occur. A small frame meeting-house was built about the year 1740, on a lot of ground granted for that purpose by Solomon Lippincott. The meeting held therein was a branch of Haddonfield Monthly Meeting until the year 1785, at which time the meetings of Woodbury and Upper Greenwich were separated, to constitute Woodbury Monthly Meeting.

In 1798, a large and commodious two-story brick meeting-house was erected, on ground granted for the use of Friends by Samuel Tonkin and Samuel Mickle. This house is located one and a half miles east of the former one. The first mentioned lot is still held for a burying-ground.

A preparative meeting existed at Upper Greenwich as early as the year 1775.

A Friend adds the following encouraging note:—

"In the year 1808 two Friends conveyed to the meeting a lot of ground, adjoining the premises, of two acres and ten perches, whereon to erect a schoolhouse, for play grounds, &c.; and the meeting, the next year, raised the necessary funds and built a large brick house for the use of the members AND THE NEIGHBORHOOD. The school is under the exclusive care of the preparative meeting. Suitable apparatus is provided for illustrating the higher branches of science, and an extensive and well-selected library established." I would say to Friends everywhere, *go and do likewise.*

IV.—PILESGROVE MONTHLY MEETING.

1794.—"At a Quarterly Meeting, held at Haddonfield, the 21st of the third month, 1794, Salem Monthly proposing for consideration the dividing of that meeting, and holding a Monthly Meeting at Pilesgrove, ... the proposal is approved, and the said meeting established. . . . . . . Samuel Roberts, Bethuel Moore, Enoch Jones, John Haines, Thomas Thorn, Samuel Webster, James Whitehall, Samuel Paul, John Stewart, Richard Wood, and Samuel Townsend, are appointed to attend the opening thereof.

"Extracted from the minutes.

"THOMAS REDMAN, *Clerk.*"

1794.—"At the close of the meeting for worship at Pilesgrove, the 24th of fourth month, 1794, a minute of the Quarterly Meeting, establishing a Monthly Meeting to be there hereafter held, was produced and read; and the Friends therein named to attend being present, the meeting of business opened accordingly."—(Pilesgrove Monthly Meeting.)

PILESGROVE—AT WOODSTOWN.

No record obtained.

UPPER PENN'S NECK.

1794.—The meeting at Upper Penn's Neck appears to have been indulged by Salem Monthly Meeting, previous to the establishment of that of Pilesgrove, in 1794. The indulgence was continued by the latter meeting, by which it was established, and a preparative meeting allowed in 1796, about which time the meeting-house was built. It was rebuilt in 1857, and occupies a conspicuous position in Pedricktown.—(See Pilesgrove Monthly Meeting.)

WOOLWICH—AT MULLICA HILL.

1797.—A Friend writes that "Liberty was granted to Friends of Woolwich to hold a meeting in the schoolhouse at Mullica Hill, to commence on the first first day of the eleventh month, 1797, and which was continued from time to time until the meeting was established. It was composed of members of Pilesgrove and Woodbury Monthly Meetings."

V.—MAURICE RIVER MONTHLY MEETING.

1805.—" Maurice River Monthly Meeting was established in 1805, and continued till 1855, when the meeting there being reduced to a few families, they were attached to Greenwich Monthly Meeting, by their own desire."—(Thomas Shourds.)

1855.—"Maurice River Preparative and Monthly Meetings, have at their own request been discontinued, and the members attached to Greenwich Monthly Meeting."—(Yearly Meeting Extracts.)

VI.—GREAT EGG HARBOR MONTHLY MEETING.

——?—"A Monthly Meeting hath been held there for some years, composed of the Friends who live there, and those of Cape May; they belong to Salem and Gloucester Quarterly Meeting."—(S. Smith.)

On the division of Haddonfield Quarter from that of Salem, Great Egg Harbor and Cape May Monthly Meeting was embraced in Haddonfield. The Monthly Meeting was discontinued in   ?

GREAT EGG HARBOR.

1702.—"The first convincement of Friends about Great Egg Harbor, was about the year 1702; since which, meetings have been settled there, and two meeting-houses built."—(S. Smith.)

It is probable that one of the houses referred to, was that at Cape May. The meeting at Great Egg Harbor has been discontinued, and the few remaining members attached to Greenwich.

CAPE MAY.

The meeting at Cape May was established early, and then formed a part of Great Egg Harbor Monthly Meeting.

CHAPTER V.

PHILADELPHIA QUARTER.

THE few Friends who had settled on the west side of the Delaware, previous to the arrival of William Penn, attended the Monthly, Quarterly, and Yearly Meetings, of Burlington, the former of which was held at various places, to accommodate the more distant members. Thus we read,

"At a Monthly Meeting, held at Upland, in the house of Robert Wade, the 15th of the 9th month, 1681."—(Burlington Monthly Meeting.)

But soon after the arrival of William Penn at the intended site of Philadelphia, in the following year, it was ordered,—

1682.—"That notice be given to Friends, the next first day, that as many as can conveniently, may meet at Shackamaxon, in order to appoint other meetings, where it may be thought meet."—(Abington Monthly Meeting.)

Accordingly, "Friends belonging to the meeting in Philadelphia, in the province of Pennsylvania, being met, in the fear and power of the Lord, at the present meeting-place in the said city, the 9th day of the 11th month, being the third day of the week, in the year 1682, they did take into consideration the settlement of meetings therein, for the affairs and service of the Truth, according to that godly and comely practice, which they had received and enjoyed, with true satisfaction, among their friends and brethren, in the land of their nativity. And did then and there agree, that the first third day in the week, in every month, shall hereafter be the Monthly Meeting day, for the men's and women's meetings for the affairs and service of Truth, in this city and county, and every third meeting shall be the Quarterly Meeting for the same."

"The next thing considered was a fit place to build a meet-

PHILADELPHIA QUARTER

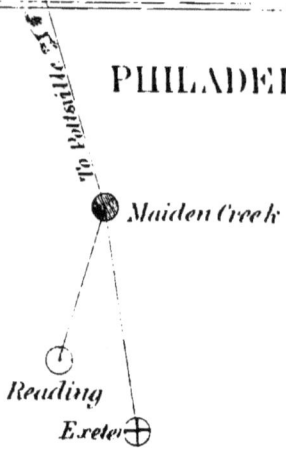

To Pottsville

Maiden Creek

Reading

Exeter

N

SCALE: 10 miles to an inch.

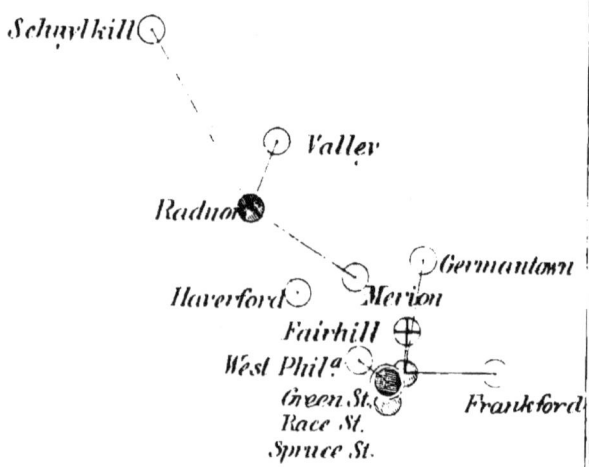

Schuylkill

Valley

Radnor

Germantown

Haverford   Merion

Fairhill

West Phil.ᵃ   Frankford

Green St.
Race St.
Spruce St.

ing-house in the city, as also the manner of building it."—(S. Smith.)

In the same year, Richard Townsend writes: "Our first concern was to keep up and maintain our religious worship; and in order thereto, we had several meetings in the houses of the inhabitants, and one boarded meeting-house was set up where the city was to be."

Although the above arrangement seems to have been made without much regard to the meetings in New Jersey, to which they had previously belonged, yet, as we have already seen, the utmost harmony continued to prevail among them.

It is probable that the same convention which established the Monthly and Quarterly Meetings, also concluded to hold an independent Yearly Meeting in Philadelphia; for it was a favorite idea with Friends of those days to hold a Yearly Meeting in each province, a Quarterly Meeting in each county, and a Monthly Meeting in each township, where Friends were sufficiently numerous to do so. It is, however, recorded,—

1683.—"At a Monthly Meeting at Burlington, the 6th of the first month, 1683, Friends in Pensylvania desireth to have a Monthly men's and women's Meetings, which was readily and freely assented to by Friends in this meeting."

I.—PHILADELPHIA MONTHLY MEETING.

1682.—"At a General Meeting, held at Salem, in the province of West New Jersey, the 11th of the second month, 1682, it was ordered that a six weeks' men's and women's meetings, for the ordering of the affairs of the Church, be kept the 24th day of the third month at William Cooper's, and the next six weeks' meeting at Thomas Fairman's, at Shackamaxon, and so in course."—(Burlington Monthly Meeting.)

By the conclusion of the meeting in Philadelphia, already

quoted, this six weeks' meeting was annulled, and the Monthly
Meeting of Philadelphia established in its place.

Reliable information is wanting to determine the location of
the "present meeting-place," the "boarded meeting-house,
which was set up in 1682, where the city was to be," as mentioned above. It is probable, however, that these phrases are
synonymous, and that the said "boarded house" was located
on Front Street, above Arch, where the Bank meeting-house
was afterwards built, in 1685.

It is said that the Assembly, which first convened in Philadelphia on the 10th of the first month, 1683, and consisted of
seventy-two members, met in the "boarded meeting-house,"
and probably continued to meet there until the erection of the
court-house in Market Street, in 1707.

1685.—"The Friends' meeting, in Front Street above Arch
Street, built in 1685, was originally intended for an evening
meeting." "The Bank meeting had its front on the Front
Street. The pediment at the front door was supported by
columns. At that door the men entered. On the southern
side was a double door, covered by a shed, by one of which the
women entered. At those doors was the entrance for men and
women to the gallery; the men going to the east, and the
women to the west. Originally the meeting had no board partition, but a curtain was used when they held a preparative
meeting. The preacher's gallery was on the north side. The
house was fifty feet front, by thirty-eight feet wide, and the
green yard in front, within the brick inclosure or wall, was
fourteen feet wide." "It was sold and taken down in 1789,
at the time it became useless, by their building 'the new meeting-house' in Key's Alley."—(Watson's Annals, p. 335.)

In 1695, the "great meeting-house," on the southwest
corner of Market and Second Streets, was built, at a cost of
six hundred and sixteen pounds. It was further enlarged in
1755.

An amusing incident occurred in one of the meetings held

here. The sleepers, if there were any in those days, were suddenly awakened by a neighboring parrot entering the house, and calling out, "Hannah Roberts! Poll wants her breakfast."

As the noise and pressure of business increased along the market-place, Friends deemed it expedient to sell the property, and remove the meeting to the yet larger house on the corner of Arch and Fourth Streets, which was built in 1804.

The Monthly Meeting of Philadelphia was held successively at the several houses above mentioned, until the division of Society in 1827. After which, it was temporarily held in Carpenter's Hall, Chestnut below Fourth Street, till the meeting-house on Cherry near Fifth Street was built, in the same year, at which place it continued to be held until the completion of the new house on Cherry Street above Fifteenth. The first Monthly Meeting held in this house was in the second month, 1857.

WEST PHILADELPHIA MEETING.

1837.—"The joint committee of men and women Friends appointed to take into consideration the opening of an indulged meeting at West Philadelphia, having twice met and deliberated thereon, feel willing to recommend to the Monthly Meeting that an indulged meeting for worship, on first day mornings, under the care of a committee, be opened at West Philadelphia, to commence, &c. &c.

"Signed, on behalf of the committee,

"SAMUEL HAYDOCK,
"JAMES MARTIN,
"SUSANNA HAYDOCK,
"MARY BIDDLE."
(Philadelphia Monthly Meeting.)

The report was adopted, and the meeting has since been regularly continued, under the care of the Monthly Meeting. For a time, it was held in a room, provided for the purpose, until a lot was obtained, and a meeting-house erected thereon. The first meeting held in the new house was on the 22d of the ninth month, 1851.

NOTE.—I shall here depart from the chronological order of the Monthly Meetings, to prevent a separation of those which belong to the city of Philadelphia.

II.—PHILADELPHIA MONTHLY MEETING (NORTHERN DISTRICT).

1772.—The meeting at the Bank meeting-house appears to have been continued after the erection of the Market Street house. And as Friends became more numerous and widely scattered, it was found expedient to increase the number of Monthly Meetings. One on the north was first held at the Bank meeting-house, on third day, the 24th of the eleventh month, 1772. Friends finding themselves greatly incommoded by the grading of the street, built a meeting-house in Key's Alley, and removed the meeting thereto in the year 1789, where it was continued till the division in 1827, at which time Friends withdrew therefrom. The property has since been sold for public school purposes.

III.—SPRUCE STREET MONTHLY MEETING.

(Formerly Philadelphia Monthly Meeting, for the Southern District, on Pine Street.)

1772.—" On the 25th day of the 11th month, being the fourth of the week, 1772, divers men and women Friends assembled in our meeting-house on Fourth Street, being the first Monthly Meeting of Friends of Philadelphia for the Southern District, appointed for the maintaining of the testimony of Truth and our Christian discipline, within the limits prescribed for the said Monthly Meeting. The extracts from the minutes of the Monthly Meetings of Friends of Philadelphia, and of the Quarterly Meeting by which it was established, were read," &c.— (Philadelphia Monthly Meeting for the Southern District.)

After the division of Society in 1827, Friends withdrew, and were temporarily joined with Philadelphia Monthly Meeting, held on Cherry Street. They subsequently purchased a lot, and erected a meeting-house, on Spruce Street near Ninth, and resumed the Monthly Meeting, which was first held therein in the year 1833, and has so continued.

PINE STREET.

1753.—According to Watson, the "Hill Meeting" on Pine Street was built in 1753. In which year, I am informed, the Yearly Meeting was held therein.

SPRUCE STREET.

1833.—See as above.

IV.—PHILADELPHIA MONTHLY MEETING, WESTERN DISTRICT, TWELFTH STREET.

1814.—"It is agreed to propose to the judgment of the Quarterly Meeting, that a Monthly Meeting be held on the fourth day preceding the last sixth day but one in the month, and a preparative meeting in the week preceding the Monthly Meeting."

The foregoing is an extract from the minute of Philadelphia Monthly Meeting, dated 27th of first month, 1814, which was sent up to, and approved by, the Quarterly Meeting, the 7th of second month, 1814. "The first Monthly Meeting of Friends of Philadelphia for the Western District, was held on the 10th of third month, 1814."

TWELFTH STREET MEETING.

1813.—So early as the year 1685, the same year in which the Bank meeting-house was rebuilt, Friends also erected the "Centre Meeting-house," on the southwest corner of Market and Broad Streets. This was intended for day meetings, while that at the Bank was for evening use. According to the original city plan, Broad Street was intended to have been where Twelfth Street now is, or midway between the two rivers. Hence it is probable that the present Twelfth Street house may stand upon nearly the same ground which its predecessor occupied.

1813. — "The present Twelfth Street meeting-house was built in 1812, and the first meeting for worship held therein on the first first day in the fourth month, 1813."

After the division in 1827, Friends who had belonged to this Monthly Meeting were joined to those of Philadelphia and Green Street.

V.—GREEN STREET MONTHLY MEETING.

1816.—"At a Monthly Meeting of Friends, held at Green Street, Philadelphia, 20th of sixth month, 1816, established by the Quarterly Meeting, agreeable to the following extracts from its minutes,—

"At a Quarterly Meeting held in Philadelphia, the 6th of the fifth month, 1816, the following proposal for establishing a Monthly Meeting, to be held at Green Street, accompanying the report from the Monthly Meeting of Friends for the Northern District, obtaining deliberate attention, is united with; and Jonathan Evans, Ellis Yarnall, Samuel Bettle, Thomas Stewardson, and Thomas Wistar, are appointed to attend the opening thereof."

"At a Monthly Meeting of Friends of Philadelphia, for the Northern District, held the 23d of the fourth month, 1816, the following report being produced and read, was united with and directed to be laid before the Quarterly Meeting for its consideration:—

"The committee of men and women Friends, appointed to consider the proposition from the Preparative Meeting of Green Street, for establishing a Monthly Meeting in that district, &c., having met and given the subject solid, deliberate consideration, are united in reporting it as their sense that a Monthly Meeting be established there, to be composed of Friends residing within the limits of that Preparative Meeting; and that it be known by the name of 'The Monthly Meeting of Friends, held at Green Street, Philadelphia,' &c. &c.

"Extracted from the minutes of the Quarterly Meeting.

"ISRAEL MORRIS, *Clerk.*"

(Green Street Monthly Meeting.)

GREEN STREET.

1814.—The meeting-house at the corner of Fourth and Green Streets, was completed in the spring of 1814.

"At a Monthly Meeting of Friends of Philadelphia, for the Northern District, held ninth month, 27th, 1814, the committee of men and women Friends, appointed to consider of and propose, &c., agree to propose to the Monthly Meeting, that meetings for worship be established there on first days, morning and afternoon, and on sixth day mornings, all to begin at the usual hour; and that Friends composing that meeting be allowed to hold a preparative meeting at the close of their meeting for worship on sixth day, in the week preceding the Monthly Meetings, to be known by the name of 'The Preparative Meeting, held at Green Street.'

"DANIEL THOMAS,
"LEONARD SNOWDEN,
"MARY TAYLOR,
"SARAH SMITH."

1814.—"At a Monthly Meeting of Friends of Philadelphia, for the Northern District, held eleventh month, 22d, 1814, an extract from the minutes of our late Quarterly Meeting was produced and read, informing that that meeting had concurred in the proposition of establishing meetings in the Green Street house, agreeable to the conclusion of this meeting in ninth month last. And as the meetings for worship, thus proposed to be established, will commence with the first first day in the twelfth month, and the preparative meeting on the twenty-third

of that month, Nathan A. Smith, Philip S. Bunting, William
Sansom, James Vaux, Thomas Stewardson, Joseph Bacon, and
Edward Randolph, are appointed to attend the opening of
them."—(Philadelphia Monthly Meeting for Northern District.)

The two ancient meetings of Frankford and Germantown,
which now compose Frankford Preparative Meeting, have been
attached to the Monthly Meeting of Green Street since the
year 1827.

FRANKFORD.

1682.—" Thomas Fairman, having removed with his family
from Shackamaxon to Oxford, there gave a piece of ground to
build a meeting-house upon, which was built accordingly very
early; first a log house, afterward a brick."—(S. Smith.)

A first day meeting had been held still earlier at the house
of Sarah Seyers, at Tacony, or Oxford.

GERMANTOWN.

1683.—It appears that the first meeting at this place was
held at the house of Dennis Conard (or, as then called, Tennis
Kundert), in the year 1683 (S. Smith says 1682). It was constituted of German Friends, who thus gave name to the place.

1854.—" Philadelphia Quarter reports that Frankford Preparative Meeting is now held alternately at Frankford and
Germantown."—(Yearly Meeting.)

FAIR HILL.

The meeting-house at Fair Hill was built many years ago,
on ground purchased by the Monthly Meeting of the People of
God, called Quakers, in Philadelphia, " for the benefit, use and
behoof of the poor people of the said Quakers, belonging to the
said meeting, forever, and for a place to erect a meeting-house
and schoolhouse upon, for the use and service of the said people,

and for a place to bury their dead." It is located in the northern precincts of the city proper, between Cambria and Indiana Streets, on the east side of the road to Germantown. No meetings have been held there for many years. The property is now known as "Fair Hill Burying-ground."

VI.—RADNOR MONTHLY MEETING—FORMERLY HAVERFORD.

1684.—"Men's meeting held at Thomas Ducket's house, in Schuylkill, the 10th of second month, 1684.

"Men's meeting held at William Shaner's house, in Radnor, the second fifth day of the third month, 1684.

"Men's meeting held at Hugh Roberts's house, in Merion, the second fifth day in the fourth month, 1684.

"Men's meeting held at John Bevan's house, in Haverford, the second fifth day of the fifth month, 1684."

Such are the first four opening minutes on the Radnor Monthly Meeting records now extant. It appears that Thomas Ducket's house, in Schuylkill, was located at the old burying-ground, at the west end of the Market Street Permanent Bridge.

From this time forward, the Monthly Meeting appears to have been most frequently held at Haverford, until,

1698.—"At our Monthly Meeting, held at Haverford, the 22d of the second month, 1698,

"It is concluded, that the Monthly Meeting for business, be kept in course here, at Merion, and Radnor," &c.—(Radnor Monthly Meeting.)

Beside their monthly meetings for business, they also had general monthly meetings, monthly meetings for worship, first day monthly meetings, &c., all of which probably meant the same thing. Thus,—

1698.—"David Lawrence and William Jenkins are ordered

to meet Friends at Darby, to remove their Monthly Meeting to another day, being it is kept the same day with our General Monthly Meeting." Yet only four months previous, the record says: "The first day Monthly Meeting at this place, Friends have thought fit to move it to the first fourth day of the week, in every month."—(Radnor Monthly Meeting.)

1700.—" At our Quarterly Meeting, held at Philadelphia, the 2d of the 7th month, 1700, the Friends from Haverford Meeting report: that the Quarterly Meeting of Chester County have sent some of their members to their Monthly Meeting, signifying the mind of their meeting, that the said Monthly Meeting in the county of Chester ought to be joined to them; which this meeting, having weighed and considered the same, came to this agreement, that Haverford Monthly Meeting hath belonged to this meeting from the first settlement, and for several other reasons, this meeting unanimously desires that the Monthly Meeting of Haverford may not be separated from this our Quarterly Meeting.—A copy, per Samuel Carpenter."—(Radnor Monthly Meeting.)

1700.—" At our Monthly Meeting, held at Haverford, the 10th of the 8th month, 1700, there was a paper drawn, in behalf of the meeting, directed to the Friends of the Quarterly Meeting for the county of Chester, which was thus:—

" ' In the Truth of God, our salutation is unto you, desiring we may be one with you in it forever. The proposal laid before our Monthly Meeting, by the Friends appointed by your Quarterly Meeting, viz., that our Monthly Meeting should be joined to your Quarterly Meeting, was laid before the Quarterly Meeting of Philadelphia, by the Friends of our Monthly Meeting appointed to attend the same, and their unanimous desire and sense, and also the general sense of this our Monthly Meeting is, that being we are joined to their Quarterly Meeting, from our first settlement, therefore, and for other reasons, we should so continue; which, in answer to your desire, we thought fit to signify unto you.

" ' Signed, &c., by
" ' THOMAS JONES.' "

HAVERFORD, MERION, AND RADNOR.

About the year 1682, and soon after, there came a large number of settlers from Wales, who, having purchased 40,000 acres of land, on the west side of the Schuylkill, settled the three townships of Haverford, Merion, and Radnor. Meetings · were undoubtedly held thus early at Friends' houses in each township, and probably at Thomas Ducket's in Schuylkill also. But we find no record of the first meetings established, or of the first meeting-houses built. The latter were probably of rude construction, and of transient duration. Hence so early as

1695.—"William Howell, William Jenkins, William Lewis, Ellis Pugh, and David Hugh, are ordered to inspect and consider what way will be most convenient to rebuild or repair this (Haverford) meeting-house."—(Radnor Monthly Meeting.)

1700.—"Stephen Bevan, Ellis Pugh, David Morris, and David Hugh, being appointed by the last Monthly Meeting to compute the charge of rebuilding the meeting-house at Haverford; and they bring an account that it will amount at least to one hundred and fifty-eight pounds."—(Radnor Monthly Meeting.)

Day, in his Historical Collections says, "One of the venerable meeting-houses founded by the early Friends from Wales, is that in Lower Merion township. It was erected, as appears by a date on the tablet, in 1695." (There must have been a previous meeting-place at Merion.)

1717.—"A letter was received from our friend Benjamin Holme, to this meeting, recommending to their consideration the stirring up of Friends, in the building of their meeting-house at Radnor, &c. This meeting, pursuant to the Radnor Friends' desire, acquiesce with them in building a new meeting-house; and this meeting appoints David Morris, David Lewis, Edward Reese, Robert Jones, Richard Hayes, and Samuel Lewis, to assist them in the contrivance of the building thereof; and meet together about it on the 21st of this instant, and bring account thereof to the next meeting."

Report.—" Some Friends of those appointed to assist Rad-

nor Friends in the contrivance of a new meeting-house there, bring account that they have accordingly met, and given them their thoughts as to the bigness and form thereof; to which Radnor Friends then present seemed generally to agree with."
—(Radnor Monthly Meeting.)

A youth's meeting is mentioned at Radnor meeting-house, to be held in the third, sixth, ninth, and twelfth months, so early as 1698.

VALLEY.

1698.—" Friends of the upper end of Merion, having acquainted this meeting that they live remote from the settled weekly meeting, proposed to this meeting to have a weekly meeting held among themselves ; and this meeting approved of the same, that they should keep it every third day of the week."

1713.—" Stephen Bevans and Lewis Walker have requested to have a meeting sometimes at the house of Lewis Walker. This meeting do condescend that Friends may keep a meeting at Lewis Walker's, the first first day of the week, in the sixth and eighth months next."—(Radnor Monthly Meeting.)

Similar requests continued to be made and allowed for several years.

SCHUYLKILL, FORMERLY CHARLESTON.

" Radnor Monthly Meeting adds to its report the following minute, which being deliberately considered was approved, women Friends concurring therein.

" The committee of men and women Friends appointed at last meeting respecting the propriety of establishing a preparative meeting at Charleston, report, that they attended that meeting, and on conferring together, were united in judgment that it would be right to accede to the proposal. This meeting, on consideration, appears to unite with the judgment of the committee, and submits to the Quarterly Meeting, that a preparative meeting be established at Friends' meeting-house in the township of

FRIENDS MEETING HOUSE. READING. PA
Built 1766

Schuylkill, to be called Schuylkill Preparative Meeting, to be held the first fifth day in the month, and opened in the ninth month next, at ten o'clock; women Friends concurring therein."
—(Radnor Monthly Meeting.)

VII.—EXETER MONTHLY MEETING (FORMERLY OLEY).

1737.—"At a Monthly Meeting, held at Gwynedd, the fifth month, the 26th, 1737, pursuant to the directions of last Quarterly Meeting's minute, this meeting, together with the Friends of Oley and Maiden Creek, have agreed that their Monthly Meeting for business be called Oley Monthly Meeting, and held the last fifth day in every month, except they discover occasion to remove it to another time. The first to be at Oley, the last fifth day in next month."—(Gwynedd Monthly Meeting.)

1742.—"At a Quarterly Meeting held in Philadelphia, the 3d day of the third month, 1742, Oley Monthly Meeting reporting that upon a division of the townships, their meeting falls into Exeter Township, whereupon it is agreed that henceforward Oley Meeting be called Exeter Monthly Meeting."—(Exeter Monthly Meeting.)

EXETER (FORMERLY OLEY).

No records obtained.

MAIDEN CREEK.

No records obtained.

READING.

1759.—"Maiden Creek representatives report that Reading Friends desire the advice of this meeting about the buying of a lot for a meeting-house. Joseph Penrose, Thomas Lea, and Mordecai Ellis, are appointed to meet said Friends at their meeting, view the place proposed, and give their opinion to next meeting, whether suitable or not."—(Exeter Monthly Meeting.)

1762.—" Maiden Creek Friends report, that the Friends of Reading being in much want of a better house to meet in, have thought of beginning to build one next summer, and desire this meeting would take the same under consideration. And it being represented to this meeting that the ground they now have seems no more than sufficient for a burying-place, and that they think it would be advisable to build a house large enough to accommodate a meeting when travelling Friends visited the place, for which reason another lot should be sought for, and a larger house built than just for their particular use: the meeting, therefore, commits the consideration of the whole to Ellis Hughes, Samuel Lea, Richard Penrose, Merrick Starr, John Scarlet, and Thomas Thomas, who are desired to visit them for that purpose, and report to next meeting."—(Exeter Monthly Meeting.)

" The first house of worship in Reading was built by Friends, on their burying-ground, in 1751. In 1766, it was pulled down, and in its place the present one-story log house was built."—(Day's Historical Collections.)

The meeting at Reading is still held by indulgence, after the lapse of more than a century.

POTTSVILLE.

1831.—" To the Quarterly Meeting: The committee to whom was verbally referred, at our last meeting, the subject of Friends' meeting-house at Pottsville, Schuylkill County, report, that a meeting-house was erected in 1831, upon a lot freely given for that purpose, containing upwards of an acre. The building is of stone, thirty-three by forty-five feet, with a basement story. The upper room is finished; and a meeting, on first day, has been regularly held in it for the last eighteen months, under the care of Exeter Monthly Meeting," &c.— (Philadelphia Quarterly Meeting, 8th of sixth month, 1833.)

CONCORD QUARTER

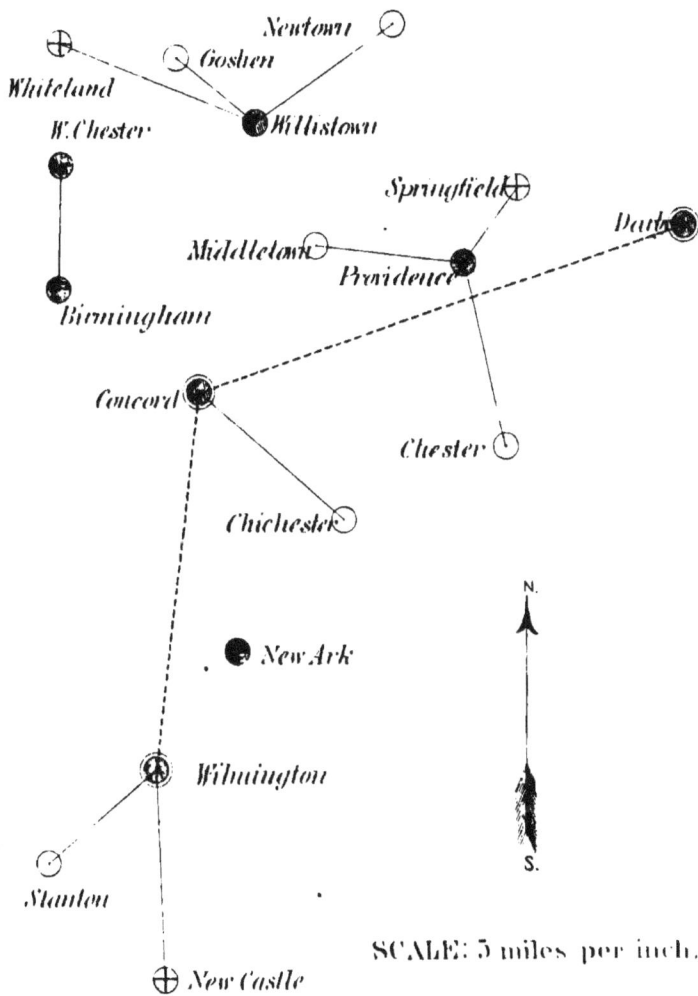

Newtown

Goshen

Whiteland

W. Chester

Willistown

Springfield

Darby

Middletown

Providence

Birmingham

Concord

Chester

Chichester

New Ark

N.

Wilmington

S.

Stanton

New Castle

SCALE: 5 miles per inch.

Owing to the removal of Friends and other causes, the meeting has been discontinued for a number of years.

CHAPTER VI.

CONCORD QUARTER (FORMERLY CHESTER).

1683.—"The Quarterly Meeting of Chester was first established the latter end of the year 1683; and the first meeting of that kind on record in this county, was held at Chester, the fourth day of the twelfth month, 1683-4."—(S. Smith.)

In 1758, Chester Quarter had become, both numerically and geographically, very large; consisting of fourteen Monthly Meetings: Chester, Goshen, Darby, Concord, Wilmington, Newark, New Garden, Nottingham, Bradford, Sadsbury, Duck Creek, Hopewell, Fairfax, and Warrington. A division was then found necessary.—(See Western Quarter.)

1800.—"The proposed alteration in the time of holding Chester Quarterly Meeting, and the changing its name to Concord, being deliberated on, is united with."—(Yearly Meeting.)

I.—CHESTER MONTHLY MEETING.

1681.—"The first Monthly Meeting of Friends at Chester, to be found on record, was held the tenth day of the eleventh month, 1681, at the house of Robert Wade, and consisted of the Friends of Chichester and Upland, or Chester."—(S. Smith.)

"The first minute of the Monthly Meeting runs thus: 'Tenth of eleventh month, 1681. A Monthly Meeting of Friends belonging to Marcus Hook, alias Chester and Upland, held at the house of Robert Wade.'"—(Bowden.)

Robert Wade came with John Fenwick to Salem, in 1675, but soon crossed the Delaware, and erected the "Essex House," on the south side of Chester Creek, called Wade's Landing. Here Friends' meetings were held, here William Penn took lodgings on his arrival, and here the first Assembly of Pennsylvania held its session, in the year 1682.

CHESTER.

1675.—"These Friends (of Chichester and Upland) had meetings for worship at each other's houses so early as 1675, in which year Robert Wade and divers others came over."—(See Salem.)

1682.—"At the Monthly Meeting of Chester, the eleventh of the seventh month, 1682, it was agreed that a meeting should be held for public worship, every first day of the week, at the court-house at Chester."—(S. Smith.)

SPRINGFIELD, PROVIDENCE, AND MIDDLETOWN.

1696.—"In 1696, the Monthly Meeting of Chester, then held at the house of Thomas Vernon, agreed that a meeting should be settled every first and fourth day of the week, at John Bowater's; another at Thomas Minshall's, every first and fifth day; and another at Bartholomew Coppock's, every first and fourth days. These meetings were called by the names of the persons where they were held; and are now the respective large meetings of Springfield, Providence, and Middletown."—(S. Smith.)

1849.—"Concord Quarter informs, that at the request of Springfield Preparative Meeting, that meeting, and also the meetings for worship held at that place, have been discontinued."—(Yearly Meeting.)

II.—DARBY MONTHLY MEETING.

1684.—"Their Monthly Meeting was settled in 1684, till

which time they were joined to Chester Monthly Meeting."—
(S. Smith.)

Bowden gives the same date. But the early records of Darby
Monthly Meeting are imperfect. Some certificates received
there from England bear date as early as 1682; but that does
not prove the establishment of the Monthly Meeting at an
earlier date.

DARBY.

1682.—"Meetings for worship were first settled in Darby in
the year 1682, and a meeting-house soon after built. The names
of some of the first settlers belonging to Darby Meeting were
John and Michael Blunston, Adam Rhodes, Henry Gibbons,
Samuel Sellers, Richard Bonsal, John Bartram, &c., who came
from Derbyshire; Thomas Worth, Samuel Bradshaw, John
Hallowell, &c., who came from Nottinghamshire; and John
Hood, William Garrett, Robert Cliff, &c., who came from Leicestershire."—(S. Smith.)

III.—CONCORD MONTHLY MEETING.

1684.—"The 'fearst' Monthly Meeting held by Friends in
Chichester, on the 17th of the first month, 1684.

" WILLIAM HOUSE,
" JOHN BEZER,
" JOHN HARDING."
(Concord Monthly Meeting.)

It appears to have been the practice of this Monthly Meeting to record the names of the members in attendance, varying,
according to the record, from two to sixteen. None but the
more experienced and exercised members were allowed to attend, and they often necessarily absent.

1686.—"It was the same year (1686) agreed, that the
Monthly Meeting formerly kept at Chichester, should from

henceforth be kept alternately at (Chi)chester and Concord; which last meeting had two years before this, set up a Monthly Meeting among themselves."—(S. Smith.)

There is probably a mistake here. As there does not appear to be any interruption in the Concord series of minutes, it is probable that Chichester should have been used instead of Chester.

The Monthly Meeting continued to be held at Chichester and Concord till 1729, since which time it has been constantly kept at Concord.

CHICHESTER.

1683.—" At the Monthly Meeting at Chester, the 11th of the seventh month, 1682, it was agreed that a meeting should be held for public worship, for the western part, at Chichester, the fifth day of the week," &c.—(S. Smith.)

CONCORD.

1684.—Bowden places the commencement of Concord meeting in 1684. Smith gives a confused history of meetings held in the vicinity, which I have not been able to unravel. Thus in 1682: " That there should be three meetings held in the week, as follows : the western part at Chichester, the fifth day of the week ; the middle meeting at Harold, at the house of William Woodmanson, the fourth day of the week ; and the eastern meeting at Ridley, at the house of John Simcock, the fifth day of the week."

This middle meeting at Harold may have been the earliest representative of Concord meeting.

IV.—GOSHEN MONTHLY MEETING.

1721.—" It was agreed to be moved to the Quarterly Meeting for their consent, that this Monthly Meeting, that was now grown large, and consisted of seven particular meetings, should be divided into two Monthly Meetings: that is to say, the particular meetings of Chester, Springfield, Providence, and Middletown, be continued one Monthly Meeting, and Newtown, Goshen, and Uwchlan be another. To this proposal the Quarterly Meeting agreed, and the one continued its former name of Chester Monthly Meeting; the other was called Goshen. The first whereof was held in the sixth month, 1722."—(S. Smith.)

1800.—"Goshen Monthly Meeting informs they have united in removing their Monthly Meeting to Willistown, which they propose to take effect in the first month next, &c., which this meeting unites with."—(Concord Quarterly Meeting.)

N E W T O W N.

1696.—"At our Monthly Meeting, held at Haverford, the fourteenth day of the eleventh month, 1696, William Lewis, and some other Friends, having proposed to this meeting to settle a meeting at Newtown, they are left to their freedom therein."—(Radnor Monthly Meeting.)

1697.—"Thomas Jones is ordered by this meeting to acquaint Friends of Chester Meeting that the meeting at Newtown is done by the consent of this meeting, in order to have their approbation therein."—(Radnor Monthly Meeting.)

G O S H E N.

1703.—"At a Monthly Meeting, held at Springfield, &c., it was agreed that, to answer the request of Friends at Goshen, a meeting for worship should be held the last first day of the tenth, first, fourth, and seventh months, at the house of David Jones; and on every first day of the week, throughout the year, at Goshen meeting-house. It was also agreed that the weekly meeting, throughout the year, should thereafter be kept the sixth day of the week."—(S. Smith.)

W I L L I S T O W N.

1767.—It appears that a meeting for worship was held and

a meeting-house built thus early, as the records show that Benjamin Hibbert and Mary Garrett were married at Willistown meeting-house the nineteenth day of the tenth month, 1767.

1788.—"The committee, on the request from Willistown, having had a weighty conference on the subject of establishing a meeting there, and being favored with a comfortable calm, which hath tended to the uniting of our hearts together, do agree to report that we are free that the Quarterly Meeting should grant them their request." "Which, being attended to, was approved, and the said meeting allowed of, to be held on the first and fifth days of the week, &c., agreeable to their request; and the clerk is requested to furnish Goshen Monthly Meeting with a copy of this minute.

"Taken from the minutes of Chester Quarterly Meeting, held the 11th of tenth month, 1788.

"JOSHUA SHARPLESS, *Clerk.*"

(Goshen Monthly Meeting.)

WHITELAND.

1816.—The meeting of Whiteland was first held in the eleventh month of this year.

"At a Monthly Meeting, held the 30th of fourth month, 1817, the Friends appointed in the tenth month last, to attend the opening of the meeting in East Whiteland, produced the following report," &c.—(Goshen Monthly Meeting.)

"The Preparative Meeting at Whiteland was allowed by Concord Quarterly Meeting in 1822. In 1843 it was discontinued, at its own desire, and the members attached to Goshen Preparative by the same authority. And, in 1847, Whiteland Meeting was in like manner laid down."—(See Goshen Monthly Meeting Records.)

V.—BIRMINGHAM MONTHLY MEETING.

1815.—"At Birmingham Monthly Meeting, held the 7th of

the twelfth month, 1815, the following minute of Concord Quarterly Meeting, respecting the establishment of this meeting, was read, and the Friends therein named attended:—

"Concord Monthly Meeting reports they were united in proposing to the Quarterly Meeting the establishing a new Monthly Meeting, to be composed of Birmingham and West Chester Preparative Meetings, and that it be known by the name of 'Birmingham Monthly Meeting,' and held alternate at Birmingham and West Chester, &c. &c.; which, coming weightily before this meeting, is united with, and the following Friends are appointed to attend said meeting at the opening thereof, viz. : Abraham Pennel, Edward Garrigues, Samuel Canby, Jacob Hibbard, Thomas Smedley, and Joseph Malin.

"Extracted from the minutes.

"NATHAN SHARPLESS, *Clerk.*"
(Birmingham Monthly Meeting.)

BIRMINGHAM.

1704.—"John Bennet and Elizabeth Webb, on behalf of Friends, inhabitants of the upper part of Birmingham and Brandywine Creek, with the advice of the Preparative Meeting of Concord, did request of this meeting that they might have a meeting at John Bennet's house this winter time, because of their far living from Concord meeting."—(Concord Monthly Meeting.)

Bowden gives 1718 as the time of the establishment of this meeting. The meeting-house was built this year.

1726.—"Birmingham makes application to this meeting for the privilege of keeping a preparative meeting, &c., which this meeting allows of."—(Concord Monthly Meeting.)

WEST CHESTER.

1810.—In the year 1810 a meeting was indulged near West Chester, composed of some Friends belonging to Goshen, Bradford, and Birmingham meetings. In 1813, the meeting was established by Concord Monthly and Quarterly Meetings, and the following year was allowed to hold a preparative meeting.

VI.—WILMINGTON MONTHLY MEETING.

1750.—"At a Quarterly Meeting, held at Concord, for the county of Chester, the 14th of the third month, 1750, the Friends appointed to meet and sit with the Friends of Newark Monthly Meeting, to consider whether it will be of the most service to Friends, and conducive to the prosperity of Truth, for the said Monthly Meeting to be divided into two, report, they met accordingly, and considered the whole affair, and are of opinion it would be better to settle a Monthly Meeting for Friends of New Castle and Wilmington Particular Meetings, than that the Monthly Meeting of Newark should circulate to Wilmington, &c.

"This meeting, after a mature consideration of the affair, do allow that New Castle and Wilmington particular meetings be made and embodied into a Monthly Meeting for discipline, separate from the Centre and Kennet Particular Meetings, which remain and is continued a Monthly Meeting as heretofore.

"Examined, per JACOB HOWELL."

(Concord Quarterly Meeting.)

NEW CASTLE.

1684.—John Hussey, John Richardson, Edward Blake, George Hogg, Benjamin Swett, and other Friends, being settled in and near New Castle, held meetings for worship several years at a private house in said town ; it was first set up by the authority of the Quarterly Meeting at Philadelphia, the 2d of the first month, 1684, and continued till 1705, when a lot of ground was purchased and a meeting-house built.

For further particulars, see Newark Meeting.

1758.—"At our Quarterly Meeting, held at Concord, the

18th of the eleventh month, 1758, the Friends appointed to visit New Castle Preparative Meeting (at the request of Wilmington Monthly Meeting), report that they generally met, and had a meeting with them, and also attended Wilmington Monthly Meeting; and found it necessary to advise New Castle Friends to resign their right of holding a preparative meeting, and join with that of Wilmington. This meeting concurs therewith, and directs that New Castle Preparative Meeting be discontinued accordingly."—(Concord Quarterly Meeting.)

"And it was the advice of the same committee to Friends of this meeting, that we tenderly labor with them to submit thereto, unless such labor should stir them up to more diligence to attend their meetings for the future, and therein seek, in a right manner, for a true qualification to discharge the care of such meeting properly."—(Wilmington Monthly Meeting.)

Friends having been for some time all removed from New Castle, the Monthly Meeting of Wilmington has recently sold the meeting-house, but retains the burial-ground, through respect for the remains of those who have been interred there.

WILMINGTON.

1738.—"Several Friends being settled at Wilmington, in New Castle County, viz., William Shipley, Joshua Way, Thomas West, David Ferris, Joseph Hews, and divers others, they, in 1738, requested liberty to have a meeting for worship settled among them, which was allowed, and first held at the house of William Shipley. But in the same year, they provided a house for a meeting-place, in which they met till the year 1748, when their large meeting-house was built. In 1750, they and Friends of New Castle were constituted a Monthly Meeting. Prior to this, they belonged to Newark Monthly Meeting: subsequently, they constituted a branch of Concord Quarter."

STANTON (FORMERLY WHITE CLAY CREEK).

1772.—"The Friends appointed to meet with Friends at Christiana Bridge, &c., report, that it is their mind that the meeting had best grant them their request; and on considering the case, it is agreed to allow said Friends to hold a meeting for worship on the first and fourth days of every week, until next Monthly Meeting, &c., at the house of Hannah Lewden, at the bridge aforesaid."—(Wilmington Monthly Meeting.)

1781.—"At Chester Quarterly Meeting, held at Concord, thirteenth of eighth month, 1781,

"The committee appointed to visit Friends at White Clay Creek report, they all attended, and had a solid opportunity with them, and endeavored to feel after the mind of Truth. And on conferring together, they think it would be best to allow them to hold a meeting agreeable to their request; which being considered and spoken to in this meeting, is agreed to.

"Copied by order of the meeting.

"THOMAS LIGHTFOOT, *Clerk.*"

(Concord Quarterly Meeting.)

In 1781, White Clay Creek Meeting was established by consent of Chester Quarter. In 1784 they were allowed the privilege of holding a preparative meeting; and in 1803, at their own request, the name of the meeting was changed from White Clay Creek to that of Stanton.

CHAPTER VII.

BUCKS QUARTER.

1684.—"Whereas, heretofore, from the first settlement of this county, there was only one Monthly Meeting within the said county. At the Yearly Meeting held at Philadelphia, in the seventh month, 1683, it was then agreed, that the said Monthly Meeting, for the ease and benefit of Friends, should

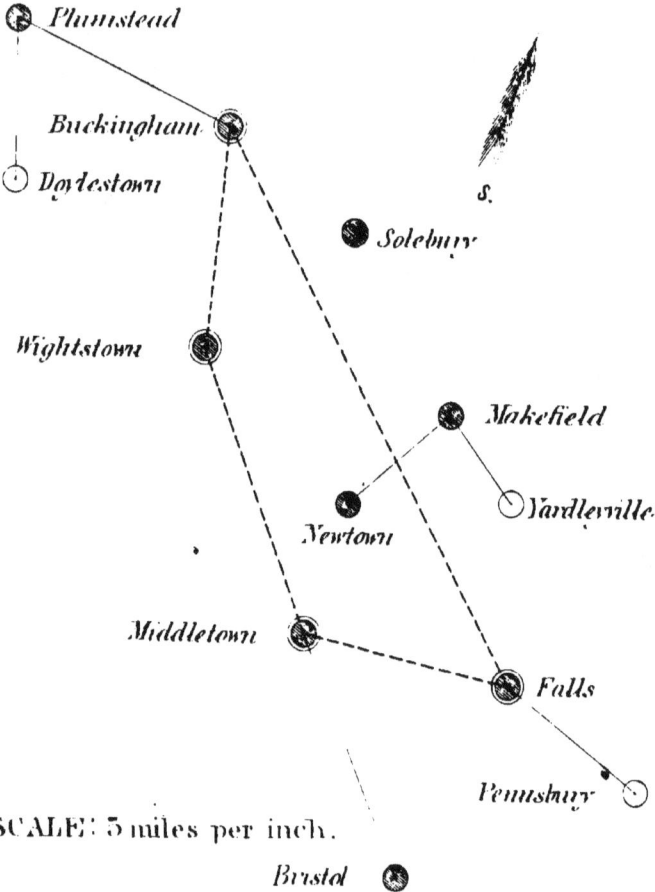

Kingwood

Plumstead

Buckingham

Doylestown

Solebury

S.

Wightstown

Makefield

Newtown

Yardleyville

Middletown

Falls

Pennsbury

SCALE: 5 miles per inch.

Bristol

be divided into two parts: the one to be held about Neshaminy; and the other near the river Delaware. And that the
said meetings shall meet together once every quarter; which
was accordingly observed."

"At a Quarterly Meeting held at William Biles's house, the
seventh of the third month, 1684; being the first Quarter
Meeting held in the aforesaid county, after the aforesaid agreement was made."—(Bucks Quarterly Meeting.)

Although the meeting-houses at the Falls and at Neshaminy
(Middletown) had both been built for several years, yet the
Quarterly Meeting continued to be held at the houses of William Biles, Nicholas Waln, Richard Hough, Joshua Hoopes, and
others, up to the year 1696. From that time it alternated between the two meeting-houses till 1722, when it began to circulate to Wrightstown; and in 1736 the circle was extended to
Buckingham, as at present.

In several instances the minutes establishing Monthly Meetings end thus: "and every third meeting shall be the Quarterly
Meeting." (See Philadelphia.) Bucks Quarter appears to have
been so held for some years.

1686.—"Whereas it is found inconvenient that the business
of the Monthly and Quarterly Meetings should be performed
both at one and the same meeting, it is agreed that from henceforth the respective Monthly Meetings of this county be kept
distinct from the Quarter Meeting, as well in the month the
Quarter Meeting falls, as other months; and that the Quarter
Meeting for the future be kept on the third weekly fourth day
in the month," &c.—(Bucks Quarterly Meeting.)

I.—FALLS MONTHLY MEETING.

1683.—"At a meeting at William Biles's house, the second
day of the third month, 1683, then held to wait upon the Lord
for his wisdom, to hear what should be offered, in order to
inspect into the affairs of the Church, that all things may be

kept sweet and savory to the Lord, and, by our care over the
Church, helpful in the work of God; and we, whose names
are as follows, being then present, thought it fit and necessary that a Monthly Meeting should be set up, both of men
and women, for that purpose; and that this meeting be the
first of the men's meetings after our arrival into these parts.
The Friends present,—

> " WILLIAM BILES,
> " WILLIAM DARK,
> " LYONEL BRITANY,
> " WILLIAM YARDLEY, -
> " JAMES HARRISON,
> " PHINEAS PEMBERTON,
> " WILLIAM BEAKS."
> (Falls Monthly Meeting.)

FALLS.

1680?—"Meetings for worship were very early established
about the Falls, even before the land bore the name of Pennsylvania; and the Friends who were settled from Bristol upwards used to attend the meetings for business at Burlington.
Their own meetings for worship used to be held at the houses
of some of the inhabitants, viz., William Yardley, James Harrison, Phineas Pemberton, William Biles, William Dark, Lyonel
Britany, William Beaks, &c. The first Falls meeting-house was
built in 1690."—(S. Smith.)

New York and New Jersey Colonies having been settled
prior to that of Pennsylvania, some Friends obtained patents
from Edmund Andros, and located themselves on the west side
of the Delaware, before the grant was made to William Penn.

PENNSBURG.

1814.—"The committee appointed to take into consideration the subject proposed by Friends in the neighborhood of
John Comfort's, respecting their holding an indulged meeting

there, have all, except one, met with the applicants, and weightily considered the subject ; and it appears to be the prevailing sense of the committee that an indulged meeting be granted them, under the care of a committee, to be held in the schoolhouse in said neighborhood ; . . . . which was generally united with by the meeting, and Joseph Taylor, &c., appointed to attend the opening, and extend such care as may appear to them needful."—(Falls Monthly Meeting.)

II.—MIDDLETOWN MONTHLY MEETING.

1783.—"At the Yearly Meeting held at Philadelphia, in the seventh month, 1683, it was then agreed that the said Monthly Meeting (at the Falls) should be divided into two parts ; the one to be held about Neshaminy," &c.—(See Bucks Quarter.)

"At our Monthly Meeting, holden at Nicholas Waln's, the first day of the eleventh month, 1683."

1857.—"Bucks Quarter reports that Middletown Monthly Meeting will, in future, be held alternately at Middletown and Bristol."—(Yearly Meeting.)

MIDDLETOWN (FORMERLY NESHAMINY).

1682.—"Meetings for worship were first settled at Neshaminy in 1682, and held at the houses of Nicholas Waln, John Otter, and Robert Hall, till 1690, when their first meetinghouse was built."—(S. Smith.)

1722.—"At this meeting, the having a preparative meeting settled, belonging to this Monthly Meeting, was moved, considered, and agreed on," &c.—(Middletown Monthly Meeting.)

This meeting, being first held "about Neshaminy," was hence called "Neshaminy Meeting." It was first mentioned as Middletown Meeting in 1706, and so continues.—(See Bucks Quarterly Meeting for that year.)

BRISTOL.

1704?—"Meetings for worship at Bristol were sometimes held at Friends' houses till 1710, when a meeting-house was built, and a meeting settled therein."—(S. Smith.)

Prior to 1788, Bristol Friends had belonged to Falls Monthly Meeting. At their own request, they were then transferred to Middletown; and it was agreed

" That all the property which the said Preparative Meeting are now in possession of, or hold as a meeting, ought to be held and enjoyed by them as heretofore."—(Bucks Quarterly Meeting.)

III.—BUCKINGHAM MONTHLY MEETING.

1720.—"Whereas Friends of Buckingham, who have hitherto belonged to Falls Monthly Meeting, being now pretty much increased in number, and having for a long time, with some hardship, travelled a great way, move to have a Monthly Meeting of their own. Notwithstanding the Falls Friends are loath to be deprived of their good assistance and company, yet this meeting, having taken their request and reasons into consideration, consents to their proposal, and allows them to have a Monthly Meeting of their own."—(Bucks Quarterly Meeting.)

In 1724, Wrightstown Preparative Meeting claimed that the Monthly Meeting should sometimes come to them, but "Middletown not condescending to go up to Wrightstown once in three months, as formerly proposed, Wrightstown Friends are now left to their liberty to join with Buckingham Monthly Meeting on equal terms, as proposed."—(Bucks Quarterly Meeting.)

Thenceforward, Buckingham Monthly Meeting alternated to Wrightstown, until the latter was constituted a separate Monthly Meeting, in 1734, from which time it was held alternate at Buckingham and Plumstead, as at present.

BUCKINGHAM.

1701.—" Application being made by the new settlers above Wrightstown to have a meeting for worship weekly among themselves and others that might think fit to visit them, they are at present left to their liberty."—(See Bucks Quarterly Meeting.)

1705.—" Falls Monthly Meeting proposed the building a meeting-house at New Buckingham, which this meeting approved, and left the care of it to Falls Meeting."—(Bucks Quarterly Meeting.)

" The meeting-house at Buckingham was built in 1706, and a new one in 1729."—(S. Smith.)

The latter was burned in 1768, and another erected, at a cost of seven hundred and thirty-six pounds, fourteen shillings. In the year —— the present commodious house was built, of which a Friend writes, " Buckingham Meeting-house justly deserves especial notice, as being one of the most substantial and imposing-looking country meeting-houses which I have ever seen in seven of our States."

PLUMSTEAD.

1727.—" In Plumstead, in 1727, Friends first held their meetings at private houses during the winter season. In 1730, a constant meeting for worship was there settled. Their meeting-house was built in 1750." (1752, the date on a stone.)— (S. Smith.)

DOYLESTOWN.

1834.—" Several Friends residing in and near to Doylestown, made application to Buckingham Monthly Meeting for liberty to hold an indulged meeting on first days in the village, under the care of the Monthly Meeting. The meeting appointed a committee, &c., who reported favorably. Meetings were held in a room rented for the purpose. The following year a meeting-house was erected, which, with the improvements, cost $1654.50."—(Samuel Hart.)

IV.—WRIGHTSTOWN MONTHLY MEETING.

Buckingham Monthly Meeting had been held at Wrightstown and Buckingham; but Plumstead, being equidistant with Wrightstown, claimed that the Monthly Meeting should be kept constant at Buckingham for their convenience. Plumstead was now placed in the same relation to Wrightstown that the latter had been to Middletown ten years before. "But a debate arising thereupon, and Wrightstown Friends not at all condescending thereto.—(Buckingham Monthly Meeting.)

1734.—"It is the agreement of this meeting that the said meetings do part, and Wrightstown be a Monthly Meeting of themselves; and Buckingham and Plumstead have a Monthly Meeting between themselves."—(Bucks Quarterly Meeting.)

WRIGHTSTOWN.

1686.—"In the year 1686, James Radcliff, a noted public Friend, removed to settle at Wrightstown, near John Chapman's. For the ease of those two families, a meeting was held sometimes at their houses, which continued for the most part till about 1690."—(S. Smith.)

1686.—"The Monthly Meeting ordered that there be a meeting established at Wrightstown, to be held once a month, for the convenience of Friends there."—(Middletown Monthly Meeting.)

A meeting-house was built in 1721, and, the following year, a Preparative Meeting was granted to be held therein.

QUAKERTOWN MONTHLY MEETING (FORMERLY KINGWOOD; STILL EARLIER, BETHLEHEM).

1744.—"At our Monthly Meeting, held at Bethlehem, the 10th day of the seventh month, 1744." Again,

1748.—"At our Monthly Meeting, held at Kingwood, the 10th of the first month, 1748."—(Kingwood Monthly Meeting.)

The name was changed in 1747, in consequence of a division of the township of Bethlehem, &c. The Monthly Meeting was composed of Kingwood and Hardwick meetings, and belonged to Burlington Quarter. In 1759, the Monthly Meeting alternated with Hardwick till 1797, when the latter was created a Monthly Meeting with the help of Mendham.

In 1786, on the request of Shrewsbury Quarterly Meeting, and with their own consent, the Monthly Meetings of Hardwick and Kingwood were transferred thereto by Burlington Quarter. But, in 1832, Kingwood requested to be joined to Bucks Quarterly Meeting, which was effected in the following year.

1859.—" Bucks Quarterly Meeting informs that the name of ' Kingwood Monthly Meeting of Friends,' has been changed to that of 'Quakertown Monthly Meeting of Friends, New Jersey.' "—(Yearly Meeting.)

QUAKERTOWN.

Chesterfield records mention the appointment of overseers for Bethlehem Meeting so early as the year 1731; and, in 1736, a Friend was named there for another purpose. In 1747, the name was changed to Kingwood; and, in 1859, this name was again changed to Quakertown. Kingwood Preparative Meeting was established in 1756.

V.—SOLEBURY MONTHLY MEETING.

1811.—"The committee appointed to propose a time for opening Solebury Monthly Meeting, &c., reported that Solebury Monthly Meeting be opened in the 7th month next, &c.; which was approved, and William Lownes, Jonathan Kirkbride, Moses Comfort, William Blakey, Jeremiah Crosdale, John

Watson, John Buckman, Thomas Atkinson, Jesse Heston, Stephen Wilson, Daniel Carlisle, and Robert Smith, are appointed to attend the opening thereof.

"Extracted from the minutes.

"SAMUEL GILLINGHAM, *Clerk.*"

(Bucks Quarterly Meeting.)

SOLEBURY.

1805.—"The committee appointed to take into consideration the request of Solebury Friends, of having a meeting settled near the corner of John Blackfan and Moses Eastburn's lands in Solebury, are united in granting their request. Which report the meeting confirms; and appoints the following named Friends to procure suitable ground to build upon; to suggest a plan for building; to estimate the expense which it is probable will arise in the execution, and to see what aid can be obtained to carry it into effect, viz.: Aaron Paxson, Samuel Johnson, Samuel Gillingham, Oliver Hampton, John Watson, John Blackfan, Matthew Hutchinson, Isaiah Michener, Edward Good, John Malone, Daniel Carlisle, and Robert Smith."—(Report.)

"The members intending to constitute that meeting have presented a plan of a house, to be about sixty-three feet long, and thirty-six wide, to be erected nearly on the model of Buckingham meeting-house; which we estimate, with the contingent expenses, will cost £1500 in the execution, and themselves subscribed £1346 15s. to carry it into effect. This plan has received our full concurrence; and it is our judgment, and we wish to impress it on all the members of the meeting, that their liberality merits the concurrent pecuniary aid of their brethren, particularly that branch of the meeting from which they are about to separate, to complete the design, and place them in as comfortable a situation as those will be left in from whom they have separated."—(Buckingham Monthly Meeting.)

1806.—"Solebury Preparative Meeting in Bucks County was first established and held in a new commodious house for that purpose, near the centre of Solebury Township, by members of Buckingham Monthly Meeting ; and first held 30th of 12th month, 1806."

VI.—MAKEFIELD MONTHLY MEETING.

1820.—The Monthly Meeting of Makefield was constituted by a division of Falls Monthly Meeting, and opened in the 7th month, 1820. It was composed of Makefield and Newtown meetings, and held alternately.

MAKEFIELD.

1750.—" The Friends of Makefield having represented their being heretofore exposed to difficulty in attending meetings in the winter season ; and this meeting taking the same into consideration, does, agreeable to the request of the said Friends, consent that there may be held a meeting for worship the first first day in each month at Benjamin Taylor's, and the third first day in each month at Benjamin Gilbert's," &c.—(Falls Monthly Meeting.)

1752.—" The meeting-house at Makefield being so far finished as to be fit to meet in, the Friends there request leave to hold their meetings there, both first and week days, &c. ; which request is allowed by this meeting." —(Falls Monthly Meeting.)

NEWTOWN.

1815.—Middletown Monthly Meeting granted Friends of Newtown the indulgence of a meeting for worship on first and third days, in the year 1815.

Two years after, the meeting was established with the privilege of a preparative meeting, which was then joined to Wrightstown.

When Makefield Monthly Meeting was opened in 1820, Newtown Preparative became a constituent thereof.

YARDLEYVILLE.

1857.—"At Makefield Monthly Meeting of Friends, held 8th of tenth month, 1857, the committee to whom was referred the request of the Friends of Yardleyville and vicinity, having several times met and conferred together on the subject of their appointment, have mostly united in reporting that their request be granted, and that they be indulged in holding a meeting on first and fourth days of the week in that place, for the space of six months, under the care of the Monthly Meeting.

"Which being considered, was united with, women Friends also uniting. Zephania Mahan, William Cadwallader, Joseph Paul, John Mahan, and Joseph Flowers, are appointed to attend the first meeting, to be held on the first first day in the eleventh month next, and to extend such further care as they may think necessary for the encouragement of Friends composing that meeting."—(Makefield Monthly Meeting.)

This meeting is still continued by the indulgence of the Monthly Meeting.

CHAPTER VIII.

ABINGTON QUARTER.

1786.—"The minutes of the Quarterly Meeting of Philadelphia relative to the institution of another Quarterly Meeting within the limits of that, and the report of their committee thereon being read, obtained the solid attention and concurrence of this meeting. To attend the opening thereof, the following Friends are named, viz., Robert Kirkbride, Oliver Paxson, Eli Yarnall, Thomas Lightfoot, George Churchman, Thomas Pimm,

ABINGTON QUARTER

SCALE: 5 miles to an inch.

Stroudsburg ⊙

Richland ⊙

N.

S.

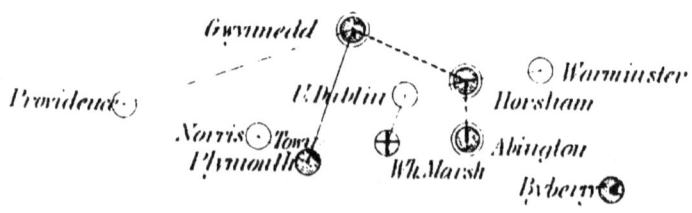

Gwynedd ⊙

Providence ⊙

Warminster ⊙

N.Dublin ⊙

Horsham ⊙

Norris ⊙ *Town*

Abington ⊙

Plymouth ⊙

Wh.Marsh ⊕

Byberry ⊙

Benjamin Clarke, John Hoskins, William Jackson, Jr., David Cope, Mark Reeve, Benjamin Reeve, Benjamin Shotwell, and Joseph Stackhouse.

"The said new Quarterly Meeting to be composed of the Monthly Meetings of Abington, Horsham, Gwynedd, and Richland, and known by the name of Abington Quarterly Meeting."—(Yearly Meeting.)

I.—ABINGTON MONTHLY MEETING.

1683.—"At a Quarterly Meeting of Friends, in the city of Philadelphia, in the sixth month, 1683, it was then and there agreed and concluded that there be established a first day meeting of Friends at Tookany and Poetquesink; and that those two make one Monthly Meeting, men and women, for the ordering of the affairs of the Church."

"At a Monthly Meeting, the 3d of the seventh month, 1683—at a Monthly Meeting of Friends in Truth, of the inhabitants about Tookany and Poetquesink Creeks, being met together for the service of Truth, and the better ordering and governing of the affairs of the Church."—(Abington Monthly Meeting.)

1683.—"There were now three particular meetings belonging to this Monthly Meeting, viz., one held at the house of Sarah Seyers, which afterwards became Oxford Meeting; one at John Hart's, Poetquesink, which afterwards became Byberry Meeting; and one at Richard Waln's, which afterward became Abington Meeting."—(S. Smith.)

The Monthly Meeting circulated variously at those several places until 1702, "where and when it was agreed to be kept at Abington, and has so continued ever since."—(S. Smith.)

ABINGTON.

1683.—"In the year 1683 a meeting of worship was settled among the Friends at Cheltenham, to be held at the house

of Richard Waln. At this place and parts adjacent, lived, very
early, a good body of Friends. It was at first called Dublin
Meeting."—(S. Smith.)

II.—GWYNEDD MONTHLY MEETING.

1714.—"At the Monthly Meeting held at Radnor meeting-
house, the ninth day of the tenth month, 1714, it is left for
further consideration what time to appoint the Monthly Meeting of Gwynedd and Plymouth; which was left to the appointment of this meeting by the Quarterly Meeting.

"Gwynedd and Plymouth Friends, after consideration what
day is suitable for their Monthly Meeting, propose the last
third day in every month; which this meeting acquiesces with."
—(Radnor Monthly Meeting.)

PLYMOUTH.

1685.—James Fox and other Friends settled about Plymouth
in the year 1685?, and held meetings at Fox's house. But they
soon after removed from the place, and were succeeded by David
Meredith and several Friends, who attended Merion Meeting.

1702.—"Friends about Plymouth of the other side of the
Schoolkill, propose to have a meeting on first days at Hugh
Jones's, ... and a weekly meeting the fifth day, to be kept
by course at David Williams's, at Hugh Jones's, at Lewis
Thomas's; which this meeting consents to, if the Quarterly
Meeting approve thereof.

"The Quarterly Meeting have approved that Friends of Plymouth should keep their first day meeting as proposed."—(Radnor Monthly Meeting.)

1703.—"The Quarterly Meeting approved that Friends of
Plymouth meeting continue their first day meeting; and it was
so settled. It is ordered that Plymouth Friends keep their
Preparative Meeting the last weekly meeting before the Monthly
Meeting."—(Radnor Monthly Meeting.)

1699.—"There is a General Meeting appointed at Gwynedd, the second weekly third day of every month, at the desire of Friends there."—(Radnor Monthly Meeting.)

1703.—"Gwynedd Friends desire their Preparative Meeting removed from their General Meeting day to the last weekly third day in the month; which was approved."—(Radnor Monthly Meeting.)

"A meeting-house was built in the year 1700, and a larger one in 1712; and the meeting held therein on the 19th of the 7th month in that year."—(S. Smith.)

PROVIDENCE (MONTGOMERY COUNTY).

Record of this meeting not obtained.

NORRISTOWN.

1854.—"The establishment of a meeting, proposed to be held in Friends' new meeting-house in the borough of Norristown, being introduced by the following address, signed by members residing in said borough and its vicinity; upon consideration, the meeting united in judgment that the application be granted," &c.—(Gwynedd Monthly Meeting.)

III.—RICHLAND MONTHLY MEETING.

1742.—"The Introduction. Inasmuch as it hath pleased God, the author of all our mercies, to increase the number of Friends belonging to our meeting at Richland, and the adjacent places thereunto belonging; many of the elders growing in years, and the youth coming up; and also living far remote from Gwynedd Monthly Meeting whereunto we belonged; and the difficulty we sometimes had to attend the same: under these considerations, a concern came upon Friends here, to make application to the Monthly Meeting, to have a Monthly

Meeting established among ourselves, desiring their consideration and concurrence to propose our request to the Quarterly Meeting at Philadelphia ; which, after deliberate consideration of the Monthly and Quarterly Meetings, our said request was allowed of and granted.

"At a Quarterly Meeting, held at Philadelphia the 1st of the 9th month, 1742, the motion from Gwynedd Monthly Meeting, for the Friends at the Swamp being a Monthly Meeting of themselves, to be held the third fifth day of the week, monthly, is granted.

"Copy.   "SAMUEL PRESTON, *Clerk.*"
(Richland Monthly Meeting.)

RICHLAND.

1710.—"Richland, formerly known only by the name of the 'Great Swamp,' was first settled by a few families of Friends, about the year 1710. They soon after had a meeting for worship settled among them. Some time after, increasing in bigness, they had a preparative meeting of business set up by authority of Gwynedd Monthly Meeting, to which they belonged till 1742."—(S. Smith.)

STROUDSBURG.

1809.—The meeting at Stroudsburg was indulged by Richland Monthly Meeting in 1809, and, two years after, a prepative meeting was established there, and is so continued.

IV.—HORSHAM MONTHLY MEETING.

1782.—"Horsham, in the county of Philadelphia, in Pennsylvania, 1782.

"On the 29th day of the eighth month, 1782, being the fifth day of the week, a considerable number of men and women Friends, members of the Preparative Meetings of Horsham and Byberry, also a committee appointed by the Monthly Meeting of Abington, and divers Friends of a committee of the Quarterly Meeting of Philadelphia, each consisting of men and women, assembled at the meeting-house of Friends in Horsham aforesaid, when, after a seasonable time of silent retirement and acceptable ministerial labor, the following minutes of the said Monthly and Quarterly Meetings were read, &c.

"After which, the women Friends retired into a separate apartment of the said meeting-house, in order to consider and conclude upon the necessary matters for the future orderly management of the affairs of Truth, to come under their particular care. And the men Friends proceeded on the proper consideration of such matters as were most immediately necessary for the future conducting of the weighty affairs of the said Monthly Meeting."—(Horsham Monthly Meeting.)

The Monthly Meeting continued to be held alternate at Horsham and Byberry until 1810, when the latter became a Monthly Meeting.

HORSHAM.

1716.—"Friends of Horsham made application for a constant meeting, to be kept on first and sixth days, during the winter season, which was granted." And in

1717.—"Friends of Horsham request a preparative meeting, which is granted to them."—(Abington Monthly Meeting.)

"It is agreed that there be two overseers chosen for Horsham Meeting, viz., John Michener, Thomas Iredell."—(Abington Monthly Meeting.)

Preparative Meetings did not formerly preserve any record of their proceedings. Horsham record was begun in the year 1769.

The meeting was probably held at private houses till the year 1724, when "application being made by Horsham Friends for some assistance towards the finishing their new meeting-house, the meeting having taken it into consideration, orders, that the other four meetings shall assist those Friends of Horsham."—(Abington Monthly Meeting.)

In 1803, a new and commodious house was erected, seventy-two by forty feet.

UPPER DUBLIN.

1813.—" George Shoemaker informs that a considerable number of our members have been convinced, and have thought right to lay before this meeting, for consideration, the propriety of holding an indulged meeting for worship within our limits on the western side." "Benjamin Lloyd, &c., were appointed to take the matter under consideration, and report their sense to next meeting."

1814.—Report, that they "feel unity with the proposal;" and that "Phœbe Shoemaker, having offered a piece of ground for the purpose of building on, we concur with accepting of it, and indulging said meeting as soon as a house is prepared."—(Horsham Monthly Meeting.)

The report was adopted, and a meeting-house, forty feet square, erected for the accommodation of the meeting; and "that it be distinguished and called by the name of 'Upper Dublin Meeting;'" and also, "that they have the privilege of holding a Preparative Meeting for discipline."—(Horsham Monthly Meeting.)

WARMINSTER.

1840.—" We, the undersigned, members of Horsham Particular Meeting, taking into consideration the distance which many of us reside from said meeting, have believed that a benefit would arise to Society if a meeting of worship could be established among us. Therefore we request, for ourselves and families, the privilege of holding an indulged meeting, for public worship, in Warminster township, in the county of Bucks, and wish the meeting to take the subject under their deliberate consideration.

"Signed by

"DANIEL LONGSTRETH,"

(And nine others.)

(Horsham Monthly Meeting.)

The request was granted, ground purchased, and a meeting-house erected. In 1841, the meeting was established, and a Preparative Meeting allowed.

WHITEMARSH.

——?—A small meeting-house has existed at this place for a number of years, the property of Friends, but is not used, except for meetings specially appointed to be held there.

V.—BYBERRY MONTHLY MEETING.

1810.—The Preparative Meeting of Byberry was separated from Horsham and constituted a new Monthly Meeting in the year 1810. We have no records.

BYBERRY.

1683.—"At a Quarterly Meeting of Friends, in the city of Philadelphia, in the sixth month, 1683, it was then and there agreed and concluded that there be established a first day meeting at Poetquesink," &c.—(Abington Monthly Meeting.)

"In the year 1683 a meeting of worship was settled among the Friends at Poetquesink, which was held at John Hart's house, and which afterwards became Byberry Meeting."— (S. Smith.)

1701.—The Preparative Meeting of Byberry appears to have been established about the year 1701.

The new stone meeting-house was built in 1714, and an addition added in 1753. In 1808 another meeting-house was erected, "about sixty-six feet by thirty-six."

CHAPTER IX.

WESTERN QUARTER.

1758.—" Our Quarterly Meeting, consisting of fourteen Monthly Meetings, whose business to it abounding beyond the work of one day, the same has been for some years a particular concern of this meeting; and divers expedients have been proposed, if practicable, to keep together longer, and also gain more time for the work of the discipline. Yet the inconvenience arising from want of time to transact business in, seems not remediable any other way than by dividing into two Quarterly Meetings; which having been repeatedly discussed and considered by committees, and also in our meetings, it now appears to be the unanimous sense of Friends to divide as follows, viz. :—

" That Newark, New Garden, Nottingham, Bradford, Sadsbury, Duck Creek, Hopewell, Fairfax, and Warrington Monthly Meetings, should compose a Quarterly Meeting, to be held at London Grove meeting-house, &c., to be known by the name of the Western Division of Chester County. And that the other five Monthly Meetings, viz., Chester, Goshen, Darby, Concord, and Wilmington, should remain a Quarterly Meeting as before," &c.—(Chester Quarterly Meeting.)

1758.—" Whereas, at the Yearly Meeting of men Friends, held at Burlington, in the ninth month last, upon application made by Chester Quarterly Meeting for a division thereof into two quarterly meetings; the Yearly Meeting concurred with the proposal, and agreed to establish one, by the name of the Western Quarterly Meeting, to be held for the present at London Grove meeting-house, in the county of Chester aforesaid, on the third second day of the week, in the second, fifth, eighth, and eleventh months, until further direction. In pursuance whereof—

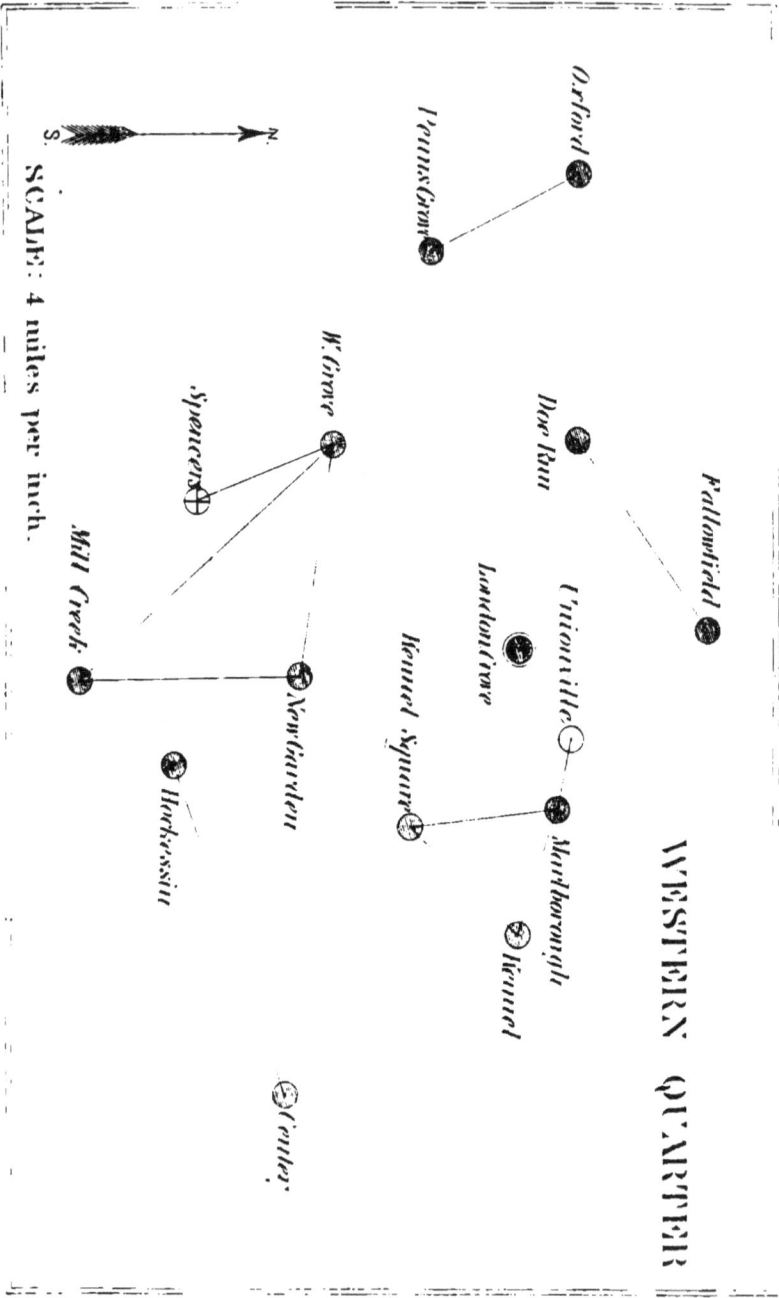

WESTERN QUARTER

Orford

PennsGrove

Doe Run

Fallowfield

W. Grove

Spencers

Unionville

LondonGrove

Kennel Square

Marlborough

Kennel

Mill Creek

NewGarden

Hockessin

Center

N

S.

SCALE: 4 miles per inch.

"The first Quarterly Meeting of Friends, held at London Grove aforesaid, was on the 20th of the 11th month, in the year of our Lord, 1758."—(Western Quarterly Meeting of Women Friends.)

As few opportunities occur of quoting from the records of women's meetings, I do so with pleasure in the foregoing instance. For the information of the uninitiated, I may mention, that so soon as Friends had fully organized their meetings for discipline, separate meetings for women were established, usually at the same time and place as those of the men, allowing each separately to transact their appropriate business, or jointly to labor for the promotion of the general concerns of Society. In the latter case, they generally united with their brethren, by appointing committees to accompany and assist in the service. The treatment of offenders of their own sex was more especially left to themselves.

I.—KENNET MONTHLY MEETING (FORMERLY NEWARK, OR ORIGINALLY, NEW CASTLE).

There was probably a Monthly Meeting held at New Castle for some time previous, of which no record remains. The first minute extant, does not seem like the opening of a new Monthly Meeting.

1686.—"At the Monthly Meeting held at the Widow Welsh's, Edward Gibbs and Edith Crawford proposed their intentions of marriage with each other, the man producing a certificate from the Monthly Meeting in Maryland, signifying his clearness."—(Kennet Monthly Meeting.)

1687.—"This meeting, taking into consideration the matter of the men's meeting, which hitherto hath been kept at New Castle, and finding, upon due consideration, that it may be more convenient for the present, that it be kept twice on the other side of Brandywine, and the third, which will be the Quarterly Meeting, to be kept at New Castle."—(Kennet Monthly Meeting.)

Friends of New Castle, perhaps not liking the removal of the Monthly Meeting from them, grew careless of attendance, and were several times requested to attend, but they still not complying, the following minute occurs,—

1689.—"The Monthly Meeting being held at Morgan Dewitt's, debated concerning the deficiency of Edward Blake and others, formerly belonging to the meeting at New Castle, in not answering the desire of the meeting, by coming hither, on this side Brandywine Creek, but have notwithstanding absented themselves. The meeting therefore appoints that the next Quarterly Meeting be held on this side Brandywine, where it will fall in course."—(Kennet Monthly Meeting.)

From this time, the Monthly Meeting was most frequently held at "Valentine Hollingsworth's at Newark," often at other Friends' houses, and a few times at New Castle, up to 1704, when,

1704.—"This meeting orders, that our next Monthly Meeting be held at the Centre, which is supposed to be George Harlan's ould house."—(Kennet Monthly Meeting.)

The last Monthly Meeting held at Newark, was in the year 1707. From the building of the meeting-house at Centre, in 1708, it was generally held there, a few times at New Garden, until the separation of that meeting in 1718. It was first kept at Kennet, in 1721, and after 1726, once in three months. These removes were, however, made by the special appointment of the meeting, from month to month.

1729.—"The settlement of the Monthly Meetings to be sometimes at Kennet, have been under the consideration of this meeting, and the concurrent conclusion of this meeting is, that it is settled every other time at Kennet, until further order."—(Kennet Monthly Meeting.)

1760.—"Agreeable to our request, the Quarterly Meeting has allowed of the alteration of the name of our Monthly

Meeting, from Newark to that of Kennet; which is to be its name till further orders."—(Kennet Monthly Meeting.)

After the separation of Centre Monthly Meeting in the year 1808, Kennet Monthly Meeting alternated to Marlborough ; and when Kennet Square Meeting was set up in 1820, the Monthly Meeting circulated there also.

NEW CASTLE.

1684.—" John Hussey, John Richardson, Edward Blake, George Hogg, Benjamin Swett, and other Friends, being settled in and near New Castle, held meetings at each other's houses, which was established by the Quarterly Meeting at Philadelphia. In 1705 a lot of ground was purchased, and a meeting-house built."—(S. Smith.)

As the settlement of Friends above the Brandywine increased, and the meeting established at Newark, the meeting at New Castle declined, and was finally dropped in 1758, its members attending Wilmington Meeting. The meeting-house has recently been sold by Wilmington Monthly Meeting. The graveyard is still held, on account of the remains of the dead deposited therein.

NEWARK.

1682.—" About the year 1682, several families of Friends arrived and settled on the east side of Brandywine, in New Castle County, viz., Valentine Hollingsworth, William Stockdale, Thomas Connoway, Adam Sharpley, Morgan Drewitt, Valentine Morgan, Cornelius Empson, and others ; and held a meeting for worship at said Valentine Morgan's [Hollingsworth's ?] and Cornelius Empson's, until the year 1688, when said Valentine [Hollingsworth ; the Monthly Meeting minute is clear] gave that piece of ground for a meeting-house and graveyard, which was known by the name of Newark Meeting ; which lasted till 1754 ; when they being suited with a better conveniency, it was laid down."—(S. Smith.)

KENNET.

1707.—"Vincent Caldwell, Thomas Wickersham, Joel Bailey, Thomas Hope, Guyan Miller, and others, being settled in Kennet and the east end of Marlborough, had liberty to keep a meeting for worship sometimes at private houses. In the year 1710, a piece of land was purchased, and a meeting-house built; which was enlarged in 1719; in 1731 it was further enlarged."—(S. Smith.)

MARLBOROUGH.

1799.—The meeting at Marlborough was constituted of members taken from Kennet and London Grove, and was first held in a schoolhouse near Richard Barnard's. In 1801, the joint committee reported in favor of establishing the meetings; which was confirmed by the Quarterly Meeting as a branch of Kennet Monthly Meeting. The following year a Preparative Meeting was admitted there.

KENNET SQUARE.

1812.—This meeting was at first an indulgence to some members of Centre, Kennet, New Garden, and London Grove Monthly Meetings; and held at the house of John Phillips, near Kennet Square. In 1814, it was proposed by the said Monthly Meetings to the Quarter, to establish the said meeting, with the privilege of a Preparative Meeting, and to be united to Kennet Monthly Meeting.

1814.—"At the Western Quarterly Meeting held the seventeenth of the eighth month, 1814,

"The committee on the request of Friends in the vicinity of Kennet Square report, that it is their prevailing judgment that it will be best their request, as noted in the minute of seventh month last, should be granted; which is concurred with by the Quarterly Meeting," &c.—(Kennet Monthly Meeting.)

The meeting-house was built in Kennet Square the same year.

UNIONVILLE.

1845.—"The committees of men and women Friends, respectively appointed by the Monthly Meetings of Kennet and London Grove, report, that having generally met, and had a full conference with the principal part of those members of the two Monthly Meetings which are embraced in the application, and after a time of solid consideration (the said committees acting conjointly), were much united in believing that it would be right to grant the request; and that an indulged meeting, to be called Unionville Meeting, be accordingly held in the house already provided," &c.

"Which, on deliberate consideration, was united with, Women's Meeting also concurring; and the following Friends appointed to unite with women Friends, to attend the opening of said meeting, and have the general oversight thereof, conjointly with a committee of Kennet Monthly Meeting," &c.— (London Grove Monthly Meeting.)

II.—NEW GARDEN MONTHLY MEETING.

1718.—"Our request to the last Quarterly Meeting, concerning the parting of our Monthly Meeting into two Monthly Meetings, was granted. Therefore, it is agreed," &c.—(Kennet Monthly Meeting.)

"At our Monthly Meeting of New Garden, held at New Garden, the 12th of the fifth month, 1718, being the first held distinct from Newark."—(New Garden Monthly Meeting.)

The Monthly Meeting was sometimes held at Nottingham, till the establishment of that Monthly Meeting, in 1729. Thenceforward it alternated to London Grove, till 1792, when a Monthly Meeting was set up at that place. From that time, it was held alternate at New Garden and West Grove, till 1845, when it began to circulate to Mill Creek, and so continues.

NEW GARDEN.

1712.—"In the year 1712, several Friends, viz., John Miller, John Lowdon, Michael Lightfoot, James Starr, Thomas Garnet, and others, being settled in New Garden, they mostly frequented Kennet Meeting, till about the year 1714 or 1715, when a meeting was settled there, and a meeting-house built, which continued till about the year 1743, when a larger house was built."—(S. Smith.)

1715.—"Friends belonging to New Garden First Day Meeting, having requested of this meeting the liberty of holding a Preparative Meeting at the meeting-house of New Garden, this meeting approves of their request, and grants them the liberty of holding such a Preparative Meeting."—(Kennet Monthly Meeting.)

In 1743, the south end of the present brick edifice was erected in room of the former log one. The north end was added about the year 1790.

Tradition says that the original house was of hewn logs, tenoned into guttered corner-posts; and when taken down, it was re-erected for a barn by William Miller, son of John, who then occupied the Avondale Farm. In —— it was again taken down, and converted into fuel, by a succeeding occupant, to the regret of the venerable Jacob Lindley, whose religious reminiscences are said to have been so excited, that he almost deemed it sacrilege to burn that temple, made with hands which had witnessed his early devotions; but his remonstrance did not avail to place it

"Above the reach of sacrilegious hands."

WEST GROVE.

1787.—The Jacksons, Micheners, Puseys, Prestons, and many other families of Friends, having settled about West Grove, a meeting-house was built, and a meeting indulged therein by New Garden Monthly Meeting, in the year 1787.

The following year, the Monthly Meeting proposed to the Quarter to establish the new meeting, whose committee reported that,

"'After divers opportunities had with friends there, in weightily considering the proposals, and freely conferring together thereon among ourselves, now unite in believing that, under every consideration, it may be best for the Quarterly Meeting to concur in the establishment of a meeting there. Which is submitted, &c. Signed (by eight men and six women) the 15th of second month, 1789.' Which, being considered, is concurred with."—(Western Quarterly Meeting.)

A Preparative Meeting was allowed at West Grove, in the year 1790.

In 1831, a new meeting-house was erected, some distance from the former, and the meeting has since been held therein.

SPENCER'S (INDULGED).

1813.—Samuel Spencer, John Hallowell, Francis Good, and other Friends, living in the lower part of New London, remote from West Grove Meeting, were indulged to hold meetings for worship in Spencer's school-house. It was opened the 10th of the first month, 1813. In 1833, the week-day meeting was discontinued, and that on first days in 1836,—the members returning to West Grove, where they had formerly belonged.

MILL CREEK.

1838.—James Thompson, and thirty-two other Friends, produced a written request to New Garden Monthly Meeting for the indulgence of a meeting for worship in Mill Creek Hundred, to be composed of members of New Garden, Centre, and Wilmington Monthly Meetings. The following report of the joint committees of men and women, from each of those meetings, "on deliberation, was adopted:"—

"*To New Garden Monthly Meeting.*

"At a meeting of the joint committees of men and women

Friends of New Garden, Centre, and Wilmington Monthly Meetings, held at James Thompson's, 16th of tenth month, 1838, to consider the proposition of a number of Friends belonging to those meetings, to hold an Indulged Meeting, at such time and place as may be thought best, having nearly all met, and weightily considered the subject, are united in judgment that the request of those Friends should be granted. Said Indulged Meeting to be under the care of New Garden Monthly Meeting.

"Signed by direction and on behalf of the committee, by

"SARAH MICHENER,

"SARAH WILSON,

"MARTHA HILLIS,

"JONATHAN LAMBORN,

"EPHRAIM JACKSON,

"BENJAMIN FERRIS."

(New Garden Monthly Meeting.)

1841.—In this year a commodious meeting-house was built; and the meeting being the same year established, with the privilege of a Preparative Meeting, was removed thereto,—having been previously held at the house of James Thompson.

III.—LONDON GROVE MONTHLY MEETING.

1792.—"We, the committee appointed to consider the proposal which came from New Garden Monthly Meeting, in the eighth month, last year, respecting a division thereof into two Monthly Meetings, having a considerable number of us, at different times, visited the Preparative Meetings and Monthly Meetings, and paid close attention to the subject, and being now met in a solid conference thereon, are generally united in the prospect of a division; and have not, in the present circumstances, seen any other method for it than the way proposed, viz., that New Garden and West Grove Meetings make up one Monthly Meeting; and the members of London Grove

Preparative Meeting another,—which we submit to the Quarterly Meeting.

"Signed on behalf of all who were present (thirteen men and seven women Friends) by

"ABRAHAM GIBBONS,

"MARY JACKSON.

"Which being several times read, and many uniting sentiments expressed, is concurred with," &c.—(Western Quarterly Meeting.)

LONDON GROVE.

1714.—"In the year 1714, Francis Swayne, John Smith, Joseph Pennock, William Pusey, and several other Friends, being settled at Marlborough, &c., kept a meeting for some time at John Smith's house, until about the year 1724, when a meeting was settled there, and a meeting-house built in London Grove Township."—(S. Smith.)

1714.—"Friends of Marlborough request of this meeting to have a meeting at the house of John Smith, one first-day in the month, and every other sixth-day, for half a year. And this meeting, having taken the same into consideration, have consented that it go to the Quarterly Meeting for approbation." —(Kennet Monthly Meeting.) It was granted.

1724.—"Friends of Marlborough Meeting (with the consent of New Garden Monthly Meeting) request of this meeting, that they may have liberty to build a meeting-house on the corner of London Grove Township, joining to Marlborough, in order to keep a meeting there," &c.—(Chester Quarterly Meeting.)

A larger one was built in 1743, and replaced by the present commodious one in 1818, for the accommodation of the Quarterly Meeting also.

IV.—CENTRE MONTHLY MEETING.

1808.—Kennet Monthly Meeting having proposed for the consideration of the Quarterly Meeting, to divide the Monthly

Meeting; Kennet and Marlborough Meetings to compose one, and Centre and Hockesson another, to be called Centre Monthly Meeting ; and the committee of the Quarterly Meeting having reported favorably, the proposal was concurred with.

" The committee have visited all the Preparative Meetings belonging to that meeting, and also the Monthly Meeting, and have endeavored to attend to the state and situation of each ; and after solidly considering the same, do agree to report, that we are united in believing that it may be of advantage to that meeting to be divided into two separate Monthly Meetings, agreeable to their request, &c.

    " Signed, &c., by

" HANNAH JACKSON,
" ELIZABETH PENNOCK,
" GEORGE CHURCHMAN,
" JOHN KINSEY."
(Kennet Monthly Meeting.)

The Monthly Meeting is held alternate at the two houses, Centre and Hockesson.

CENTRE.

1687.—"About the year 1687, George Harlan, Thomas Hollingsworth, Alphonsus Kirk, William Gregg, and other Friends, settled on the west side of Brandywine."—(S. Smith)

    They attended Newark Meeting until

1687.—" At the request of Friends beyond Brandywine, to have a meeting there this winter season ; to which Friends are willing, and thereto consent."

1689.—" George Harlan desires the concurrence of Friends, on behalf of the families on the other side of Brandywine, for the holding a meeting for this winter season among themselves, by reason of the dangerousness of the ford ; to which this meeting agrees and consents."—(Kennet Monthly Meeting.)

1690.—" George Harlan laid before this meeting, to have a meeting kept constantly over Brandywine. The meeting condescends thereto."—(Kennet Monthly Meeting.)

    The meeting-house was built about the year 1708.

HOCKESSON.

1737.—"Henry Dixon, John Baldwin, John Dixon, and divers other Friends, being settled in Mill Creek Hundred, New Castle County, in 1737, a meeting for worship was established among them. It is known by the name of 'Hockesson Meeting;' so called from an Indian town that was formerly near that place."—(S. Smith.)

Yet we find an earlier date recorded.

1730.—"Newark Preparative Meeting signified that the Friends of Mill Creek Hundred request to have a week-day meeting settled among them; with which this meeting is so fully satisfied, that we grant them the liberty to keep a meeting at the house of William Cox upon the sixth day of the week, every week, until further order."

In 1737, a first and week-day meeting was settled among them, and the following year a meeting-house was erected, which was enlarged in 1745. In 1786, the Preparative Meeting of Centre and Hockesson was divided into two; one being held at each meeting-place.

V.—FALLOWFIELD MONTHLY MEETING.

1811.—"At the Western Quarterly Meeting, held the 20th of second month, 1811, 'We, of the committee appointed in the eighth month last, respecting the division of London Grove Monthly Meeting, most of our number having visited the meetings proposed to be separated, after a free communication of sentiments thereon, are united in believing that it might tend to the promotion of Truth for the division to take place in the manner proposed by the said meetings, &c.

" 'Signed on behalf of the committee,

" 'ALICE LEWIS,
" 'ALICE JACKSON,
" 'JAMES JACKSON,
" 'DAVID WILSON.'

"Which, being deliberately considered, is concurred with, and John Parker, Jacob Lindley, James Wilson, Jonathan Grave, Joseph Bernard, Robert Clendenin, Lydia Phillips, Mercy Brown, Elizabeth Way, Rebecca Chambers, Anna Balance, and Miriam Lamborn, are appointed to attend the opening of said meeting.

"Extracted from the minutes.

" Enoch Lewis,
" Elizabeth Way,
" *Clerks.*"
(Western Quarterly Meeting.)

The Monthly Meeting was to consist of Fallowfield and Doe Run Preparative Meetings.

FALLOWFIELD.

1792. — Many Friends, the Bakers, Harlans, Trumans, Mades, &c., who had settled in Fallowfield, belonged to London Grove Monthly Meeting, and before its establishment, to New Garden ; which latter meeting had already indulged them with the privilege of holding a meeting for worship, at the house of George Welsh. The indulgence was renewed by London Grove Monthly Meeting.

1792.—" George Welsh, on behalf of the Friends of the Indulged Meeting in Fallowfield, informs, that they have lately conferred together, and were generally desirous of being allowed the liberty of holding their meetings longer. Which coming under consideration, is granted." — (London Grove Monthly Meeting.)

Having erected a meeting-house in 1794, the Friends of Fallowfield then requested the establishment of a meeting therein ; which, being approved by the Monthly Meeting, was sent to the Quarter, whose committee of women friends reported :—

1795.—" That some of their number attended most of the

meetings there since last quarter, in company with men Friends; and after solidly conferring together, were united in judgment, that their request might be granted. The case coming weightily before us, some solid remarks were made, and concurring sentiments expressed. This meeting unites with men Friends in granting their request."—(Western Quarterly Meeting, Women Friends.)

DOE RUN.

1805.—"A request of a number of Friends for holding a meeting for worship in Friends' school-house in Londonderry Township, being laid before this meeting, &c., 'We, the committee, &c., had a conference with them; and after solidly considering the matter among ourselves, are generally free that they may be left at liberty to hold it for a time, under the care of the Monthly Meeting, or a committee thereof.

" ' Signed, on behalf of the committee,

" ' ELIZABETH PENNOCK,
" ' HANNAH WALTON,
" ' JOSEPH SMITH,
" ' EDWARD BROOKES.' "
(London Grove Monthly Meeting.)

This meeting was composed of members of London Grove and New Garden Monthly Meetings, requiring their joint action, which does not appear as above.

In 1808, it was established as a branch of Fallowfield Preparative Meeting, and a meeting-house built the same year. The right of membership for twenty-five members of New Garden, was transferred to London Grove by a general certificate.

A Preparative Meeting was established in 1811, at the same time with Fallowfield Monthly Meeting, and was united thereto.

VI—PENNSGROVE MONTHLY MEETING.

1842.—"Minutes were received of the proceedings of New Garden and Fallowfield Monthly Meetings, having in view the establishment of a new Monthly Meeting out of parts of those meetings, to be called Pennsgrove, to be opened at Oxford meeting-house in the third month next, and to be held alternate at Oxford and Pennsgrove. Which claiming, &c., is approved; and Jonathan Lamborn, Eusebius Bernard, Charles Buffington, David Wilson, Joseph Chandler, Ruth Pyle, Asenath Tigert, Martha Lamborn, Dinah Phillips, Rebecca Pierce, Ann Chandler, Ann Hadley, and Eliza Way, are appointed to attend the opening of said meeting.

"Extracted from the minutes,

"RICHARD M. BARNARD,
"AMY PENNOCK,
"*Clerks.*"
(Western Quarterly Meeting.)

The Monthly Meeting is composed of Pennsgrove and Oxford preparatives, and held alternate.

PENNSGROVE.

1820.—On the request of John Hambleton, Joseph Brown, Nathan Sharpless, and divers other Friends, with their families, New Garden Monthly Meeting indulged them the privilege of holding a meeting at the house of Joseph Brown, in the year 1820, which was soon after removed to John Hambleton's, as being more convenient.

In 1828, the meeting was discontinued at John Hambleton's, and kept at the house of Samuel Hadley, under the care of a joint committee of men and women Friends. In 1829, the meeting was established, with the privilege of holding a Preparative Meeting, and so continued till 1833, when the meeting-house was built and the meeting held therein.

OXFORD.

1828.—Thus early, Fallowfield Monthly Meeting had indulged Samuel Gatchel, Asa Walton, Isaac Clendenin, Mahlon Brosius, William Brosius, with their families, and divers others, to hold meetings in a house of Asa Walton's, in Colerain Town-

SOUTHERN QUARTER

GeorgesCreek ⊕

SCALE: 12 Miles per inch.

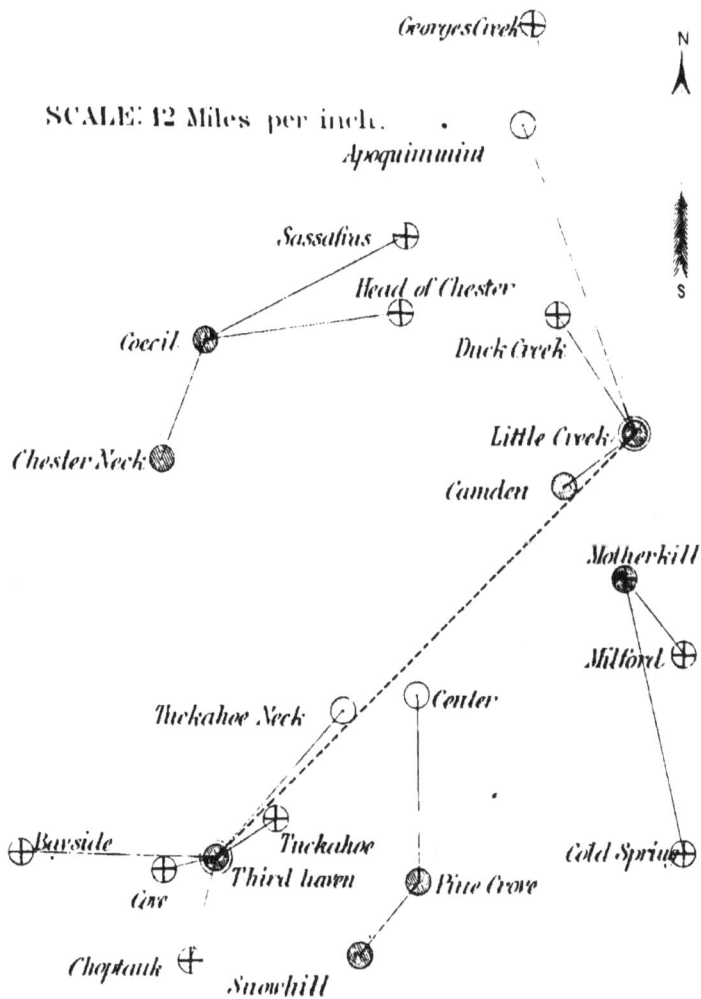

Apoquinimint ⊙

N

S

Sassafras ⊕

Head of Chester ⊕

Cecil ⊗

Duck Creek ⊕

Chester Neck ⊗

Little Creek ⊗

Camden ⊙

Motherkill ⊗

Milford ⊕

Tuckahoe Neck ⊙

Center ⊙

Bayside ⊕

Tuckahoe ⊕

Cold Spring ⊕

Cove ⊕

Third haven

Pine Grove ⊗

Choptank ⊕

Snowhill ⊗

ship, Lancaster County. This was continued from time to
time till 1839, when the present meeting-house in Upper
Oxford was built, and the said meeting established by the
Quarterly Meeting to be held therein, with the privilege of
holding a Preparative Meeting, as a branch of Fallowfield
Monthly Meeting.

CHAPTER X.

SOUTHERN QUARTER.

So early as 1675, a General Meeting of Friends in Maryland was called by John Burnyeat, which was also attended
by George Fox and his companions, soon after their arrival
from Barbadoes. This meeting continued to be held half-
yearly, alternate at West River and on the Eastern Shore,
and was composed of Herring Creek Quarterly Meeting, on
the west, and Choptank, on the east side of the Chesapeake.

The meetings on the Eastern Shore were eventually turned
over to Philadelphia Yearly Meeting. Hence, they claim a
notice in this place.

My notes, taken from the records of the Half-Year's Meeting of Maryland, mostly relate to transactions which belonged
to the Eastern Shore, and therefore more properly belong to
this narrative.

1679.—" At a Man's Meeting, at Howell Powell's, the 4th
of fifth month, 1679, the Half-Year's Meeting at West River
advised, that Friends on this side should appoint a Quarterly
Meeting, for the easing of the Monthly and Half-Year's Meetings, that so they may not be so much concerned in outward
matters.

" It is agreed, that a Quarterly Man's and Woman's Meeting be kept every second sixth day after the Monthly Meeting,

at Tuckahoe, at the house of William Stephens, Jr., at the
Island Creek."—(Thirdhaven Monthly Meeting.)

1681.—" At our Quarterly Meeting, at John Edmondson's,
the 24th of fourth month, 1681, it is assented to and concluded,
that a Half-Year's meeting-house be built upon the most convenient point for a good landing; and respecting Richard
Mitchell, for convenience of passage over the creek.

" The house to be built forty feet long and twenty-two feet
wide, and twenty feet long and twenty-two feet wide against
the broad side of the forty feet house, in the form of a T, and
to be good substantial work, and be partitioned most suitable
for the accommodation of Friends, both at the Half-Year's and
Quarterly Meeting, according to the discretion of the following
Friends: William Southbee, Richard Mitchell, Lovelace Gorsuch, Ralph Fishburn, Bryan Omelia, John Edmondson."—
(Thirdhaven Monthly Meeting.)

The meeting-house was not completed till the year 1684, as
the record sets forth.

1684.—" At our Yearly Meeting, at our meeting-house at
Thirdhaven Creek, the 7th day of the eighth month, 1684, it
is agreed by Friends of the Eastern Shore, with the consent of
this meeting, that, for the future, all Monthly and Quarterly
Meetings usually kept on the Eastern Shore, above Somerset
County, at other places, be henceforth kept at the meeting-
house at Thirdhaven Creek."—(Thirdhaven Yearly Meeting.)

Prior to this date, the record calls the meeting a " Half-Year
Meeting;" henceforward it is denominated a "Yearly Meeting," as here above quoted, but still held half-yearly.

The Southern Quarterly Meeting, properly so called, was
not established until the year 1790.

A Quarterly Meeting had long been held at Choptank and
Thirdhaven, on the Eastern Shore of Maryland, which, in connection with Herring Creek Quarter, on the western side of
the bay, constituted Maryland Yearly, or rather Half-Year
Meeting.

I.—THIRDHAVEN MONTHLY MEETING (FORMERLY CALLED
TREDHAVEN).

1676.—"At our Man's Meeting, at Wenlock Christison's,
24th of first month, 1676."

This is the earliest record extant of this Monthly Meeting,
but it had probably existed for some time, and was held at
private houses, or perhaps at Choptank, till Thirdhaven house
was built, in 1684.

The meetings around Thirdhaven were numerous, some of
them only transient, and not all in existence at the same time.
It is probable they all belonged to the one Monthly Meeting
up to 1698, except the three last. Among them we may mention Choptank, Tuckahoe, Bayside, and Betty's Cove; Cecil,
Chester River, and Sassafras; Marshy Creek, Northwest Fork,
Centre, and Tuckahoe Neck. The three last belonged to the
Society of Nicholites, till their union with Friends, about the
commencement of the present century.

A few notes are all that my scanty means will afford in relation to those meetings. I give the earliest notices in my
possession.

TUCKAHOE.

1676.—A burial-ground was fenced at Tuckahoe in the year
1676. In 1752, a Preparative Meeting was settled. In 1828,
it was discontinued; and in 1839, the meeting for worship also
was dropped.

BAYSIDE.

The Preparative Meeting at this place was discontinued in
1826; the meeting for worship was also dropped, and the members attached to Thirdhaven Preparative Meeting, in 1841.

BETTY'S COVE.

1676.—Mention is made of this meeting in 1676. Two years
after, the Half-Year's Meeting was held there, and, for its

further accommodation, the house was ordered to be "lofted and partitioned, with falling windows, hung with hinges." But the meeting was soon after removed to John Edmondson's house (at Tredhaven), and the order countermanded. The meeting was discontinued early.

CHOPTANK.

1684.—Mentioned in this year; probably much older. In 1734, the Monthly Meeting was removed from Choptank to the new meeting-house at Thirdhaven. Choptank Preparative Meeting was dropped in 1806, and the meeting for worship, in 1834.

TUCKAHOE NECK.

1798.—This meeting was originally of the Nicholites, and probably was instituted about a hundred years ago. In 1798, the members joined Thirdhaven Monthly Meeting of Friends, and transferred their property thereto, as elsewhere mentioned.

GREENSBOROUGH (FORMERLY QUEEN ANN'S, OR TRANSQUAKING).

1701.—The first notice observed was in 1701. The meeting was laid down in 1807.

II.—CECIL MONTHLY MEETING.

1698.—"At our Monthly Meeting, held at our meeting-house, in Cecil County, the 9th of ninth month, 1698, it being our first Monthly Meeting, desired by Friends of Cecil and Chester Meetings, and granted by the Yearly Meeting at Thirdhaven, that Friends of Cecil and Kent Counties should have a Monthly Meeting established among them."—(Cecil Monthly Meeting.)

If the notes furnished are correct, both Cecil and Chester Meetings reported their state to Thirdhaven Monthly Meeting in 1701.

In 1848, the Monthly Meeting began to be held alternate at Cecil and Chester, and so continues.

`CECIL.

Records wanting.

CHESTER.

This and the preceding were established early.

The Preparative Meeting, at the head of Chester, was laid down in 1840, and the members joined to Cecil.

SASSAFRAS.

1679.—"At Cecil Monthly Meeting, the —— of tenth month, 1738, John Browning and Joshua Vansant were appointed to take a deed from William Stoopes for a piece of land on the head of Swan Creek, near the head of Sassafras, for the purpose of building a meeting-house for the people called Quakers."—(Cecil Monthly Meeting.)

The foregoing meetings were all within the State of Maryland, and situate on the Eastern Shore of the Chesapeake Bay. Under the old *regime* of a Yearly Meeting to a State, they were united with meetings on the Western Shore; while other contiguous meetings on the Delaware side of the peninsula were turned to Philadelphia Yearly Meeting.

III.—CAMDEN MONTHLY MEETING (FORMERLY DUCK CREEK).

1705.—"Anthony Morris and Richard Gaw, having lately been down visiting Duck Creek and thereabouts, inform this meeting that the said Friends request that there is need of a Monthly Meeting to be held among them; which this meeting, upon further consideration, doth admit of."—(Chester Quarterly Meeting.)

1705.—"The tenth month, 19th, 1705. This day was held

the Monthly Meeting of Friends at Duck Creek; it being the first Monthly Meeting, by approbation and order of the Quarterly Meeting of the people called Quakers, at Chester, in Chester County, Pennsylvania, for the establishing and keeping up of the good order of Truth," &c.—(Camden Monthly Meeting.)

In 1830, the Monthly Meetings of Duck Creek and Motherkiln were united in one, under the name of "Camden Monthly Meeting," and thenceforward held alternate at Camden and Little Creek.

DUCK CREEK.

1852.—The Preparative Meeting at this place was laid down in 1852, and its members joined to that of Little Creek. An Indulged Meeting for worship was still allowed, for the accommodation of Friends in and near to Smyrna.

APPOQUINIMINK (FORMERLY GEORGE'S CREEK).

1703.—"Friends of George's Creek had a meeting among them at times, for many years, before 1703."—(S. Smith.)

1703.—"John Ashton being present, and laying before this meeting the request of Friends of George's Creek, concerning settling a meeting thereaway, we find nothing to the contrary but it may be convenient; therefore refer it to the consideration of the Quarterly Meeting."—(Kennet Monthly Meeting.)

1707.—The meeting at George's Creek was established in 1707.—(See Camden Monthly Meeting.)

1762.—"Several of the Friends nominated to visit the Preparative Meeting of George's Creek, report, they have complied therewith; and likewise some Friends visited the Monthly Meeting at Duck Creek, and recommended them to comply with the advice heretofore given by this meeting, with respect to visiting the Preparative Meetings belonging thereto; which,

with hopes it may tend to some advantage, is left at present."—
(Western Quarterly Meeting of Women.)

1772.—"The Friends appointed to visit George's Creek
Preparative Meeting, &c. It is their sense and judgment, that
some circumstances which appear, do render them incapable of
holding a Preparative Meeting to reputation ; on consideration
of which, this meeting concurs with their report. Men Friends
having discontinued the Preparative Meeting accordingly."—
(Western Quarterly Meeting of Women.)

1783.—"We, of the committee to take into consideration
the report from Duck Creek Monthly Meeting, for the removal
of George's Creek Meeting to a place near Appoquinimink
Bridge for trial, have attended to the appointment, and agree to
report, that we think they may be indulged with their request,
when they may procure a place for holding said meeting, &c.
(Signed by nine men and three women.) Which, being considered, is approved, and the proposal of that meeting concurred with."—(Western Quarterly Meeting of Women.)

1830.—In 1830, Appoquinimink Preparative Meeting was
united to that of Duck Creek.

CAMDEN.

I have no information respecting the first establishment of a
meeting at this place.

LITTLE CREEK.

1710.—The meeting at Little Creek appears to have been
settled in 1810.—(See Camden Monthly Meeting.)

IV.—MOTHERKILL MONTHLY MEETING (FORMERLY MURDER KIL).

1788.—"The committee appointed, &c., unite in believing
that it may be profitable for a division (of Duck Creek Monthly
Meeting) to take place, agreeably to their request. Motherkill

8

and Cool Spring Preparative Meeting to constitute a Monthly
Meeting, to be held at Motherkill, &c.

"ELIZABETH WICKERSHAM,   "SAMUEL HOPKINS,
"MARY SWAYNE,   "WILLIAM LAMBORN,
"HANNAH LINDLEY,   "AMOS HOLLINGSWORTH,
"REBECCA PRESTON,   "DANIEL THOMPSON,
"WILLIAM EDDINGS,   "BENJAMIN HOUGH,
"JOHN TRUMAN,   "HUMPHREY MARSHALL."
"SAMUEL WALLACE,

"Which being solidly considered, is concurred with; and John
Parker, Joseph Preston, William Harvey, Joshua Pusey, Humphrey Marshall, Isaac Coates, and Abraham Gibbons, together with Margaret Marshall, Hannah Pusey, Margaret Cook,
Frances Hopkins, Rebecca Chambers, and Elizabeth Brown, are
appointed to attend at the opening of the meeting at Motherkill."—(Western Quarterly Meeting, Men's and Women's.)

The Monthly Meeting of Motherkill was joined to that of
Duck Creek in 1830, and the name changed to Camden
Monthly Meeting (which see).

A Friend writes: "The name of said Monthly Meeting I find
to be variously spelled on the Quarterly Meeting records;
which would be of very little importance, if they did not convey ideas essentially different from each other. By way of
explanation, it may not be improper to state that Delaware
having been settled by the Swedes, their word for stream, or
creek, was in many instances retained with an English prefix,—
as 'Broad kil;' and that a bloody battle fought by the Indians
on the banks of one of those streams, gave it the name of
Murderkil, which name was also imparted to a district of
Kent County lying on said stream, and known as Murderkil
Hundred, where the Friends' meeting-house was located in
which the meeting under consideration was held. The Friends,
being a murder-hating, peace-loving, and simple-minded people,
and not approving of the word *murder*, adopted in lieu thereof
that of *mother*, as a prefix to *kil*, making the name of *Motherkil*

for their meeting. But the word *kil* is often, and I believe mostly, spelled *kill*, which, in combination with *mother*, makes a very inappropriate name for a Friends' meeting, more objectionable than the one intended to be softened and improved. It is sometimes written *Motherkiln*, a name that conveys a totally different idea, and is not objectionable in itself."

MOTHERKILL.

1760.—"Pursuant to appointment, we met with some of the Friends of Motherkill and Titberry, at the place proposed by them to build a meeting-house; and, after viewing the place had an opportunity of sitting with them, and some conversation on the occasion; and they appearing to be unanimous respecting the place, and satisfied concerning the title, we were of opinion it might be of service to grant their request; and this meeting grants their request."—(Western Quarterly Meeting.)

In 1828 the meeting for worship at Motherkill was discontinued, and the members thereof joined to that of Camden.

COLD SPRING.

1720.—"On application of this (Duck Creek) Monthly Meeting to the Quarterly Meeting of Chester, Friends of Lewistown and those about or near Cold Spring had their meeting for worship set up in the year 1720."—(S. Smith.)

It is probable that a meeting had been held at Lewes some time before, perhaps since 1712.

MILFORD (MISPILLION, FORMERLY MUSHMELON).

1760.—"Mushmelon and Cedar Creek Friends request liberty to build a meeting-house."—(Western Quarterly Meeting.)

1832.—This year Milford Preparative Meeting was discon-

tinued, and the members thereof united to Camden Preparative;
and the following year the meeting for worship was also dropped.

V.—NORTHWEST FORK MONTHLY MEETING.

1800.—"At a Monthly Meeting held at Northwest Fork
Meeting-house, the 16th day of the seventh month, 1800, by
appointment of the Southern Quarterly Meeting, as appears by
the following minutes:

" The committee on the proposition of establishing a Monthly
Meeting at Northwest Fork, &c., were united in believing it
would tend to the promotion of the cause of truth for a meeting
to be held there, called Northwest Fork Monthly Meeting, and
composed of Center, Northwest Fork, and Marshy Creek Preparative Meetings; which is concurred with, and William
Dolby, Nathaniel Luff, John Bowers, Tristram Needles, and
Joseph Turner, appointed to attend the opening of said meeting.

" Extracted from the minutes,
" SAMUEL TROTH,
" Clerk."
(Northwest Fork Monthly Meeting.)

Since the year 1839, the Monthly Meeting has alternated
between Northwest Fork and Marshy Creek (now Snow Hill).

SNOW HILL (FORMERLY MARSHY CREEK).

1727.—The first report from Marshy Creek to the Monthly
Meeting of Thirdhaven was in 1727. In 1848 the meeting
was removed to another locality, and the name changed to
Snow Hill.

PINE GROVE (FORMERLY NORTHWEST FORK).

1798.—The meeting at this place belonged to the Society
of Nicholites until about the year 1798, when they generally
went over to Friends, carrying their property with them. In
1848 the meeting was removed to another district, and the
name changed to that of Pine Grove.

HADDONFIELD QUARTER

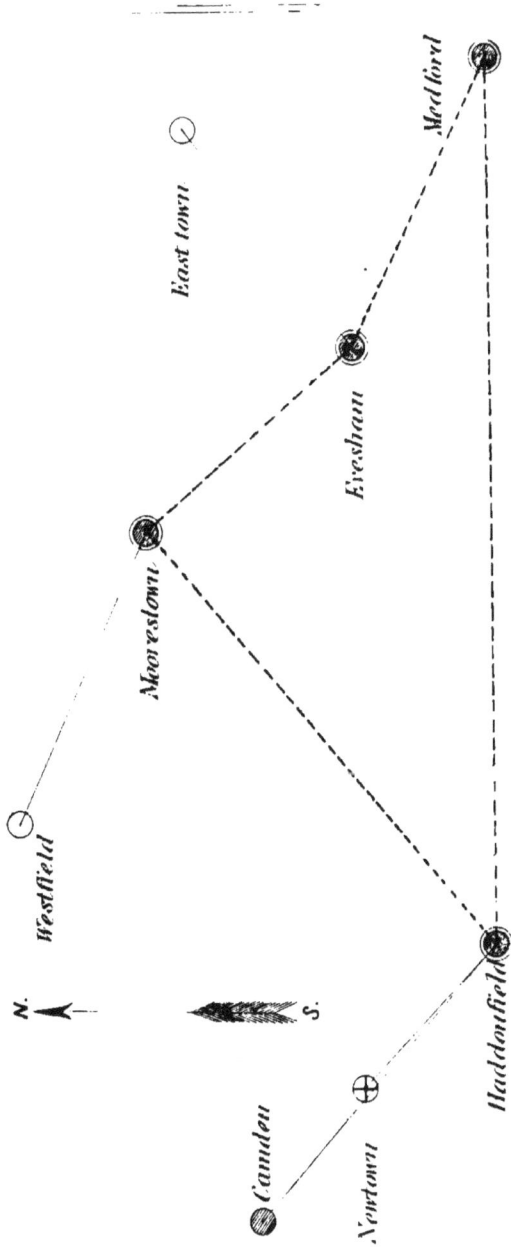

N.

S.

Westfield

Camden

Newtown

Moorestown

East town

Evesham

Haddonfield

Medford

CENTRE.

1798.—This, too, was originally a Nicholite Meeting, and was transferred about the same time and in the same manner as the preceding one.

TUCKAHOE NECK.

1798.—This, like the two preceding meetings, originally belonged to the Nicholites, and was transferred to Friends as they were.

CHAPTER XI.

HADDONFIELD QUARTER.

1794.—"By a minute of the Quarterly Meeting of Gloucester and Salem, it appears that meeting agreed to propose to the Yearly Meeting to constitute · two Quarterly Meetings within their limits. One to be composed of the Monthly Meetings of Evesham, Haddonfield, Great Egg Harbor, and Cape May, to be distinguished by the name of Haddonfield Quarterly Meeting, to be held at Haddonfield in the third and ninth months, and at Evesham in the sixth and twelfth months," &c. &c. "Which being united with and confirmed, a committee was appointed," &c.—(Yearly Meeting.)

The Quarterly Meeting appears to have been held alternate at the two places mentioned, until the year 1831, when it began to circulate to Haddonfield, Moorestown, Medford, and Evesham, as at present.

I.—HADDONFIELD MONTHLY MEETING (FORMERLY GLOUCESTER).

1695.—"The Monthly Meeting of Gloucester, from the year 1695, was held alternate at Newton and the house of

Thomas Shackles (perhaps near to Haddonfield), until the twelfth month, 1721, when it was held in the meeting-house at Haddonfield, which was built in the forepart of that year, on ground given by John Estaugh, for the accommodation of the Monthly and Quarterly Meetings."—(S. Smith.)

The Monthly Meeting is now held alternate at Haddonfield and Camden.

CAMDEN.

1681.—"At a Monthly Meeting at the house of Thomas Gardner, in Burlington, the 5th of seventh month, 1681, it is ordered that Friends of Pine Point have a meeting on every fourth day, and to begin at the second hour, at Richard Arnold's house."—(Burlington Monthly Meeting.)

1682.—"At a General Meeting held at Salem, in the province of West New Jersey, the 11th of the second month, 1682, it was ordered that Friends at Arwamus and those at Shackamaxon do meet together once a month. . . . The first meeting to be at William Cooper's, at Pine Point, at Arwamus," &c.—(Burlington Monthly Meeting.)

Although the meeting at Arwamus had for many years ceased to exist, it seems natural to consider the present Camden Meeting as the phœnix from its ashes. Subsequent to the division of Society in 1827, Friends belonging to Newtown held their meetings at Camden, soon after which time the meeting-house was built, on land given for the purpose by Joseph W. Cooper.

NEWTON, OR NEWTOWN.

1682.—It appears, from a statement recorded by the junior member of the company, that in the year 1682, Mark Newby, Thomas Thackara, William Bates, with their families, and George Goldsmith and Thomas Sharp, the latter a young man, settled at Newton, where they were joined by Robert Zane. "And immediately," says Sharp, "there was a meeting set up and kept at the house of Mark Newby, and in a short time it grew and increased."

"The meeting-house was built on land bought of Thomas Thackara, in 1687."—(S. Smith.)

HADDONFIELD.

1721.—Both the village and the meeting took their name from the well-known Elizabeth Haddon. The meeting-house was erected on land given by her and her husband, John Estaugh, in the year 1721. A meeting had probably been held previous to that date at Friends' houses, perhaps at Thomas Shackles.

II.—EVESHAM MONTHLY MEETING.

1760.—" *The introduction.*—It having been observed by some Friends of Evesham and Chester Meetings, the great increase of a hopeful and rising generation among us, and the comfortable increase of our meetings for worship, from hence a concern arose for their further advancement in the blessed Truth; and having by experience seen the need and use of church discipline, and the necessity of waiting for Divine aid in the management thereof; and observing the increase and multiplicity of business at Haddonfield Monthly Meeting, of which we are members, by reason whereof our affairs could not be carried on with that improving calmness and deliberation which the nature of the service required; and being concerned that generations to come may ask and seek for the good old way, and may walk therein by a clear illumination of mind and simplicity of manners;—under these considerations a concern arose to request that Evesham and Chester might be constituted to hold a separate Monthly Meeting; which, after several years' deliberation, and a firm persuasion that it might be for general service, was accordingly done, as the minutes do set forth."

" The said request was laid before the Quarterly Meeting

held at Haddonfield, third month, 1759, and was kept under the consideration thereof until the third month, 1760, when the said request was granted."—(Evesham Monthly Meeting.)

1760.—"Agreeably to the direction of the Quarterly Meeting held in the ninth month last, Friends of Evesham and Chester held their Monthly Meeting at Evesham, on the 9th of tenth month, 1760, it being the fifth day of the week after the first second day, according to appointment; and Thomas Redman, Josiah Albertson, Joshua Stokes, William Wilkins, and Joshua Lord, Sen., by appointment of the Quarterly Meeting, with several other Friends, accompanied us; which said meeting is now settled under the same regulations as other Monthly Meetings."—(Evesham Monthly Meeting.)

EVESHAM.

1694.—"The first account of meetings held at this place is of one held at the house of William Evans, in the year 1694, which was probably continued till the building of the meeting-house." "The meeting-house at Evesham was built about the year 1698, and meetings for worship then established there."—(S. Smith.)

The Preparative Meeting at Evesham was established at the same time of the Monthly Meeting, in 1760.

EASTON.

1803.—"Friends who live within the vicinity of Easton schoolhouse request that two meetings in a month, for three months, may be held at that place, &c.; which claiming the consideration of the meeting, was granted."—(Evesham Monthly Meeting.)

The meeting was continued by indulgence till 1810, when it was established, with the privilege of a Preparative Meeting. The Preparative Meeting was discontinued in 1827. And in the present year (1859), " Friends were united in believing that

there was such a small number of Friends there that it would
be best to discontinue the meeting for worship at that place;"
which was accordingly done.—(See Evesham Monthly Meeting
Records.)

III.—MEDFORD MONTHLY MEETING (FORMERLY UPPER EVESHAM).

1793.—" We, the committee to take into consideration the
subject of the proposed division of this meeting, &c., report:
That we have generally united in proposing that Friends con-
stituting the meeting held at Cropwell unite with those of Upper
Evesham, in holding a Preparative and Monthly Meeting at
said house, to be known by the name of Upper Evesham
Monthly Meeting; to be held," &c.—(Evesham Monthly
Meeting.)

1850.—"Haddonfield Quarter reports that Medford Monthly
Meeting have changed the title of their meeting from Upper
Evesham to Medford."—(Yearly Meeting Extracts.)

MEDFORD (FORMERLY UPPER EVESHAM).

1760.—" Friends from the Preparative Meeting at Evesham
request that a meeting for worship might be held at the
school-house near Robert Braddock's, on the first first-day and
on the second sixth-day in each month; which was granted,"
&c.—(Evesham Monthly Meeting.)

This meeting was continued by indulgence for many years;
but in

1774, " the Friends belonging to the school-house meeting
requested some advice and assistance with respect to building
or enlarging their meeting-place; therefore, Thomas Evans,
Thomas Wilkins, William Forster, William Rogers, or any
other Friends that are free to attend, are appointed to go and
sit with them, and give them what advice and assistance they
find needful."—(Evesham Monthly Meeting.)

The meeting-place was enlarged in the following year, and obtained the name of "Upper Evesham." In 1783, the meeting was established with a Preparative Meeting.

CROPWELL.

1786.—"A request, by direction of the Preparative Meeting of Evesham, in favor of holding a meeting for worship in a schoolhouse, lately erected near Cropwell Creek, signed by the principal part of men and women Friends that are likely to constitute the same, being produced, and several times read, the meeting unites in deferring the further consideration thereof to next meeting."

It is probable that some members of the Monthly Meeting of Haddonfield were united in the request, as it was finally granted, on the favorable report of a joint committee of the two Monthly Meetings.

It does not appear that the meeting has been kept up by Friends since about the year 1827.

IV.—CHESTER MONTHLY MEETING, AT MOORESTOWN.

1803.—"The Preparative Meeting of Westfield propose, for consideration, whether there would not an advantage arise from a division of this Monthly Meeting; which, on deliberation, is referred to the consideration of next meeting."

1803.—"The report of the committee, relative to a division of this Monthly Meeting, being again read and considered, was approved, and the substance thereof directed to be forwarded in the report to our next Quarterly Meeting, viz., that the Preparative Meetings of Chester and Westfield unite in holding a Monthly Meeting at Chester, on the third day of the week following the second second day in each month, &c., to be known by the name of ' Chester Monthly Meeting.' "

" The minute of our last Quarterly Meeting was read, setting forth that meeting's concurrence therewith; and the Monthly Meeting of Chester is thereby established and confirmed, agreeably to the proposition in our report to the Quarterly Meeting."—(Evesham Monthly Meeting.)

MOORESTOWN (FORMERLY CALLED CHESTER).

1721.—Samuel Smith says, the meeting-house at Chester was built and the meeting settled there in 1721. But the Chesterfield records mention assisting Chester Friends to rebuild their meeting-house, which had been burned in that year. The meeting had probably existed prior to that date.

The Preparative Meeting of Chester was granted to be held in 1760.

In 1803, Evesham Monthly Meeting reported:—

"One new meeting-house erected for the accommodation of Chester Particular Meeting, in lieu and near the place of the old one."—(Evesham Monthly Meeting.)

WESTFIELD.

1794.—"A proposition was made, from the Preparative Meeting of Chester, to hold meetings for worship at Friends' lower schoolhouse, within the limits of said meeting; not only to accommodate divers members, living somewhat remote from said Preparative Meeting, but those of other professions, living contiguous thereto; which, being attended to with a good degree of solid weight, there appeared a general concurrence with holding one at the place proposed next first day, at the eleventh hour. And John Collins (and others) were appointed to the oversight thereof, and report to next meeting."—(Evesham Monthly Meeting.)

The meeting at Westfield was continued, from time to time, under the care of the Monthly Meeting, up to the year 1801, when a meeting-house was erected, and the meeting established, with liberty to hold a Preparative Meeting.

The meeting-house was accidentally burned in the present year (1859), and is now rebuilt.

CHAPTER XII.

CALN QUARTER.

1800.—" The proposals from Philadelphia, Chester, and the Western Quarters, relative to the establishment of a Quarterly Meeting at East Caln, to be denominated East Caln Quarterly Meeting, composed of Bradford, Sadsbury, Uwchlan, and Robeson Monthly Meetings, being now deliberately considered, and a concurrence therewith expressed, it is concluded that the said meeting be opened on the 14th day of the eighth month, 1800."—(Yearly Meeting.)

Caln Quarterly Meeting was composed of parts of the three quarters above named, who all united in the application. Bradford and Sadsbury belonged to the Western, Uwchlan to Concord, and Robeson to Philadelphia Quarter.

I.—BRADFORD MONTHLY MEETING.

1737.—" This meeting, after due consideration, do grant and allow to Friends of Bradford and Caln Particular Meetings, liberty of keeping and holding a Monthly Meeting for discipline and church affairs, and to be called and known by the name of Bradford Monthly Meeting."—(Chester Quarterly Meeting.)

1846.—" Bradford Preparative Meeting requests the Monthly Meeting be held alternately at Romansville and Caln; to be held at Romansville on the even months, and to commence next month (tenth): with which this meeting unites."—(Bradford Monthly Meeting.)

EAST CALN.

1716.—" In 1716, the Friends of Caln Township, with the allowance of Concord Monthly Meeting and Chester Quarterly,

CALN QUARTER

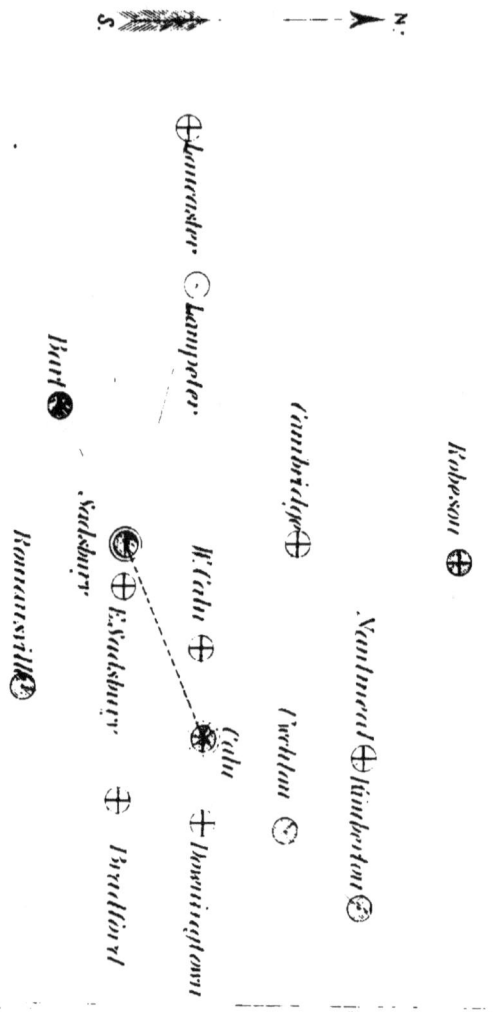

N.

S.

SCALE: 5 miles per inch.

Robeson

Lancaster

Lampeter

Cambridge

Nantmeal Timberton

Vincent

Bart

W. Caln

Salsbury

E. Salsbury

Caln

Lancasville

Downingtown

Bradford

had a meeting of worship settled among them, and about that time built the meeting-house."—(S. Smith.)

1716.—"This meeting, pursuant to the advice of the last Quarterly Meeting, doth settle a Preparatory Meeting at Caln, in the valley, and to be kept on the first day before the Monthly Meeting," &c.—(Concord Monthly Meeting.)

BRADFORD.

The older Monthly Meeting records often contain much good penmanship and correct diction, according to the forms of speech then used. But there are exceptions, where the true meaning is obscure, as will appear from a few instances under this head.

1716, eighth month.—"Kennet Preparative Meeting moved here for a meeting to be settled in the Forks of Brandywine twice every week, for this winter season, which this meeting leaves till the next Monthly Meeting for a further consideration."—(Kennet Monthly Meeting.)

1716, ninth month.—"The motion from Kennet Preparative Meeting to the last Monthly Meeting, concerning the Friends living up Brandywine keeping meetings for this winter time in the forks of the said creek, near William Marshall's, is ordered to be laid before the Quarterly Meeting."—(Kennet Monthly Meeting.)

1716, tenth month.—"The request of the Friends in the Forks of Brandywine is not approved by the Quarterly Meeting for the present."—(Kennet Monthly Meeting.)

1722, second month.—"The Friends within the Forks of Brandywine made application to the Preparative Meeting of Kennet for a meeting once in two weeks, which case was referred to this meeting for further consideration, and every fifth day in the week, except Preparative Meeting week."—(Kennet Monthly Meeting.)

1722, fourth month.—"The request of the Friends in the Forks of Brandywine, after consideration in this meeting, referred it to the consideration of the Quarterly Meeting, which was granted to be held the year about (the whole year), as formerly allowed in the winter season."—(Kennet Monthly Meeting.)

1722.—"Abraham Marshall, Peter Collins, Jeremiah Dean, and several other Friends, being settled in and near the Forks of Brandywine, belonged to Kennet Meeting till the year 1722, when they requested a meeting to be settled among them, which was allowed, and held in a house belonging to Abraham Marshall, till about the year 1727, when a piece of ground was purchased and a meeting-house built."—(S. Smith.)

1726.—"Friends belonging to the Forks First Day Meeting require a Preparative Meeting, which was laid before this meeting for consideration, and is granted."—(Kennet Monthly Meeting.)

WEST CALN.

1756.—"The Friends appointed to visit West Caln Meeting report, that they met most of the members, and are of opinion that they may have leave to hold a meeting for worship, as heretofore; with which this concurs, and do establish said meeting by the name of West Caln Meeting."—(Chester Quarterly Meeting.)

DOWNINGTOWN.

1811.—"The proposal from Uwchlan Monthly Meeting for establishing a Preparative Meeting at Downingtown, claiming the consideration of this meeting, is united with," &c.

"Transcribed from the minutes of Caln Quarterly Meeting, held the 14th of second month, 1811.

"JAMES COOPER,
"*Clerk.*"
(Uwchlan Monthly Meeting.)

CAMBRIDGE.

1825.—"The committee, on the request of Isaac Haines and Jacob Haines, inform that Bradford Monthly Meeting has granted an Indulged Meeting to continue one year, which meeting they all attended except one; and having a satisfactory conference with said families, report as their sense, that they be left at liberty to meet with said Indulged Meeting on the first and fifth days of the week; with which this meeting unites."—(Sadsbury Monthly Meeting.)

1852.—"The meeting for worship at Cambridge is discontinued."—(Yearly Meeting Extracts.)

ROMANSVILLE.

The meeting at Romansville was first set up by the indulgence of Bradford Monthly Meeting, in the year ——. In 1846 the Monthly Meeting began to be held there in alternate months.

II.—SADSBURY MONTHLY MEETING.

1737.—"As Friends increased, and spread themselves back in the uncultivated woods, it became necessary to have meetings settled at suitable places for worshipping the Divine Being; and, in process of time, the meetings of Sadsbury and Leacock were settled for that service,—the respective members thereof being a branch of New Garden Monthly Meeting; and as they increased, this difficulty of attending their Monthly Meeting likewise increased; and, judging themselves in a capacity to hold a Monthly Meeting, made a request to their said Monthly Meeting, held at New Garden, the 24th day of the seventh month, in the year 1737, to have a Monthly Meeting settled among them. Which said meeting took it into consideration, and, at their next Monthly Meeting, sent the request to the ensuing Quarterly Meeting, held at Concord the 14th day of the ninth month, for their approbation; which meeting, after consideration thereof, allowed the said Friends, members of Sadsbury and Leacock Particular Meetings, liberty of holding a Monthly Meeting on the first second-day of the week in every month until further orders, and to be called by the name of Sadsbury Monthly Meeting. . . . In consequence whereof, the said Friends of Sadsbury and Leacock Particular Meetings met at their meeting-house at Sadsbury, in the county of Lancaster, in the twelfth month following, and held their first Monthly Meeting."—(Sadsbury Monthly Meeting.)

The Monthly Meeting was held alternately at Sadsbury and Leacock, until 1751, when the meeting-house and meeting were removed from Leacock to Lampeter, and the name of the meeting changed. Thenceforward the Monthly Meeting was held alternately at Sadsbury and Lampeter till 1840; from which time it circulated at the three places until 1854, when it was withdrawn from Lampeter, and held alternately at Sadsbury and Bart. Sadsbury Monthly Meeting was a branch of Chester Quarter up to 1758. When the Western Quarterly Meeting was established it became a branch thereof, and so remained till the establishment of Caln Quarter in the year 1800.

SADSBURY.

1724.—"In the year 1724, Samuel Miller and Andrew Moore made application, on behalf of themselves and their friends settled about Sadsbury, for liberty to build a meeting-house, which being granted by the Quarterly Meeting, they built one in 1725, which goes by the name of Sadsbury Meeting."—(S. Smith.)

COLUMBIA (FORMERLY HEMPFIELD).

1728.—In the year 1728, Robert Barber, Samuel Blunston and John Wright, together with their families, removed from Chester, and settled at Columbia, where they had purchased one thousand acres of land. They no doubt held meetings for worship at their houses at this early date. A meeting-house of squared logs appears to have been built very early.

Sadsbury Monthly Meeting has a long series of minutes about "Hempfield Friends," "Hempfield Meeting," &c., which must have been the one now called Columbia. The earliest notice which I have seen of Hempfield, is the following:—

1754.—" Thomas Minshall requests to come under the care of Friends. Peter Worrall and Isaac Whitelock, are appointed to desire him to attend our next meeting; also to let Hempfield Friends know that we expect them to come under our care."—(Sadsbury Monthly Meeting.)

Those Friends appear to have held meetings in their own way, but refused subordination to any other. After labor by the Monthly and Quarterly Meetings " they refused to request any privilege, but thought they would hold meetings as they had done formerly." But at length,

1758.—"A copy of a minute of the Quarterly Meeting was produced here, concerning Hempfield Friends, permitting them to hold meetings for worship on first-days, at their meeting-house; and to be a branch of Lampeter Preparative and Sadsbury Monthly Meeting, therefore . . . are appointed to give them a copy thereof, and inform them how they stand." Who " report they are not willing to be accountable to any meeting, except the widow Barber."

1761.—" The Friends appointed on a visit to Hempfield Friends, report:—They say they are resolved to hold meetings, and are all of one family, and cannot report."

During the many years of this laborious concern, numbers of the more obstinate were disowned for various offences, up to about the year 1773. My notes do not extend further, until in

1799.—" From Lampeter report it appears, that application is made to this meeting in writing, by Friends of Hempfield, requesting the privilege of holding an Indulged Meeting on first and week days at Columbia."

" Which, after a communication of sentiments, is agreed to by the meeting, and . . . are appointed in conjunction with women Friends, to attend at the opening thereof," &c.—(Sadsbury Monthly Meeting.)

Three years after this request of Hempfield Friends to have an Indulged Meeting at Columbia, another minute notes "the Indulged Meeting of Hempfield." They were undoubtedly one and the same; Columbia is in Hempfield Township.

In 1810, the meeting at Columbia was established by Caln Quarter, and in 1812 they were allowed the privilege of a Preparative Meeting.

LEACOCK.

Hattell Varman, William Evans, and several other Friends having settled in Leacock,

1729.—"Sadsbury Preparative Meeting requested on behalf of Friends who live beyond Pequea, to have a meeting at the house of Hattell Varman every sixth-day of the weeks; which this meeting allows."—(New Garden Monthly Meeting.)

In 1732 Leacock Meeting was established, by the consent of Chester Quarter, and the following year allowed to hold a Preparative Meeting, which, like the foregoing, was a branch of New Garden Monthly Meeting until 1737, when they were erected into a Monthly Meeting.

1748.—"The affair of moving Leacock Meeting-house coming under consideration, it is concluded to lay it before the Quarterly Meeting for their approbation."

1751.—"Leacock Friends having moved their meeting, according to the liberty formerly allowed them, so our next Monthly Meeting is to be held at Lampeter, where their meeting-house is now fixed."—(Sadsbury Monthly Meeting.)

LAMPETER.

The early history of this meeting is to be found in that of the preceding one, being merely a continuation thereof under another name.

1851.—"A minute was received from Lampeter Preparative

Meeting, requesting the Monthly Meeting to lay that meeting down, and unite its members to Sadsbury Preparative Meeting; which request was granted by this meeting."—(Sadsbury Monthly Meeting.)

LANCASTER.

The meeting at Lancaster was established, by the consent of Chester Quarter, in 1755. In 1766, the Yearly Meeting recommended its subordinate branches to raise money " to enable Lancaster Friends to finish their meeting-house."

1779.—" This meeting agrees to request the advice of the Quarterly Meeting respecting the waste condition of the meeting-house and graveyard at Lancaster."

1780.—" Our Quarterly Meeting, some time past, appointed a committee to view the meeting-house at Lancaster, who made report that, according to their sense, it would be best to shut up the large house, repair the small apartment, and fence up the burying-ground; which the meeting concurred with, and appointed," &c.

1784.—"As report is made that week-day meetings are *weakly* attended at Lancaster, this meeting more closely enjoins it on the committee, before appointed on that account, to take the case strictly under their notice."—(Sadsbury Monthly Meeting.)

1788.—" On consideration of the subject committed to us, respecting the repairs proposed to be done to Friends' Meeting-house in the borough of Lancaster, it is agreed to recommend that, for maintaining the reputation of Society, there be applied out of the general stock the sum of one hundred pounds, to assist the Western Quarterly Meeting in repairing the said meeting-house as, or nearly as, proposed by the united committee of the Meeting for Sufferings and the Western Quarter, in their report of the 11th of fourth month last to the Meeting for Sufferings; which we submit to the Yearly Meeting." (Signed by twenty-one Friends.)—(Yearly Meeting Extract.)

1798.—"The case of Lancaster Meeting, by Lampeter's re-

port, coming under consideration, from the number of Friends
that have or are about to remove therefrom, this meeting appoints . . . . in conjunction with women Friends, to have the
care and oversight thereof."

1802.—" The committee appointed, &c., unitedly agree to
report, that most of our number have attended there since last
Monthly Meeting, and divers of us at several times before ; and
after weightily and solidly considering the subject, are of the
mind that it would be right to acquaint the Quarterly Meeting
therewith, as we feel a tenderness in expressing that it is our
sense that it would be seasonable to discontinue that meeting.
Signed," &c.—(Sadsbury Monthly Meeting.)

1802.—" At Caln Quarterly Meeting, held 13th of fifth
month, 1802, the following report of the committee relative to
Lancaster Meeting, being read and deliberatively considered, is
united with, viz.: The committee appointed to take into consideration the state of Lancaster Meeting, as represented in
the report from Sadsbury, having met and attended said meeting, and after conferring with what members were present, and
taking circumstances relative thereto into consideration, unanimously agree to report, as our sense, that it will be best to
discontinue said meeting, and unite the members thereof to
Lampeter; which we submit to the Quarterly Meeting. Signed,"
&c.—(Caln Quarterly Meeting.)

1802.—" This meeting received the foregoing minute of the
Quarterly Meeting, which is united with and . . . . . . are
appointed to sit with Friends in their meeting at Lancaster, on
next sixth-day, and inform them of the result of the Quarterly
Meeting; from that time that meeting to be discontinued."—
(Sadsbury Monthly Meeting.)

The decline of the meeting at Lancaster, as in many other
places, did not indicate a decline of the Society, but was owing
to the removal of its members.

The Meeting for Sufferings, in a minute of advice, subsequently issued, observes :—

" As the estate was originally obtained for the use and benefit of such of our religious Society as should reside in the borough of Lancaster, it appears incumbent to recommend that the said Monthly Meeting (Sadsbury) do always exercise a becoming religious care that the whole of the premises be kept in decent order; and that the internal arrangement of the house be so constructed or adapted to be suitable for the members of our Society to hold religious meetings in, whenever there may be an opening therefor;" and, "that Friends there may always maintain a diligent care and concern, that the property be preserved in good order, and that the uses to which it may be applied be always such as to comport with our religious profession and principles."—(See Sadsbury Monthly Meeting.)

Since 1827, "Orthodox Friends" have assumed the entire charge of this property; and a correspondent writes, "How far the above recommendation has been complied with, may be inferred from the fact, that, a few years since, the Lancaster property was disposed of to the fraternity of Odd Fellows, and a fantastic-looking structure may now be seen, dedicated to midnight orgies, on the spot where Friends once reverently met to worship the Father in spirit and in truth. Alas, how sad to contemplate!"

EAST SADSBURY.

In 1810, Friends of East Sadsbury requested liberty of an Indulged Meeting, to be held in a school-house near the turnpike, which was granted; but they not providing suitable accommodations, the Monthly Meeting thought proper to withdraw it in 1813. In 1819, the same Friends renewed their request for an Indulged Meeting in Joseph Cooper's school-house, which was allowed.

1820.—"Sadsbury Monthly Meeting now offers, for our consideration, a proposal for the establishment of a meeting for religious worship, to be held in Sadsbury Township, on, &c., to be called 'East Sadsbury;' which, being deliberately considered, is united with, and the meeting established."—(Caln Quarterly Meeting.)

1858.—"The committee, in the case of East Sadsbury Meeting, report, that a part of their number had a conference with the Friends of that meeting, and were united in the belief that it would be right to grant their request (that their meeting be laid down, and the members joined to Sadsbury Meeting), which is satisfactory to this meeting. East Sadsbury Meeting is therefore laid down," &c.—(Sadsbury Monthly Meeting.)

BART.

1820.—"We, the committee appointed on the application of a number of members of Sadsbury Particular Meeting, requesting the privilege of holding a meeting in the school-house belonging to Jeremiah Cooper, having deliberately attended to the subject, unite in proposing to the Monthly Meeting to grant their request," &c.; which, having been read and considered, was adopted, women Friends uniting therewith. The following Friends are appointed to attend at the opening, viz.: Azahel Walker, Thomas Whitson, Samuel Gibbons, and John Kendall."—(Sadsbury Monthly Meeting.)

1825.—"A transcript of a minute now received from our late Quarterly Meeting is as follows :—

" 'Dear Friends: The committee on the subject sent up on your report, respecting the establishment of Bart Meeting, inform they all attended said meeting; and they were easy that the request of Friends constituting it, should be granted. This meeting, on due deliberation, united in the establishment thereof. Extracted from the minutes of Caln Quarterly Meeting, held 17th of second month, 1825.

" ' JESSE MEREDITH,
" ' Clerk.' "

(Sadsbury Monthly Meeting.)

1840.—"The following minute was received from Caln Quarterly Meeting :—

" 'Sadsbury Monthly Meeting informs that the members of Bart Meeting have applied for the privilege of holding a Preparative Meeting, to be held, &c., and to be called Bart Pre-parative Meeting, with which the Monthly Meeting united; and being considered in this meeting, was also united with. Said meeting to be opened, &c.

" ' Taken from the minutes, &c.

" 'LINDLEY COATES,

" '*Clerk.*' "

III.—UWCHLAN MONTHLY MEETING.

1763.—"On the 5th day of the first month, 1763, men and women Friends belonging to Uwchlan, Nantmeal, and Pikeland Particular Meetings, being assembled at Uwchlan meeting-house, agreeably with the intention of the following mentioned conclusion, viz.:—

"The Monthly Meeting of Goshen, consisting of the Particular Meetings of Goshen, Newtown, Uwchlan, Nantmeal, and Pikeland, taking into consideration the large extent thereof, and the numerous appearance of Friends belonging thereto, with the inconvenience that many undergo in attending the same, and the multiplicity of business abounding beyond what can be deliberately considered and expedited in one day, it was thought necessary to have the said Monthly Meeting divided into two such meetings. And accordingly a motion was made to the Quarterly Meeting held at Concord, and after deliberate consideration from time to time, the Quarterly Meeting, in the eleventh month last, did approve of the proposal of dividing as may best answer the service. And therefore it was concluded, at the last Monthly Meeting at Goshen, that the particular Meetings of Uwchlan, Nantmeal, and Pikeland do henceforth constitute one Monthly Meeting, of men and women Friends, to be known and called by the name of Uwchlan Monthly Meeting, and to be held in Friends' meeting-house there, on the fourth day of the week, next after the first second-day in each month, till further order; and, in pursuance thereof, is now held in the said meeting-house in the township

of Uwchlan, in Chester County," &c.—(Uwchlan Monthly
Meeting.)

UWCHLAN.

1720.—The Meeting of Uwchlan was established by Chester
Monthly Meeting in the year 1720.

NANTMEAL.

1750.—The Meeting in Nantmeal was set up by the same
authority as the preceding.

A Preparative Meeting was established here in 1781.—(See
Chester Quarterly Meeting.)

KIMBERTON (FORMERLY PIKELAND).

1857.—" Caln informs that Pikeland Preparative and Mid-
week Meetings have been discontinued, and the members attached to Uwchlan Preparative Meeting.—(Yearly Meeting.)

IV.—ROBESON MONTHLY MEETING.

Record not obtained.

ROBESON.

1741.—The Monthly Meeting of Exeter granted the Friends
at Robeson the privilege of holding a Preparative Meeting, in
the year 1741.—(See Exeter Monthly Meeting.)

FISHING CREEK
HALF YEAR MEETING

Williamsport 🜨 *Muncy*

Fishing Creek 🜨

Berwick 🜨

Catawissa 🜨

N.

↑

Shamokin 🜨

Roaring Creek 🜨

S

SCALE: 5 miles per inch.

CHAPTER XIII.

FISHING CREEK HALF-YEAR MEETING.

1833.—"We propose to the consideration of Muncy Friends the establishment of a Half-Year Meeting, to be held at Fishing Creek; and to be composed of Friends of that meeting and Roaring Creek," &c.—(Roaring Creek Monthly Meeting.)

The subject having claimed the attention of the Yearly Meeting, through a committee, they reported:

1834.—"That most of their number have attended said Monthly Meetings, and some of them have visited all the particular Meetings constituting them, since last year. On deliberate consideration, and with feelings of tenderness towards Friends of those meetings, we unite in proposing that their request be granted, and the said Half-Year Meeting established; at present under the care of a committee of the Yearly Meeting, and that it be called and known by the name of *Fishing Creek Half-Year Meeting*, &c.

" Which being read, was united with; and Women's Meeting also uniting therewith, a committee was appointed," &c.—(Yearly Meeting.)

I.—CATAWISSA MONTHLY MEETING.

1796.—" At a Quarterly Meeting held in Philadelphia, the 1st day of the second month, 1796—

" The following report being produced and read, is concurred with, &c.

" The committee appointed in consequence of the proposal from Exeter, relative to instituting another Monthly Meeting within their limits, &c., report, we are united in judgment, that under all circumstances it may be right to concur therewith; and that the proposed Monthly Meeting should be composed of, and include, all the members within the verge of, or belonging to, the several meetings of Roaring Creek, Catawissa, Fishing Creek, and Muncy, and distinguished by the name of Catawissa Monthly Meeting," &c.

" On the 23d day of the fourth month, 1796, and seventh of the week, a Monthly Meeting was opened at Friends' meeting-house at Catawissa," &c.

"Inasmuch as meetings of discipline have, under the influence of Divine Wisdom, been established in our Society, and the solid advantages experienced therefrom have abundantly evinced the propriety thereof: in order that a due and tender attention should be extended to the various circumstances and situation of our members, that their necessities might be timely and duly relieved, and that Friends be encouraged in orderly and circumspect walking, and when that is not the case, that they may be duly advised, and labored with, in the spirit of meekness and wisdom, is the earnest and affectionate desire of many brethren and sisters; that the members of this meeting may watchfully and diligently seek for, and follow after, the qualifying virtue of truth; that a good light may be held up to the people, which may yield cause for our members and others to praise the name of our God, who has called us to glory and virtue."—(Catawissa Monthly Meeting.)

CATAWISSA.

1787.—William Hughes, William Collins, James Watson, John Love, and some other Friends, having settled at Catawissa, held a meeting there by the indulgence of Exeter Monthly Meeting.

1853.—"Fishing Creek Half-Year Meeting informs that Catawissa Mid-week Meeting has been laid down."

And in

1856.—" Catawissa Particular Meeting has been laid down."
—(Yearly Meeting Extracts.)

ROARING CREEK.

From the settling of Catawissa Monthly Meeting, the two foregoing meetings made one preparative, till the year 1801, when they were separated into two.

LOYAL SOCK.

1797.—"The committee on the request of Friends at Loyal Sock, reported, &c.; and after deliberately considering the subject, are of the opinion that it may be right to indulge them with the privilege of holding a meeting of worship on the first day of the week, at the house of Nathaniel Pearson; which being considered, the meeting concurs therewith," &c.— (Catawissa Monthly Meeting.)

BERWICK.

1800.—In the year 1800 the same authority, in like manner, indulged a meeting at the house of Andrew Shiner, on the first day of the week.

II.—FISHING CREEK MONTHLY MEETING (FORMERLY MUNCY).

1799.—"We, the committee appointed to take the subject of dividing the Monthly Meeting into view, after having, &c., agree to report, that we are united in judgment that it will tend to the general benefit of society among us, that a new Monthly Meeting be established, to be held at Muncy, to be composed of that Preparative Meeting and Fishing Creek, &c. Which, being deliberately considered, is concurred with, and directed to be laid before the Quarterly Meeting, for the advice and concurrence thereof."—(Catawissa Monthly Meeting.)

1799.—"The proposal, brought up from Catawissa Monthly Meeting, to establish a new Monthly Meeting at Muncy, to be composed of the Preparative Meetings of Fishing Creek and Muncy, coming under renewed weighty consideration, is united with, and the following Friends appointed to attend the opening of said meeting, viz.: Arthur Howell, Samuel Smith, Cadwalader Foulke, David Evans, James Jones, Thomas Lee, and John Scarlet, Jr.

" Extracted from the minutes.

" PETER BARKER,

" *Clerk at this time.*"

(Philadelphia Quarterly Meeting.)

1856.—" Fishing Creek reports that the name of 'Muncy Monthly Meeting' has been changed to 'Fishing Creek Monthly Meeting, held at Millville.' "—(Yearly Meeting.)

MUNCY.

1796.—" Benjamin Warner, on behalf of Friends at and near Muncy, requests the continuance of their meeting on first and week-days, which is granted."—(Catawissa Monthly Meeting.)

FISHING CREEK.

1799.—" At a Quarterly Meeting, held in Philadelphia, the 6th of the fifth month, 1799, the subject brought up from Catawissa, concerning the establishment of a meeting for worship, and a Preparative Meeting, at Fishing Creek, being carefully considered, it is believed it may be safe to concur with the prospect of the Monthly Meeting therein.

" Extract from the minutes.

" JONATHAN EVANS,

"*Clerk.*"

(Catawissa Monthly Meeting.)

III.—ROARING CREEK MONTHLY MEETING.

1814.—" At a Quarterly Meeting, held in Philadelphia, the 7th of second month, 1814, in considering the request from Muncy, for establishing a Monthly Meeting, to be held at

Roaring Creek, and the report of the committee appointed thereon, the meeting was brought into sympathy with Friends in those remote parts, and concluded to grant their request, &c.
    "Extracted from the minutes.

"ISRAEL MORRIS,
"<i>Clerk.</i>"
(Roaring Creek Monthly Meeting.)

Roaring Creek Monthly Meeting was composed of Catawissa and Roaring Creek Meetings, which were now again separated, so as to constitute two Preparatives,—Berwick being joined to the former.
    For Catawissa and Roaring Creek Meetings, see above.

SHAMOKIN.

1840.—"Shamokin Friends request an Indulged Meeting for worship, to be held on the first day of the week, in a school-house near Asa T. Johns, for the ensuing six months; which request the meeting unites with, and appoints Benjamin Sharpless and William Thomas a committee to attend the opening of the said meeting. Women's Meeting concurring, appoints Mary Ellis and Sarah Hughes to join the committee of men Friends."
—(Roaring Creek Monthly Meeting.)

The Half-Year's Meeting is now composed of Fishing Creek and Roaring Creek Monthly Meetings. Catawissa Monthly Meeting was laid down in 1807, and its members joined to Muncy. In 1814, it was virtually re-established under another name,—Roaring Creek Monthly Meeting. At a later period, Muncy Monthly Meeting was discontinued, and that of Fishing Creek instituted in its stead. The cause of most of these changes is expressed in the following minute of Catawissa Monthly Meeting, previous to its dissolution :—

1807.—"As a considerable number of our members have already removed to other parts of the country, and it appearing

likely that several more families may leave this neighborhood
in the course of the summer, which occasions some doubt of
Friends remaining here being sufficient to hold a Monthly
Meeting, &c., it may be advisable to offer our situation to the
consideration of the Quarterly Meeting; a disposition prevailing
among us generally to submit to the advice and judgment of
Friends on the occasion," &c.—(Catawissa Monthly Meeting.)

RETROSPECT OF EARLY QUAKERISM.

CHAPTER I.

CHILDREN AND YOUTH.

1694.—"WE are willing and free, for the good of all, and for the opening the understandings of youth, to give a hint of some things that we know by our own experience that Truth's testimony is against—as challenging each other to run races, wrestling, laying of wagers, &c."

"It is also a very evil thing, and hateful to God and all solemn people, for children to answer their parents again forwardly and crossly. Although they think they are out of the way, they ought to answer soberly and modestly, or not at all; for parents ought to be obeyed next to God. Nor ought you to act for yourselves against them : they have taken pains and care for you when you were young and helpless, and so ought you to do for them when they are old, if there be need."

"And it behooveth all parents, masters, and mistresses, to be good examples in their families, and to watch over them for good; for it is a great grief to many of us to see and hear Friends' children, as well as others who profess Truth, so frequently use the world's language,—as *you* to a single person and among one another,—which is a certain token that they are not so much as brought up in the form of Truth, which is our duty, and ought to be our care."—(Yearly Meeting.)

1706.—"Advised, that Friends be careful not to put their children apprentices to such as are not Friends, whereby they are often led away through evil example; but, as much as in them lies, to bring up their children, and all under their care, in the fear and nurture of the Lord, that none may be blameworthy in a thing so greatly necessary."—(Yearly Meeting.)

1721.—"Advised that no Friend suffer romances, play-books, and other vain and idle pamphlets, in their houses or families, which tend to corrupt the mind of youth; but, instead thereof, that they excite them to the reading of the Holy Scriptures, and other good and religious books."—(Yearly Meeting.)

1723.—" It is recommended that such Friends as are concerned in the affairs of the Church, at Quarterly, Monthly, and Particular Meetings, be careful to act themselves in the wisdom of God, whereby they may be exemplary to the young who may be esteemed members thereof and attend the same. And as such young persons are found to be qualified, with a real sense of Truth on their spirits and subject thereunto, and thereby made capable to come up to a service in the several meetings, Friends are desired to encourage and bring them forward therein, whereby they may be helpful to the ancient."

"As to such young people as have been educated in the way of Truth, or made profession with us, if they do not continue in well-doing, but frequent scandalous or tippling houses, and delight in vain and evil company and communications, or shall use gaming, or drink to excess, or behave rudely, or such like enormities, or shall decline our plain way of speech, or imitate the vain, antic modes and customs of the times, &c.,

. . . . it is our advice and earnest desire that parents and guardians, while such youth are under their tuition, do restrain them, and not indulge them in such pride and extravagance. But if they will not be reformed, then the Overseers and other Friends shall use their endeavors to reclaim them; and if they cannot prevail, let the offenders (after dealing and admonition) have notice to be at the next succeeding Monthly Meeting, in order to be further dealt withal, in the wisdom of Truth, according to our discipline."—(Yearly Meeting.)

1724.—"And let none of them count it a light thing to reject or slight the care and concern that Friends have for their welfare and prosperity in the blessed Truth, lest they be found fighting against God, and trampling upon his testimony, in his faithful people and children."—(Yearly Meeting.)

1729.—"We beseech all Friends who are parents of children, guardians, and masters of families, to be religiously concerned, in precept and example, to nurture them up in the fear of the Lord and knowledge of his Truth; that they induce them to read the Holy Scriptures, to be frequent at meetings, and to keep them from loose, wanton, and vain books and vicious company."—(Yearly Meeting.)

1759.—"In all our cares about worldly treasures, let us steadily bear in mind that riches, possessed by children who do not truly serve God, are likely to prove snares, that may more grievously entangle them in that spirit of selfishness and exaltation which stands in opposition to true peace and happiness, and renders them enemies to the cross of Christ who submit to the influence of it."—(Yearly Meeting.)

1760.—"One prevailing danger which attends them (the youth) is the frequenting of public companies, such as are too often met with in taverns, fairs, and all places of public diversion, wherein, although they may see no harm at first, there is a snare in which many promising youth have been caught. Having been overtaken, in unguarded moments, not only with the current vanities, but even the infections of the wicked; and, as error is progressive and sin hardens the heart, they have gone on from one thing to another, till lamentable consequences have ensued. And as most disorders are more easily prevented than remedied, we advise Friends, in their Monthly Meetings, to take this matter under their care, and add their assistance, where necessary to the endeavors of individuals, to discourage it as much as in them lies."—(Yearly Meeting.)

A very large amount of salutary advice might be added, but I will close this article with a short address, which was issued

10

by Wilmington Monthly Meeting, on the approach of a public fair, in 1772.

1772.—"Beloved Youth: Feeling strong desires that you may be preserved from the ways of ensnaring folly, we have to remind you that some who have trod before you the slippery paths which you are in, for want of keeping to that state of watchfulness in which alone there is safety, have, by the prevailing leaven of evil company, been drawn aside from the narrow way, whereby they have made for themselves a long and painful wilderness of suffering to pass through, before they have come to know a state of acceptance with the Father of Mercies; and it is much to be feared that many have been so far entangled as never to have arrived at a place of rest.

" Therefore, seeing the dangers before you are so imminent, the prize for which you are to run of such infinite importance, the time allotted for you to make your calling and election sure so short, and that time so very uncertain, we feel constrained, in the bonds of unfeigned affection, to warn you to shun all light and vain company, and especially at the time of the Fair now approaching. As it is become a scene of much profanity, we think it safest that you should, as much as possible, avoid attending it. The vain fashions and follies, the idle amusements, games, and recreations of the present day, are so far beneath the dignity of the Christian spirit, that we feel a desire that you may be more and more preserved out of them. We recommend to your solid attention the solemn injunction of the royal Psalmist: 'And thou, Solomon, my son, know thou the God of thy fathers, and serve him with a perfect heart, and with a willing mind; for the Lord searcheth all hearts, and understandeth the imagination of all thoughts. If thou seek him, he will be found of thee; but if thou forsake him, he will cast thee off forever.' "—(Wilmington Monthly Meeting.)

It is a consideration which might profitably engage the attention of those who have the management and instruction of the young, how far their backslidings might have been prevented by more timely and vigilant care on their own part, and, consequently, how far they themselves are accountable to God for what may appear to others as the perverseness of those under their care. It is, indeed, recorded: "I, the Lord thy God, am a jealous God, visiting the iniquities of the fathers upon the children unto the third and fourth generation." But this seems to be rather the declaration of a prophetic truth than of the Divine justice; for it is also declared: "The fathers shall not be put to death for the children, neither shall the children be put to death for the fathers: every man shall be put to death for his own sin."

CHAPTER II.

CONDUCT AND CONVERSATION.

1694.—"Dear Friends, whatsoever we may meet withal, for the sake of our constant testimony to the Truth in all manner of conversation, and to the end that we may not faint in our minds, let us consider Him who endured such contradiction of sinners against himself, who took up the cross and despised the shame, and is now sat down on the right hand of the throne of God. This is the Captain of our salvation; let us follow him, that we may fight under his banner the good fight of faith, and in the end we may obtain the crown of righteousness, which is peace and assurance forever."—(Yearly Meeting.)

1726.—"We find a pressing concern earnestly to excite all our dear Friends, brethren and sisters, seriously to consider the state of things in this land, so lately a wilderness. When, on the one hand, we look back to the many blessings we have received, and the protection and peace we have enjoyed, how greatly doth it concern us to be humbled before the Almighty, and with grateful hearts take due heed to our walking before him; and, on the other hand, when we take a view of the great

increase of the people, and consider how many among them
appear regardless of religion, probity, and virtue, who seem to
combine, in an uncommon manner, to rush into immoralities
and tumultuous practices, using many artful ways to draw
others to fall in with them—the more, perhaps, because of the
number of Friends who are inhabitants here, and that some
are concerned in the Government, by this means, since they
cannot persecute them as in times past, to give them disturbance and trouble of another sort—how very careful, then, ought
we all to be not to countenance or connive at such doings in
the least manner, under any color or pretence whatsoever, but
to oppose and discourage them as much as in us lies."—(Yearly
Meeting.)

1732.—"I—— H—— appeared here and acknowledged
his fault (being too vain in his conversation), and to be very
sorry for it. This meeting, upon consideration, doth pass it
by."—(Concord Monthly Meeting.)

1734.—"And we earnestly caution and advise against the
inordinate pursuit of worldly riches, which, being sought within
due bounds, for the comfortable subsistence of ourselves and
families, and the charitable relief of others in necessity, is not
only lawful, but commendable; but when the mind is carried
away with the love of these things, they then become (even
though men do not transgress the bounds of justice) a clog and
hindrance in its attendance on the duties of religion, and is an
excess which ought to be guarded against."

" We seriously exhort all, that in their conversation in the
world, they keep in the fear of the Lord, and therein watch
against the enemy, that he neither entangle nor hurt their
spirits by a too near or unnecessary intimacy; for, although
such conversation may be lawful and necessary, yet, if it be
done beyond the limits of the pure fear, the spirit of the world
may seek and gain an entrance; and, being once entered, it
will insensibly dispose the mind to a condescension to and compliance with the people so conversed with, first in one thing,
then in another—in words, behavior, &c. (little things in appearance, but great things in consequence), till at length in-

difference gets up in the mind, and the testimony of Truth is by degrees let fall."—(Yearly Meeting.)

This minute describes with prophetic accuracy the cause which has pre-eminently disposed so many Friends to a compliance with the world's ways, until indifference has indeed got up, and the testimonies of Truth have been suffered to fall to the ground.

1772.—"And it is desired that, above all, we individually dwell near to the Divine principle of Truth in our own minds; a due attention to the dictates of which, would produce fruits of righteousness in precept and example, and contribute to the restoration of that primitive beauty which eminently distinguished our ancient Friends, in the first breaking forth of this day of Gospel Light among them."—(Yearly Meeting.)

CHAPTER III.

PLAINNESS.

1670.—"Son William, if you and your Friends keep to your plain way of preaching, and to your plain way of living, you will make an end of the priests to the end of the world."—(Admiral Penn.)

1682.—"Advised that male and female, both old and young, who make mention of the name of the Lord, may all take heed that they be not found in wearing superfluity of apparel; . . . but that all may be kept within the bounds of moderation, and within the limits of the spirit of Truth, and may be known to be governed by the Truth in all concerns, so shall we be to the glory of God, and the comfort of one another."—(Yearly Meeting.)

1694.—"We tenderly advise all, both old and young, to

keep out of the world's corrupt language, manners, and vain, needless things, and fashions in apparel, and immoderate and indecent smoking of tobacco.

"It is very unseemly, and not at all like Truth, to ride, or go in the streets with pipes in their mouths; for we ought, in all things, to take up the daily cross, minding the grace of God, that brings salvation, and teaches to deny all ungodliness and worldly lusts, and to live soberly and godly in this present world, that we may adorn the Gospel of our Lord Jesus Christ. So shall we feel His blessing, and may be instrumental in His hands for the good of others."—(Yearly Meeting.)

1719.—"Advised that such be dealt with as do not keep themselves and their children to moderation and plainness in gesture, speech, apparel, or furniture of houses;" . . . . "for, as those vain habits and needless fashions, by the levity too much prevalent among mankind, frequently change, so the vain and wanton mind in our youth and others is too apt to be taken with, and fall into them." . . . . . . "Also such as accustom themselves, or suffer willingly their children, to use the corrupt, and unscriptural language of *you* to a single person; or to call the week-days or months by names given them by the heathen, in honor of their gods; it being contrary to Scripture and our ancient testimony."—(Yearly Meeting.)

1726.—"As we have been redeemed from the confused doctrines of the schools, ... so has it, from the beginning, fallen closely on our elder brethren to bear testimony against all vanity and pride, all superfluity and excess; being rightly made to see, in the first place, the great necessity of sincerity and uprightness of heart towards God, and obedience to His commands; and next, how inconsistent it is with His inward work to retain or launch into the vain customs and fashions too prevalent among the professors of Christianity. For how is .it possible for a mind truly religious to be delighted with such follies? Let but our youth, or others who may now make light of such plainness in speech, and apparel, or furniture, as our elders have been led into, but seriously examine their own hearts, with due application to the grace of God placed there, and they will find that, so far as they let out the mind to such vanities, they weaken themselves in the true practice of religious duties, and lie open to further temptations and more dangerous vices."—(Yearly Meeting.)

1746.—"Though the goodness of God is such that He will, doubtless, in His universal love, visit them (the youth), and strive with them, yet, if they give way to youthful lusts, which now, as much as ever, war against the soul, and their parents neglect to do their duty in restraining them, it may be feared that the visitation of the grace of God may be bestowed on them in vain, to their own irreparable loss, and the great disappointment of their parents. We do, therefore, in the love of God, and great tenderness of spirit, beseech you to be religiously concerned, in precept and by example, to nurture them in the fear of the Lord and the knowledge of His Truth; and that you induce them frequently to read the Holy Scriptures, and such other books as tend to their instruction in true Christianity; and, as far as in your power, to prevent them reading any books of a contrary tendency."—(Yearly Meeting.)

1778.—Complaint was made against "E—— B——, for much deviating from plainness, in dress and address, and frequenting places of music and dancing."

Also against "E—— S—— and S—— S——, for deviating from plainness of dress and language, and frequenting places of music and dancing, and joining therein themselves."—(Wilmington Monthly Meeting.)

In reply, we often hear it said that *religion* does not consist in thee and thou; in the cut or color of a garment; or in the style of household furniture. That is admitted. But as the mind is brought under the influence of religion, its cravings and desires are all subjected to that divine and heavenly influence; there will be no disposition to indulge in superfluity, and extravagance, whereby others might be induced to imitate them, at a cost which their means would not justify. Indeed it is not lawful for Christians to waste their means in that way, however ample, while there are so many humane and benevolent purposes to which they may be better applied.

Though plainness is not religion, yet it is a religious duty; and religion, when properly established in the mind, will always incline us to simplicity in life and manners.

1792.—" Some explanation respecting the authority of Monthly Meetings to disown our youth, or others, who depart from that simplicity which Truth requires, and who run into and copy after the vain and extravagant fashions of the world, in their dress and address, being necessary, and coming under solid and weighty consideration, it appears to be the sense of this meeting, that if, after patient labor, in the spirit of meekness and wisdom, such cannot be reclaimed, Monthly Meetings may give forth a testimony of disownment against them."— (Yearly Meeting.)

CHAPTER IV.

CHARITY, LOVE, AND UNITY.

1687.—" We beseech all, that they hold fast the blessed unity of the spirit in the bond of peace, and be tender and very careful of breaking it; lest it be an occasion of mourning to Zion, and of rejoicing to her enemies."—(Yearly Meeting.)

1706.—" We recommend unto you fervent and inward charity one towards another, and to all men; for beside those commendations given unto charity by the Apostle, in his day, we also say by experience, that charity preventeth many evils. It keeps the peace, preserves unity, and, as it were, teaches all duty. Where charity is, there is love to God and love to man; but where that is wanting, zeal toward God fails, and neighbors and friends are also disregarded, and, instead of acts and expressions of love and good-will to all, the contrary is brought forth by such, which ought not. It is for want of charity that men speak evil of dignities, detract and lessen the name of their neighbors, and evily intreat in secret the reputation of those that think them no harm. And this is a crying evil, from which the God of Truth purges and preserves his people everywhere."—(Yearly Meeting.)

1727.—"Dear Friends, love and unity is the true ornament and bond of our Society, under our heavenly head, Christ Jesus; and without which, formality will take the place of substance, and the life and power of true religion will be withdrawn. And you are sensible that the way to stand firm in that unity and love is, for every member to have a watch over his own heart, and to examine whether he finds love to God and the brethren really established there, upon all occasions, but more especially when we meet together for worship or discipline."—(Yearly Meeting.)

1752.—"Whereas several things among us are not so well as could be desired, therefore we do think well to apply to the Quarterly Meeting for assistance, and appoint Benjamin Swett, Eliakim Garretson, Thomas Gilpin, and Richard Carson, to attend the service of the Quarterly Meeting, and carry in our report, viz.: Meetings are kept up; love and unity not so well as could be desired;—so we request the assistance of the Quarterly Meeting in settling some uneasiness that subsists among us."—(Wilmington Monthly Meeting.)

1762.—"This meeting recommends to all the Monthly Meetings to use early faithful endeavors to remove uneasiness, and inquire strictly into the cause why love and unity (as they appeared in ancient beauty among our forefathers) is now so much lost in society; and tenderly entreat Friends, in their Monthly and other Meetings, to be roused up to industry, that they may be able to bring up more satisfactory reports hereafter."—(Western Quarterly Meeting.)

1766.—"Dear Friends: We, the committee appointed by the Quarterly Meeting to your assistance, having met at the time and place appointed, and inquired into the cause of some uneasiness which hath subsisted among Friends of your meeting, and considering the necessity and importance of unity in sentiments and conduct of active members of Monthly Meetings, and viewing the general conduct of the Society in such difficult cases, as far as hath come to our knowledge, we do in much tenderness remark, that when persons having some right of membership are under immediate dealing by the Overseers, or by the Meeting, for conduct publicly reproachful, and in that situation are likely to propose intentions of marriage, they should be advised against making such proposals, until they have offered such condemnation of their misconduct as the Monthly Meeting shall think sufficient. And if, notwithstanding such advice, any person so situated shall offer such proposals, we think the Meeting should first demand such an acknowledgment, before they show so much unity as to admit of such proposals. We mention these sentiments as likely to be useful in future cases of the like nature, and without any design of bearing hard on those who, in the case under consideration, thought somewhat differently. And with respect to the degree of kindred of the parties, we find no rule in our Discipline which we think amounts to a prohibition in that case; and yet Friends who are tender in those points, should be careful in timely speaking to the parties likely to contract marriage, before their affections are too far engaged.

"Upon the whole, as we observe a decent regard to each other, in the Friends of your committee who were of opposite sentiments, we much desire that the same moderation and spirit of brotherly love may prevail and increase among you, that no root of bitterness may be nourished in any minds. Difference in sentiment among the best is common. In a case circumstanced as the above, it might reasonably be expected. May you then think of each other with tenderness, bear one another's burdens, and so fulfil the law of Christ. We conclude your affectionate friends.

"DANIEL SMITH, JR.,   "HENRY PAXTON,
"JOHN HOSKINS,   "PETER HARVEY,
"EDWARD CATHRALL,   "JOSEPH BUSBY,
"CORNELL STEPHENSON,   "CALEB CARR,
"HEZEKIAH JONES,   "FRANCIS VINCECOMB,
          "WILLIAM JONES."

(Chesterfield Monthly Meeting.)

CHAPTER V.

MINISTRY.

EVERY religious association, whether great or small, has an undoubted right to judge of, and approve or disapprove, the ministrations of its members. The early exercise of this right, and the manner of doing it, was probably derived from the example of Friends in England.

1681.—"Agreed that if any Friend have it on his mind to travel in the service of Truth to any remote parts, that before they so do they first lay their intentions before the respective Monthly Meetings they do belong to, in order to have the approbation or consent thereof."—(Yearly Meeting.)

1682.—"Whereas S—— H—— hath acted contrary to the blessed Truth, and hath rendered himself unworthy of the weighty work and service of the ministry, by giving way to [an] unbridled and a loose, gainsaying, rebellious, ranting spirit, and that a testimony, as of this meeting, be drawn and go forth against him, for the clearing of the blessed Truth and the honest professors of it of the reproach he hath brought upon it and them, by his ungodly and loose carriage."—(Thirdhaven Monthly Meeting.)

1685.—"It is agreed that Friends in the ministry do meet together on first-day morning at the seventh hour, before the public general meeting, in such place as shall be prepared by the public Friends in each town where the meeting shall be kept that year."—(Yearly Meeting.)

This appears to be the first institution of the meeting of ministers. The appointment of Elders had not yet been made.

1690.—"Some weighty, serious Friends having moved it to this meeting, that ministering Friends that have a testimony

for the Truth in meetings, may have a meeting a few hours
before the Yearly Meeting begins; which this meeting has
unity with, and does agree that Friends so qualified do meet at
the meeting-house at Thirdhaven, about the seventh hour, the
first day of the public meeting. And at William Richardson's,
about the same hour, the first day of the Yearly Meeting, when
it is on the Western Shore."—(Thirdhaven Yearly Meeting.)

1695.—"Ordered at this meeting, that Samuel Furness and
Thomas Raper assist Henry Grubb in the care of public Friends'
horses; and that Henry Grubb do bring in his account once a
quarter to the Monthly Meeting, to receive his money on said
account, or any other necessary charge."—(Burlington Monthly
Meeting.)

1699.—"It was agreed at our last Quarterly Meeting, that
some Friends be chosen at this meeting, to go along with one from
Burlington Meeting, to accompany travelling Friends as need
shall require. The Friends chosen are Robert Wilson, William
Wood, John Bunting, and John Abbott, one of which is to go
with one from Burlington, to York or Shrewsbury, as need shall
require, beginning with the first, until they have all been
once."—(Chesterfield Monthly Meeting.)

1699.—"According to the order of the Quarterly Meeting,
this meeting have chosen four men for the service of going with
travelling Friends when occasion is."—(Burlington Monthly
Meeting.)

The three preceding minutes are characteristic of the fore-
thought and brotherly kindness of the early Friends, who often
had to travel long distances through a wilderness country.
Witness the case of George Fox, George Pattison, Robert
Widders, and "some others," who journeyed from Thirdhaven,
in Maryland, to Oyster Bay, Long Island, in 1672, ten years
before the arrival of William Penn in this country.

1704.—"Elizabeth Webb requested of this meeting to give
her a few lines of her conversation since she has been among
us, for the seventh-day meeting of ministering Friends at

Philadelphia; and, according to her request, it was granted."
—(Concord Monthly Meeting.)

This is the earliest mention which I have met with, of a certificate from the Monthly Meeting to the Meeting of Ministers. Nor do I find any order of a superior meeting requiring one, until 1712. (See below.) It is probable that, for a time, all who appeared in the ministry were permitted to sit in those meetings, until, owing no doubt to some disturbing spirits thus getting in, the order, or at least the usage, was altered. John Richardson, while in Rhode Island, in 1701, says he "met with something worthy of notice."

"Being in Rhode Island, several Friends came to me, in some of the intervals of the Yearly Meeting, to inquire whether it was usual to let the young, and such as had appeared little in testimony in our part of the world, come into meetings of public Friends? I said yes, if they were of clean lives, and what they had to say approved; and it was very likely such might want advice, as much as those who were come to more experience in the work of the ministry, if not more. This was some means of enlarging the said Meetings of Ministers now coming on."

1710.—"This meeting, have taken into consideration E——— G———'s appearing in public, to the dissatisfaction of Friends, therefore this meeting doth appoint Thomas Wickersham and Samuel Graves to speak to him and labor with him, that, for the time to come, he keep silent, &c. George Harlan and Thomas Wickersham are appointed to attend the Meeting of Ministering Friends, and lay before them the dissatisfaction of this meeting concerning E——— G———'s appearing in public," &c.—(Kennet Monthly Meeting.)

1712.—"This meeting orders, that every one who frequently appears in that station (of ministers), that they request certificates, from the Monthly Meeting to which they belong, of their unity and fellowship with them in that weighty work; so that they may have them to produce to the Meeting of Ministering

Friends, as there may be occasion."—(Bucks Quarterly Meeting.)

1713.—"Therefore, John Rutledge and Ezra Crosdale do request, each of them, one (certificate) from this meeting to the Meeting of Ministering Friends."—(Middletown Monthly Meeting.)

1715.—"John Scarborough requested a certificate from this meeting to the Meeting of Ministering Friends; but the meeting being small, and none from the meeting he belongs to, therefore this meeting defers a month, and appoints Joseph Fell to inquire how Friends of that meeting are satisfied that his life and conversation agrees with his doctrine," &c.—(Falls Monthly Meeting.)

1717.—"Edmund Kinsey requested a certificate from us to the Meeting of Ministering Friends. Agreed that one be drawn in readiness against next meeting."—(Falls Monthly Meeting.)

1718.—"It was thought necessary that the Overseers of each Particular Meeting, belonging to this meeting, do meet on the seventh day morning next, to draw up something in writing to send to the Quarterly Meeting of Ministers, to give them an account of the state of the ministry among us."—(Burlington Monthly Meeting.)

I have not noticed the time when, or the authority by which, the Quarterly Meeting of Ministers was established. John Fothergill attended a Quarterly Meeting of Ministers at Neshamony the day preceding Bucks Quarter, in 1721. In 1733, Shrewsbury Quarterly Meeting requested the Yearly Meeting to allow them a Quarterly Meeting of Ministers and Elders, which was granted; "the said meeting to be accountable, as other Meetings of Ministers and Elders are, to this meeting."—(Yearly Meeting.)

1723.—"It is to be observed that the God and fountain of all our mercies has opened and is opening, in divers of our young people, a divine spring of living ministry. Therefore our earnest desire is, that both ministers and elders may be as nursing fathers and mothers to those that are young in the ministry, and with all care and diligence advise and admonish them, and, if they see occasion, reprove them, in a tender and Christian spirit; observing the rules of our discipline and counsel of Friends in that respect. As also to exhort them frequently to read the Holy Scriptures, and earnestly seek the mind of the Spirit of Truth to open the mysteries of those holy writings; and, as they keep to true patience, and submission to the will of God, and stand faithful, and abide in the simplicity of the Gospel, and be exercised in their proper gifts, keeping down to the openings of divine love and life in themselves, they will witness a gradual growth, and be content to wait for it in the will of God, and not strive to extend their declarations further than they find the life and power of God to bear them up."—(Yearly Meeting.)

"If any man speak, let him speak as the oracles of God; if any man minister, let him do it as of the ability which God giveth." When God, in mercy, shall send forth the messengers of his grace, he will assuredly furnish them the messages which they are commissioned to deliver to the people. Moses said: "I am not eloquent, but I am slow of speech, and of a slow tongue." But the answer was: "Go, and I will be thy mouth, and teach thee what thou shalt say." And Jesus Christ gave instruction to those whom he commissioned to preach the Gospel "among all nations:" "Take no thought beforehand what ye shall speak, neither do ye premeditate; but whatsoever shall be given you in that hour, that speak ye; for it is not ye that speak, but the Holy Ghost."

The wisdom and eloquence of man, all the self-acquirements which it is possible for him to attain, never did, and never will make any one a minister of the Gospel of Christ, however much they may assist when kept in entire subjection to, and in accordance with, the power of God operating in the soul. The most efficient preachers which the world has ever witnessed were illiterate fishermen, obscure husbandmen, and mechanics,

taken from the lower walks of life. Compare the preaching,
and the effects of the preaching of George Whitfield, with that
of George Fox. The former, with all his eloquence and popularity, was obliged to acknowledge : " I have carried high sail
while running through a torrent of popularity and contempt ;
I may have mistaken nature for grace, imagination for revelation, and the fire of my own temper for the flame of holy zeal ;
and I find I have frequently written and spoken in my own
spirit, when I thought I was assisted entirely by God."—
(Watson's Annals, p. 517.)

1724.—" We tenderly recommend to faithful Friends, and
especially to ministers and elders, to watch over the flock of
Christ, in their respective places and stations ; always approving themselves, by their holy examples in conversation and conduct, to be such as faithfully, and diligently walk up to the
testimony of the blessed Truth, whereunto the Lord hath
gathered us, in this his Gospel day."—(Yearly Meeting.)

1727.—" John Stackhouse, at a by-past Monthly Meeting,
and again at this meeting, hath made application for a few
lines, by way of certificate, to the Quarterly Meeting of Ministers and Elders," &c.—(Middletown Monthly Meeting.)

1728.—" Whereas Friends of Horsham, Germantown, and
Abington Preparative Meetings have signified to this Monthly
Meeting that John Cadwalader, Jr., David Dawes, Isaac Davis,
and Thomas Wood are come forth, and appear in public testimony, and that they have good unity with them, desiring that
they may be recommended to the next Quarterly Meeting of
ministers at Philadelphia ; which this meeting approves of," &c.
—(Abington Monthly Meeting.)

It appears, from the above minute, that Friends of Philadelphia Quarter, and perhaps others, had adopted the same rule
as that of Bucks (see above, 1712), prior to any action of the
Yearly Meeting in the premises, as set forth in the following
minute.

1730.—"It is the sense of this meeting (as it hath been the practice of Friends for several years past), that any person coming forth, or offering themselves in the ministry, be approved of in the Monthly Meeting to which he or she doth belong, and by them be recommended, before they are permitted to sit in the Meetings of Ministers and Elders, or to travel abroad in the ministry."—(Yearly Meeting.)

It will be observed, that by the foregoing rule, the Monthly Meetings were made the sole judges of the propriety of recommending young ministers.

About this period, Monthly Meetings sometimes reported the state of the ministry to the General Quarterly Meetings: thus:—

1738.—"As to the state of the ministry; those concerned therein are generally in love and unity with us, and one with another; are diligent in attending meetings, and their public testimony mostly well accepted."—(Burlington Monthly Meeting.)

1743.—"Whereas our friends, Peter Andrews, John Woolman, and Josiah White, have had at times a concern on their minds to appear in public, by way of exhortation to religious duties; whose appearances are generally well received: wherefore a motion was made here, that they might be recommended to sit in the Meetings of Ministers and Elders; and they are hereby accordingly recommended."—(Burlington Monthly Meeting.)

1746.—"This meeting recommends James Crues, as a member of the Meeting of Ministers and Elders."—(Chesterfield Monthly Meeting.)

1746.—"Whereas D—— S—— hath frequently appeared in our Meetings by way of testimony, to the great dissatisfaction of Friends, notwithstanding the many precautions and labors of love, which have proved ineffectual; therefore we disown her to be of our Society, until she, by unfeigned repent-

ance, comes to amend her ways; which that she may, is our
sincere desire.

"Signed on behalf of our said meeting.

"JAMES MILLER,

"*Clerk.*"

(New Garden Monthly Meeting.)

1747.—"This meeting agrees that Grace Crosdale may be
recommended to sit in the Meetings of Ministers and Elders."
Also, "that Stephen Comfort be recommended," in like manner.
—(Middletown Monthly Meeting.)

1747.—"That when the Meeting of Ministers and Elders,
within the verge of which such young ministers may appear,
shall be desirous of having them admitted to their meeting,
the same, by their direction [may] be signified, by one of the
elders, or other weighty Friend, to the Monthly Meeting, for
their consent and approbation."—(Yearly Meeting.)

In a collection of advices sent down by the Yearly Meeting
this year, after repeating that of 1730, as rendered above,
the foregoing advice was appended thereto. It goes no further
than to allow Meetings of Ministers and Elders to propose
young ministers to Monthly Meetings, for their approval and
recommendation.

1751.—"At this meeting was considered the case of Samuel
Eastburn's appearing in the ministry, for some time; and the
meeting is free that he be recommended to the Meeting of
Ministers by the elders, as usual."—(Buckingham Monthly
Meeting.)

1755.—"It is unanimously agreed that, in such places where
Monthly Meetings of Ministers and Elders have not been already settled, they ought, without further delay, to be established; and, agreeably to the rules of our discipline, that solid
women elders should be appointed to sit therein. And the
following queries were agreed to be proposed at such meeting:

"I. Are ministers and elders careful duly to attend all their
meetings for worship and discipline, bringing with them as

many of their families as they can? and are they good examples in humble waiting therein, not giving way to drowsiness?

"II. Are ministers sound in word and doctrine, careful to
minister in the ability God only gives, and thereby kept from
burdening the living?

"III. Are the lives and conversation of ministers and elders
clean and blameless amongst men, adorning the doctrines they
deliver to others, being examples of the believers in word, in
conversation, in charity, in spirit, in faith, in purity?

"IV. Do they rule their own houses well, bringing their
families up in plainness, which Truth still requires, in dress, language, and true moderation? and are they good examples in
these respects themselves?

"V. Are they peacemakers in families and in the Church,
not concerned in raising or spreading evil reports against any;
nor busy-bodies where they have no proper business?

"VI. Are they careful to maintain the discipline of the
Church in every part thereof; not to hide even their own families from Truth's judgment, if occasion be given, but impartially administer justice as faithful servants in the house of God?

"VII. Do any travel abroad as ministers without being first
recommended to and accepted by the Quarterly Meeting they
belong to, as such? and do any appoint meetings out of the
limits of the Quarterly Meeting they belong to, without a certificate from their Monthly Meeting of business, or the concurrence thereof?

"VIII. Are ministers and elders in unity one with another,
and with the meetings they belong to, harmoniously laboring
together for Truth's honor, and careful to give no just occasion
of offence to either Jew, Gentile, or the Household of Faith?

"IX. Do you watch over one another for good; to help
those that are young in the ministry in the right line; discouraging forward spirits that run into words without life and
power; advising against affectations of tones and gestures, and
everything which would hurt their service; yet encouraging the
humble, careful traveller, speaking a word in due season to them

that are weary?   And let all dwell in that which gives ability
to labor in the Church of Christ."

1756.—" This meeting now appoints a Meeting of Ministers
and Elders to be held quarterly at Burlington, &c., agreeably
to the advice of the Yearly Meeting."—(Burlington Monthly
Meeting.)

1756.—" Pursuant to the direction of the Yearly Meeting,
this meeting allows the ministers and elders to meet at New
Garden Meeting-house, on the second fifth-day of next month,
and make return to next Monthly Meeting the appointment of
said meetings for the future."—(New Garden Monthly Meeting.)

1756.—" It is recommended from our Yearly Meeting to
have a Monthly Meeting of Ministers and Elders established ;
which, after some considerable time of consideration, we consent to," &c.—(Concord Monthly Meeting.)

The above Monthly Meeting recommended to its preparatives, " also to nominate a weighty and solid man Friend in
each meeting as assistant to the elders."   No explanation appears of this procedure, unless it be found in the records of
Chesterfield Monthly Meeting for the eighth month, 1757.

" The Monthly Meetings of Ministers and Elders, being new
to several Monthly Meetings, and several Friends can hardly
approve of them, imagining they lessen the authority of the
Monthly Meetings of business, we think that an explanation of
the extent of their authority, their service, and the manner how
the reports should go up from them to the superior meetings,
would be of service to settle those that are dissatisfied, in settling the said meetings in one method throughout the limits of
the Yearly Meeting, if it was to come down by the authority
thereof ;" which was sent to the Quarter.

Two years after, the Select Meeting informed the Monthly
Meeting that there was still a dissatisfaction with them, and
requested that it might be sent to the Quarter again, with the

view of being brought before the Yearly Meeting. It is thus minuted :—

1760.—"There continues an uneasiness respecting some parts of the constitution of the Meetings of Ministers and Elders, therefore [we] desire the concurrence of the Quarterly Meeting to make application to the Yearly Meeting, concerning ministers answering for their own conduct and performance, for amendment, viz. : Where ministers and elders are uneasy with the present practice in that respect, then, and in such case, they may have liberty to apply to the Monthly Meeting for assistance, and the Monthly Meeting to have authority to appoint a number of solid Friends to sit in those Select Meetings, and assist in that weighty work of representing the state of the above Friends to the Quarterly Meeting."—(Chesterfield Monthly Meeting.)

In 1765, the Queries for Ministers and Elders were revised, and the number reduced to seven, the excluded matter being put in form of advices, to be read in the meetings.

1765.—"And it is earnestly and affectionately recommended, that ministers and elders watch over one another for good; to help those that are young in the ministry in the right line ; discouraging forward spirits that run into words without life and power ; advising against affectation of tones and gestures, and everything that would hurt their service ; yet encouraging the humble, careful traveller, speaking a word in season to them that are weary; and let all dwell in that which gives ability to labor successfully in the Church of Christ, adorning the doctrine they deliver to others, being examples of the believers, in word, in conversation, in charity, in spirit, in faith, and in purity."—(Yearly Meeting.)

1769.—"A minute of the Yearly Meeting of Ministers and Elders was received and read in this meeting, informing that they apprehend it may be of use to have queries suitably adapted to their meeting. William Edmondson, Joseph Berry,

Joseph Bartlet, and Isaac Dixon are appointed to prepare essays for said purpose, and produce them to next meeting."— (Thirdhaven Yearly Meeting.)

The Queries were essentially similar to those already given.

1776.—A complaint was made against Z—— F——, "for publicly opposing a Friend in unity, in his ministry, in a meeting for worship."—(Wilmington Monthly Meeting.)

1785.—"New Garden Preparative Meeting have had under consideration recommending Dinah Lamborn as a minister to the Select Quarterly Meeting; which, coming under solid consideration, Elizabeth Pusey, Hannah Pusey, Mary Bulger, and Elizabeth Millhouse, are appointed to join men Friends, to take an opportunity with her to deeply feel after the propriety of such a movement, and report to our next meeting."—(New Garden Monthly Meeting Women Friends.)

The committee reported, "that, to them, the service appeared weighty," and recommended another opportunity with her. The following month, "they were of the mind her case might be forwarded;" and it was accordingly done.

The prudence and deliberation displayed in this case was not unusual in those days on similar occasions, and must have greatly promoted the unity and mutual confidence so essential to the well-being of religious society.

1797.—"When the gifts of ministers are considered and approved by a Monthly Meeting, and a minute thereof forwarded to the Quarterly Meeting of Ministers and Elders, the sense and concurrence of that meeting ought to be had before such minister be reputed as a received and approved minister, or admitted to sit in the Meetings of Ministers and Elders, or travel abroad in the ministry."

Again. "The said Meetings of Ministers and Elders shall not, in any wise, take upon them, or interfere with, any part of the exercise of the discipline of the Church belonging to

the Yearly Meeting for Business, or any subordinate meeting
for discipline, nor adjourn so as to interfere with any of the
sittings of this meeting."—(Yearly Meeting.)

By the adoption of the above rule, requiring the concurrence
of the Quarterly Meeting of Ministers and Elders, the power
of Monthly Meetings to recommend ministers was greatly cur-
tailed, while that of the Select Meeting was enlarged in the
same proportion.

1806.—"When any Friend has frequently appeared in our
religious meetings as a minister, and the Preparative Meeting
of Ministers and Elders apprehends that it is seasonable that
the subject should claim the attention of the Monthly Meeting
for Discipline of which the person is a member, they are at
liberty to mention the matter therein.   And if the Monthly
Meeting, after deliberate consideration, should unite in believing
that a gift in the ministry has been committed to him or her,
a minute, expressive thereof, should be forwarded to the Quarterly Meeting of Ministers and Elders, where the case being
solidly weighed, and the sense of the Monthly Meeting concurred with, information thereof should be sent to the Preparative
Meeting of Ministers and Elders, of which the party is to be a
member; and, until the approbation of the Quarterly Meeting
of Ministers and Elders is obtained, no such Friend is to be
received as a minister, nor permitted to sit in the Meetings of
Ministers and Elders, nor travel abroad as a minister."—(Discipline, 1806.)

Sad experience has long taught us that there is a constant
tendency among all privileged classes, both in civil and religious society, to extend their privileges, to the hurt and oppression of the communities which tolerate them.   The testimony has gone forth, from the lips of many martyrs, that
those who professed to be ministers of the Gospel of Christ
were too often the foremost in making these encroachments.
Hence, there is wisdom in guarding every avenue which may

lead to a violation of the rights of the people. A heaven-appointed and well-regulated ministry is one of the brightest ornaments and greatest blessings which a religious society can possess; while a self-constituted, and domineering one, is the worst form of tyranny to which man can be subjected.

Friends will ever do well to profit by a world-wide experience, and to study the lessons which it teaches. Perhaps there is no acknowledged authority in our Society so proper and so convenient to judge of the qualifications of ministers as the Monthly Meetings. In 1730, our Yearly Meeting decided, " that any person coming forth, or offering themselves in the ministry, be approved of in the Monthly Meeting to which he or she doth belong, and by them be recommended," &c. The power of the Monthly Meeting was then absolute.

In 1747, it was directed, " that, when the Meeting of Ministers and Elders shall be desirous of having them admitted to their meeting, the same, by their direction, be signified to the Monthly Meeting for their consent and approbation." Here the power of the Monthly Meeting was made to depend, in the first instance, on the desire of the Meeting of Ministers and Elders.

But, in 1797, it was further ordained that, when a minute of such consent and approbation of a Monthly Meeting shall be " forwarded to the Quarterly Meeting of Ministers and Elders, the sense and concurrence of that meeting ought to be had before such minister be reputed as a received and approved minister." And the same rules were embodied in the Discipline of 1806, and are still maintained. It will be readily seen that the recommendation of ministers is now placed entirely in the Select Preparative and Quarterly Meetings, with the single exception that Monthly Meetings have the negative power left to refuse to concur with the recommendation of the Select Preparative. If the latter meeting does not see proper to introduce the case, or if the Select Quarter refuses to approve the recommendation, the Monthly Meeting is altogether powerless.

It seems to be a common usage of society, that, when a

minister transgresses the order, and falls under the cognizance of a Meeting of Discipline, that he or she thereby forfeits the previous recommendation; but when such minister has become burdensome, and appears to have lost his gift in the ministry, the rule is different.

The power to approve, certainly implies the power also to disapprove. Hence the time was when Monthly Meetings could release their ministers by withdrawing their recommendations. They no longer possess that power. The case must first be taken up by the Select Preparative Meeting, carried thence to the Select Quarter, and, when there determined, be sent down to the Monthly Meeting for its further care; "and he or she ought, from that time, to refrain from attending any such Select Meetings, until they shall be again recommended or appointed, as at first." Hence it follows that the Select Preparative and Quarterly Meetings possess the absolute and uncontrollable power to deprive any of its members of their recommendation as ministers, before any action has been had in the Monthly Meeting. The only safeguard left to the Monthly Meetings will be found in the judicious appointment of elders.

CHAPTER VI.

ELDERS.

THE term Elder has long been applied to those of riper years and more knowledge and experience in conducting the affairs of the Church; but we now come to use it in a more specific sense. This is the earliest proposition for the appointment of elders.

1714.—"This meeting requests, that the Quarterly Meeting be desired to request the Yearly Meeting to order the Monthly

Meetings, to choose out of them two or more elderly Friends
out of each meeting, to attend the Meetings of Ministering
Friends."—(Kennet Monthly Meeting.)

This curiously constructed tautological minute was probably
predicated upon, and partly copied from, one brought up by a
Preparative Meeting.

1714.—" *To the Quarterly Meeting, &c.:*
" Dear Friends,—After the salutation of our dear love to you
by this, you may understand that it hath been moved in this
meeting, concerning having some elders appointed by each
Monthly Meeting, that are not concerned in public testimony,
to sit with ministering Friends in their meetings ; which case
we have considered, and are of opinion that it would be of
very good service, and refer it to you, for your consideration.
" Signed by appointment of our said meeting, by
" JAMES STARR,
Clerk."
(Kennet Monthly Meeting.)
1714.—" This meeting being under a weighty consideration
of the service that may be in some select elders from the
Monthly Meetings being appointed to sit with the ministering
Friends, in their Particular Meetings, in order to be assistant
in making their returns to their Yearly Meeting, and other
matters which they may be assistant in, it is the mind of this
meeting that the representatives do lay it before the next
Quarterly Meeting, for further consideration."—(Middletown
Monthly Meeting.)
1714.—Chester (now Concord) Quarterly Meeting, proposed
for the consideration of the Yearly Meeting, " that some
elders, or ancient Friends, be appointed by every Monthly
Meeting to sit with the ministers in their meetings."—(Concord Quarterly Meeting.)
1714.—" Middletown Monthly Meeting hath laid before this
Meeting, that they have had under their consideration that it
may be of service that there be select members chosen out of

each Monthly Meeting, to meet and sit with ministering Friends in their respective meetings. This meeting has taken it into consideration, and orders that it be laid before the Yearly Meeting, for their concurrence."—(Bucks Quarterly Meeting.)

1714.—"This meeting agrees, that each Monthly Meeting (where meetings of ministers are, or may be held), shall appoint two or more Friends, to sit with the ministers in their meetings ; taking care that the Friends chosen for that service, be prudent, solid Friends, and that they do carefully discharge their trust in such matters, and in such manner as the Monthly Meeting shall from time to time see occasion to appoint them."—(Yearly Meeting.)

1714.—"Thomas Wickersham and Michael Lightfoot are appointed to sit with the ministering Friends in their meetings."—(Kennet Monthly Meeting.)

1714.—Recommended from the Yearly Meeting, "that it would be of service to Truth, to appoint some weighty, honest Friends, to sit with, and be assisting to, the ministering Friends in their meetings. Therefore, this meeting appoints William Blakey, George Clough, Robert Fletcher, Joshua Hoopes, Joseph Fell, and Thomas Watson, Jr., for that service."—(Falls Monthly Meeting.)

1714.—"This meeting doth appoint Thomas Baynes and John Penquite (according to the order of the Yearly Meeting), to sit with the ministers in their meetings ; and that there be a new election every year, or oftener if there be occasion."

And in 1715.—"Adam Harker and Stephen Twining are appointed to sit with the ministers for the ensuing year, or until others be appointed in their stead."—(Middletown Monthly Meeting.)

1717.—"New Garden Preparative Meeting, have offered Caleb Pusey to sit with ministering Friends in their meetings (which this meeting approves of), instead of Michael Lightfoot." —(Kennet Monthly Meeting.)

1719.—"Friends having concluded at this meeting to make choice of some Friends to attend the meetings of our minister-

ing Friends, have chosen,—for Oxford Meeting, Edmund Orp-
wood ; for Germantown, Peter Shoemaker ; for Abington,
Morris Morris; for Byberry, Abel Hinkson; and for Horsham,
Richard Kenderton.—(Abington Monthly Meeting.)

And in 1720, "It is agreed that Edward Busby do give his
attendance with ministering Friends when they do meet quarterly.

And in 1722, "Joseph Elgar is chosen to accompany ministering Friends in their Quarterly Meetings."

1723.—"This meeting hath thought fit to appoint our
Friends and elders, Richard French and Benjamin Blake, and
request that they will meet with our several meetings of ministering Friends held at Burlington, at the times agreed to by
the General Meeting of Ministering Friends."—(Chesterfield
Monthly Meeting.)

1738.—"This meeting thinks proper to answer the Quarterly
Meeting's request, to desire the Overseers of each Particular
Meeting to think of some Friends that will be proper to serve
as elders to sit in the Meeting of Ministers."—(Burlington
Monthly Meeting.)

1740.—"This meeting being informed that doubts have
arisen concerning the intent of the minute of 1714, about the
appointment of elders to sit with ministers in their meetings,—
this meeting, for the removing thereof, declares it as their
opinion, it ought to be understood to extend to the appointment
of prudent, solid women Friends, as well as men."—(Yearly
Meeting.)

1778.—"This meeting having, some time ago, recommended
to the Quarterly Meeting of Ministers and Elders, Hannah
Carter as an elder, do now discontinue her from being a member thereof."—(Concord Monthly Meeting.)

1782.—"Birmingham Preparative Meeting proposes our
friend, Hannah Carter, being reinstated in the station of an
elder; which was done."—(Concord Monthly Meeting.)

1783.—"The committee appointed to join with the members
of the Select Meeting, to consider of suitable persons to name
for elders, report," &c.—(Wilmington Monthly Meeting.)

The last minute is of so extraordinary a character as to claim the special consideration of the reader.

1786.—"London Grove Preparative Meeting proposes Hannah Pusey for an elder, to sit with Friends in their Select Meetings; which coming under solid consideration, Ann Lamborn, Susanna Harlan, Mary Swayne, Jr., and Hannah Jackson, are appointed to join men Friends, to take a solid opportunity with her, and report their sense to next meeting:" when "they were of the mind her case might be forwarded;" which was accordingly done.

The many advantages resulting from a well-regulated ministry, sustained, or restrained, as occasion may require, by "prudent and solid Friends chosen for that service," is unquestionable. But such is "frail humanity," that there is scarcely an authoritative body in any association of men, who do not, sooner or later, require a check to the encroachments of their power. It seems, therefore, unwise for society to let go its means to control this mischievous tendency in every department of its organization. We hope none will conclude that when once appointed to the station of elders, they are placed beyond the reach of Monthly Meetings; for if such meetings have a purpose to fulfil by the appointment, they certainly are competent to inquire whether that purpose has been fulfilled, and to take all necessary measures for its accomplishment, and it is their duty to do so. Nor do we find any authority upon our records for the assumption that Monthly Meetings cannot release its elders, whenever they may have lost their service in the Church. The functions of an elder may be so exercised as to do much good or much harm. If fitly chosen and rightly qualified, they will feel it to be an incumbent duty to "take the oversight of the flock of Christ, not by constraint, but willingly; not as lords over God's heritage, but as good examples: to help the weak, confirm the feeble-minded, and labor to gather the scattered, and the other sheep not yet of Christ's fold, under him, the one Shepherd; when, being fed in the pastures of life, they may, when he shall appear, receive a crown of glory that fadeth not away."—(London Epistle, 1727.)

The almost absolute power given to the Meetings of Ministers and Elders, either to recommend or to release ministers, is certainly liable to abuse, and when abused must be productive of the most disastrous consequences. Monthly Meetings possess the means of preventing this abuse, by the judicious selection and timely change of their elders. It is perhaps the most important appointment they are required to make, and the duties of the station the most responsible of any which society imposes upon its members.

1829.—"It is recommended to our Monthly Meetings that a committee be appointed at least once in four years, and as much oftener as the occasion may require, to consider the propriety of changing the elders, and of bringing forward well-qualified Friends to fill that station."—(Yearly Meeting.)

CHAPTER VII.

DISCIPLINE.

I PROPOSE to give sundry advices with reference to the administration of the Discipline, together with such testimonies and acknowledgments as do not seem to have any more appropriate place.

Under the difficulties of immigration into a remote wilderness country, Friends found it necessary to dispense with the mere formalities of order and church government, and in a more summary way to establish such meetings as they most immediately felt the want of. Hence the first meetings for discipline were Monthly Meetings, the executive branch of Society organization. Their knowledge of the rules observed in England, and their attention to the pointings of Divine Truth, naturally led them into the same order of procedure therein.

In 1672, William Edmundson appointed a "Men's Meeting" in Virginia, "things being much out of order among them;" the object of which was, "to lay down a method to provide for our poor widows and fatherless children; to take care that no disorders were committed in our Society; and that all lived orderly according to what they professed."—(See Journal, p. 71.)

1675.—"It is our judgment and testimony, in the word of God's wisdom, that the rise and practice, setting up and establishment of men's and women's meetings in the Church of Christ, in this our generation, is according to the mind and counsel of God, and done in the ordering and leading of his eternal Spirit; and that it is the duty of all Friends and brethren in the power of God, in all parts, to be diligent therein, and to encourage and further each other in that blessed work; and particularly that Friends and brethren, in their respective counties, encourage their faithful and grave women in the settlement of the said meetings.

"Advised that the Church's testimonies and judgments against disorderly and scandalous walkers, as also the condemnations of the parties restored, be recorded in the respective Monthly Meetings, for the clearing of Truth, Friends, and our holy profession, to be produced and published by Friends for that end and purpose, so far only as in God's heavenly wisdom they shall see needful."—(London Advices.)

1676.—"At our Man's Meeting at Wenlock Christison's, &c., it was concluded by the meeting that the meeting at Belty's Cove should be to ceil the gable-end and loft with, and clapboard, and make a partition between the old room three feet high, ceiled, and with windows to lift up and down, and be hung with hinges, according to the discretion of Bryan Omealy and John Pitts, who are appointed to have the oversight of the same."—(Thirdhaven Monthly Meeting.)

1676.—"At a Man's Meeting at John Pitts's, it is agreed that John Taylor do keep Friends' books, and write the concerns of Friends in their Men's Meeting; this order to be entered in all the Monthly Meeting books, day of month, and account of all things Friends were concerned in ; the Friends' names that did go to exhort such as do walk disorderly ; the answers of such as were spoken to, and also the time set down ; also such as declare their intentions of marriage ; if any man or woman hunt after one another, and then leave one another and go to others."—(Thirdhaven Monthly Meeting.)

1677.—"The meeting requested Thomas Taylor to write, as from them, to Q—— W——, of Sassafrax, and to admonish and exhort him to keep to meetings, they understanding his remissness in that matter."—(Thirdhaven Yearly Meeting.)

1681.—"It is ordered by this meeting that henceforward there be no meeting erected or altered, before the knowledge and consent of the Monthly Meeting they belong to, or the Quarterly Meeting."—(Burlington Monthly Meeting.)

Only two months previous to the date of this minute, the Monthly Meeting "unanimously agreed" to hold a Yearly Meeting within less than two months after the said date, and yet assumed to make a rule of Discipline for the establishment of meetings.

1684.—"At a Quarterly Meeting held at William Biles's house, &c., after the conclusion of the meeting, L—— B—— brought in his paper of condemnation for quarrelling and fighting with some of his servants ; and, at his request, it was read and accepted, and he advised to read it according,—as he said it had been on his mind, both in the meeting and court."—(Bucks Quarterly Meeting.)

1686.—"Some discourse hath been at this meeting, touching such as hold discourses, either private or public, in meetings of business, having no relation to the business on hands, and run in and out, to the annoyance of the meeting. It is ordered that such may be spoken to, as a warning, that Friends may behave themselves decently in their duty towards God and man."

"It is also agreed that the men and women meet distinctly

apart from one another, from this time."—(Abington Monthly Meeting.)

1687.—"Inasmuch as the next Quarterly Meeting and Philadelphia Fair fall both on one day, it is agreed to propose the deferring of it for one week, and it be signified to Neshamony Friends for their concurrence."—(Falls Monthly Meeting.)

The Falls and Neshamony Monthly Meetings then constituted Bucks Quarter, and felt competent to determine the time of holding it.

1689.—"Ordered, that all belonging to this meeting shall come, every one, a day, to work at the meeting-house; and that four come of a day, until the work be done."—(Darby Monthly Meeting.)

1691.—"Whereas, it is observed that divers are slack and backward in coming to meetings,—as W—— C——, I—— B——, W—— B——, and their wives,—it is agreed that Joseph Kirkbride and Richard Hough speak to them, and stir them up to their duty therein; and that Thomas Janney do speak with R—— B—— on the same account."—(Falls Monthly Meeting.)

1691.—"It is ordered that Friends of the Monthly Meeting, for time to come, do always inspect and take care who there be that stay and attend the meeting; to the intent that none that are of an airy spirit may be suffered to stay there, but that they may be spoke to (if any such there be) by some Friends to withdraw."—(Middletown Monthly Meeting.)

1692.—"This meeting is informed that what is said in the meeting is carried abroad, and perverted and made evil use of, which is a grief to us, and causeth Truth to be evil spoken of; therefore, this meeting hath taken it into serious consideration, and have ordered Nicholas Newlin and Nathaniel Parke to make inquiry who the person is, and order him to appear at the next meeting."—(Concord Monthly Meeting.)

It was the usual custom in those days for the Monthly Meet-

12

ing to require the attendance of offenders, and then resolve itself into a committee of the whole, to treat with them. Hence, it assumed the character of a confidential private interview between the parties, the occurrences of which could not with decency and propriety be divulged. This was, no doubt, the reason why those "of an airy spirit" were excluded from the meetings.

1693.—"It is ordered by this meeting, and consent of the townships of Haverford and Radnor, in pursuance of a law in that case made, that the inhabitants of the two townships should pay one shilling in the hundred towards the taking of wolves,— William Howell and William Jenkins, for Haverford, and David Meredith and Stephen Bevan, for Radnor, to receive the said taxes."—(Radnor Monthly Meeting.)

1694.—"We are sensible one great hurt is, the late coming to meetings. And that all that walk disorderly, should be tenderly dealt withal, in the same love wherewithal God hath loved us ; but, if they cannot be reclaimed, they ought to be denied, and Truth cleared. So, dear Friends, keep your meetings in the authority, wisdom, and power of the Truth, and unity of the blessed Spirit, and endeavor to keep out all contentions, personal reflections, heats, and passions. Let all be done in meekness, and the God of peace be with you."—(Yearly Meeting.)

1698.—"This meeting desires that John Stacy may be agreed to cover this meeting-house; and John Pemberton has promised 300 30d nails, and, 1000 received, and 4000 10d; and Thomas Edmundson has promised to give timber to cover it."

"John Stacy having covered and ceiled our great meeting-house, there is due unto him 2500 pounds of tobacco; which is to be paid as follows :

"Choptauk 500 lbs., Thirdhaven 1000 lbs., Bayside 500 lbs., Tuckahoe 500 lbs."—(Thirdhaven Monthly Meeting.)

1699.—"The meeting having under consideration the indecent sitting and settling of our meetings, doth order, that

public Friends do sit in the galleries, and the elder Friends
with them, or before the galleries; and that our women Friends
take one side of the house, and the men the other; and that
all sit with their faces towards the galleries; and that the
meeting be kept below, and a fire made above, for such as are
weak through sickness, or age, or otherwise, to warm at, and
come down again modestly; and keep the meeting soberly,
without going out any more than necessity requires."—(Middletown Monthly Meeting.)

1701.—"Advised, that all meetings orderly established be
duly attended, both on first and week-days; and that when met,
all may know a travail and right exercise of mind, which will
repel and drive away all indisposition; so will God have the
worship of his own establishing, which is performed in his
Spirit and Truth, the rewards of which are life and peace.
But those that give way to a heavy, sleepy spirit, are great
lets and hindrances to the work, as well as great weights and
burdens to the faithful, and are giving renewed evidence against
themselves, of their disregard to the worship of God, and are
doing his work negligently."

"Be careful that those meetings whose institution was
chiefly for the necessary order and discipline of the Church, be
kept in that authority in which they were established; the
use of which is so great, that we cannot but earnestly recommend it to your care. And where any have been negligent, or
averse to promoting the service of those meetings, death and
carnality have manifestly been the consequence."—(Yearly
Meeting.)

1701.—"The greater part of the members of this meeting
being called away upon a business relating to the government;
therefore it is adjourned until to-morrow, being the fifth of
this month."—(Middletown Monthly Meeting.)

The burden and responsibility of the government at that
time rested upon Friends, and they no doubt felt it to be a
religious duty to attend to the proper choice of persons to administer it.

1702.—"This meeting, taking into consideration the sleepy, drowsy spirit that attends too many that come together among us to worship God; in a true concern for the prosperity of Truth, and as much as may be, to put a stop to such things for the future, it is ordered, with unanimous consent, that each particular Friend do give an account to the Monthly Meeting how things have been with them for the month past; and when any have been guilty, to admonish them to take more care for the future; that so Truth may prosper among us, and the oppressed be eased."—(Falls Monthly Meeting.)

Cases of immoral conduct were common at this period, which need not be introduced here; but it is worthy of remark, that they were generally among those who, disregarding the salutary restraints of society, were in the practice of mingling with and following the fashions and customs of the people of the world,—a caution which should not be neglected.

1719.—"Where any, professing Truth, are guilty of any gross or notorious crimes, or such other disorders and indecent practices as shall give or occasion public scandal, such, after dealing with by the Overseers, or other Friends, as advised and directed, if they are brought to a sense thereof, either by such dealing or by compunction, or true sight in themselves (which is more commendable), ought to appear as soon as possible at the Monthly Meeting whereunto he or she belongs; and, to the end that the scandal may be removed, and our holy profession cleared, as much as in them lies, there to acknowledge the offence, and condemn the same in writing, under his or her hand, to the satisfaction of the said meeting. And let such acknowledgment and condemnation be published by the said meeting in such manner as that it may probably reach as far, and become as public, as the offence hath been. And when any offender refuseth so to acknowledge and condemn the fault, then the said meeting ought speedily to testify, upon record, against him or her, and the fact, and publish such testimony, so far as shall appear requisite for the clearing of Truth.

"But if the offence committed be only against the Church, and not of public scandal, in that case, acknowledgment and condemnation by the party under hand, and the same entered in the Monthly Meeting book only, is sufficient, without further publication. And, upon the offender's refusing so to do, the meeting ought, after deliberate dealing and due admonition, to testify against them, according to the nature of the offence, and enter the same on their own minutes, whereby such persons stand disowned, until they shall repent and give satisfaction."

1719.—"Advised that such be dealt with as frequently neglect and do not in due time attend meetings,—those on week-days, as well as those on first-days,—but stay away on light, trivial, or ordinary occasions, and stir them up to more diligence,—a constant, or frequent neglect thereof, being a mark of declension; and, when it becomes remarkable, such ought to be dealt with and admonished the more earnestly."— (Yearly Meeting.)

1719.—"Agreed, that no Quarterly Meeting be set up or laid down, without the consent of the Yearly Meeting; no Monthly Meeting, without the consent of the Quarter; nor any Preparative, or other meeting for business or worship, without application of the respective Monthly Meeting to, and having the consent of, the Quarterly Meeting.

"These meetings are subordinate and accountable thus: the Preparative to the Monthly; the Monthly to the Quarterly; and the Quarterly to the Yearly Meeting. So that, if the Yearly Meeting be at any time dissatisfied with the proceedings of any of the Quarterly Meetings, or a Quarterly Meeting with the proceedings of any Monthly Meeting, or a Monthly Meeting with any Preparative within their respective limits, such meeting or meetings ought, with readiness and meekness, to render a satisfactory account accordingly.

"And, because many inconveniencies and delays have happened, where Friends, whose duty it is or who have been appointed to attend Monthly, Quarterly, or Yearly Meetings, or where any have been chosen to end differences, or to do any service in or on behalf of said meeting; it is, therefore, earnestly desired and advised by this meeting, that all Friends do carefully attend such meetings and services.

"And, when any Friends who stand appointed do come and sit down in any of the said meetings of business, that they do not withdraw from or leave the same until the business is finished; unless they first give the meeting a satisfactory reason for so doing.

"And, when any are appointed to any service, that they cheerfully and carefully attend the same, unless prevented by sickness or other extraordinary occasion, of which either themselves or some Friend, at their request, ought to render to the said meeting a satisfactory account."—(Yearly Meeting.)

1721.—"Advised, that Friends keep all our meetings in the wisdom of God and unity of His blessed spirit, wherein they were created and settled; and continue your godly care and service therein, for the good ends for which they were first instituted. And keep all contentions, reflections, and smitings out of your meetings; and keep down and out of all heats, and passions, and doubtful disputations; and suffer no turbulent, quarrelsome, contentious persons among you in ordering the affairs of Truth, that they may be managed in the peaceable, tender spirit and wisdom of Jesus Christ, with decency, forbearance, love, and charity towards each other. . . . . . That so we may all walk by the same rule, and every one come up in their respective duties and proper services in the Church of Christ. And, while we do so act with love and freedom, no person or meeting hath reason or can have occasion to set up different orders; because we all seek and aim at the best things. If, at any time, there should be found cause for further consideration on any point or practice of discipline, and it shall be regularly brought into the Yearly Meeting, it is not to be doubted but their weight and concurrence will be had therein, whenever it shall be seen to be of benefit, in that wisdom which the Lord may afford and will always give to his Church, as they seek it rightly."—(Yearly Meeting.)

1722.—" W—— B—— appeared and delivered a paper condemning his forepast actions, which was accepted; and the said W—— B—— is ordered to be present at the reading of the said paper in two public meetings,—the one at New Garden, the other at Nottingham."—(New Garden Monthly Meeting.)

1723.—" Some members of our Monthly Meeting have been so disorderly as to carry some discourse out of our last Monthly Meeting, and wrest it in discourse with others that are not members of this meeting. Therefore, each Preparative Meeting is desired to take care, in their quarters, to find out the disorderly person or persons, and bring them to the next Monthly Meeting, to give an account of themselves." —(New Garden Monthly Meeting.)

1724.—" Advised, that Friends, in meetings for business, watch over their own spirits, that no indecent warmth get in, whereby the understanding may be hurried and hindered from a regular judgment on the affair before the meeting ; so that it may be seen by all that the restoring spirit of meekness and Christian love abounds, before church censure comes, and that a Gospel spirit is the spring and motive to all our performances, as well in discipline as worship."—(Yearly Meeting.)

1725.—" A—— W—— hath allowed his daughter to lodge a considerable time in one house with N—— R——, without any other in the house with them, which hath produced very bad effects ; and this meeting, considering the carelessness of the said A——, thinks we can do no less than desire him to forbear coming to meetings for business, until Friends are better satisfied of his sincerity to the Truth and the care of his family."—(New Garden Monthly Meeting.)

1726.—" Advised, that Friends, in their respective Quarterly and Monthly Meetings, as they find occasion, do cause former epistles, or extracts of such parts of them as regards any growing or rising evil, to be read in the Youth's Meetings, particu-

larly those given forth in the years 1721, 1722, 1723."—
(Yearly Meeting.)

1727.—"The Preparative of Newark presents Joseph Un-
derwood, to have the privilege to sit in our Meetings for Discipline, which is allowed."—(Kennet Monthly Meeting.)

1729.—" Sadsbury Preparative Meeting complained of J——
H—— and his wife, for spreading a report of young J——
M——'s wife, as though she were drunk. The Friends of that
meeting did inspect it, and do not find that it is true. The
said J—— H—— and his wife stand still in the vindication of
their report, which seems to be the effect of envy. Therefore
this meeting appoints," &c.

Two months after. " The Friends that were appointed to
speak to J—— H—— and his wife, have given an account
that they hope things are pretty well settled."—(New Garden
Monthly Meeting.)

1739.—"It is agreed that persons who have committed any
public offence, that when they offer satisfaction to the meeting
they bring in the papers themselves."—(Chesterfield Monthly
Meeting.)

1739.—"R—— T—— acknowledges that he hath joined
himself to another Society, and thinks that he shall not come
to our meetings any more. Therefore this meeting doth esteem
the said R—— to be no member of our Society."—(Concord
Monthly Meeting.)

1739.—"The Friends appointed to visit those Friends who
have been remarkable for neglecting our meetings for worship
and discipline, report, that they have visited several of them;
and to some it seems a matter of indifferency, and to others a
matter of principle, not so to assemble. The latter argue
much for an inward retirement of mind, and express, in words,
great attainments therein. But this meeting, judging it our
Christian duty, as well as commendable and profitable practice,
to be diligent in the assembling of ourselves together, in order
to concur with our persons, as well as our spirits, in waiting
upon God, and worshipping him in the immediate movings and
drawings of his Spirit, and for maintaining a joint and visible

fellowship, and bearing an outward testimony for God. And we have a testimony in our hearts against that spirit which leads us from assembling ourselves together for the purposes aforesaid. Therefore," &c.—(Kennet Monthly Meeting.)

Those persons were finally disowned. How similar is the situation of some in our day? They argue for "inward retirement," and express "great attainments therein;" but, like them, they neglect assembling together, "as a formality not worthy of their compliance."

1740.—"Concord and Birmingham Preparative Meetings complain against some of our young Friends, viz., I—— G——, G—— G——, S—— P——, Jr., T—— I——, and I—— B——, for assenting and assisting to a forward and unadvised action, in going to correct a man for beating his wife, which practice is contrary to our principles ; for which the said persons have offered their acknowledgment for their offence, which is accepted."—(Concord Monthly Meeting.)

1740.—"This meeting declares it as their sense, that such persons who neglect assembling themselves together for the worship of God, and contend against that necessary duty, and refuse to give satisfaction for such misconduct, be publicly testified against, as in cases of public scandal."—(Yearly Meeting.)

1743.—"Touching the manner of making acknowledgments, or papers of condemnation, for offences against the Church, it is the sense of this meeting, that the offenders do attend the Monthly Meeting, together with their papers of condemnation, where it is practicable."—(Yearly Meeting.)

1751.—"Friends,—Whereas I contended with my neighbor, W—— S——, for what I apprehended to be my right, by endeavoring to turn a certain stream of water into its natural course, till it arose to a personal difference ; in which dispute, I gave way to warmth of temper so far as to put my friend W—— into the pond ; for which action of mine, being contrary

to the good order of Friends, I am sorry, and desire, through
Divine assistance, to live in unity with him for the future.

                    " From your friend,
                                        " J—— W——."
                    (Wilmington Monthly Meeting.)

1752.—" It is agreed, that our next Monthly Meeting be
held on the fifth day after the election."   Again,

1753.—" It is agreed that our next Monthly Meeting be held
on the fifth day of the week, instead of the second, on account
of the election."—(Sadsbury Monthly Meeting.)

Friends of our day will do well to remember the change of
circumstances since that period.   Then, Friends had for a long
series of years administered the government, and, of necessity,
acted in the legislative and executive departments, agreeably
to the peaceable and Christian principles which they professed.
But the ingress of other people, and the influence of the adverse
policy of the neighboring colonies, had created a war spirit in
Pennsylvania, which was now striving for the ascendency.
Truth required that Friends should sustain their position by
the choice of proper officers.   But when that ascendancy was
gained in 1756, the case was entirely changed.   The government became a military one, administered on the anti-Christian,
war principle, and the officers, when elected, were military officers.   Elections no longer turned upon the choice of a pacific
or a warlike policy, but upon the mere preference given to this
or that party, or one or the other candidate,—all equally
military and alike willing to persecute Friends, and violate
their rights of conscience.   Under these circumstances, many
conscientious Friends resigned their seats in the Legislature,
and no longer felt themselves at liberty to participate in the
affairs of government.

1758.—" Dear Friends, in a deep sense of the suffering of
Truth, in divers branches of its testimony,—by the too great
neglect of the discipline and advices of this meeting, which, if
received and attended to in true love and charity, would pre-

serve from slighting and laying waste that precious testimony given us to bear, and for which our forefathers and elders suffered so much, and some of them even sealed with their blood,—we fervently exhort Friends to arise and rebuild the waste places, each cheerfully doing their proper part of the work, remembering that the service is the Lord's. May we all, therefore, diligently wait on him for the renewal of heavenly virtue, and the influence of that wisdom which is from above, faithfully laboring to restore those that are overtaken in faults; and, after having thus discharged our duty, be careful to place judgment on such as cannot be reclaimed in the authority of Truth."—(Yearly Meeting.)

1760.—" This meeting, taking into consideration the various circumstances of Friends among us, doth appoint William Shipley, Vincent Bonsall, Daniel Byrne, Francis Way, and Robert Richardson, to inquire whether there be any among us who are not capable of giving their children learning suitable to fit them for business; and whether there be any who launch into trade and business beyond their ability to manage, or by any imprudent ordering of their outward affairs, are in danger of bringing reproach on the profession we make; and whether there be any who are not punctual to their promises, or careful in paying their just debts; and where any deficiency appears in these respects, to assist, caution, or reprove, as the case may require."—(Wilmington Monthly Meeting.)

1672.—" On receiving members into Society, it hath been the usual practice of this meeting to receive them first under care, and then, in future, as they conduct, to receive them into full unity, and admit them to sit in Meetings of Discipline; which, being considered here, it is the unanimous mind of Friends, that when any person makes application to be admitted a member of the Society, and the Monthly Meeting is satisfied of his life and conversation, and receive him, that then he shall be deemed a member in unity, and have privilege to sit in Meetings of Discipline."—(Sadsbury Monthly Meeting.)

It is proper that all the branches of the same religious or-

ganization should observe the same standard of fitness for
membership, both in receiving and disowning members; otherwise, those having a low standard may certificate members to
others of a higher grade, where they could not be consistently
received, and clashing would be the consequence.

1763.—"Where any are found wholly to absent themselves
from our religious meetings, the Monthly Meetings, after due
deliberation, and having fully discharged their duty towards
them, and finding their endeavors to reclaim them ineffectual,
may testify against them, as regardless of their religious duty."
—(Yearly Meeting.)

1763.—Concord Monthly Meeting complained against "R——
P—— and J—— L——, for backbiting and using abusive language."

After much labor had been bestowed upon them, the meeting
requested the assistance of the Quarterly Meeting, whose committee made the following report. The parties were disowned
after a treatment of nearly two years :—

"It is our opinion that Concord Friends have been put by
their proper business, in the case of J—— L—— and R——
P——, by giving way to their outward appearance of love and
friendship being restored between them, when their hearts have
been evily affected towards each other. And, as we fear the
testimony of Truth has suffered by too much delay, we think
that, unless something more of love appears between them than
has heretofore done, Friends should testify against them.

" Joshua Baldwin,	" Amos Garret,
" Evan Jones,	" Thomas Massy,
" John Hibbert,	" Abraham Bonsall,
" Nathan Garret,	" Joseph Lees,
" John Perry,	" Griffith Minshall,
" William Lewis,	" Daniel Burns."

(Concord Monthly Meeting.)

1763.—"Stephen Comfort and Robert Collinson are appointed to visit such as are delinquent in the attendance of religious meetings, and endeavor to stir them up and encourage them to more diligence, as they, in the wisdom of Truth, may be enabled."—(Middletown Monthly Meeting.)

1763.—"The Preparative Meetings returned Jacob Dingee, William Trimble, William Peters, Abraham Darlington, and George Entriken, for the necessary undertaking of stirring up the delinquents in their duty of attending religious meetings, as they, in the wisdom of Truth, may be directed."—(Kennet Monthly Meeting.)

1763.—"J—— W—— (a representative) acquainted a Friend that outward business prevented his attending both now and at last meeting; which reason, not being satisfactory to the meeting, it is desired that Friends of Deer Creek do give the necessary caution and advice to him on the occasion; and also, it is desired, that Monthly Meetings would be careful to appoint such Friends representatives who may not let small matters hinder their attendance."—(Western Quarterly Meeting.)

Very appropriate advice, and much needed by those who, often too hastily, offer names on the appointing of committees.

1765.—"With much affection and tenderness, we recommend to each Quarterly and Monthly Meeting, and to each individual member who has the least desire to be useful in the Church, that, in all their deliberations and conclusions, whether public or private, you may retain a single eye to the power of God and the prosperity of our Zion; gathering inward to the divine principle, to know from what spring and motive you act. And, as this is experienced to influence the mind, partiality and every wrong bias will be avoided, and a living concern will subsist for the welfare of the whole body; that unity and concord may be maintained through every part, on the right foundation."—(Yearly Meeting.)

1765.—"Whereas, W—— M—— hath had his education

among us, and been deemed a member of our Society, but for
want of enough regarding the dictates of Truth in his heart,
which would have preserved him from evil, and enabled him to
live a life of integrity and self-denial, he hath given way to his
libertine inclinations, so far as to neglect his lawful business,
and too much practice jockeying or dealing in horses, and
several other things tending to a vain and idle life; whereby
he involved himself in debt, and became unable to satisfy his
creditors, by paying their just demands; and hath also, for a
considerable time, almost wholly absented himself from our
religious meetings, and doth not keep to the plain language,
nor appear convinced of the necessity thereof; all which
being reproachful, we disown him," &c.—(New Garden Monthly
Meeting.)

W—— M—— was descended from worthy and exemplary
ancestors in the Church; but the licentiousness of the age,
aggravated by peculiarly unfavorable circumstances of a local
character, led him, and very many of his contemporaries, into
ruinous practices, which ought to be held up as a beacon-light,
to warn others of the dangerous rocks whereon they made ship-
wreck.

1766.—"The committee appointed to view and compare the
accounts [sent up] to last meeting, &c., propose to this meeting's consideration, 'whether, in this time, wherein weakness
and deficiencies prevail, it might not be useful closely to recommend to all the Monthly Meetings a strict and narrow inspection into the particular state of their Preparative Meetings, and
the conduct of Overseers and other active members, to know
how far a regular care is taken at home to remedy the defects
that have often been hinted to this meeting;' which, being
weightily spoken to, and the proposal favored by many Friends,
the subject is accordingly recommended to the several Monthly
Meetings, in order that a solid inspection may be made into
the situation of things as proposed."—(Western Quarterly
Meeting.)

1777.—"The meeting being sensibly favored with the calming influence and seasoning virtue of Truth, it is unanimously agreed to recommend this weighty subject to the deep attention and speedy care of Quarterly Meetings, that they may appoint suitable Friends in each of them as committees, to visit the Monthly, Preparative, and Particular Meetings, or families of Friends, as Truth may point out the way; for reformation with respect to the due and wakeful attendance of all our religious meetings; plainness of speech, behavior, apparel, and household furniture, with other deficiencies mentioned in the answers to the queries which are the cause of the present concern and exercise."—(Yearly Meeting.)

This concern was promptly responded to by Quarterly and Monthly Meetings, as many of their records show, and much labor bestowed in order to promote a "reformation;" but the minutes are too voluminous for insertion.

1778.—" S—— D——, under a sense of her own transgression, attended this meeting and offered a paper in order to acknowledge and condemn the same.

" Whereas, I, the subscriber, for want of giving heed to the dictates of Truth in my own heart, which would have preserved me from evil, have, in a most sorrowful manner, deviated therefrom, and given way to a libertine disposition in keeping company with a man in no way suitable for me ; and was led away in such a manner as to be guilty of fornication. It is with shame and sorrow of heart that I thus expose myself; but it has often come before the view of my mind that the taking of the accursed thing formerly, although hid, even under ground, yet it was a hindrance to the battle of the Lord going forward. So I have been ready to conclude, that my endeavoring to keep this a secret might, in a spiritual sense, be a hindrance to the battle in this our day. And it is the sincere desire of my mind, that Infinite Goodness, which has been graciously pleased to visit me and set my sins in order before me, may not leave me nor forsake me ; and that every-

thing in me that is sinful or displeasing in his sight may be
stoned, and the stump and root thereof be burned as with fire,
and that I may witness my sins to be washed away. Then I
shall have more comfort than I sometime ago had, when I
thought the time had come wherein I must appear before Him
who knows the secrets of all hearts, and is of purer eyes than
to behold iniquity with approbation. Oh, that I may often
think of the distress that I was then in, for it passed through
my mind, with many other things, that there was a woe pronounced against those that made the outside of the cup and
platter clean, while the inside was full of hypocrisy; and it
seemed to me that they were those who had the favor of man,
but not of God. Now, as I felt myself, through my misconduct (though in a secret manner), disowned from the true
unity of Friends, yet I think I can say that I am heartily
sorry for all such misconduct as I have been guilty of, and do
wish that Friends may find freedom so far to pass by my
offence as to continue me under their care, hoping my future
conduct may better deserve it.   S—— D——.''
   (Wilmington Monthly Meeting.)

   Let none despise this humble penitent. It certainly mani-
fests a deep sense of religious duty, and a large amount of
moral courage for her to offer such a humiliating acknowledgment where there was no accuser; and, though some may
think she was not required to make the disclosure, yet all
must award her entire sincerity, and admit that she was im-
pelled by a strong sense of duty. May we all be alike faithful to our manifested duties, remembering with her that there
is One '' who knows the secrets of all hearts, and is of purer
eyes than to behold iniquity with approbation.'' And, though
no human eye may have witnessed it, sin, of whatever kind,
ever will ''disown us from the true unity of Friends'' and of
the ever blessed Truth.

   1780.—'' The committee appointed in that weighty service
of reformation, with respect to the due and wakeful attendance

of our religious meetings, plainness of speech, behavior, apparel, and household furniture, with other deficiencies complained of in the answers to the queries, report, they attended to the service, and visited one another several times, and find that there appears a willingness in most to endeavor to remedy deficiencies; and many things that appeared superfluous have been removed or altered. But there doth not appear that lively concern on the minds of all for returning to that primitive plainness and simplicity which Truth led our forefathers into, that would be profitable; which is under care of the committee."— (Sadsbury Monthly Meeting.)

Committees of this sort appear to have been appointed in all the Quarterly and Monthly Meetings, and continued for many months. In many instances they commenced their labors among their own members, and with those who stood high in their respective meetings.

1792.—"On attending to the state of the Church as represented in the reports, a lively concern arose, under which it is apprehended that an appointment of a committee to visit the several Quarterly, Monthly, and Preparative Meetings, as Truth may open the way, may conduce to the promotion of our several religious testimonies and the benefit of individuals. The following Friends are therefore appointed to the service, viz.: Nicholas Waln, Caleb Cresson, James Thornton, William Blakey, Oliver Paxson, Joshua Sharpless, Samuel Canby, Abraham Gibbons, Isaac Coates, Warner Mifflin, Daniel Cowgill, George Dillwyn, Benjamin Clarke, John Collins, William Rogers, Benjamin Reeve, Isaac Martin, Abraham Hibbard, John Simpson, John Hoskins, James Pemberton, Huson Longstreth, and Mark Miller."—(Yearly Meeting.)

1800.—"It is believed it will tend to most satisfaction, and consist with general union, to adopt the following report :—

" 'The committee appointed on the proposition from Burlington Quarterly Meeting having met, and divers other brethren attending, after a free communication of sentiments, agreed with much unanimity to propose, that the publishing of testifications and papers of acknowledgment, at our meetings for public worship, should in future be discontinued.'"—(Yearly Meeting.)

CHAPTER VIII.

OVERSEERS.

It appears to have been the practice of Friends, from a very early period, to appoint some of their number to preserve good order, but without the specific name of overseers. Preparative Meetings seem to have grown out of those appointments, and will be best noticed in that connection.

1681.—"At a General Meeting, held in Burlington the last day of the sixth month, 1681, it is ordered, that each Monthly Meeting do appoint two persons to follow reports, in order to find out the reporters; and to minister justice upon all such reports, that may tend to defamation or slander of any Friend or person; and also such reports as may be spoken out of Friends Men's and Women's Meetings."—(Burlington Monthly Meeting.)

1682.—"At our Quarterly Meeting at John Edmondson's, &c., the advice of the Half-Year's Meeting, that two Friends should be appointed in each respective meeting to inquire into its well-being, and to end differences, if possible, among them, that the work of peace may go on, and those Friends give an account to the Half-Year's Meeting; and this meeting appoints William Lockwell, William Southbee, for Tuckahoe; Howell Powell, Lovelace Gorsuch, for Choptank; Bryan Omealy, Richard Mitchell, for Betty's Cove; Ralph Fishburn, William Jones, for Bayside."—(Thirdhaven Monthly Meeting.)

1695.—"Advised that such as come late to meetings, or, when they come there, fall asleep, or be restless, or not stay in the meeting, but go forth, or otherwise behave themselves unbecoming our holy profession; that, as soon as meeting is over, they be admonished thereof by such as are appointed to take care of such things; and that two or more men and women, out of their respective meetings, be from time to time chosen for that service; and such as will not receive their admonition, on their report to the said Monthly Meeting, to be further dealt with, as Friends in the wisdom of God shall see meet to direct."—(Yearly Meeting.) (Friends' Library.)

This date accords with my notes, but it appears most likely that it was first issued in 1694 and repeated this year.

1695.—"Whereas there were formerly appointed* two Friends of this meeting, to inspect and see that all professing Truth do walk accordingly, in sobriety and plainness; and that it may be the better known what the said Friends do therein, it is agreed that the Monthly Meeting make inquiry monthly, and that they give an account thereof."—(Falls Monthly Meeting.)

1695.—"The Yearly Meeting paper being read, brought a concern upon the meeting, and, according to the advice of Friends in the same, we choose William Hughes, Robert Pyle, and John Kingsman, for Chichester Meeting; George Pierce, Thomas King, and Nicholas Pyle, for Concord Meeting; to admonish Friends and young people, in any case where they come short in the good order of Truth."—(Concord Monthly Meeting.)

1695.—"Some papers being brought from the Yearly Meeting, wherein are contained many and weighty particulars relating to an honest, plain, and upright life and conversation, among all that make profession of Truth; it is the care of this meeting to appoint Ezra Crosdale and Stephen Wilson to take care and inspect among Friends, and Friends' children; belong-

---

* The minutes of several months of this and the preceding year are not found on the record. The appointment was probably made in one of those months.

ing to this meeting; to advise and admonish according as they, in the wisdom of God, shall see needful and find occasion; and that they make return or report how they find things at every Monthly Meeting."—(Middletown Monthly Meeting.)

In the year 1699, James Dickinson addressed an epistle to Friends in the American Provinces, inculcating the necessity for maintaining a strict and holy discipline in the Church. It was read in Bucks Quarterly Meeting, and probably in others.

1699.—"And in order thereto, we (in England) are in the practice of appointing two or more faithful Friends in every Particular Meeting, to take inspection into the conversation of Friends, how they walk as becomes Truth; and these Friends of every meeting, which we call a Preparative Meeting, because it fits those that are appointed to give a true account to the Monthly Meeting, that often consists of several, and takes a great deal of work from the Monthly Meetings; things being done without going thither."—(Gough III, p. 521.)

. 1700.—"In pursuance of the order of the Yearly Meeting, for the preserving of the unity, and the more decent behavior to be kept and preserved among Friends, according to the Truth, this meeting have ordered those Friends, viz., eight men and eight women, to meet on the first fifth-day before every Monthly Meeting, to hear and consider of matters that may be for the service of Truth," &c.—(Concord Monthly Meeting.)

1701.—"It is agreed upon at this meeting, that a Preparative Meeting be established on the Weekly Meeting day that happeneth next before the Monthly Meeting; and that those Friends that are appointed to be overseers, do attend to that service."—(Abington Monthly Meeting.)

1701.—"Agreed at this meeting, that a Preparative Meeting be established; and that the same be observed and kept upon the last fourth-day in every month, as soon as the meeting for worship is over." And six months after, it was "ordered that the Preparative Meeting of Men and Women Friends be apart by themselves."—(Darby Monthly Meeting.)

1701.—"Ordered, that William Garrett and Edmund Cartledge inspect into the orderly walking of Friends, as it was given forth by Friends here at the Yearly Meeting, 1695, and from the Quarterly Meeting at Pardsay Cragg, in old England, in 1699; and that those things therein expressed be put in practice."—(Darby Monthly Meeting.) (See Epistle from Pardsay Cragg, at the end of this article.)

1701.—"Ordered, that Valentine Hollingsworth, George Harlan, George Hogg, and John Bruster be overseers in the Weekly Meetings."—(Kennet Monthly Meeting.)

1701.—"The Friends appointed to attend the Quarterly Meeting, having laid before it the intention of Friends of this meeting of keeping a Preparative Meeting; which was accordingly entered there, and it was left to Friends here to appoint the time as they thought most convenient.

"That Friends keep their Preparative Meetings after their Weekly Meetings in each Particular Meeting belonging to this Monthly Meeting; and that they keep it at their next Weekly Meeting, before the Monthly Meeting; and that they meet at the eleventh hour; and that Friends' intention of marriage be laid before the Preparative Meeting before they bring it before the Monthly Meeting; and that all differences that cannot be ended and decided by the endeavors of Friends appointed, as by the settled and approved order of Friends, be brought before the Preparative Meeting before it be brought to the Monthly Meeting."—(Radnor Monthly Meeting.)

The name of overseers occurs several times under this date, but not earlier, that we have seen. Up to this period, Preparative Meetings appear to have been held by persons appointed in the capacity of overseers. The name at least may have been taken from John Dickinson's Epistle; but it appears, by the discipline of 1704, that the Yearly Meeting clearly distinguished between the service of the overseers and of the Preparative Meeting. It recommended,

1704.—"That the elderly and other Friends, both men and women, in unity, and who may have a sense of Truth's service, do make some stay and inquire into the service of the said meeting, &c., whether there be anything for them to offer to the next Monthly Meeting." And also,

" That there be two sober and judicious men Friends, and also two women, chosen from time to time by every Monthly Meeting, to be overseers in each of the Preparative Meetings ; to continue so long at one time as may by them be seen needful for the service of Truth ; which overseers, at the request of the said Monthly Meeting, shall be ready to give an account of their several services and duties as is hereafter mentioned."
—(Discipline, 1704.)

1705.—"John Blunston and John Hood were ordered to attend the Quarterly Meeting and to lay before it the manner of our Preparative Meeting, and to know their approbation about it."—(Darby Monthly Meeting.)

The meeting had accepted the rule of discipline of the preceding year in an advisory sense, and kept the Preparative Meeting in the " manner" formerly adopted. We have not seen the decision of the quarter, but two months after,

" The chosen number of Friends for the Preparative Meeting are discharged ; and it is ordered by this meeting, that the elderly Friends, and others in unity, shall, upon the same days, make some stay to consider of all such matters as may come before them."

A commendable instance of the condescension and harmony which characterized the Friends of that day, and is deserving of imitation in all future time.

In 1719 the last advice was again sent down, with the following additions :—

1719.—" And, although it is a duty incumbent on meetings and every faithful member, where any disorder or unbecoming practice comes to their knowledge, to advise and admonish or deal with such as are guilty of them; yet, that some may not be overlooked or neglected, it is and ought to be more particularly and directly the business and service of the overseers." And,

"It is the advice of this meeting, that, in speaking to or dealing with any, it be done in a Christian spirit of love and tenderness, laboring in meekness, by laying the evil before them, to bring such persons to a sense of it in themselves, that they may be restored, if possible. And, although such as transgress or lose their hold on Truth are apt to oppose or be testy, while they are in that condition, yet we ought patiently and meekly to instruct and advise them; that so we may not only have a testimony of peace within ourselves, but that it may likewise so affect the spirit of the Friend spoken to, that he may be sensible we have performed a truly Christian duty and an office of brotherly love towards him. After which tender dealing, if any reject the admonition, counsel, or advice given them, the overseers, or such as so deal with them, are to acquaint the next Monthly Meeting thereof, that further care may be taken with such, according to the established rules among Friends."—(Yearly Meeting.)

1723.—The Yearly Meeting again recommended "That each Monthly Meeting, as often as there may be occasion, appoint at least two overseers for each Particular Meeting, who are to be diligent in putting our discipline and directions by Epistles in practice; and make report of their proceeding when the meeting requires the same."—(Yearly Meeting.)

1739.—"Recommended to the several Monthly Meetings within the verge of this meeting, once in each quarter of the year, and at such other times as they shall think fit, to call upon the respective overseers to know in what manner they have discharged their trust; and, to this end, that such queries be proposed to them as the meeting shall judge proper."—(Yearly Meeting.) See Queries.

In those times, many of the offences committed against the

order and discipline of the Church were of a minor grade. The name "overseer" does not often occur; yet appointments were made to perform duties which are now enjoined upon them. Those duties are variously expressed by different meetings, all signifying the same thing. In one they were to "follow reports ;" another, "to end differences ;" another, "to admonish unbecoming behavior ;" another, "those who came short in the good order of Truth ;" and another, "to inspect into the orderly walking of Friends." This last is perhaps the full expression of the duty of an overseer ; or, to which may be added, that of answering the state of the members to the Monthly Meetin Darby Monthly Meeting, however, gave its appointees a more detailed charge, by committing to them a paper.

"From our Quarterly Meeting at Pardsay Cragg, the 12th of the eighth month, 1699.

"Dear Friends and Brethren : Unto you is the salutation of our dearest love, in the sweet fellowship of the Gospel of Peace : desiring that grace, mercy, and peace may be increased in and amongst you, and in all the Churches of Christ. Having a weighty sense upon us for the honor of God, and that a holy discipline, in the pure wisdom and love of God, may be kept up and practised in all the churches, we thought good to recommend unto your care these following minutes to be put in practice :—

"1. To see that Friends be diligent in coming to their Week-Day Meetings, and to stir up those that are backward.

"2. That Friends be careful to keep to their Monthly Meetings, to attend the affairs and service of the Truth.

" To counsel and admonish Friends to keep out of superfluity in meat, drink, and apparel, at all times ; especially at marriages, births, and burials.

"4. That Friends everywhere be careful to behave themselves orderly in their words, carriage, and deportments, upon all occasions, as to answer the witness of God in those whom they may converse with.

"5. That Friends launch not out into trading and business,

beyond what they are able to manage; nor break their promises, in paying of their just debts and contracts; nor that none practice any clandestine way of trading, which is to the great dishonor of Truth and scandal to religion, which the testimony of Truth is gone forth against.

"6. That Friends be careful to keep out of the abuse of smoking and chewing of tobacco, especially in markets and public places; and that such render a reason why they take it, and to observe convenient times and places.

"7. If there be any Friends who be masters of any trade, and want apprentices, or the children of Friends to be put forth to any trade, that they do first acquaint the Preparative, Monthly, and Quarterly Meetings therewith, before they take those that are not Friends, or put forth their children to such.

"8. That care be taken that all Friends be careful not to give way to sleep or drowsiness in public meetings for worship or business, but to watch against it, for it is a dishonor to such as profess the Truth.

"9. That Friends be careful to keep out of tattling, talebearing, backbiting, whispering, and meddling themselves in other men's matters, where they are not concerned; which things may tend to the sowing of discord, and raising strife among brethren.

"10. That care be taken, where any difference happens to arise among Friends, that they be advised speedily to end the same; otherwise to refer themselves to the judgment of two or more honest Friends; and if they cannot agree, then to report the same, first to the Preparative Meeting; and if there they cannot be agreed, the said meeting is to report the same to the Monthly Meeting to which they belong, and so to the Quarterly Meeting, if need require.

"11. That care be taken, and Friends advised that have real estates, not to put away or dispose of them to their children or other relations, which may prove injurious to themselves, and Truth suffer thereby, before they first acquaint the Preparative and Monthly Meetings therewith.

"12. That care be taken that Friends who have children

train them up in the fear of the Lord, and that they restrain them from vice and wantonness, and keeping of company with such as teach the vain fashions and corrupt ways of the world, to the misspending of their precious time and substance, and to the dishonor of Truth and grief of faithful Friends.

" 13. That Friends do not remove themselves from the place of their last abode or settlement, before they acquaint, and have the advice of, the said meetings.

" 14. It is likewise advised, that no Friend commence or defend any suit at law against any person, before they lay their present case before the Preparative and Monthly Meetings; save only they that may be concerned to defend, may give appearance, if need requires, or, in case of necessity, upon a bond or just debt."

CHAPTER IX.

CERTIFICATES.

It is the reasonable duty of an order-loving, religious society, when any of its members remove to another meeting, to furnish them with a certificate of their membership and circumspect walking; and such has been the early and continued practice of Friends.

1679.—" At a Man's Meeting, at Howell Powell's, the 25th of first month, 1679, this may certify all Friends whom it may concern, that William Berry, Jr., of Maryland, by and with the consent of his father and mother-in-law, is intended to take shipping and go for Ireland; his father and mother desiring it may be for his good every way. This testimony we have for him, that, as far as we know, he has behaved himself as a dutiful son to his parents, and walked blameless in the Truth, so far as made known."—(Thirdhaven Monthly Meeting.)

1682.—"From Suttle Monthly Meeting, the 7th of the fourth month, 1682. These are to certify all those whom it may concern, that it is manifested to us that a necessity is laid upon several Friends belonging to this Monthly Meeting to remove into Pennsylvania, and particularly our dear friend Cuthbert Hayhurst, his wife, and family, who has been, and is, a laborer in the Truth, for whose welfare and prosperity we are unanimously concerned; and also for our friend Thomas Wrightsworth, and also his wife; Thomas Walmsly, Elizabeth his wife, and six children; Thomas Croasdale, Agnes his wife, and six children; Thomas Stackhouse and Margery his wife; Nicholas Waln, his wife, and three children; Ellen Cowgill and family; who, we believe, are faithful Friends in their measures, and single in their intentions; to remove into the aforesaid Pennsylvania, in America, there to inhabit, if the Lord permit. And we do certify unity with their said intentions, and do desire their prosperity in the Lord; and hope what is done by them will lead to the advancement of the Truth, in which we are unanimously concerned with them."

(Signed by eleven Friends.)

The Friends named in the above certificate came over in the ship "Welcome," in company with William Penn.

1682.—"Agreed that all young persons that are single and profess the Truth, both male and female, do take care to procure certificates from the Monthly Meetings they belong to, both of their conversation and clearness of any person relating to marriage."—(Yearly Meeting.)

1683.—"It being ordered by the Yearly Meeting, that all Friends that come into this province shall bring in their certificates to every Monthly Meeting, this meeting doth order William Yardley to publish the said order in the Particular Meetings belonging to this Man's Meeting."—(Falls Monthly Meeting.)

1684.—"Dear Friends: Whereas, Adam Roades, son of John Roades, of Wingreanes, in the county of Darby, having a mind to transport himself into the . . . . . country, we certify that he hath behaved himself as a loving, sober young man, and, to the best of our knowledge, is clear from all women; and Friends have had love and unity with him, and in this we part with him, still wishing his preservation and prosperity.

"From our Monthly Meeting at Whitt Led, in the county of Darby, this 14th of the fifth month, 1684."—(Darby Monthly Meeting.)

1687.—"This meeting orders that all Friends belonging to this meeting shall bring in their certificates, or verbal testimony of Friends that live here, of their good lives and conversation in Old England, to the next Monthly Meeting; and also that Philip Roman doth publish it in Chichester Meeting, and Nicholas Newlin doth publish it in Concord Meeting."

The next month, several certificates were given in; and "John Harding, John Kingsman, Philip Roman, and Francis Chadsy, gave this meeting satisfaction, by testimony of Friends and one for another, of their honest conversation and unity with Friends from whence they came."—(Concord Monthly Meeting.)

1719.—"Where any Friends remove their habitation, . . . they ought to apply for, and, if no objection against it, to have a certificate of their good life, and conversation, and circumstances, according to Truth and justice, as they may deserve," &c.—(Yearly Meeting.)

1722.—"And as the ancient and continued use of certificates hath been of great service in preserving our unity and reputation as a people, so we are of one mind with our brethren in England, to encourage and advise to the careful observance of it."—(Yearly Meeting.)

1744.—"This meeting, having deliberately considered the matter of Friends removing from one Monthly Meeting to another, do agree that it is a fault for any Friend to remove, as aforesaid, without first applying for a certificate," &c.—(Falls Monthly Meeting.)

1750.—"This meeting is of opinion, that where it appears any person, removed from the meeting he belonged to, hath neglected to deliver his certificate to the meeting to which it is directed, it is the duty of the said first meeting to send a copy of the certificate after them ; . . . . . in order to which, copies should be kept of all certificates that are granted."— (Yearly Meeting.)

1761.—" I—— C——'s certificate is returned from Exeter Monthly Meeting, by reason the settlement of his outward affairs was not ascertained in said certificate."—(Concord Monthly Meeting.)

1786.—" Men Friends informed this meeting that they proposed declining to appoint a man Friend to assist women in drawing certificates of removal for single women ; but that one or more should be appointed in each branch (for them) to apply to occasionally ; which, being considered, is united with."— (New Garden Monthly Meeting of Women.)

CHAPTER X.

FAMILY VISITS.

1709.—" It having been proposed that there is a necessity for some Friends to be appointed in each quarter of this meeting, to visit every particular family of Friends, and inquire into their state in relation to the Truth ; and this meeting, having weightily considered the matter, do agree that it be absolutely necessary, and that it will be of service to the Truth," &c.—(Falls Monthly Meeting).

1713.—" This meeting appoints John Lowdon, Abraham Marshall, John Smith, and George Robinson, with the company of the Overseers, to go and visit the families of Friends belonging to this meeting, and make report, after it is done, whether the Book of Discipline be put in practice."—(Kennet Monthly Meeting.)

1717.—" This meeting agrees, that such Monthly Meetings

as do see a service therein, may appoint honest, faithful, and discreet Friends, to visit families within the compass of such meetings, respectively."—(Yearly Meeting.)

1723.—"Forasmuch as we have accounts from divers places, that visiting families has proved beneficial both to the visitors and the visited, where Friends are in the practice of it; therefore, we can do no less than earnestly recommend the said service to the general practice of Friends, both men and women, as the respective Monthly Meetings shall direct and appoint. And we desire that none be discouraged, but seek the Lord for assistance, and they will feel love to flow towards God's people and children; and as they abide in that love, they will witness a providential hand to direct and give them acceptance where they come."—(Yearly Meeting.)

1733.—"Under due consideration of the service there may be in visiting the families, in the spirit of love and true Christian charity, in order to the stirring one another up to the maintenance of our Christian testimonies by an agreeable life and conversation, this meeting approves of the Friends mentioned at the last meeting, for that service,—the said Friends signifying some drawing in their own minds that way,—viz., Henry Oborn, Benjamin Mendenhall, John Townsend, Benjamin Cook, and William Pimm."—(Concord Monthly Meeting.)

1737.—"Forasmuch as the Gospel order established among us, looks only into offences and immoralities already committed, Friends have been led into the practice of visiting particular families, for the prevention of the many prevailing evils by a timely caution; which labor of love having had a good effect, we earnestly recommend the continuance of it."—(Yearly Meeting.)

1747.—"This meeting recommends it to the several Quarterly and Monthly Meetings within the verge of this meeting, to revive and continue the practice of appointing solid, weighty Friends and elders, with some of the ministers, to visit the particular families within their respective meetings; the good effect of which wholesome and serviceable part of our ancient practice and discipline, hath been often attended with the Divine blessing, to the great satisfaction of those concerned therein; and hath been a means of preventing many growing inconveniences and customs among us, which it may be difficult guarding against in a more public manner."—(Yearly Meeting.)

1753.—"Where any Monthly Meetings are backward in undertaking the discharge of this duty, through a diffidence in the members of their being duly qualified for it, or the number of weighty Friends and elders being small, the Quarterly Meetings are desired to assist such meetings, by inciting and engaging some experienced Friends of other meetings to join with them therein."—(Yearly Meeting.)

1756.—"The present state of the Church requiring the most weighty and solid attention of the faithful, it is the earnest desire and expectation of this meeting, that a care be continued on the minds of Friends to enter into this necessary service, in such places where it has not been lately performed, and to repeat it in others, as they may be assisted and directed in the wisdom of Truth."—(Yearly Meeting.)

1757.—"The Friends appointed to visit the families within the limits of this Monthly Meeting, reported, that they had performed the service to their satisfaction; and as to the visited, there appeared to be a general satisfaction."—(Darby Monthly Meeting.)

1778.—"The extracts of last Yearly Meeting being produced, and that part read relating to the youth, it revived a concern which prevailed in the Yearly Meeting, for the advancement of righteousness, and the benefit of the rising generation, both with respect to their pious education in Friends' families, as also their school education; which was recommended to the attention of Quarterly Meetings, that they might appoint suitable Friends in each of them, as committees to labor for a reformation in that, as well as for a due and wakeful attendance of our religious meetings, plainness of speech, behavior, apparel, and household furniture, with other deficiences, as contained in the answers to the Queries.

"And our Quarterly Meeting having appointed a committee of thirteen Friends, to take those matters under their care and labor, as they in the wisdom of Truth may be enabled, this

meeting, taking into consideration the appointment of a committee to join in the service aforesaid, agreeably to the advice
of the committee of the Quarterly Meeting, many of whom
attended this meeting, do appoint Amos Davies, Amor Hollingsworth, Isaac Chandler, Enock Wickersham, Thomas
Chandler, and Joshua Way, therefor."—(Kennet Monthly
Meeting.)

For the Yearly Meeting's minute here referred to, see under
"Discipline, 1777." The Quarterly and Monthly Meetings
appear, generally, to have responded to the call of the Yearly
Meeting.

1779.—" The committee appointed to promote a reformation,
reported in writing, that they have continued to meet once a
month, in order to confer on the weighty subjects committed to
their care, and, as way opened, from time to time have visited
divers families within the compass of each Particular Meeting ;
first, to the overseers in their families, who generally unite
with us in the concern and labor; have also visited divers other
families ; and some of us have of late joined with some of the
Quarterly Meeting's Committee, in a visit to the families of
Friends that fill the foremost stations in society.

" In which we have had satisfaction, and believe the Truth
has owned the labor. The committee is continued, and David
Graves added at his own request."—(Kennet Monthly Meeting.)

1782.—" We, the committee to promote a reformation as
directed by the Yearly Meeting, have continued to give attention to this weighty concern ; as way opened, have visited all
the families belonging to this meeting, and ninety of them since
our last report ; and although we were impressed with a deep
sense of our incapacity to forward so great a work, yet as our
eye was kept single to the Shepherd of Israel, we have been
helped thus far to discharge this important trust, to the peace
of our own minds, and believe that a fresh visitation was
vouchsafed to many of the youth, and some further advanced
in years. And as we had, in the performance of this service,

often to view the desolations of our Zion, and some sense given of the state of things among us, we are free to make a few remarks thereon.

"Notwithstanding there are, we trust, a considerable number belonging to this meeting who are earnestly concerned to come up in the footsteps of the flock of Christ's companions, and that they may, in all respects, exhibit an example which may convey an inviting language to others to come up to the mountain of the Lord; yet the spirit of the world, having too much had the ascendency, whereby wrong things crept in among us, the effects thereof are yet obvious in the houses and among the children of some who are in a good degree sincere. And with sorrow it may be observed, that the worldly spirit and the love of money remains too prevalent in some, whereby the sight of many is dim in regard to the beauty of holiness, and the necessity of doing whatsoever they do for the glory of God, and for the spreading the precious testimonies of Truth in the earth.

"And further, notwithstanding the concern of Society, and the extensive labor which hath been bestowed, both publicly and privately, in order that we might come out of the world's spirit, ways, customs, and fashions, it is lamentable to view some of our youth, of both sexes, who, by their conduct and appearance, abundantly manifest that they are not redeemed therefrom, but are in the air gratifying that eye which is never satisfied with seeing, but ready to imitate every vain fashion which the unstable mind may invent. And we wish we had cause to believe all parents were clear in these respects.

"Thus we thought best to be somewhat particular, in order that the concern may, in a clear, weighty manner, come before the Monthly Meeting for consideration; and may wisdom be felt after to point out what may be best for carrying on this desirable and necessary work, that no inconsistencies may remain among us; and that none of us, who have indeed been favored above all the families of the earth, may remain as stumbling-blocks in the way of such of our youth or others who, under the tendering visitation of Divine Goodness, may

14

be inquiring the way to Zion ; or to any who, in these times of shaking, may see the insufficiency of their foundation, and be induced to look towards us.

"Signed, on behalf of the committee, by

"JOEL BAILY,

"EDITH BAILY."

(New Garden Monthly Meeting.)

There is probably no duty resting upon our religious Society more imperatively called for, which would be more productive of good results, than that of visiting families, so often recommended and so successfully practised by our forefathers, but now so much neglected. As an excuse for this neglect, we are sometimes told that the service is a delicate one ; that those who engage in it must have clean hands. This is certainly very desirable, but ought not to be deemed indispensable. Such a conclusion is based upon a mistaken view of the true nature and design of religious society, the essential end of which is mutual help and encouragement ; that whatever advantages the clean-handed, the upright, the strong in faith, may possess, yet even the licentious, the doubting, the halt and lame, may profitably admonish, and receive admonition from, each other.

When a religious concern is felt to visit families, whether it be by a committee of the Monthly Meeting, by a minister bearing a certificate of approbation to a neighboring meeting to visit the families thereof, or merely the individual concern of a Friend to visit a fellow-member and inquire after his spiritual welfare, if the concern is properly abode under and submitted to, strength will be afforded to perform the required service. By yielding too readily to discouragements, Friends are too much disposed to put by concerns of this nature, to the manifest injury of the cause of Truth. A Friend writes to us that —— and —— have recently visited the families of their Monthly Meeting, the first visit of the kind for thirty-nine years. In commenting on the benefits experienced from this visit, he says :—

"The frequent attendance of our Friends from neighboring meetings has a strong tendency to cement and strengthen. I verily believe that if concerned Friends would cast off the lethargy which so much prevails, and not allow themselves to rust out, their hands would no longer hang down; their lights would be placed on a candlestick, and not under a bushel; while others, seeing their humility and zeal for the cause of righteousness corresponding with their good works, would be greatly strengthened and encouraged. If we were thus faithful, we should often feel constrained to go and sit with our Friends in the neighboring meetings as our fathers did formerly, where, peradventure, we might be favored to experience together an anointing with the oil of gladness. Thus we should find the interest of the young people and some of riper years would be greatly increased, to the enlargement of our meetings; and the growth and extension of the testimonies we profess to maintain would be the golden fruits."

The above suggestion is deserving of the serious consideration of every religiously-concerned member of our Society.

— — ..

CHAPTER XI.

MUTUAL HELP.

THE principles professed by Friends, when properly lived out, naturally lead to industry and frugality. While they lessen the wants, they furnish the means to supply them. Hence, they need not and do not have many poor among them; but causes beyond individual control or human foresight may sometimes occasion destitution. It has ever been the practice of Friends to look after and support their own poor, without any charge to others.

The devastations of war, of pestilence, or the failure of crops may sometimes expose large communities to present want, while casualities of a local nature may similarly affect individuals for a season.

The necessity for expending large sums of money for Society purposes, building meeting-houses, &c., may also become oppressive when borne by the parties immediately concerned.

In all such cases Friends have contributed with a liberal hand.

1678.—"It was agreed that a collection be made once a month for the relief of the poor, and such other necessary uses as may occur. The persons appointed to receive it are John Woolstone and William Peeche, to be collected the first day before the Monthly Meeting."—(Burlington Monthly Meeting.)

1680.—"It was now concluded, that because some, through sickness, weakness, or death of relations, may be reduced to want or distress, care should be taken to administer present supplies; and John Hart and Henry Waddy, for the upper part of the county, and Thomas Bowman and Henry Lewes, for the city and lower part of the county, were appointed to visit the poor and sick, and administer what they should judge convenient, at the expense of the Monthly Meeting."—(Philadelphia Monthly Meeting.)

1683.—"William Biles hath this day acquainted the meeting that T—— A——, of Neshamony, hath made him acquainted that he is in want as to his outward concerns; and he, with some others, had took his condition into their consideration, and have bought him a cow and calf,—the price is five pounds,—and do desire this meeting's assistance towards the payment of said cow and calf; to which this meeting doth consent, and doth appoint the Friends subscribed to take care to raise the money Friends are willing to contribute towards the said five pounds.

"For Neshamony.—JOHN OTTER,
"ROBERT HALL,
"For the Falls.—JOHN BROOKES,
"PHINEAS PEMBERTON."
(Falls Monthly Meeting.)

1687.—" T—— A—— saith that both he and his family
are so weak that they are not able to thresh a little corn, nor
hath gotten any hay for his cattle, and therefore desires some
assistance from Friends; whereupon the meeting requested
Phœbe Blackshaw to acquaint him, if any man could be had
to assist him, they would take care to see him satisfied."—
(Falls Monthly Meeting.)

We do not know at what time men and women began to hold
their meetings distinct. It is likely Phœbe Blackshaw lived
near to T—— A——'s place of residence.

1693.—" Henry Baker informed this meeting that he believed J—— C——'s family lived in necessity, and are short
of corn and other necessaries; wherefore their condition is
referred to the next Quarterly Meeting."—(Falls Monthly
Meeting.)

1697.—" It was ordered by the Quarterly Meeting, that
every Monthly Meeting subscribe and contribute unto the great
want and necessity of Friends and others in the Eastern country of New England, by reason of the Indians making inroads
upon them, burning and destroying the habitations and the
lives of many, and by reason of the failing of their crops; in
concurrence with which order, £37 5s. 3d. have been subscribed."—(Concord Monthly Meeting.)

In such cases of extensive suffering, it was usual for the
Yearly or Quarterly Meeting, as the case might be, to send
the information down to the smaller branches, where greater
or less sums would be raised.

In the above case, we observe that—

Falls Monthly Meeting gave £15 16s. 8d.

Abington   "   "   £12   4s. 0d., &c. &c.

1699.—" J—— P—— being in necessity of a cow, having
lost one, and being in necessity of milk for his children, this
meeting have lent him £5 for one year to buy one. Also, it is

ordered, that Robert Pyle shall take a bond of him, in the meeting's behalf."—(Concord Monthly Meeting.)

1701.—"Information being given to this meeting that W—— P—— is very poor and in necessity, this meeting orders Joseph Kirkbride, Samuel Dark, and Peter Worral, to get a good pair of leather 'briches,' and a good warm coat and waistcoat, one pair of stockings and shoes, for the said W—— P——, and make a report of the charge to the next meeting."—(Falls Monthly Meeting.) .

1703.—"A committee was appointed to relieve a poor Friend who had broken his leg. They reported that they had agreed to pay the doctor £18; which was approved, and ordered to be done."—(Falls Monthly Meeting.)

1714.—"Germantown Meeting reported having lent a woman Friend three shillings, she not being willing to accept it as a gift."—(Abington Monthly Meeting.)

1719.—"A—— P——'s condition is such that he is reduced to poverty, and doth stand in need of some assistance, particularly a cow; therefore, this meeting doth appoint John Dawson to procure one. . . . . He bought one of John Bye, and the price was three pounds and ten shillings; which this meeting orders to be paid."—(Falls Monthly Meeting.)

1721.—"The cow formerly lent to A—— P—— by this meeting, is referred to Buckingham Monthly Meeting for further order and disposal, as they think most convenient."—(Falls Monthly Meeting.)

The cow was loaned to A—— P—— for two years, when she was to be returned. But, by a division of Falls Monthly Meeting, he (A. P.) fell to the lot of Buckingham Monthly Meeting, and the right of the cow was transferred by the foregoing minute. She was afterward loaned to him for another year, by a minute of the latter meeting. Tradition says he did not provide well for her, and she was taken from him, fed, and slaughtered, and the beef given to such persons as had none.

1721.—"It is advised by this meeting, that all poor Friends

among us may be taken due care of, and that none of them be
sent elsewhere for relief, according to Friends ancient care and
practice."—(Yearly Meeting.)

1732.—"Kennet Preparative Meeting reported· that J——
C——, Jr., and his wife, want relief; therefore, the meeting
appoints Abraham Marshall, Peter Collins, William Harvey,
Ellis Lewis, Christopher Wilson, and Gayon Miller, to see how
affairs are with them."

"They find that they have necessity of a house to live in,
and have ordered one to be built."

"The charge of building I—— C——'s house amounts to
£1 18s. 8d.; which this meeting orders to be paid."—(Kennet
Monthly Meeting.)

1756.—"Thomas Bulla and Isaac Whitelock are appointed
to go to the back inhabitants, and distribute our collections
among the distressed poor which are driven from their habitations by the Indians."—(Sadsbury Monthly Meeting.)

1759.—"Our Preparative Meeting have agreed with Alexander Foreman to keep N—— M—— (a poor Friend) one
year, with sufficient meat, drink, washing, and lodging, shaving,
and leading him to meetings, for fifteen pounds, ten shillings:
provided said N—— continues in usual health, as heretofore."
—(Wilmington Monthly Meeting.)

During the disturbance which preceded and accompanied
the War of Independence, much suffering was the consequence
among the poorer classes, especially in the frontier settlements.
In 1775, Kennet Monthly Meeting acknowledges the reception
of "subscription papers for the relief of the distressed inhabitants of Massachusetts, and other parts of New England," and
made an appointment accordingly.

1775.—"The Friends appointed to take in subscriptions for
the relief of the poor and destitute of New England, reported,
they have taken in subscriptions to the amount of £33 14s."
—(Darby Monthly Meeting.)

1776.—"This meeting received a written account from a

member of the Meeting for Sufferings in New England, concerning the necessities and distresses of the poor thereaway, and a distribution of a considerable sum of the money contributed by Friends in Pennsylvania and the Jerseys; and of the care taken in the distribution, not to do anything that might give reproach to our Society; which, it appears, hath been well approved by the contending parties, and gratefully received by the poor, who were mostly those of other societies."—(Western Quarterly Meeting.)

1778.—"The committee appointed in 1775 to take in subscriptions and collect money for the poor and suffering inhabitants of New England and other places, by the present calamitous state of public affairs, report,—that they have collected one hundred and eighty-eight pounds eighteen shillings; which they have paid into the hands of John Reynolds, treasurer, and have produced three receipts for the same, viz. :

"1775, 8th mo., 7th, one for £100   0s. 0d.
"1776, 9th mo., 26th, one for   83 7s. 8d.
"1778, 3d mo., 25th, one for   5 10s. 6d.—£188 18s."
(Wilmington Monthly Meeting.)

About the year 1801, the Continental wars and the failure of crops caused much want and suffering among many in England and Ireland. The Yearly Meeting of Philadelphia, in its Epistle to London, says :—

1801.—"Our minds have been impressed with humble thankfulness, in the remembrance of the many favors we enjoy from the All-bountiful Hand ; under which sensations, a disposition became prevalent to share with you a portion of the abundance with which we have been blessed."—(Philadelphia Epistle.)

"The committee appointed to promote subscriptions for the relief of our brethren in Great Britain and Ireland, report that they have collected from Friends of

"New Garden Meeting,   .   . $84 12
"West Grove   "   .   .   . 122 13
"By Women, ...   42 50—$248 75."
(New Garden Monthly Meeting.)

The records, now before me, further show that London Grove Meeting gave $384 23.

Kennet Monthly Meeting (men), . . $324 75
"   "   (women), . 93 75—$418 50
Middletown, Bucks County, ... 447 85

In this way there appears to have been contributed, within the limits of the Yearly Meeting, the sum of £5691, or $15,176. The following documents, forwarded from the Meeting for Sufferings in London, will show how it was received and disposed of:—

"MEETING FOR SUFFERINGS, the 5th of third month, 1802.

"The following report, from the committee on the Pennsylvania donation, was brought in and read: 'One of the correspondents is desired to send a copy of it to the correspondents in Philadelphia.

"'J. G. BEVAN.'"

"COMMITTEE ON THE AMERICAN FUND,
5th of the third month, 1802.

"To the Meeting for Sufferings:

"Pursuant to instruction, this committee has entered on the distribution of the fund raised in America, and made such an appropriation as appeared to it most accordant with the views of the benevolent contributors.

"In order to obtain the information necessary for its guidance, a letter was sent to a number of judicious Friends in different districts of the Yearly Meeting, including Ireland, inviting them to make inquiry after suitable objects, and proposing certain questions, the answers to which might assist the committee in a just and feeling distribution. And, as it was deemed important that the care of Monthly Meetings over their poor should be in no degree relaxed, discouragement was offered to the presentation of cases supplied through that channel.

"From accounts thus collected, the committee has already apportioned the sum of five thousand and ninety-four pounds, to six hundred and sixty-one cases, including eighteen hundred and eighty individuals; and it has reason to apprehend that not a few more are likely to be brought forward.

" On remitting the money to the Friends through whom it was proposed to be handed, request was made that the whole assigned to each respective case might be handed at once; and that the feelings of none might be hurt by disclosing to others what was severally distributed.

" The committee has reason to believe that its views have been, in general, carefully complied with; and while it contemplates with comfort the assistance that has been yielded, it considers it but just to our American brethren warmly to acknowledge their benevolence and sympathy, and to add, that the cases which have been brought to view, and the gratitude and thankfulness which have been expressed, abundantly evince the importance of the aid that has been administered.

     " Signed by direction of the committee.

                     " GEORGE STACEY."

CHAPTER XII.

MARRIAGES.

In the early period of our history, the proper ordering of marriages occupied a large share of the attention of Monthly Meetings. The acknowledged importance of suitable marriage relations, and the constant liability to be led into hasty and ill-advised connections, rendered this care necessary.

The following is the earliest marriage certificate that we have seen :—

1677.—" This is to satisfy whom it may concern, that Abraham Strand and Parlo C. Nicholson take each other as husband and wife, this 25th day of the ninth month (called November), in the year 1677, before us, who are witnesses hereunto, in our meeting at Salem, West Jersey.

"Signed by

"SAMUEL NICHOLSON,	"RICHARD GUY,
"RICHARD ROBERSON,	"PETER CORNELIUS,
"THOMAS STORLEY,	"EDWARD BRADWAY,
"MARY SAUNDERS,	"HANCE STRABO,
"PRUDENCE WADE,	"NATHAN SMART,
"MARGARET SIMMS."—(Salem Monthly Meeting.)	

1678.—"Obadiah Judkins and Obedience Jenner acquainted this Meeting, and also Women's Meeting, with their intentions of coming together as husband and wife, according to the order of Truth. Now, inasmuch as the young woman. is but lately come forth of England, and Friends have no certain knowledge of her, the advice of Men and Women's Meeting is, that they forbear, and proceed no further, till a certificate be procured out of England from the meeting where she last belonged unto, of her being clear from others, and as to the manner of her life and conversation, that so the Truth may be kept clear in all things; both the parties being willing to submit to the same, and also to live apart in the meantime."—(Thirdhaven Half-Year's Meeting.)

1683.—"This day we received an account from the Friends of the Men's Meeting at Burlington, concerning their proceedings with Samuel Dark, relating to marriage, &c.

"To our dear friends and brethren of the Monthly Meeting for the County of Bucks, in Pennsylvania.

"Dear Friends,—With love unfeigned, in the holy covenant of life do we greet, and in duty salute you, blessing God for that holy communion and fellowship which he hath graciously brought his people up to, and doth defend and preserve them in, where being kept, our greatest care will be for the honor of God and the good of his people.

"Dear Friends, we are comforted concerning many of you, being fully assured of your integrity and service in the Lord, and are glad our lot has fallen so near each other, and do desire that in this service and work of God which he is carrying on as well here as elsewhere, it will make glorious in his time, that we may be all packed together, and knit by that holy bond which the strongest powers of darkness are not able to break.

" Dear Friends, as to the business of Samuel Dark and his friend, we are informed that he hath a certificate come, and therefore our exercise as to that is nearly ended; yet still we are desirous, according to our former intentions, to give you a naked serious account; wherefore we have laid such an injunction upon all, of having certificates when their marriages were presented, that came single and marriageable into this country.

" We had many marriages that came before us, where little could be certified concerning the persons, yet earnestly pressing the accomplishment of the matter, which became a great strait and exercise to honest Friends, on whom God had laid the care of his honor; but for a time permitting such marriages, constantly expressing ourselves not satisfied therewith, still desiring that care might be taken for the future, that things too doubtful and dangerous might not be put upon us; requesting the care and help of Friends in England, to inform such as came over that they might bring certificates with them, giving notice, through our respective meetings, that it was expected; also informing all how they might be helped by the Monthly Meetings here, in their sending; yet, notwithstanding, it was no better, and the old practice continued and grew among us, and the burden of the upright grew with it; some alleging, that such and such were passed, and why not we ?

" So that finding it of that dangerous consequence, and that it strengthened the wrong part and hurt the good, we can say, in the sight of God and his people, a necessity was laid upon us to do what we did, singly eyeing the glory of God and advancement of Truth in it. So, not doubting that we shall be felt and credited, and strengthened by you herein, we subscribe ourselves, by order and on behalf of our Men's Monthly Meeting, held at Burlington, the 2d of the sixth month, 1683, your friends and brethren, in the love and travail of the Truth,

" Samuel Jennings,
" Thomas Budd."
(Falls Monthly Meeting.)

1684.—" It is agreed that all professing Truth, before they proceed in marriage, do publish their intention before the men and women at our Monthly Meeting."—(Chesterfield Monthly Meeting.)

1684.—" Richard Hough and Margaret Clows have again appeared in the meeting, and do desire the meeting's consent to take each other in marriage. And Friends ordered to make inquiry do say that they find nothing, but they are both clear; therefore, the meeting doth leave them at liberty to proceed in marriage; and doth order Thomas Janney and William Yardley to see the same orderly done and performed."— (Falls Monthly Meeting.)

1684.—" John Pemberton, of Tuckahoe, Talbot County, cooper, and Margaret Matthews, of the same place and county, spinster, having declared their intentions of marriage with each other before several public meetings of the people of God, called Quakers, of the county aforesaid, according to the good order used among them, whose proceedings therein, after deliberate consideration thereof, they appearing clear of all others, were approved by said meeting. Now, these are to certify all whom it may concern, that, for the full determining their said intentions, this 11th day of the fourth month (commonly called June), in the year 1684, they, the said John Pemberton and Margaret Matthews, appeared in a solemn and public assembly of the said people, and others, met together for that end and purpose, at the public meeting-house of the said people, and, according to the example of the holy men of God recorded in the Scriptures of Truth, he, the said John Pemberton, taking the said Margaret Matthews by the hand did openly declare as follows :—

" ' Friends, you are here witness, in the presence of God and this assembly of his people, I take this maid, Margaret Matthews, to be my loving and lawful wife, promising to be a true and faithful husband unto her, till death shall us part.' And then and there in the same assembly, she, the said Margaret Matthews, did in like manner declare : ' Friends, before God and you his people, I take John Pemberton to be my husband, promising to be a loving and faithful wife until death shall us part.' And the said John Pemberton and Margaret Matthews, as a further confirmation thereof, did then and there set their hands.

"JOHN PEMBERTON,

her

"MARGARET ⋊ MATTHEWS.

mark.

" And we whose names are hereunto subscribed, being present among others at the solemnization of said marriage and subscription in manner above said, thereto have also to these presents subscribed. (William Berry," and twenty-seven others.)—(Thirdhaven Monthly Meeting.)

Women appear to have subscribed their maiden names to marriage certificates up to 1686, when they began to assume the name of the husband. There are some peculiarities in this certificate, though nearly approaching the present form.

1688.—" The Quarterly Meeting being held at Edward Blake's, at Newcastle, Edward Blake and Hannah Decow, appearing before the meeting, signified their intentions of marriage. The meeting appoint Cornelius Empson and Robert Ashton to make inquiry concerning the clearness of the said Hannah; and John Alloway and George Hogg to make inquiry concerning the clearness of Edward Blake; and to make report thereof to the next Monthly Meeting. Likewise Cornelius Empson and Robert Ashton are desired by this meeting to send to the said Hannah Decow's brother (living at Burlington) an account of her intentions, and to hear his opinion thereof; that the next Monthly Meeting may be satisfied concerning it."—(Kennet Monthly Meeting.)

1688.—" J—— R—— signified to this meeting that he was inclined to marry T—— B——'s daughter, and desired the meeting's advice; which advises that he refrain her company at present, and wait to feel the Lord carry it on in his own time. With the advice of his friends he is satisfied." But, only

seven months after, we read: "J—— R—— and M——
B—— laid their intentions of marriage before the meeting."
—(Thirdhaven Monthly Meeting.)

1688.—"William Homes and Joan Davis came before this
meeting and signified their intentions of marriage. It is
ordered, that the meeting send a few lines to the meeting at
Salem, to inquire of the clearness of said Homes, he coming
thence last; and also, that Thomas Connoway and Thomas
Pierson make inquiry at Newcastle and at Christiana Creek
concerning the clearness of the said couple."—(Kennet
Monthly Meeting.)

The manifested care of early Friends to ascertain that parties proposing marriage were clear of similar engagements with
others, indicate the licentiousness of the age in that particular.
The attempts made in England to invalidate marriages accomplished by the order of Friends, was another reason why they
should be conducted with strict decorum.

Persons not members sometimes wished to accomplish their
marriage among Friends, and were permitted to do so. Thinking, perhaps, that the sanction of their solemnities would
strengthen the bond of union, and render the marriage covenant more sacred. Thus—

1689.—"William Hughes and Sarah Bezar declared their
intentions of marriage with each other, it being the second
time. The Friends ordered to inquire of their clearness, life,
and conversation, report to this meeting they find nothing to
obstruct. And whereas the young man, heretofore, had been
given to be something wild, he of late years was become more
sober, it was proposed by Friends to the young man and woman, whether he did believe it was the Truth we professed and
walked in, according to our measure; further showing, that if
we did not walk in the Truth according to our measure given
to us, we were but a community of men and women, and not a
Church of Christ, and then marriage would be as well by the
law of the province as among us. And your coming to us to

profess your intentions of marriage, and desiring our consent, is, as we are a Church of Christ, which we cannot be without we walk in Truth, therefore, whether thou dost believe it is the Truth we profess and walk in? His answer was, Yes, he did believe it is. Also the young woman was asked the same; she answered the same: Yes, I do believe it is. Whether you do believe that this way of marriage among Friends is according to the order of Truth? Whether you do believe it is your duty thus to proceed? They both answered, Yes. Friends said, as Paul to the Church of the Romans (14 : 1) : ' Him that is weak in the faith receive you, but not to doubtful disputation.' "—(Concord Monthly Meeting.)

1692.—" William Dixon informs this meeting that his daughter-in-law is stolen away, and married by a priest in the night, contrary to his and his wife's mind; and that he has opposed the same, and refused to pay her portion, for which he is cited to appear before the Commissary-General. Now he desires to know whether the meeting would stand by him, if he should sue the priest that so married her? The meeting said it would stand by him, and assents to it; he taking their advice from time to time."—(Thirdhaven Monthly Meeting.)

Formerly, as at present, Monthly Meetings were careful that the rights of the children of widows should be properly secured in case of their marrying.

1693.—" Randall Maillin and Mary Connoway laid their intentions of marriage before this meeting. It is appointed that Mary Sharpley and Cassandra Druitt do make inquiry concerning the clearness of the woman, and that Randall bring a certificate touching his own clearness to the next Monthly Meeting.

" Randall Maillin, before this meeting, doth promise to pay, or cause to be paid, the full sum of six pounds, at or before the first day of the next first month, for the use of the children of Mary Connoway, the said Randall's intended wife.

" Thomas Hollingsworth, before this meeting, doth promise

to pay, or cause to be paid unto Mary Connoway, the full sum of four pounds, at or before the 10th of the next first month, for the use of her children.

" I, Mary Connoway, doth set out one mare and her increase for the use and benefit of my children, leaving the mare in my brother Thomas Hollingsworth's custody, desiring him to look after her and her increase from this time forward, for the use above mentioned."—(Kennet Monthly Meeting.)

1694.—" Take heed of giving your sons and daughters, who are believers and profess and confess the truth, in marriage with unbelievers; for that was forbidden in all ages, and was one main cause that brought the wrath of God upon old Israel. See how good Nehemiah was concerned when he saw the Jews had married wives of Ashdod, of Ammon, and of Moab, and that their children spake half in the speech of Ashdod, and could not speak in the Jews' language, but according to the language of each people.

" It is unbecoming those who profess the Truth to go from one woman to another, and keep company and sit together, especially in the night season, spending their precious time in idle discourse, and drawing the affections one of another, many times when there is no reality in it. As one said in his day: ' These things make more like Sodom than saints, and is not of God's moving.' Therefore we exhort all to be careful in these weighty matters, and that both males and females be clear of one before they become concerned with another, and first take the advice of parents or guardians ; for disobedience to parents was death by God's law, and must needs bring death upon the innocent life now, in those that are found in such practices."—(Yearly Meeting.)

1701.—" This meeting being informed that E—— B—— is going to take M—— H—— to her husband, being not in unity with Friends, orders Joseph Kirkbride and Richard Hough to go to E—— B—— and speak to her about it."—(Falls Monthly Meeting.)

1703.—" I—— C—— brought a paper to this meeting, condemning the evil action of being married by a priest, to a man out of the profession of Truth; she is advised to go to the priest and there condemn it before him publicly."

Some Friends agreed to accompany her, who reported that "it was done effectually."—(Thirdhaven Monthly Meeting.)

1704.—" George Hogg and Hannah Cole, laying their intentions of marriage before this meeting (it being the third time), the Friends appointed to make inquiry on the man's behalf, find nothing but what he is clear in relation to marriage.

"And further, Friends that were appointed brought two letters, one from the young woman's father, signifying that he knoweth nothing but that she is clear, and likewise a letter from Randall Janney, which signifieth so far, that he had knowledge of her for six years before she left England.

" The which, with other circumstances, manifestly appeared to the meeting that she is clear in relation to marriage.

" But, forasmuch as she hath not, according to the good order among Friends in that case made and provided, brought with her a certificate of her clearness in relation to marriage from England along with her, this meeting cannot have further unity with their proceedings in marriage, for want thereof, no otherwise than by way of permission."—(Kennet Monthly Meeting.)

1705.—" Whereas, this meeting having had something laid before it, depending between J—— H—— and R—— H——, concerning some engagement of marriage between them, without the consent of parents, the young man and the young woman being here present, hath given discharges one to the other, and have fully cleared each other before this meeting."—(Kennet Monthly Meeting.)

1705.—" Whereas, several marriages that hath been permitted among us have proved hurtful, it is the sense of this meeting, that all persons purposing to propose their intentions of marriage, ought to acquaint the overseers of each Monthly Meeting, at least a week before the said meeting; and that the overseers acquaint the meeting before the parties propose their intentions."—(Bucks Quarterly Meeting.)

"This is very well approved of, and ordered to be put in practice."—(Falls Monthly Meeting.)

1706.—"Advised, that none professing Truth may keep company with women in an unseasonable and unseemly manner, which has not a tendency toward virtue, but rather a snare of the enemy, taking occasion thereby to beget hurtful lusts in the heart, which greatly war against the soul and have brought many to ruin before they have been aware."—(Yearly Meeting.)

1714.—"Agreed that it be recommended to the Quarterly Meetings, that according to the ancient decent practice among Friends, they take care that such men and women Friends as do make suit, or concern themselves in proposals of marriage one to the other, do not dwell together in the same house from the time they begin to be so concerned, until their marriage is consummated."—(Yearly Meeting.)

1716.—"Advised, that Friends everywhere avoid all extraordinary provision at their marriages ; and also, as much as may be, avoid inviting such as are not Friends, or that will not be under our Discipline."—(Yearly Meeting.)

1716.—" To the Monthly Meeting, &c. Inasmuch as it hath been requested of me why I was not married according to the order used among us, my reasons are great. I would I had them not to excuse myself in this behalf, they are so plain and so manifest, having been unlawfully concerned with her that is now my wife before marriage. For the which deed I am right sorry, as God knows.

"This I give forth for the clearing of Friends and the Truth. As witness my hand,

"T—— S——."

(Kennet Monthly Meeting.)

1719.—" Advised, that such be dealt with as keep company with those not of our profession in order for marriage, and such as marry out of the unity of Friends, or by any other method than the orderly and decent way used among Friends ;

and such as go themselves, or suffer their children to go to such marriages.

"It is further advised, that the said consummation be performed decently, gravely, and weightily; and that the parties themselves, their parents, or any others concerned, do take care at the houses or places where they go to, or are, after the meeting is over, that no reproach arise, or any occasion be given, by any intemperate or immoderate feasting or drinking, or by any unseemly wanton discourses or actions, but that all behave with such modesty and sobriety as becomes a people fearing God. And in order thereto, and for the assistance of those immediately concerned, let there always be two men and two women Friends, appointed by the Monthly Meeting where the marriage is allowed, to attend the same, and take care, as much as in them lies, that all be done, and that all behave as above advised. And if by them, or any other Friends, anything to the contrary is observed, that they speedily, or as soon as with convenience and decency they can, take such aside as make such breach upon good order, moderation, or modesty, and, in brotherly love and tenderness, admonish and caution them to a better behavior, and to be more watchful over their words and actions."—(Yearly Meeting.)

1720.—"Whereas J—— B——, being educated in the way of Truth as professed by us, the people called Quakers, but without regard to his profession of religion and education, and also contrary to the advice of the apostle (which is, 'Be not unequally yoked,' &c.), let out his affections in relation to marriage to a woman of another persuasion; and although his friends and relations did labor much with him, both before and after marriage, laying before him the evil effects of such marriages, which often tend to breed contention and confusion in families; yet, notwithstanding all their advice, their labor of love he did reject. And so we can do no less than testify against him and such practices, as being out of unity with us, earnestly desiring that the Lord may be pleased to bring him to a sense of his outgoing, and that he may find true repentance.

"Signed in behalf and by appointment of our Monthly Meeting of New Garden, the 10th of the tenth month, 1720.

"WILLIAM BAELS,	"CALEB PUSEY,
"JAMES STARR,	"JOHN SMITH,
"SAMUEL LITTLER,	"THOMAS LIGHTFOOT,
"JOHN WILLEY,	"SIMON HADLEY,
"FRANCIS HOBSON,	"THOMAS JACKSON,

"JOHN CHURCHMAN."

(New Garden Monthly Meeting.)

1723.—"Whereas I gave consent to my daughter to marry, contrary to the order of Friends, to one that was not in unity with them, which was a grief to them, and a letting the testimony of Truth fall, which I ought to have kept up, for which I am truly sorry, and I hope others will take warning not to do the like. So I give this as a testimony against myself. Witness my hand,

"E—— P——."

(New Garden Monthly Meeting.)

1726.—"J—— S—— appears here, and desires the objections to be heard which obstructed his proceeding (in marriage with S—— H——) last meeting, which was here set forth; and after some debate, found that he is a man of contrary principles, and his conversation very unfit and unbecoming a Christian. Therefore we deny the said J—— S—— the privilege of proceeding any further among us in that affair."— (Kennet Monthly Meeting.)

A Friend requested a certificate to another Monthly Meeting, in order for marriage; but an objection being made, he made the following acknowledgment:—

1740.—"Whereas I was too forward and hasty in making suit to a young woman after the death of my wife, having made some proceedings in that way in less than four months, which I am now sensible was wrong. As witness my hand,

"R—— H——."

(New Garden Monthly Meeting.)

1740.—" Women's Meeting complain against M—— (W——
that was, but now) H——, for going to be married by a priest,
and marrying in a very uncommon way,—by putting off her
clothes, and putting on a shift,—in order to screen her husband from her former husband's debts."—(Concord Monthly
Meeting.)

Some may think that the record of this ridiculous proceeding need not have been preserved here; but as a historical
fact it is instructive.   Being a novel case, the advice of the
Quarterly Meeting was obtained; which was, that an acknowledgment might be received from her, " if she was sincere."
After much labor, she was disowned.

While we pity the mental and moral darkness which would
allow a woman thus to unwoman herself, and which a proper
education would have effectually prevented, we cannot but
despise the duplicity of those priests, whose education must
have taught them better than to countenance such a supersti-
tious and unseemly practice.   Yet this seems not a solitary
case.   Watson says, that " in 1734, a widow of Philadelphia
was married in her shift, without any other apparel upon her,
from a superstition, prevalent then, that such a procedure
would secure her husband, in the law, from being sued for any
debts of his predecessor.   Kalm, in 1748, confirms this fact
as a common occurrence, when her husband dies in debt.   She
thus affects to leave all to his creditors.   He tells of a woman
going from her former home to the house of her intended husband in her shift only; and he meets her by the way, and
clothes her before witnesses, saying, 'he has lent them.'"—
(Watson's Annals, p. 650.)

1757.—" The Friends appointed to inquire the reasons why
I—— H—— and R—— R—— did not appear at our last
meeting, report that they have altered their minds, and have
discharged each other from under hand."—(Wilmington
Monthly Meeting.)

This couple had proposed marriage at a previous meeting, and it became the duty of Friends to inquire into the matter.

1769.—C—— D—— and A—— D—— (widow), having proposed marriage, she declined proceeding, and a committee was appointed "to inspect into the cause of her disreputable conduct;" who reported "that she renders no sufficient reasons; . . . . wherefore, until she makes suitable satisfaction, this meeting cannot have full unity with her."—(Concord Monthly Meeting.)

1780.—"A weighty concern attended this meeting, respecting the making large and unnecessary entertainments at marriages accomplished among us; as also the continuation thereof more than one day; which, after a time of mature deliberation, it appeared the united sense and judgment of this meeting, that such things are of a disorderly tendency, and ought to be wholly discouraged among us."—(Evesham Monthly Meeting.)

1780.—"I—— A—— produced a paper of acknowledgment, condemning her misconduct in attending at a marriage feast of a member of our Society, who had accomplished his marriage contrary to the rules of our discipline."—(New Garden Monthly Meeting, Women Friends.)

This was as it should be. Every one knows that the ground of objection to members attending the disorderly marriages of members, is the encouragement which is thus afforded to the disorder. The flimsy expedient of stepping aside, so as not actually to witness the marriage ceremony, but otherwise to give it all the encouragement they can, will neither satisfy a pure conscience, or render its possessor less liable to the censure of the discipline. The first violation is in nowise mitigated, while hypocrisy is added to the offence.

1789.—"I—— T—— requested a certificate to New Garden Monthly Meeting, in order for marriage with S—— W——. Amos Harvey and Jacob Way were appointed, &c.;

. . . report there appears an obstruction; therefore, James
Jackson, William Lamborn, and Enoch Wickersham, are appointed, &c.; . . . . report the obstruction is not removed;
which appears to be a claim of a young woman, not in membership, of a prior engagement of marriage by him to her, which
she is not free to release; and this meeting, considering the
case as a manifest breach of our Discipline, continues the same
Friends to take a solid opportunity with him, and endeavor
to convince him of the evil and inconsistency of his conduct; and
also to take an early opportunity with the young woman whom
he hath requested a certificate in order for marriage with, and
inform her of the true state and situation of the case."—(Kennet Monthly Meeting.)

1792.—"Concord Preparative Meeting complains of J——
P—— S——, for breach of his marriage covenants, in refusing
to live with his wife, as a faithful husband ought to do."—
(Concord Monthly Meeting.)

1838.—"To Kennet Monthly Meeting:

" The committee appointed on the subject relating to requests for certificates, in order for marriage, having generally
met in conference, and deliberately considered the subject,
agree to report, that they are much united in believing that
the ancient practice of giving the name of the young woman to
the Monthly Meeting, and having it inserted in such certificate
when granted, is an excellent order, and one that becomes the
open, candid mode of procedure, which ought to characterize
the movements of this Society.   They are also much united in
judgment that such practice is in accordance with the spirit and
intention of our Discipline.   They therefore propose, in all
cases where certificates are requested in order for marriage,
that the name of the young woman be given to the Monthly
Meeting, and inserted in the certificate when issued.

" Signed on behalf of the committee.

" MOSES MENDENHALL,
" THOMAS JENKINSON,
" JAMES MEREDITH."
(Kennet Monthly Meeting.)

I have extended these notes beyond the usual limit; but, perhaps, have not exceeded the transcendent importance of the subject, as it relates either to social and religious prosperity, or to individual happiness. As far as practicable, we have embraced the divers forms under which Meetings for Discipline may have the subject of marriage presented to them. To the attentive reader they will afford "food for reflection," though sometimes served up in the coarser utensils of the kitchen.

CHAPTER XIII.

BURIALS.

1676.—If I have correctly read the extracts taken for me from Thirdhaven Monthly Meeting record, that meeting recommended "Friends to buy convenient burial-plates," to be placed upon the coffins of their dead. Possibly it was then the general custom. See a minute below, of Concord Monthly Meeting, for 1729.

1711.—"Philadelphia Quarterly Meeting requested to know how far Friends may be concerned in the burials of those that are not in communion with us? It was thought necessary to exhort Friends to keep themselves and their children from going with the dead into any of their worship-houses; and avoid, as much as may be, to hear any of their sermons; that Friends may be careful to discharge their conscience in the sight of God, and wait for wisdom and counsel from him; that so Truth, in all things, may be honored by them, and no offence justly given to those that are not of us."—(Yearly Meeting.)

Those who are familiar with the grounds of Friends' testimony against a man-made and hireling ministry, will readily perceive the consistency, even if they do not approve of the foregoing advice; and no others can be considered qualified to judge thereof.

1719.—"Whereas, at some burials, where people may come far, there may be occasion for refreshment, yet let that be done in such moderation, and the behavior of all Friends be with such gravity and sobriety as becomes the occasion; and, if any appear otherwise, let them be reproved and dealt with, as is advised in cases of misbehavior or indecencies at marriages. And it may be further noted, that any excess in this case, and the making so solemn a time as this ought to be, and really is, in its own nature, to appear as a festival, must be burdensome and grievous to the sober Christian mind, which will, of course, be under a far different exercise at such times.

"Friends are desired, therefore, to have great care herein, and use all endeavors everywhere more and more to break from and avoid that offensive and unsuitable custom of large provisions of strong drink, cakes, &c, and the formal and repeated servings and offers thereof. This indecent and in-discreet custom and practice has run to such excess, that invitations being made to greater numbers than their own or neighbor's houses can contain, the very streets and open places are made use of for the handing about burnt wine and other strong liquors. And, besides the indecencies above mentioned, the custom of waiting for the last that will please to come (though ever so unseasonable), and the formality of repeated servings to each, breaks in upon another decent order among Friends,—of keeping to and observing the time appointed."—(Yearly Meeting.)

We may hope the time has passed never to return, when such excesses will be again perpetrated; yet there is ordinarily, even in our day, much that is to be regretted, and much that is inconsistent with the solemnity of the occasion, in regard to the provisions for eating.

1727.—"Nottingham Preparative Meeting proposes John

White and James King to oversee at burials of Friends."—
(New Garden Monthly Meeting.)

I am not informed how general such appointments may have
been, prior to the recommendation of the Yearly Meeting in
1729; but many of our disciplinary rules appear to have
been adopted by some of our Monthly Meetings before any
action was taken upon them by the Yearly Meeting.

1729.—" This meeting recommends to the care of Friends
that they observe decency and moderation in their interments,
that the becoming solemnity may not appear as a noisy
festival. And, when wine or other strong liquors are served
(which many sober-minded amongst us think needless), that it
be but once; and that some solid Friends be appointed by
the respective Monthly Meetings, to attend at funerals; to
move for bearing out the corpse seasonably,—about an hour
after the appointment made to meet at the house."—(Yearly
Meeting.)

1729.—" Whereas, it hath been upon the minds of some
Friends to suppress all superfluous practices of putting of
names and dates upon coffins; and it is the mind of this meeting
that, for the future, Friends desist from all such idolatrous
practices."—(Concord Monthly Meeting.)

1735.—" Notwithstanding the provision made by our Book
of Discipline, and the advice of Friends on that occasion,
greater provisions for eating and drinking are made at marriages and burials than is consistent with good order. It is
therefore recommended to the several Quarterly and Monthly
Meetings to be careful in those particulars, and to deal with
such who may transgress therein."—(Yearly Meeting.)

1750.—" Advised, that Friends be concerned frequently to
call upon the overseers, or other Friends appointed within the
respective meetings, to prevent the unnecessary use of strong
drink at burials; and to see that the time fixed be observed;
and to inquire whether they discharge their duty therein."—
(Yearly Meeting.)

1790.—" A concern appeared in our last Quarterly Meeting, that burials at our several graveyards should be punctual to the hour appointed; and especially those on our meeting days, so as not to interfere with the time appointed for our religious meetings; and likewise, that a solemn pause should be made at the interment of the dead."—(Concord Monthly Meeting.)

1792.—" To prevent the introduction of improper interments among us, it is recommended that two or more Friends be appointed to the care of our several burial-grounds, by the Preparative or Monthly Meetings, as the case may require; and that no person who is not in membership be buried therein, without a permit in writing, to be signed by one or two of those Friends; who should also take care that our burial-grounds be properly inclosed and kept in decent order."—(Yearly Meeting.)

The custom which long prevailed, of converting the solemn burial-service at the house of mourning into a noisy bacchanalian festival, presents an anomaly difficult to trace to its origin; it has probably existed in all nations, varying in form, of which the Irish wake and the Indian dance are examples.

When a king dies and the heir-apparent assumes the regal vesture, we can perceive his motive for proclaiming a general amnesty, or for granting special pardon,—the hope to gain popular favor and prop a tottering throne. May not the custom in question have sprung from a kindred motive, to atone for past offences, to appease vindictive feelings, or to secure the prayers of the populace for the soul of the departed?

There is still much of this idolatrous and demoralizing custom remaining; the sumptuous preparations too often made, and the light and airy conduct of many who attend, are altogether inconsistent with the solemnity of such an occasion.

The friends of the deceased may sometimes feel a pride in the numbers who have gathered to the sumptuous feast, or followed them to the grave; but when we look over the crowd thus assembled, whether at the house of mourning, in the funeral procession, or when gathered around the grave, and watch their behavior and listen to their frivolous and irrelevant discourse, we will sometimes have to form a low estimate, either of their esteem for the dead, or their respect for the living. Such conduct is highly unbecoming the occasion, and is as a dagger in the soul of the true mourner.

We would strongly recommend an increase of the practice prevalent among Friends in some places, of removing the deceased into the meeting-house at the hour appointed, and making that the place of gathering. An opportunity would be thus afforded for all to sit down in a quiet, solemn manner, until the hour of interment arrives, when the body could be carried out and buried.

By this means the family would be exempted from much of the bustle and confusion of the usual method, their friends would find more ample and comfortable accommodations, and more than all, the company could enjoy the advantages of a religious opportunity, at a time when the mind ought to be peculiarly susceptible of solemn religious impressions. May we not hope that Friends will yet more consider this matter?

1847.—" *To the Monthly Meeting :*—

" We, the committee appointed at our last to take into consideration the subject of parades at funerals in our graveyards, and the officiating of hireling ministers, and other violations of our Discipline, having conferred together, agreed to propose to the Monthly Meeting, that all those having the oversight of the several graveyards belonging to the Monthly Meeting, together with the grave-diggers, be instructed to inform all persons applying for the interment of their dead, that all interments must be done in accordance with Friends' order, without parades or the introduction of a hireling minister to officiate in the yard; and further, we are of the mind that no interment ought to take place during the sitting of any of our meetings. All of which are respectfully submitted. Signed, on behalf of said committee, the 31st of tenth month, 1847, by

" HIRAM JOHN,

" PERRY JOHN."

(Roaring Creek Monthly Meeting.)

Before dismissing this subject, I am willing to offer, for the consideration of Friends, a few extracts from the recommendations adopted by the three Monthly Meetings in Philadelphia, in the year 1850, relative to making interments at Fair Hill Burial-ground :—

" That all extravagant expenses in interments, and that everything tending to lessen the solemnity on such occasions, be avoided."

" That funerals be conducted without ostentation in the adornment of coffins, and that no parade of Lodges or Societies be permitted, or any hireling ministers, as such, be allowed to officiate at the house or ground."

" That, either at the house or in the procession, Friends should be watchful not to enter into conversation, but to demean themselves soberly, that their gravity may bespeak their sense of the solemnity of the occasion."

" With respect to the practice of looking into the grave, we think it best to revive the report adopted by the three Monthly Meetings of Philadelphia in 1791 : ' It is recommended that Friends discontinue the practice of looking into the grave after the body has been placed in the earth.' This recommendation was again revived by a joint committee of the five Monthly Meetings, in 1827."

The query has often arisen, " Why seek ye the living among the dead ?"

CHAPTER XIV.

REMOVALS.

1683.—" William Southbee laid his intentions before this meeting, of removing to Delaware River, for the meeting's approbation. The meeting having considered the same, it is the unanimous sense of this meeting, that William Southbee is at present in his place, and hath a service for God here; for which consideration, at present Friends cannot consent to his removal."—(Thirdhaven Yearly Meeting.)

1686.—"Nathaniel Cleve proposes to this meeting his mind to remove to Pennsylvania, desiring this meeting's advice. The meeting refers him to our next Yearly Meeting for advice."—(Thirdhaven Monthly Meeting.)

1719.—"We advise, that when any Friends remove their habitation, . . . that they first acquaint the Monthly Meeting whereunto they belong, thereof, in order for their brotherly advice and counsel in that respect."—(Yearly Meeting.)

1769.—"As some of the members of our religious Society, by suffering wrong motives to govern in their conclusions to remove from one place to another, have suffered loss, and divers of them have deprived their families of the benefit of attending our religious meetings, Monthly Meetings are desired to enjoin the due observance and practice of the ancient wholesome rule," &c. (See above, 1719.) . . . "And that elders, overseers, and other concerned Friends, when they hear of any Friends inclining to remove, be enjoined, in brotherly love, to advise them to consult their Monthly Meeting, agreeably to this necessary rule."—(Yearly Meeting.)

1775.—"Benjamin Townsend informs this meeting of the probability of his removing some distance from home, and desires Friends' advice therein."—(Concord Monthly Meeting.)

1778.—"Daniel Brett and Benjamin Hough informed this meeting that they have thoughts of removing out of the verge thereof, and desire the advice of Friends' therein."—(Wilmington Monthly Meeting.)

1779.—"Joseph Thompson and Hannah his wife, having thoughts of removing to North Carolina, requests Friends' advice therein. This meeting appoints Hannah Jackson, Elizabeth Millhouse, Dinah Lamborn, and Margaret Cook to join men Friends in a solid opportunity with them, in order to dip into the concern, and advise them as they may think best." —(New Garden Monthly Meeting of Women.)

1780.—"Caleb Pennock and Ann his wife, likewise Samuel Pennock and Mary his wife, having thought of removing their rights from us to Kennet Monthly Meeting, requested our certificates in order to be joined thereto.   Sarah Pusey, Hannah Swayne, Ann Lamborn, Alice Pyle, Margaret Cook, and Mary Bulger, are appointed to join men Friends in conferring with them, and solidly considering of their motives, and advise accordingly."   "The Friends to confer with Caleb and Samuel Pennock and their wives, report, that they, with men Friends, had a solid opportunity with them, and gave them such counsel and advice on the occasion as they were enabled, and left it to their consideration to do as they should find freedom in future." —(New Garden Monthly Meeting, Women Friends.)

1792.—"Joshua Pusey requests Friends to advise and confer with him, in regard to removing himself from his present habitation."—(New Garden Monthly Meeting.)

The advantages which would result to those who contemplate changing their place of residence, by attending to this safe and brotherly mode of proceeding, is too obvious to need further illustration.

CHAPTER XV.

WIDOWS AND ORPHANS.

IT is gratifying to find, under our colonial governments, when the laws were defective and the courts imperfectly organized, that Friends should have come forward to take care of widows and orphans, and to look after their estates, that they might not be wasted and lost.   A few extracts may suffice.

1678.—"The meeting seriously weighing and considering the great care and respect that ought to be had, and inspection in relation to, the estates of orphans, and the orphans also committed unto Friends, the meeting hath thought fit that one of every meeting be made choice of; and that they do make in-

quiry into the estate, usage, and condition of the orphans and
their estates, and to give an account to every respective Half-
Year Man's Meeting; that so the said orphans, so committed
to the care of Friends, may be carefully instructed in the way
of Truth, and that they be in nowise abused, nor their estates
wasted, and that poor orphans may be provided for."—(Thirdhaven Half-Year Meeting.)

1680.—"Abraham Strand redeemed a child intrusted with
a Friend out of hard servitude, and coming to some loss thereby, the meeting doth agreee to pay him, the said Abraham
Strand, two hogsheads of tobacco; that is, one from the
Eastern Shore, and one from this [Western] side, in consideration of the said loss."—(West River Half-Year Meeting.)

1731.—"It is the judgment of this meeting that for the
future we have a Yearly Meeting for Widows and Orphans, to
be held on the second day of the week yearly, in the time of
the Yearly Meeting in this house."*

1732.—"At a Yearly Meeting for the care of widows and
orphans, at our meeting-house, at the head of Thirdhaven, it is
the judgment of this meeting that James Wilson and John
Stephens address the court with a petition, setting forth our
right to our deceased Friend Josiah Parrot's son, and employ
counsel to plead to the same, at the public charge of Friends."
—(Thirdhaven Yearly Meeting.)

Reports were received from Cecil, Tuckahoe, Treadhaven,
Choptank, and Transquaking, all on the Eastern Shore.

Similar meetings continued to be held for many years, but
were probably found less needful as the courts became better
organized. But so late as

1755.—"There being very great omissions in many in not
accounting for the state of the widows and orphans, this meeting thinks proper to appoint Joseph Richardson and Philip
Thomas, Jr., to let the several Monthly Meetings on the West-

---

* The meeting-house at the head of Thirdhaven Creek.

ern Shore know of the said omissions by writing, and to advise them to put the Friends, appointed in the several Weekly Meetings, upon being more diligent in the discharge of their duty; and James Wilson and Isaac Williams to do the like to the Monthly Meetings on the Eastern Shore."—(Thirdhaven Yearly Meeting.)

Although I could cite many instances of care within our own Yearly Meeting limits, yet it is probable that the greater providence of William Penn had provided more for the security and comfort of widows and orphans, and therefore left less for the meetings to supply in Pennsylvania than in the other provinces.

CHAPTER XVI.

SCHOOLS.

THE fundamental principle maintained by Friends,—the immediate revelation of God in the soul,—so abundantly experienced in the patriarchal ages, and so manifestly inculcated by Jesus Christ and his early followers, has been long denied to exist in later days by most other Christian professors;—hence it is obvious that Friends have assumed a higher ground of religious faith and practice, and a more spiritual mode of worship, in accordance with the declaration, that "God is a Spirit, and they who worship Him, must worship Him in spirit and in truth."

Friends are, moreover, distinguished from most other religious professors by the testimonies which they have hitherto borne against all war and violence, all oppressions, all excess and intemperate indulgence in the use of temporal goods and enjoyments; and, consequently, for their opposites, peace, brotherly love and kindness, liberty, plainness, simplicity, and moderation in all things.

The [parent is the natural guardian and instructor of the child, appointed so to be by God himself; and, as it is the parent's duty to serve God aright, and to follow and obey His requirements in all things, so it is his duty faithfully to lead, educate, and instruct his tender charge : "to train him up in the way he should go, and when he is old he will not depart from it." Duty to the child is duty to God; and neglect of the one is also neglect of the other ;—they are inseparable; and that which is the duty of an individual is equally the duty of numbers, whether great or small, when associated in religious society.

Friends have ever been aware of their peculiar position, and of the necessity which existed for them to provide a carefully-guarded religious education for their children and youth, in accordance with their principles and testimonies; without which, the seductive influences of the world's ways and customs would continually operate to unfit and disqualify them from coming up to fill the position which their fathers occupied, as able testimony-bearers to the Truth, and faithful watchmen on the walls of our Zion.

In agreement with the views here presented, Friends have long been concerned to establish and maintain schools at their own cost, and under their own direction and control, for the education of their children. Not, however, so much for the purpose of giving them religious instruction in schools, as to be able to exclude therefrom any influences which might poison their tender minds, and lead them away from the simplicity of the Truth.

1683.—"At a council held in Philadelphia, the 20th of the tenth month, 1683, present,—

"William Penn, Proprietor and Governor; Thos. Holmes, Wm. Haigue, Lasse Cock, Wm. Clayton.

"The Governor and Provincial Council, having taken into their serious consideration the necessity there is of a schoolmaster for the instruction and sober education of youth in the town of Philadelphia, sent for Enoch Flower, an inhabitant of

the said town, who, for twenty years past, hath been exercised
in that care and employment in England; to whom, having communicated their minds, he embraced it upon these following terms:
To learn to read English, 4s. by the quarter; to learn to read
and write, 6s. by the quarter; to learn to read, write, and cast
accounts, 8s. by the quarter; for boarding a scholar,—that is to
say, diet, washing, lodging, and schooling,—ten pounds for one
whole year."—(Colonial Records, i, 91.)

1693.—"Agreed at this meeting, that Benjamin Clift teach
school a year, beginning the 20th day of the seventh month,
1693, and to have £12 0s. 0d."—(Darby Monthly Meeting.)

1746.—"We desire you, in your several Monthly Meetings,
to encourage and assist each other in the settlement and support of schools for the instruction of your children, at least to
read and write, and some further useful learning, to such
whose circumstances will permit it. And that you observe, as
much as possible, to employ such masters and mistresses as
are concerned, not only to instruct your children in their learning, but are likewise careful in the wisdom of God and a spirit
of meekness, gradually to bring them to a knowledge of their
duty to God and one another; and we doubt not such endeavors will be blessed with success. And, on the contrary, we
think there is too much cause to apprehend that some children, by the evil examples and bad principles of their schoolmasters, have been learned with those principles, which led
them to bad practices in the course of their lives."—(Yearly
Meeting.)

1751.—"The consideration of the proposal made last year,
concerning the settling of schools in the country, being resumed, and, inasmuch as our elder brethren in London have
likewise recommended the consideration of this weighty affair,
after some observations and reasons offered to urge the necessity thereof, it is agreed, that it be again recommended to
the Quarterly and Monthly Meetings to encourage their respective members to exert themselves as fully therein as their
present circumstances will permit; and to think of methods

by which this good work may be effected in time."—(Yearly Meeting.)

1778.—" It is the sense of this meeting that Friends having united with others in employing such persons for masters who have not submitted to the operation of Truth, hath had a tendency to strengthen a disposition in our youth to avoid the cross and unite with the spirit of the world, whereby many hurtful and corrupt things have gained ground among us.

" The consideration of the importance of training up our youth in useful learning, under the tuition of religious, prudent persons, suitably qualified for that service, came weightily before the meeting. . . . . We therefore think it necessary that it be recommended to the Quarterly and from thence to the Monthly and Preparative Meetings, that the former advices of collecting a fund for the establishment and support of schools, under the care of standing committees appointed by the Monthly or Preparative Meetings, should generally take place. . . . .

" We also think it necessary that this weighty concern should in future become the continued care of the Yearly Meeting, by an annual query, so that the matter may rest on a solid foundation, and every possible encouragement and assistance may be afforded to Friends in the settlement of schools, providing masters, &c., through the whole extent of the Yearly Meeting.

" And, notwithstanding some difficulty may appear in the raising a sufficiency fully to answer the end proposed, yet, as improvements of this kind have often arisen from small beginnings, it is desired that Friends be not discouraged by their inability; but, having faith in the Divine blessing being conferred on their benevolent intentions, would begin by making some provisions, agreeably to the circumstances of their respective meetings; that, in the compass of each meeting where the settlement of a school is necessary, a lot of ground be provided sufficient for a garden, orchard, grass for a cow, &c., and that a suitable house, stable, &c., be erected thereon. There are but few meetings but which may, in labor, in materials, or money, raise so much as would answer such a charge."

"And here a sorrowful occasion occurs, which we desire to mention with caution and tenderness; that is, the backwardness, so apparent among us, to contribute that part of our substance which the circumstances of things and the necessities of the people have, on different occasions, made necessary. If this had not been the case, a matter of so great importance as the virtuous education of our youth would not have been neglected for so long a course of years, after such pressing advices had been so expressly handed down from the Yearly Meeting. Hence arises a query, how far our neglect of applying to the necessary service of our fellow-men such part of the goods many have laid up in store, is one of the causes of the deep affliction which now so feelingly attends? and how small a portion of what has been forcibly taken from many (if it had been seasonably and cheerfully contributed), would have answered the several good purposes which have either been refused or neglected by us?"—(Yearly Meeting.)

Allusion is here made to the suffering which Friends were then under on account of military requisitions (see Sufferings); and it may be well for us of the present day to consider how far we may be subjecting ourselves to some afflictive dispensation by a similar neglect.

1779.—"This meeting, being further fervently concerned for the pious education of our youth, and their preservation from the corrupt conversation prevailing, and the various temptations to which they are exposed, again earnestly recommend this important matter to the deep and solid attention of parents, and all others who have the weighty trust of the youth committed to them, with fervent desires that it may deeply impress the minds of Friends in general; and that Quarterly and Monthly Meetings may dwell under a living concern and exercise, and, n the influence of Divine wisdom, proceed to fulfil the weighty advice recommended on this subject by the meeting in the last and foregoing years."—(Yearly Meeting.)

1787.—"Attention being given to the general account of care exercised in most parts for the promotion of well-regulated schools, for the instruction of the youth in useful learning, there appears a ground of hope that the momentous concern is gradually making way in the minds of Friends.

" And a desire prevailing that our brethren everywhere may be encouraged to persevere in this desirable work, a continued close regard to its importance, and the evil consequences resulting from a neglect of it, is earnestly urged afresh to the vigilant care of concerned Friends in each Quarter, to be extended not only to the children of Friends in more easy circumstances in life, but also to the offspring of such as are poor, and of the black people, whose condition gives them a claim to that benefit, consistent with the sense of this meeting, contained in the repeated advices given forth."—(Yearly Meeting.)

1792.—"We, the committee appointed at the request of Kennet Preparative Meeting, respecting the establishing a school within the verge thereof, . . . find they have purchased a piece of ground, &c., about two miles and a half westerly from Kennet Meeting-house, adjoining the public road leading to Nottingham," &c.—(Kennet Monthly Meeting.)

1796.—"The committee to whom was referred the preparing a plan to raise a fund for the benefit of schools, reported, &c., a plan for raising a fund for the benefit of schools within the bounds of Kennet Monthly Meeting, whereby Friends may have an opportunity of manifesting their benevolent intentions by subscribing thereto :—

" 1. That each subscriber to this plan pay, at the time of subscribing, or give his or her note to the Treasurer and Clerk of the Trustees, or their successors, appointed by Kennet Monthly Meeting to have the care of this fund, for a sum of money, payable at any time not exceeding three years after date, with interest of five per cent. per annum, paid annually for the same.

" 2. The Treasurer shall have a book for the purpose, and

keep fair entries of all money due and received; likewise of all money expended; and his receipt shall be a sufficient discharge for any money paid to him for the use of schools.

" 3. Whenever the Treasurer shall receive any new subscription, or any money for the benefit of the schools, he shall report the same to the next meeting of the Trustees of the said schools.

" 4. When the Trustees receive any money for the use of schools, they shall, as soon as they conveniently can, put the same to interest on good security; or they may purchase land or ground-rent therewith, as shall appear best for the time being.

" 5. The Trustees shall, as soon as they see occasion, apply the interest arising from this fund to schooling the children of such poor people, whether Friends or others, as live within the verge of the aforesaid Monthly Meeting; provided such children comply with the rules of the schools.

" 6. We recommend it to each other, as often as we find an increase of property and openness of heart, to add something more to our subscriptions; whereby it is hoped the Monthly Meeting may, in time, be enabled more fully to comply with the advice of the Yearly Meeting in 1778 respecting schools.

" 7. And as a variety of circumstances may in future occur, which the human eye cannot foresee, nor understanding conceive; therefore, the Trustees shall, from time to time, manage this fund, as shall appear to them best to promote the welfare of the said schools and the poor thereunto belonging; also, if the interest may be to spare, they may assist therewith in keeping the school-houses in repair, and in paying the salaries of schoolmasters or schoolmistresses within the verge of the said meeting; provided the principal be not thereby lessened.

" 8. If, at any time, the Trustees may not all judge alike how they ought to proceed, in such cases they are to apply to the aforesaid Monthly Meeting for assistance.

" 9. The Trustees shall, from time to time, be accountable to the Monthly Meeting of Kennet for their management of the fund, as directed in the minute of their appointment.

"Signed, by order of Kennet Monthly Meeting, held the 15th of twelfth month, 1796, by

" CALEB PENNOCK,

" *Clerk.*"

The records of Concord, Wilmington, and perhaps many other Monthly Meetings, contain nearly similar plans for the establishment of school-funds, and give evidence of their successful application. The Trustees of Kennet were renewed by the following minute in

1804. — " Kennet Preparative Meeting proposes Robert Lamborn, Caleb Hoopes, and Moses Mendenhall, Jr., for Trustees in the care of their school-fund, and Isaac Bennet for Treasurer; Hockessin proposes Caleb Sharpless, Ephraim Jackson, and Stephen Wilson, Trustees, and James Phillips for Treasurer; Marlborough proposes Joseph Barnard, Enoch Wickersham, and David Chalfant, Trustees, and Richard Barnard, Jr., for Treasurer; which, being considered, is united with, and they appointed to said service. Marlborough also informs that they have entered into a subscription toward their school-fund, which at present amounts to five hundred and seventy-six dollars ($576)."—(Kennet Monthly Meeting.)

1808.—" The Meeting for Sufferings having stated in their minutes, that some in membership with us have placed their children at colleges and other seminaries out of our religious Society, in order to give them what is termed a polished education; the subject engaging the solid consideration of the meeting, viewing the youth of both sexes thus situated as very likely to have their minds imbued with sentiments and principles which strengthen them in vain desires after exaltation and grandeur, and often lead them from the salutary restraints inculcated by our religious profession, it is desired that tender caution and counsel be extended to such parents, and others, who may be in danger of erring in this way."—(Yearly Meeting.)

1819.—"Marlborough Meeting informs that their school-fund is increased to $1064 49," &c.—(Kennet Monthly Meeting.)

CHAPTER XVII.

QUERIES.

MONTHLY, Quarterly, and Yearly Meetings must very early have experienced the want of an acquaintance with the state and condition of their subordinate branches, to obtain which they had recourse to interrogatories, beginning with the smaller and thence ascending to the larger assemblies.—(See Overseers, &c.)

1707.—" The Yearly Meeting paper of Discipline being produced, it is agreed that Samuel Darke, &c., do draw several other particulars necessary to ask the Overseers monthly, and bring them to the next Monthly Meeting, in order to be recommended to the Quarterly Meeting for approbation."—(Falls Monthly Meeting.)

1708.—" There being several particular questions relating to discipline, which was thought needful to ask the Overseers, drawn up and presented to this meeting, and they being read, were approved; and it is agreed each Monthly Meeting have a copy of them, and that the Overseers of each Monthly Meeting answer to them, and the representatives to the Quarterly Meeting."—(Bucks Quarterly Meeting.)

In those days a Quarterly Meeting was mainly a kind of general Monthly Meeting, and performed very similar functions, but possessed the religious weight and experience of the several Monthly Meetings combined, and hence its conclusions were deemed to be more authoritative and obligatory by them.

The following minute shows the care and concern experienced by Friends in those days, and the extraordinary labor which they performed."

1711.—"Forasmuch as the last Yearly Meeting had a concern upon them to recommend the putting in practice more strictly the particulars mentioned in the Book of Discipline, it is therefore agreed, that care be taken accordingly; and in order thereto, this meeting recommends the following method, viz. :

"That this Quarterly Meeting do, henceforth, from time to time, inquire of each Monthly Meeting's Representatives, how the Book of Discipline, and that which relates thereto in the general testimony, which according to former advices is to be quarterly read in our meetings for worship, be kept to and put in practice; but particularly how these following matters or articles therein contained, are observed and kept, viz. :

"That against proposing marriages without Friends' consent, and that about burials being kept solid and grave; that about parents' and masters' care to keep children and servants from hurtful principles and practices, and that they marry with none but Friends;* that against unseasonable keeping company with women, or at all, in order for marriage, with such as don't profess Truth.

"That against inviting servants to marriages, except near relations. That against going to the marriages of any that profess Truth, but marry not among Friends. That of keeping company in order for marriage with any one's servant, without leave of master or mistress. That about being clear of one before being concerned with another. That of being too hasty in marriage after the death of husband or wife, and against

---

* Friends in those days were a laboring people, and they brought up their children to labor. By another rule, they placed them as apprentices (or servants), "among Friends." Hence, in respect to wealth and family, the servant might equal or exceed the master; indeed, the invidious distinction of rich and poor was hardly known among early Friends, and cannot exist in the true Church of Christ. Two servants of John Fenwich, in 1675, married two of his daughters.

marriage with [by] priests. That against giving occasion of public scandal, and that against all disorderly walkers in general. That about Friends putting their children to apprentices, or otherwise to be brought up by those who are not Friends. That about parents causing their children often to read the Holy Scriptures, and to let them know some degree of writing; and that they be bred up in some useful employment. That against drinking to excess, swearing, cursing, lying, &c. That against superfluity of apparel and furniture, in all its branches. That against calling the days and months contrary to Scripture, and against calling them by the names of the idol gods of the heathen. That about speaking the plain Scripture language of *thee* and *thou.* That against buying and trading beyond abilities, and of not keeping to our words and promises. That about attending Weekly Meetings, and against disorderly going in and out; and against sleeping in meetings. That against smoking tobacco in streets, roads, and public houses, except privately. That against talking and tale-bearing. That against giving any just occasion of trouble to the government, and against our refusing to pay its tributes or assessments. That against selling rum to the Indians, and against buying Indian slaves. That against brother going to law with brother, as explained or amended by the last Yearly Meeting held at Burlington. That against challenging to fight, &c. That against keeping vain or loose company, in fairs, markets, drinking-houses, or any other places, &c. That against vain and frothy discourses, drinking to excess, and against a vain custom of drinking healths, as it is called, and against drinking one to another.

"And it is this meeting's further advice, that all the Preparative Meetings within the limits of this meeting do, also, duly and in order, as above set down, inquire into all the above particulars, that they may be the better enabled thereby to give the respective Monthly Meetings, when called upon as above advised, a faithful account of the state of each of the said particular Preparative Meetings. And when at any time any member is found deficient, as to his duty and circumspect

walking, in any of the aforesaid, or any other particular thing,
that then such be dealt with in the fear of God, and in true
brotherly love, and according to the directions of the said Discipline Book. And that copies of this be sent by the clerk to
each Monthly Meeting, and that each Monthly Meeting let
each Preparative that respectively belongs to them have a copy
also."—(Concord Quarterly Meeting.)

It would be well if Friends would compare the Christian care
and watchful regard which the meetings in those days exercised over their members, and seriously inquire why there has
been so much declension among us in this respect. Let none
excuse themselves by throwing the blame upon the meetings,
for we must remember that a meeting is nothing else than the
members who compose it. If the members will properly discharge their duties, the meetings will not be found deficient.

1712.—The representatives to the Quarterly Meeting were
directed to report: "That the heads of the Book of Discipline
have been read in this meeting, and that the Particular Meetings being called, and examined upon every article therein contained, and account being given that things are in the general
pretty well; and that when anything hath happened that is
amiss, care is taken for amendment therein."—(Concord Monthly Meeting.)

1714.—"Dear Friends: After the salutation of our dear
love to you, by this you may understand that our meetings are
pretty well kept to, and Friends are in love and unity in general; and care is taken that the discipline be put in practice."
—(Kennet Monthly Meeting.)

1718.—"The state of this meeting is as followeth: In a
general way, peace and unity is preserved among us; and when
anything is out of order, care hath been and is taken to rectify
what is amiss."—(Chesterfield Monthly Meeting.)

1719.—"John Roberts, Richard Hayes, Reece Thomas,
Rowland Ellis, and Lewis Walker, are appointed to attend the
next Quarterly Meeting at Philadelphia; and we are comforted,

that love and condescension are in some good degree among us, and we desire that the Lord may increase it among us here, and among us everywhere."—(Radnor Monthly Meeting.)

1721.—"The Friends appointed to attend the Quarterly Meeting are,—John Carver, John Knowls, Anthony Clinker, Evan Loyd, and Robert Fletcher; who are to report the present state of the meeting, which is: that meetings are kept up, and Friends in love and unity, and Discipline kept to in a good degree."—(Abington Monthly Meeting.)

1725.—"The queries being read, the overseers report they have nothing at present to offer."—(Middletown Monthly Meeting.)

This is the earliest notice I have seen of "the queries being read." The Yearly Meeting, held at Thirdhaven in the same year, has the following minute:—

1725.—"This Yearly Meeting orders these eighteen queries following, to be recommended to the Quarterly and Monthly Meetings for the ordering of the Discipline; and that they be inquired into in the Monthly Meetings, as they, in the wisdom of Truth, shall seem convenient."—(Thirdhaven Yearly Meeting.)

1741.—"The Friends appointed to consider what queries may be suitable to interrogate overseers with, report that they are of opinion that they may be drawn out of the Book of Discipline."—(Darby Monthly Meeting.)

This minute, in connection with the preceding one of Concord Monthly Meeting, may explain the character and design of the questions usually asked the overseers; as, also, the following:—

1706.—"Robert Pyle and George Pierce are appointed to go down to Nottingham, and take with them the order of the Quarterly Meeting for the settling of a meeting there; and also, the several heads out of the Book of Discipline, so far as may suit their circumstances, in order for the settling of a Preparative Meeting, and the carrying on a Church government among them, according to the good order of Truth."— (Concord Monthly Meeting.)

From all of which, it is evident that the questions asked were in reference to the support of the testimonies of Friends, and to the maintenance of the Discipline; they being systematized and extended, but not essentially changed, by the subsequent action of the Yearly Meeting, which follows:—

1743.—"This meeting directs that the following queries may be read in the several Monthly and Preparative Meetings within the verge of this meeting, at least once in each quarter of the year; to the end that the overseers, or other weighty Friends, may make such answers to them as they may be able to do, and their respective circumstances may require. The members of such meetings may, by this means, be from time to time reminded of their duty.

"I. Are Friends careful to attend their meetings for worship, both on first-days and other days of the week appointed for that service? and are they careful to meet at the hour appointed? Do they refrain from sleeping in meetings? or do any accustom themselves to snuffing or chewing tobacco in meetings?

"II. Do Friends keep clear of excess, either in drinking drams or other strong drink?

"III. Are there any who keep company, in order for marriage, with those who are not of us, or with any others without the consent of parents or guardians?

"IV. Do Friends keep clear from tattling, tale-bearing, whispering, backbiting, and meddling in matters wherein they are not concerned?

"V. Are there any Friends that frequent music houses, or go to dancing or gaming?

"VI. Are Friends careful to train up their children in the nurture and fear of the Lord, and to restrain them from vice and evil company, and to keep them to plainness of speech and apparel?

" VII. Are the poor taken care of and are their children put to school and apprenticed out (after sufficient learning), to Friends? and do Friends put their own children out to Friends, as much as may be?

"VIII. Are there any who launch into business beyond what they are able to manage, and so break their promises, in not paying their just debts in due time? And where differences happen, are endeavors used to have them speedily ended?

" IX. Are there any belonging to this meeting that are removed without certificates? or are there any from other parts appearing as Friends, and have not produced a certificate?

" X. Are Friends clear of depriving the King of his duties?

" XI. Do Friends observe the former advices of the Yearly Meeting, not to encourage the importation of negroes, nor to buy them after imported?

" XII. Are Friends careful to settle their affairs and make their wills in time of health?

" The Overseers and other Friends are earnestly desired to take due care in all the foregoing particulars, to advise or deal with such as are in the breach of these or any other branch of our discipline."—(Yearly Meeting.)

The foregoing queries appear to have had a twofold purpose; first, to remind Friends of their duties as members of social and religious society; and second, to enable meetings to judge how far Overseers discharged the responsible duties submitted to them.

1744.—" This being the time the queries ought to have been read, but the meeting was thin, it is desired that they be read next Monthly Meeting, before the men and women part."— (Burlington Monthly Meeting.)

From all the foregoing, it appears that the inferior meetings were not required to send their answers up to the superior ones.

But in 1755, this important duty was enjoined upon them; thus enabling superior meetings to judge of the state of their subordinates, and to perform their legitimate functions, by encouraging, assisting, advising, or admonishing them as occasion might require.

1755.—"Agreed, that the following queries be read in the respective Preparative and Monthly Meetings next preceding the Quarterly Meetings, and be distinctly and particularly answered to, by the Overseers or other solid and judicious Friends, and such particular and distinct answers, transmitted from the Preparative to the Monthly, and from thence, in writing to the Quarterly Meeting."—(Yearly Meeting.)

Since the above period the queries have been occasionally modified to suit the varying circumstances of society, which need not be specially noticed here.

Few opportunities have presented to make extracts from the records of Women's Meetings, though sometimes possessing peculiar interest, as the following document will show.

1764.—"From women Friends of the Western Quarterly Meeting, held at London Grove, the 20th of the eighth month, 1764.

" To Women Friends at the next Yearly Meeting to be held in Philadelphia :—

" Dear Friends,—This meeting having received reports in answer to the twelve queries from all the meetings belonging thereto, except Hopewell in Virginia, and a concern having increased in this meeting of late, that Friends of our sex may come up in the discharge of their duty more generally and fully than heretofore ; which concern has been blessed, at times, with the covering of Divine goodness among us, whereby the strength of the mourners in Zion has been measurably strengthened and encouraged still to an increase of care.

" And it has been apparent, in divers places within the verge of this meeting, that where the solemn inquiries into the state

17

of the Church, by our queries, have been the most carefully attended to, and endeavors used, not to hide, but to point out to superior meetings, pretty closely, the state of affairs, laboring for amendment from time to time where deficiencies appear ; in those places the necessity of further endeavors for a reformation has seemed still greater to many. It is from these considerations a remnant are induced to believe it necessary we should be more particular than formerly in opening the real state of things amongst us, although some of our deficiencies may be thereby discovered to the Yearly Meeting, which we hope may obtain the sympathy of the body of concerned Friends, and not at all obstruct the growth and promotion of our zeal.

"According to the reports, our first-day meetings are mostly attended by Friends pretty generally, except one belonging to Fairfax Monthly Meeting ; though some are not so timely and diligent even then as could be wished ;—that week-day meetings, considering the number of professors, are still for the greater part small, and remarkably so in some places ; several having been quite neglected, as to women Friends, once in each place. Many also remain negligent in attending their Meetings for Discipline ; yet a considerable number of Friends are concerned to keep up their meetings for both worship and discipline. Sleepiness is complained of as prevailing over some, almost in every meeting, although we hope a concern is rather increasing to discourage that, and to stir up the negligent to their duty in attending meetings, by suitable admonitions extended to such as are faulty. Respecting which matters, it appears to us that most of our meetings have been heretofore deficient in care.

" A good degree of love and unity is reported to exist amongst Friends ; with some care, mostly to discourage talebearing, &c., and to end differences when manifest ; yet there have been some hints of concord and unity not sufficiently prevailing in divers meetings, from different causes. And care remains with many to observe a good degree of moderation and temperance on most occasions ; except that a remnant are fearful the anxious pursuit of this world's treasure, rather beyond the bounds of true moderation, is hurtful to a number among us. Many appear to be concerned to example and train up their children in plainness of speech, behavior, and apparel; and yet, from the conduct and appearance of a large number of our youth and others, it is also apparent that a religious concern to maintain the primitive testimonies of Truth in simplicity has been, and is yet, too much wanting; on account of whom it is apprehended by some of us that the spirit and friendship of this world hath in a great measure taken place, instead of the important doctrine of true self-denial. Our reports generally mention a care subsisting towards the poor, and placing out of children, though some we fear are deficient therein; and that disorderly proceedings in marriage are discouraged mostly, with an account of care extended towards those that transgress or connive at the same.

"The religious education of the negroes that remain in slavery amongst us is still too little regarded;—otherwise they are said to be mostly pretty well provided for with outward necessaries. Some unfaithfulness has appeared respecting the anti-Christian demands for a hireling ministry. Some good degree of care, in other respects, remains on the minds of a number of Friends to conduct according to our Christian profession; and those are sensible that great improvement is necessary, before clear reports can be given of our care being duly taken to regularly maintain all the extensive parts of our Discipline.

" We find but few meetings have been engaged in the service of visiting families since last year, though a remnant has had to believe it has been favored with the ownings of Divine goodness when rightly engaged in. Divers Monthly Meetings have given a satisfactory account of visits they have had from a committee appointed by the Yearly Meeting for that purpose; others say little, as they have had only a small part of such visits, especially some distant, remote meetings, where, we believe, there is a remnant that would joyfully receive visits of that kind, if it was agreeable to the mind of Truth to continue such visits."—(Western Quarterly Meeting of Women Friends.)

CHAPTER XVIII.

INDIANS.

IT is impossible, within our limits, to do more than furnish a few notes in relation to Friends and the Indian natives; whole volumes would be required to do justice to this interesting subject.

1719.—"Advised, that such be dealt with as sell, barter, or exchange, directly or indirectly, to the Indians, rum, brandy, or any other strong liquors; it being contrary to the care Friends always had since the settlement of these countries, that they might not contribute to the abuse and hurt those poor people receive by drinking thereof, being generally incapable of using moderation therein; and, to avoid giving them occasion of discontent, it is advised that Friends do not buy or sell Indian slaves."—(Yearly Meeting.)

1722.—"When way was made for our worthy Friends, the proprietors and owners of lands in these provinces, to make their first settlements, it pleased Almighty God, by His overruling providence, to influence the native Indians so as to make them very helpful and serviceable to those early settlers, before they could raise stock or provisions to sustain themselves and families; and it being soon observed that those people, when they got rum or other strong liquors, set no bounds to themselves, but were apt to be abusive, and sometimes destroyed one another, there came a religious care and concern upon Friends, both in their meetings and legislature, to prevent those abuses" (here the advice of 1687 is repeated); "and where any, under our profession, shall act contrary thereunto, let them be speedily dealt with and censured for their evil practices."—(Yearly Meeting.)

1734.—"To New Garden Monthly Meeting:—

"Whereas, it hath been reported that I sold the Indians rum, which I acknowledge to be true, and am heartily sorry for.

"D—— B——."

1759.—"He is the God of the spirits of all flesh, and deals with His people agreeable to that wisdom, the depth whereof is to us unsearchable. We in this province may say He hath, as a tender and gracious Parent, dealt bountifully with us, even from the days of our fathers. It was He who strengthened them to labor through the difficulties attending the improvement of a wilderness, and made way for them in the hearts of the natives, so that by them they were comforted in times of want and distress."—(Yearly Meeting.)

This sentiment cannot fail to be strongly impressed upon the mind of every one, who will impartially study our colonial history.

1794.—"The interesting concern under which this meeting, from time to time in years past, has been exercised, and wherewith the minds of many Friends have been so deeply affected in relation to the former and present condition of the Indian natives, and with reference to events and occurrences respecting them through a long course of years, being in a solid manner, at a preceding sitting, weightily revived and spread with life over the meeting:—to give the subject more fully that weight and deliberate consideration its importance calls for, a number of Friends were named, and also to report their sense, whether a fund might not be fitly appropriated for the desirable purpose of promoting the civilization and well-being of the Indians; who now accordingly produced their report, which, being read, is united with, being as follows:—

"'To the Yearly Meeting now sitting: The committee appointed on the interesting concern for promoting the welfare of the Indian natives, report, that at several meetings, in which

we have had the company of divers concerned brethren not
particularly named to the service, we have deliberately considered this important subject, which hath for a series of years
deeply exercised the minds of many Friends, and been latterly
revived in the Yearly Meeting with increasing weight.   Our
minds have been measurably drawn into sympathy with these
distressed inhabitants of the wilderness, and on comparing their
situation with our own, and calling to grateful remembrance
the kindness of their predecessors to ours, in the early settlement of this country; considering also our professed principles
of peace and good-will to men, we were induced with much
unanimity to believe that there are loud calls for our benevolence and Christian exertions, to promote among them the
principles of the Christian religion, as well as to turn their
attention to school-learning, agriculture, and the useful mecha-
nical employments, especially as there appears in some of the
tribes a willingness to unite in the exercise of endeavors of this
kind.   We believe that this end may be much promoted, under
the Divine blessing, by a recommendation from this meeting to
the several Quarterly Meetings, that a liberal subscription be
set on foot, and a fund raised, to be under the direction of a
special committee to be appointed by the Yearly Meeting, in
order that these pious purposes may be carried into effect as
early as practicable, and the apparent friendly disposition of
government towards this desirable object be improved.   And
conceiving that the subject is of sufficient magnitude to claim
the attention of our religious society in different parts of this
continent, we think it may be useful to hint the substance of
this concern in the epistles to the respective Yearly Meetings.'
   " Conformable whereunto, a committee was appointed for the
effecting of this beneficial purpose."—(Yearly Meeting.)

   In this way the diffusive charities of the Gospel were spread
far and wide, until the concern engaged the united attention
of Philadelphia, Baltimore, New York, and Genesee Yearly
Meetings for a series of years; and resulted in reinstat-
ing the Seneca nation of Indians in the possession of lands,

from which they were about to be perfidiously expelled, and
which secured to them a high degree of civilization, and the
social and domestic comforts of a more settled mode of living.
This labor of love is still continued by most of the Yearly
Meetings named.

CHAPTER XIX.

TRADING.

1695.—"Advised, that none trade, by sea or land, beyond
their abilities; and that Friends keep to a word in their dealings, as much as may be; and if any are indebted, at home or
abroad, and answer not the same in due time, that such be
admonished thereof, that Truth may not be reproached, and
people, whether rich or poor, kept out of their just debts."—
(Yearly Meeting.)

1701.—"Advised, that all Friends be careful to preserve
the reputation that Truth hath given them, in complying with
their words and promises to their utmost power, and not to
be lavish or rash in their promises, and slack in their performances, which often brings great disappointments, and gives
great offence; and not to trade beyond their own abilities, to
the hazard of the estates of others; nor to suffer their minds
to be defiled with the earth, nor oppressed with the weight
thereof; remembering that the earth was made for the service
of man, and not man to be a servant to the earth. Dear
Friends, be serious, deep, and searching in this point, and consider how ignoble and debasing a thing it is for man to invest
that noble, gracious, primitive institution, in which man was
advanced to a divine dominion over the visible creation, now to
prostrate and yield himself a slave to that over which he once
was, and still should be, a lord.

"And that none under the profession of Truth, who are

indebted to others of the same profession, make use of that as a protection to them; thereby uncivilly and unjustly hoping to be out of the reach of civil authority, and, therefore, careless in discharging their duty."—(Yearly Meeting.)

1710.—"It is the advice of this meeting to the several Quarterly Meetings, that care may be taken that substantial Friends be appointed to visit every family among us where they think there is occasion to suspect they are going backward in their worldly estate, and to inquire and see how things are with them; and, if they will not take the advice of Friends, then to give them Gospel order, and proceed therein against them; which the Quarterly Meetings are advised to recommend the care thereof to the several Monthly Meetings.

"And, dear Friends, this meeting being under a holy care and deep exercise for the glory of God, the honor of our holy profession, and safety and growth of every member of the body, do desire and counsel all Friends, in the love of our God, and for their own good, that they keep to such lawful and honest employments as they well understand and are able to manage, for the necessary support of themselves and families, and not to launch out beyond their abilities, especially on such credit as Truth may have given them with their brethren or others, and more at their hazard who trusted them than their own."—(Yearly Meeting.)

1713.—"Advised, that all Friends be very careful in making and vending all provisions and the other commodities for transportation, taking care that the same be good and of due fineness, measure, and weight."—(Yearly Meeting.)

1719.—"Advised, that such be dealt with as trade by sea or land, or buy, bargain, or contract beyond their abilities; and such as keep not their words, promises, or engagements, in their dealings, and do not pay or satisfy their just debts, according to time agreed on. These being a reproach to Truth, and a manifest injury and injustice, advice to all such should be speedily given; and, if they do not reclaim, amend, and duly answer, they are to be further proceeded against."—(Yearly Meeting.)

1724.—"And whereas, in this time of general ease and liberty, too many under our profession have launched forth into the things of this world, beyond their substance and capacity to discharge a good conscience, in the performance of their promises and contracts, as well as their just debts, to the great scandal of our holy profession, and involving themselves, their families, and others, in great sorrow and inconveniences,—it is, therefore, our earnest desire that all Friends, everywhere, be very careful to avoid all inordinate pursuit after the things of this world, by such ways and means as depend too much upon the uncertain probabilities of hazardous enterprises ; but rather labor to content themselves with such a plain way and manner of living as is most agreeable to the self-denying principle of Truth which we profess, and which is most conducive to that tranquillity of mind that is requisite to a religious conduct through this troublesome world."—(Yearly Meeting.)

1737.—" It is our advice, when any professing Truth finds himself not able to comply with his contracts, that he call his creditors and declare his condition in time ; and, by showing the honesty of his intentions, may clear the Society of any scandalous imputations ; and when any so circumstanced refuses to do so, let him be duly censured."—(Yearly Meeting.)

1755.—" It is a Truth that ought always to be strongly impressed upon our minds, that it is by the peculiar indulgence of Divine Providence we are favored with the blessings of peace, liberty, and plenty, in the extensive manner we have long enjoyed them. Considerations of this kind, if faithfully retained, would lead every one of us to be exceeding cautious how we give any occasion to our neighbors, or others, to represent us as a Society degenerated from that integrity, justice, and uprightness" (mentioned above).—(Yearly Meeting.)

1795.—"A—— S—— attended this meeting, and offered a paper condemning his misconduct in consenting to the sale of four barrels of flour in the West Indies, which had not the quantity in them, expressed by the brand."—(Wilmington Monthly Meeting.)

CHAPTER XX.

LAW.

1679.—" To prevent what suits of law may be prevented,— we knowing that Friends going to law, though our cause may be just, yet the Truth seldom gains ground thereby, and that true love and unity may be kept up among us, and we may stand justified,—we desire that care may be taken that no Friend go forward in any suit of law without the advice and consent of a Man's Meeting;* except he be maliciously arrested suddenly, so that he cannot have time before he may be bound to answer them, to take the counsel of three or four Friends; and if they find the matter may make against the Truth, if it be possible, let it be ended.   Friends may remember that Jacob, the peaceable man, bowed to Esau for peace sake, and because he would not be hindered in his journey; and truly, dear Friends, many of us have experienced that suits of law never furthered our journey, but rather set us backward; and we believe that if this be put in practice, that Truth and Friends may find a benefit by it; for a Friend that may be brought into trouble of law, he relating the matter honestly and fairly to Friends, he will certainly find a great benefit, whether the matter go for or against him,—if it cannot be otherwise ended.   So, the Lord grant that we may all be preserved in true wisdom, and that will keep us in true moderation."—(Thirdhaven Monthly Meeting.)

1681.—" It is ordered that if any differences do arise betwixt any two persons that profess Truth, that they do not go

---

* Man's Meeting, as here used, and elsewhere, appears to be synonymous with Monthly Meeting of Men Friends.

to law before they first lay it before the particular Monthly Meeting that they do belong unto."—(Yearly Meeting. See Burlington Monthly Meeting.)

1681.—"At a Monthly Meeting held at Upland, in the house of Robert Wade, the 15th of the seventh month, 1681,—

"It is generally agreed and ordered, that if anything fall out, by way of controversy, betwixt Friend and Friend, that if they cannot end the matter between themselves, then to refer it to two Friends, or more, to see if they can end it; then, if not, to bring it to the Monthly Meeting, there to be ended."— (Burlington Monthly Meeting.)

The only records which I have seen of the Yearly Meeting held in Burlington in 1681, are recorded in Burlington Monthly Meeting book.

The few Friends living at Upland (now Chester), at first belonged to Burlington Monthly Meeting, which appears to have been sometimes held there. This explanation will remove the apparent anomaly of the two preceding minutes.

1710.—"It is the sense of this meeting (according to the epistle that was sent to us from London), that in all stations and conditions, whilst we are in unity with the body of Friends, we be very careful that we act, nor do anything contrary to the principle or discipline of Truth, because there is no person that is a member that is exempted from the censure of the Church.

"As to Friends going to law one with another, it is the sense of this meeting that such things may not be admitted among us, but that as one party is ever in the wrong, that they may be found out and proper advice given and justice demanded; which, if neglected or refused, let such be testified against, as unworthy of our communion, and that without too much delay; that where the law of God, of righteousness, and Truth doth not take place in the heart, the law of men may curb and punish the wrong and injustice."

"Yet nevertheless, in cases of executors, attorneys, factors, or the like, when both parties are agreed, but cannot effect the right and just part without a judgment of law in some temporal court, which, if necessary, must be had for the legal security of one or both, this meeting thought fit to declare, that any Monthly Meeting may judge of such necessity, and as they see cause, suffer the parties to have legal proceedings, so as not to reproach the Truth by contention or otherwise; being at the request of them both, and no other way to obtain their right and safety."

"But, if any fall short in his temporal affairs by some unforeseen and unavoidable accident (not having intruded into things out of his way, as aforesaid), and shall offer his all to his creditors, and when that falls short, his person also, at their disposal, let such have compassion among you, and aid, as an object of Christian charity, and help him as a brother: he hath done what he can, and we can expect no further from him."—(Yearly Meeting.)

1719.—In cases of debtors absconding, bankrupts, &c., the Monthly Meetings may "permit, or hold excused, such as shall appear to them really necessitated to proceed otherwise." And executors, administrators, &c., "may be permitted to have the matter tried at law, or rather first determined in our friendly way, and then by consent, confirmed by a judgment, as the meeting may see occasion upon the matter to advise and direct; with this caution and care, that the parties on both sides concerned therein, do still appear and behave towards each other in brotherly love. And in the setting forth or management of the case, or asserting what they apprehend their rights, that it be done with decency and moderation, without letting in or showing anger or animosity, or using any provoking or unbecoming language. For as a bitter or indecent behavior will cause the Truth of our holy profession to be evil spoken of, so on the contrary, a Christian, prudent, and meek deportment will bear a becoming testimony even in courts, and show that nothing but the nature of the case and our common station with our neighbors under the laws of the nation, bring any of us there.

"And as it is our duty to seek peace with all men, and to avoid giving provocation, or just offence to any, it is advised that Friends do avoid going to law with others not of our persuasion, angrily or in a passion, or without due consideration, good grounds, and having first, in a friendly way, shown his opponent the justness of his cause, and having offered (where he safely may), if the other make any reasonable objection, to put the matter to a neighborly reference. So also that Friends give no just occasion to such to go to law with them, but carefully to comply with their promises and contracts; and, where they have any reason for objecting to the demand, that they show a willingness and readiness to agree it peaceably between themselves, or to submit to a reference."

"It is the sense of this meeting, according to the advice of the holy Apostle, and the ancient, comely, and Christian practice, that at no time brother go to law with brother, before he be disowned, or upon apparent and urgent necessity, as heretofore limited and expressed, shall be permitted by the Monthly Meeting so to do.

"But, if any professing Truth shall arrest, sue, or implead at law any other person making the same profession, before he hath proceeded in the method herein mentioned, or is so permitted by the meeting, such ought to be dealt with as other disorderly persons, and give satisfaction to the meeting by condemning his or her so doing. And, in case of refusal, after deliberate dealing and waiting with such, they are to be disowned by the meeting whereto he or she doth belong.

"And, where any differences happen, let all Friends proceed in this manner, viz.: the party who finds he hath reason of complaint, first, himself calmly and friendly to speak, or, if he lives at a distance, write to the party by whom he apprehends himself injured or to be in danger of suffering in his just rights, and endeavor, by gentle means, in a brotherly and loving manner to obtain his rights. But, if they do not prevail, or if the same be refused or neglected, then let him (or, if they live at a distance and belong to different meetings, some Friend whom he may write or empower on his behalf)

take one or two with him, either the overseers or other discreet,
judicious Friends, and, in like friendly manner, make claim or
demand; which Friends, so accompanying the complainant,
are to use their endeavors and give their utmost assistance to
have the matter justly and expeditiously ended, either by the
parties themselves or by the immediate assistance of those
Friends; who, if the matter appear plain and easy, or to be
an uncontested debt, or that it be a bond against which no
reasonable objection is made by the debtor, are to advise the
party complained of to make satisfaction, without carrying
the matter further, either by arbitration or the meeting. But
if there do appear in the matter to be either unsettled difference in accounts, or reason of debate, then, if they cannot
persuade the determination thereof by the parties themselves,
or cannot procure the same by their advice and assistance,
they are to admonish and persuade the parties to choose
referees or arbitrators, and they engage themselves to stand
to and abide by the determination of such referees or arbitrators, as usual in such cases.

"If either of the said parties refuse such advice, or endeavors to end the difference, he or she so refusing may be complained of to the respective Monthly Meeting; and notice is to
be given him or her of such intention of complaint, that they
may attend (as they ought to do) the meeting at the time appointed. . . . Then the meeting (to avoid as much as possible the contention and indecent noise which some, in those
cases, are apt to fall into) is to direct the hearing and determination thereof out of the meeting. And in order thereunto,
the parties may nominate, and each choose, one or more
Friends, as the importance of the matter may require; and the
meeting add one or more Friends to them, as they see occasion,
for the determining of the said difference by majority.

"But if the parties refuse or decline to attend, and so to
nominate or choose, then the meeting is to nominate and appoint a sufficient number of Friends to hear and determine the
same. And the Friends so chosen, either by the parties or by
the meeting, ought, as speedily as may be, to agree upon and

appoint time and place, and duly attend the same for that purpose, and continue the same by adjournments (as short as they conveniently can), if they see occasion in the nature of the complaint, or for evidence, or for further necessary inquiry so to do, using all caution and care to avoid unnecessary delays, and to make the determination within the time appointed, so as to report, if possible, to the successive Monthly Meeting.

" If either party refuses to attend the arbitrators, and submit their case, or [to] stand to and abide the award, judgment, or determination of the Friends so nominated, chosen, or appointed, such person must be dealt with as one disorderly, and that regards not peace either in himself or in the Church, and that slights the love, order, and unity of the brethren. And, after due admonition, if he or she persists therein, let such be disowned and testified against by the meeting. After which, the other Friend may seek his remedy against him or her (so disowned) at the law.

" But if any do find themselves aggrieved by such judgment, determination, or award, and do apply to the respective Monthly Meeting for a rehearing, before the said judgment or determination be confirmed by the said meeting, let the same be allowed ; except in the case where bonds are or may be entered into by the parties to abide such judgment, in which case the same ought to be final."—(Yearly Meeting.)

1734.—" Leacock Preparative Meeting acquainted this meeting that there is some difference between J—— S—— and his brother J——. They both now appearing here, were advised to choose arbitrators to refer their business to, which they did ; and the Friends they chose were Joseph Sharp, Simon Hadley, William Miller, and Benjamin Fredd, which are desired to give account of their proceedings to our next meeting.

" They are bound by bonds to stand by the award of the Friends.

" They have agreed, and given each of them a copy of their award under their hands and seals."—(New Garden Monthly Meeting.)

1735.—" Whereas O—— J——, a member of this meeting,

hath, contrary to the good order and discipline used among us for the reconciling of our differing members, refused the leaving a certain controversy between him and the executors of Moses Mendenhall, deceased, to be decided by arbitrators, and also refuseth to comply with the judgment of those Friends appointed by this meeting in the case, notwithstanding he hath been several times visited in order to prevail with him to comply with the advice of said Friends, but those labors of love not any way prevailing with him to submit to our rules; therefore this meeting doth hereby declare him, the said O——J——, to be no member of our religious Society, until he, from a sense of his error, do make such an acknowledgment as may be to the satisfaction of this meeting."—(Concord Monthly Meeting.)

1736.—"The Friends appointed to treat with G—— D—— report, that she is not willing to choose persons to hear and determine the said difference. This meeting appoints John Bezer, William Peters, John Newlin, on her part; John Chadsey chooses Abraham Darlington, Edward Brinton, John Townsend, on his part."—(Concord Monthly Meeting.)

1756.—"Isaac Williams requests that this meeting grant him liberty to seek methods, as the law directs, for the recovery of some small debts, that he has due to him from sundry persons who are not Friends; which this meeting grants."—(Thirdhaven Monthly Meeting.)

CHAPTER XXI.

GOVERNMENT.

1701.—"Dear Friends and Brethren: We recommend to you peace and concord, as the great fruits of charity, without which we are nothing; and that we labor to approve ourselves men of peace and makers of peace, which is our ornament, duty, and ensign, as the disciples of Jesus. If any be otherwise, the Church of Christ have no such custom, nor can they therein be countenanced or suffered; but so it is, to the grief of our hearts and scandal of our profession, some laying claim to the same, in diverse provinces within the verge of this meeting, having been too factious and troublesome in the government, under which they ought peaceably to live, &c. &c. By God's help, we have now, for many years, approved ourselves peaceable subjects to them whom God, in his providence, hath set over us; first, to the King as supreme; and next, to those in authority under him; being subject, not for wrath, but conscience (for there is no power but of him), rendering unto all their dues, tribute to whom tribute, custom to whom custom, fear to whom fear, honor to whom honor; but when, at any time, it hath pleased God to suffer the rulers that hath been placed over us to impose anything against our allegiance to God, we have patiently suffered under them, till the Lord hath been pleased to open their understandings, and mollify their hearts towards us; and this we also recommend to be continued among us."—(Yearly Meeting.)

1710.—"As to matters of government, we advise all Friends concerned therein, whether in legislation or administration, may be very careful to act according to Truth, and the testimony of it, in all things; and not think to excuse contrary practices by any temporal station, or evade the due censure of Truth on pretence of any conjunction with such as may take liberty to act such things as consist not with our holy communion, profession, and Discipline; for, notwithstanding any such station, where any offend, the judgment of Truth must go out against them."—(Yearly Meeting.)

1746.—"Dear Friends: Under an humbling sense of the great favor of the Almighty, in blessing us, in these provinces, with the continued enjoyment of outward peace and tranquillity, and of many valuable privileges, we earnestly beseech you frequently to commemorate the gracious dealings of the Lord with us, and to make your children, and those under your care, acquainted therewith, that they may be incited to a reliance on that ancient Arm of Power which hath protected and preserved the righteous through all generations, and will still be manifested to those whose only dependence is thereon."—(Yearly Meeting.)

1758.—"As the maintaining inviolate the liberty of conscience, which is essential to our union and well-being as a religious society, evidently appears to be an indispensable duty, this meeting doth, with fervent and sincere desires for the present and future prosperity of Truth among us, and for the preservation of individuals on the true foundation of Christian fellowship and communion, caution, advise, and exhort Friends to beware of accepting of, or continuing in office, or station in civil society or government, by which they may be in any respect engaged in, or think themselves subjected to, the necessity of enjoining or enforcing the compliance of their brethren or others with any act which they conscientiously scruple to perform; and if any professing with us should, after the loving advice and admonition of the brethren, persist in a conduct so repugnant to that sincerity, uprightness, and self-denial, incumbent on us, it is the sense and judgment of this meeting, that such persons should not be allowed to sit in our Meetings for Discipline, nor be employed in the affairs of Truth, until they are brought to a sense and acknowledgment of their error."—(Yearly Meeting.)

1763.—"It remains to be the sense of this meeting, that, under the present circumstances of the Church, there is an undoubted necessity for such a Christian labor as is recommended by the minute of this meeting in the year 1758, in order to remove the painful occasion of uneasiness, which still continues to subsist in divers places, through the execution of some offices in civil government by some of our brethren in profession, whereby they are subjected to the necessity of exposing others to suffering on the account of the free exercise of their consciences."—(Yearly Meeting.)

1764.—"It is earnestly and affectionately recommended to the Quarterly and Monthly Meetings, and to Friends individually, to bear in mind the spirituality of our profession:

that, by living near the Divine principle of Truth, our testimony thereto may be preferred to every temporal consideration, and the benefits and honors of the world neither sought after nor too readily accepted of by any of us; and as the execution of offices of trust, and the acting in stations in civil government hath been for some time past, and continues to be, attended with great difficulties under the present circumstances of public affairs, Friends, in their Quarterly and Monthly Meetings, are desired to excite each other to care and circumspection, and timely to caution their members against accepting of offices in the legislative or executive parts of government.''

'' The former advices of this meeting, in the year 1710, on this subject, are particularly recommended to the observation of Friends, with this further admonition: that they be not accessory in promoting or electing any of our brethren to such offices, which may immediately lead them into the danger of deviating from the essential care, incumbent on all, of maintaining true Gospel unity and fellowship in the Church, and with each other; and that the same be manifested in the whole tenor of our conduct and conversation.''—(Yearly Meeting.)

1770.—'' This meeting finds a further engagement, earnestly and affectionately to desire that Friends in all places may be particularly careful to live near the Divine principle; which, if faithfully attended to, will preserve us in a conduct becoming our holy profession, and teach us to avoid mixing with those who are not convinced of our religious principles in their human policy and contrivance, and to seek after quietude and stillness of mind: in order that, under the direction of true wisdom, we may be enabled to administer advice to any of our brethren who may be inadvertently drawn aside to join with or countenance, by conversation or otherwise, the commotions prevailing. Thus we may demonstrate to the world our regard to our Christian testimony and profession, and give no just cause to any to accuse us of deviating from the principles and conduct of our worthy predecessors, who, in times of the greatest difficulties, manifested union among themselves;

and that they steadily preferred the cause and reputation of Truth to every other consideration."—(Yearly Meeting.)

Whatsoever we do by another, we do ourselves. The moral responsibility is the same. Hence, the conclusion is obvious, that we cannot consistently give our suffrage to others to fill any office, the duties of which we could not conscientiously discharge.

CHAPTER XXII.

APPEALS.

1711.—"Where arbitrators have been chosen by the parties differing, and bonds entered, if the arbitrators do not agree, and the Monthly Meeting gives judgment in the case, the person so aggrieved may have liberty to appeal."—(Yearly Meeting.)

1719.—"If any persons are dissatisfied with or think themselves aggrieved by the testimony or judgment entered against them in a Monthly Meeting, they may have liberty at the same, or the next, or the third Monthly Meeting, but not after, to notify their intentions of making application to have the cause heard at the next Quarterly Meeting. Which notification the said Monthly Meeting should enter on their minutes, and appoint four or more Friends (not excluding others) to take a copy of the meeting's records, signed by the clerk in the case, and therewith attend the said Quarterly Meeting; and there, on the Monthly Meeting's behalf, show the reasons for what is done as occasion may require, submitting the same to the said Quarterly Meeting.

"And then the said Quarterly Meeting is to hear, consider, and determine or confirm the same, as they, in the wisdom which God shall afford them, see most just, necessary, and convenient.

"And, if the parties should be dissatisfied with the judg-ment or determination of the said Quarterly Meeting, and do notify, at the same or next Quarterly Meeting, but not after, their intention of making application for a hearing at the next Yearly Meeting, then that the Quarterly Meeting do in like manner make entry thereof; appoint four or six Friends to attend the Yearly Meeting with the records of both the Monthly and Quarterly Meetings, signed as aforesaid, and to speak to the matter there ; where the same is to be finally determined."—(Yearly Meeting.)

The rule here stated was originally designed for cases of difference about worldly matters, where Monthly Meetings had given judgment; but it has, by common consent, been applied to other cases,—such as the disowning of members, where a party has felt aggrieved by the judgment of a Monthly Meet-ing. In a case of individual difference, the meeting is not a party ; but in case of disowning an offender, the Monthly Meeting becomes a direct party in the issue ; and is equally liable to be aggrieved by the judgment of the Quarterly or Yearly Meeting, in case of appeal, as the appellant. Such meetings ought therefore to sit on the case as a court of chan-cery, and to render a just judgment between the parties, as in the other case. This is believed to have been the intention of the Society when the rule was adopted, and the early practice of meetings under it. But many Friends, perhaps many meetings, now take a different view, as though no one was interested or could be aggrieved but the appellant; however gross the offence or direct the proof, they are not willing to take it into the account. They look entirely to the proceed-ings; if there is anything found in them that is informal, either by omission or commission, from inadvertence or igno-rance, it is sufficient to reinstate the appellant, and return him to Society, sometimes to the injury both of the meeting and the individual.

Now, in such a case, the Monthly Meeting become the ag-grieved party ; and what is the remedy ? Why, as it was

manifestly the duty of the meeting to hear the parties impartially, and to render a just judgment between them, and,
having failed to do this, there can be no good reason shown why
the suffering party (though it be a Monthly Meeting) may not
carry an appeal to a superior meeting under the rule. The
right has been denied, but has never been disproved; it has
been asserted and has been exercised, as the following case
will show :—

A—— P—— having been disowned by Middletown Monthly
Meeting, appealed to the Quarterly Meeting of Bucks, and was
reinstated on a report in her favor, signed by seven out of a
committee of twelve Friends.

1758, fourth month.—" Friends having more fully considered
the consequence of the judgment of our last Quarterly Meeting,
in regard to A—— P——'s appeal, do unanimously agree to
appeal therefrom, to the next Yearly Meeting, and orders that
the Quarterly Meeting be notified thereof."—(Middletown
Monthly Meeting.)

1758, fifth month.—The Quarterly Meeting minuted the
case, and "recommended to Friends of that Monthly Meeting
to consider further, whether some other expedient may not be
fallen on to their satisfaction, and report their determination to
our next Quarterly Meeting."—(Bucks Quarterly Meeting.)

1758, sixth month.—" This meeting, having maturely considered the reason and justice of our appeal to the Yearly
Meeting in A—— P——'s case, as proposed to the last
Quarterly Meeting, do unanimously agree to prosecute the
said appeal, of which the Quarterly Meeting is to be acquainted
on our part."—(Middletown Monthly Meeting.)

1758, eighth month.—The Quarterly Meeting being so informed, appointed a committee " to attend the Yearly Meeting,
with copies of the minutes of this meeting, and also all papers
in the hands of the clerk that relate to the same."—(Bucks
Quarterly Meeting.)

1758, eleventh month.—The Yearly Meeting returned the
case to the Quarter by a committee to assist in the settlement

thereof, and "in order to the amicable accommodation of the affair," the quarter nominated a committee, which was "desired to meet at such time and place as may be agreeable to the committee of the Yearly Meeting, and join them for the good purpose for which they were appointed."—(Bucks Quarterly Meeting.)

1759, second month.—"The committee appointed by the Yearly Meeting to assist the Quarterly Meeting in the affair, jointly report, that they have conferred on the subject of their appointment, and have agreed on a testimony which they think may be safe and proper for Middletown Monthly Meeting to issue against her; which was annexed to the report and read in this meeting, and approved. Whereupon, Middletown Monthly Meeting is desired to deliver her a copy."—(Bucks Quarterly Meeting.)

1759, third month.—"The representatives to our last Quarterly Meeting produced from thence the reports of the committees of the Yearly and Quarterly Meetings, in the case relating to A—— P——, wherein they unanimously agree that this meeting had acted agreeably to justice and the rules of our Discipline, in testifying against the said A——; but as some expressions in our said testimony did not sit easy on some of their minds, they unanimously agreed on another form, which they having subjoined, recommended it to us to publish against her, in lieu of that which we had prepared.

"All which, the said Quarterly Meeting approving, have desired us to furnish her with a copy of the said last testimony. Wherefore, John Gregg is appointed to give her a copy thereof accordingly."—(Middletown Monthly Meeting.)

1759, fifth month.—"Middletown Monthly Meeting reports, that a copy of the testimony, as approved of by the last meeting, hath been delivered to A—— P——, and that she was acquainted with her right to appeal."—(Bucks Quarterly Meeting.)

The course pursued for the harmonious settlement of this perplexing case is suggestive of instruction. It shows that

Monthly Meetings as well as individual members have their rights; that they may be aggrieved, and that they are entitled to redress.

Perhaps few cases of an appeal from the judgment of a Monthly Meeting occur, wherein it would not be of advantage for the Quarterly Meeting to return the case to the meeting from whence it came, with a solid committee to advise and assist in a renewed consideration of the subject. By such a procedure, the Monthly Meeting and the appellant would both have an opportunity afforded them to correct any erroneous step, or to make any concession which their conduct might require; and the parties would be left with a better feeling towards each other, than would likely exist where a superior meeting had made an arbitrary decision of the case. It would not often happen that such a decision would be necessary, unless one of the parties were wilfully perverse, or where some abstruse and perplexing question was involved.

An appeal is in some degree of the nature of a suit at law, and, unless conducted with extreme caution, produces the same baneful results. Where they do not spring from, they are too apt to create parties, and to produce feelings subversive of the very purpose for which religious society was instituted. A compulsory settlement will seldom restore harmony between the parties, or afford the satisfaction which might be anticipated. It is exulted in as a victory by the one, and felt to be a humiliating defeat by the other; feelings which can be productive of no good. The whole subject is deserving of attention.

CHAPTER XXIII.

AFFIRMATIONS AND OATHS.

1682.—"That all witnesses coming, or called to testify their knowledge in, or to any matter or thing, before any court, or before any lawful authority, within the said province, shall there give or deliver in their evidence or testimony, by solemnly promising to speak the truth, the whole truth, and nothing but the truth, to the matter or thing in question."—(Penn's Laws.)

1696.—"Whereas divers dissenters, commonly called Quakers, refusing to take an oath in courts of justice and other places, are frequently imprisoned and their estates sequestered, by processes of contempt issuing out of said courts, to the ruin of themselves and families; for remedy thereof, be it enacted, &c., that every Quaker who shall be required, upon any lawful occasion, to take an oath in any case, where by law an oath is required, shall, instead of the usual form, be permitted to make his or her solemn affirmation or declaration, in these words following, viz.:—

"I, A—— B——, do declare, in the presence of Almighty God, the witness of the truth of what I say.

"Provided that no Quaker, or reputed Quaker, shall, by virtue of this act, be qualified, or permitted to give evidence in any criminal causes, or serve on any juries, or bear any office or place of profit in the government," &c. &c.—(English Law.)

In 1705, Queen Anne in council annulled the colonial law of affirmations, whereby Friends on this side the Atlantic appear to have been subjected to the Act of Parliament just quoted, which was rather a modified oath than an affirmation, and unsatisfactory to many Friends, "by reason of the sacred name being comprised therein, which they, considering as an appeal to the Divine Being, thought it bordered too near upon an oath, and were not free to use it. Others, less scrupulous, gratefully accepted the favor, conceiving it only in the light of a very solemn affirmation."—(Gough, III, 462.) Hence the following advices were issued:—

1710.—"The solemn affirmation is a thing of the greatest moment. We exhort all to be very careful about it, and renew unto you the sum of the advices of the Yearly Meeting of London therein; that Friends be charitable one to another about it; they that can take it not to censure or reproach those who cannot; and those who cannot, to use the like caution and regard to those who can, till further relief can be had for us all."—(Yearly Meeting.)

1718.—"It is recommended to Quarterly and Monthly Meetings that caution be given to all Friends, as well those in the magistracy as others, to be very careful that they stand clear in all cases, as well against administering as taking oaths." —(Yearly Meeting.)

The Colonial Assembly "made divers attempts from time to time for reviving the aforesaid privilege, but without success, till the year 1725, when an act prescribing the forms of fidelity, abjuration, and affirmation, instead of the forms before required, having been passed in the province, was ratified by the King in council, and thereby became perpetual."—(Proud, II, 191.)

In an epistle of caution to Friends against the abuse of the favor thus granted, the London Yearly Meeting remarks:—

1725.—"Beside the inward engagement of this Divine law ('the law of the spirit of life in Christ Jesus'), to speak and act according to Truth, there is at this time also an outward engagement, which the government hath laid upon us, not only by the favor of this act, but also by the manner wherein they have conferred it; for in the preamble it is said, 'It is evident that the said people called Quakers have not abused the liberty or indulgence allowed to them by law;' which testimony of the legislature concerning our use of the late solemn affirmation, upon twenty-five years' experience, ought at least to stir up all Friends to great watchfulness and care in the use of this further ease and relief, that this testimony may be continued, and thereby confirm the government in their favorable sentiments concerning us."

Considerable efforts and expenditures were required to gain the royal sanction to this reasonable measure, as shown by the following minutes :—

1726.—" Ordered by the Quarterly Meeting, 'That every Monthly Meeting should make a subscription towards the charge of gaining the royal assent to the Affirmation Act, as others have done.' "—(Buckingham Monthly Meeting.)

1726.—" The Governor and General Assembly of the Province having passed a law for the ease of Friends, relating to a solemn affirmation, the getting of which to be confirmed hath cost some Friends considerably, it is therefore requested by this meeting that a free contribution be made by each Particular Meeting for the defraying that charge, and bring it to next meeting."—(Falls Monthly Meeting.)

The ratification of the law of affirmations did not take place in the Province of New Jersey till the year 1732.—(See Proud, II, 192.)

Difficulties commenced very early in regard to the taking and administering of oaths. In the beginning, the governments of New Jersey and Pennsylvania were principally administered by Friends; of a class, too, who felt concerned to maintain their Christian testimony against oaths inviolate. But soon others began to come into authority; some who still made professions of the Truth, but did not practice it; and others, who made no profession with Friends, were in favor of oaths. The unsettled state of the laws in relation to affirmations must also have greatly embarrassed Friends, and increased their difficulties in this respect.

1732.—"The Quarterly Meeting of Chester requests to know the mind of this meeting, 'Whether justices, being Friends, and sitting on the Bench when oaths are administered, are clear of administering the same, although there may be other justices on the Bench who make no scruples of conscience to take or administer oaths? And also how far a clerk, being under the notice of Friends, and acting therein, is clear?' "—(Yearly Meeting.)

This was obviously a close question, and as such was referred by a committee to the next Yearly Meeting. They reported:—

1733.—" That they have unanimously agreed, that oaths administered by clerks or others, under the notice of Friends, either in courts or elsewhere, is a violation of our ancient testimony, and that such persons ought to be dealt with as offenders; nor did it appear to them that such justices, who are Friends, sitting on the Bench when oaths are administered, are clear in respect to administering the same, unless there be a number of other justices, not of our Society, also sitting on the Bench, sufficient to authorize the doing thereof, without the concurrence of those who are Friends; that they were very sensible of the weight and importance of this part of the matter referred to them, and how nearly we, as a society of people, may be affected by it, not only in a religious, but civil capacity; and therefore, that they wished some expedient may be found out, by act of Assembly, or otherwise, to remove this difficulty; but, if that cannot be, they think the preservation of our ancient testimony inviolate ought to take place of all other considerations."—(Yearly Meeting.)

The Yearly Meeting recommended the subject to " the care of such Friends who have any share in legislation, or interest with the legislators, to endeavor to remove this difficulty, by an act of Assembly for that purpose."—(Yearly Meeting.)

1738.—"Nothing having been as yet done, i. e. by act of Assembly, relating to the affair of oaths, administered in courts and elsewhere, by some professing with us, it is again recommended to the care of Friends, pursuant to former minutes; and, in the meantime, Friends of the several Quarterly and Monthly Meetings are advised to be careful, within the verge of their respective meetings, to deal with such persons as shall offend therein."—(Yearly Meeting.)

1761.—"At Chester Quarterly Meeting, held at Concord, the 9th of second month, 1761, in answer to the application from Chester Monthly Meeting:—this meeting is desirous that all Friends do avoid accepting any office in civil government, so as to subject them to the necessity of balking that testimony which the Lord called our predecessors in profession to bear to the world relative to oaths and swearing; and which testimony they nobly maintained, at the utmost expense, even to blood and treasure. That any under our name should, now-a-days, so far deviate from the footsteps of the faithful, as to be in the practice of directly administering oaths, or subscribing, without exception, 'sworn before me, or us,' to any instrument of writing, is just matter of concern to this meeting, which declares it to be their judgment, that such conduct is subject to censure.

" Copy of the minute.

"AARON ASHBRIDGE,
"Clerk."

(Darby Monthly Meeting.)

1762.—"Recommended, that the care of Friends, where occasion requires it, may be exerted to labor in Christian love, to convince such of their error who are deficient in respect to our testimony against oaths; and, when these endeavors prove unsuccessful, that Friends proceed according to our Discipline; and, it is likewise further desired, that all Friends may be particularly careful that they be not accessory in promoting or choosing their brethren in such offices which may subject them to the temptation of deviating from our Christian testimony in this or any other branch thereof."—(Yearly Meeting.)

1762.—"J—— T—— so far condemns his having administered an oath, as to declare himself determined not to accept of any office for the future which may subject him to the necessity of doing it, and that he now sees the practice inconsistent, both with the rules of Society and the convictions of his own mind."—(Middletown Monthly Meeting.)

1771.—"The remissness, in respect to our testimony against oaths, being particularly considered, the Quarterly and Monthly Meetings are again earnestly desired seriously to attend to the support of this part of our Christian testimony. Many Friends at this time, being seriously affected to observe, by the accounts now sent, that there are members remaining in some places, who, preferring the temporary honors and profits of this uncertain life, are led into a disregard of the solemn injunction of our blessed Lord, and the doctrine of His Apostles, against swearing, which, we have grounds to believe, was the testimony and practice of believers in ancient times carefully to observe, and which our worthy predecessors in the Truth were zealously concerned to promote and maintain through much reviling, persecution, and suffering; and, we are convinced, it remains to be our duty to support this part of our Christian testimony. Faithful Friends, in their several meetings, are affectionately excited to unite in extending their brotherly labor and endeavors towards those who are the occasion of this exercise, in order to convince them of their deviation; and, if any continue in the practice of taking or administering oaths, after being thus lovingly treated with, Quarterly Meetings are requested and enjoined to give their seasonable assistance in further endeavors for the restoration of such members; and, if this additional labor proves unsuccessful, it is the sense of this meeting, that the rules of our Discipline, already established, should be enforced against them, as persons regardless of the unity of their brethren and our ancient testimony.

"And in order to prevent, as much as possible, such occasions of weakness, and that we may be qualified uniformly to support this part of our Christian testimony, we find it necessary again to exhort Friends, in all places, carefully to avoid electing or promoting their brethren to such stations in civil government which may subject them to the temptation of violating it; and where any members show an inclination or desire of soliciting or accepting of such offices, faithful Friends should take timely care to discourage and caution them against it."—(Yearly Meeting.)

CHAPTER XXIV.

ALLEGIANCE AND ABJURATION.

THE Revolutionary War gave occasion for the enactment of laws imposing a "test" oath or affirmation, abjuring the King, and declaring allegiance to the American cause, and enforced by penalties, and, in some cases, by disabilities.

1778.—"On consideration of what is necessary to be proposed to Friends on the subject of declaration of allegiance and abjuration, required by some late laws by the Legislatures who now preside in Pennsylvania and New Jersey, we are united in judgment, that, consistent with our religious principles, we cannot comply with the requisitions of those laws, as we cannot be instrumental in setting up or pulling down any government; but it becomes us to show forth a peaceable and meek behavior to all men, seeking their good, and to live a sober, useful, and religious life, without joining ourselves with any party in war, or with the spirit of strife and contention now prevailing. And we believe that if our conduct is thus uniform and steady, and our hope fixed on the Omnipotent Arm for relief, He will, in time, amply reward us with lasting peace; which hath been the experience of our Friends in time past, and, we hope, of some now under suffering."

"And as, in some places, fines and taxes are and have been imposed on those who, from conscientious scruples, refuse or decline making such declarations, it is the united sense and judgment of this meeting, that no Friend should pay any such fine or tax."—(Yearly Meeting.)

By the test-law, a fine was imposed upon any person who should teach a school, without having subscribed thereto. In a remonstrance from the Meeting for Sufferings, they thus speak :—

1779.—"Our predecessors, on their early settlement in this part of America, being piously concerned for the prosperity of the colony and the real welfare of their posterity, among other salutary institutions, promoted at their own expense the establishment of schools for the instruction of their youth in useful and necessary learning, and for their education in piety and virtue, the practice of which forms the most sure basis for perpetuating the enjoyment of Christian liberty and essential happiness. By the voluntary contributions of the members of our religious Society, schools were set up, in which their children were taught; and careful attention has been given to the instruction of the children of the poor, not of our Society only, but our liberality hath been extended to the poor children of other religious denominations generally, great numbers of whom have partaken thereof; and these schools have been in like manner continued and maintained for a long course of years."

The following narratives of sufferings are taken from the Minutes of Conference, mentioned under Sufferings, but seem properly to belong here. Many examples might be cited. The laws were very severe; but it is obvious that the officials often used them for the purpose merely of extorting money. Failing to do this, they would let their victims go.

1778.—" Lancaster County, ss.
" Whereas, John Hollingsworth, Thomas Buckman, and Charles Dingee are now confined in the jail of the county aforesaid, for not taking or subscribing an oath or affirmation of allegiance, by several Acts of Assembly of this Commonwealth heretofore required, under pain of imprisonment; and whereas, the said laws are, by an Act of General Assembly of this Commonwealth, dated the 5th day of December, 1778,

repealed, so far as respects their persons; these are, therefore, to require you forthwith to discharge the said John Hollingsworth, Thomas Ruckman, and Charles Dingee out of your custody;—their paying your fees; there being no other charge against them, or either of them, respectively, than is mentioned in their mittimus.

"Given under our hands and seals this 16th day of December, 1778.

"WILLIAM HENRY,
"MICHAEL HUBLEY,
"CHARLES HALL.

"To the keeper of Lancaster Jail."

"I do hereby certify that the above is a true copy of the original order to me directed.

"ANDREW CUNNINGHAM.

"17th of twelfth month, 1778."

A difficulty still existed. They could not pay the jail-fees, any more than the fines, consistent with their conscientious convictions of duty; as is well set forth in the following paper:—

"Friends,—We saw your order to the jailor, and have read and maturely considered the contents thereof, and cannot find the least freedom in complying therewith (we mean in paying the jailor's fees) for the following reasons, viz. :—

"1st. And principally, because the same that constrained us from complying with the requisitions of the magistrates who committed us, in consequence whereof we have been confined, doth now prohibit our paying any fees as a recompense of reward to the jailor, for his being made the instrument of our (as we think) unjust and altogether causeless restraint; having never been convicted in our consciences (or by a public trial in a court of justice among men) of the breach of any laws in travelling to do our necessary and therefore lawful business.

"2d. Because we desire to make manifest to the world that the principles we do, as a people, make profession of, are the

19

dictates of the spirit of the Prince of Peace, which our worthy ancestors did suffer for; and that it is also the spirit of Truth, which would lead into all truth, those that principally mind and attend to its dictates, and is the comforter of those that are willing to suffer for it, rather than violate and grieve its sacred impulse; and believing also that the same spirit is the Spirit of Infinite Wisdom, and therefore cannot err. And, as we have felt that peace which the world can neither give nor take away, in a consolatory manner since our confinement, [we] are therefore confirmed that our conduct in the premises hath been and will be owned by the Divine Master and Governor of the universe. To conclude, we rather choose to be the Lord's freemen, and (as to our bodies) our keeper's prisoners still, than balk the testimony our blessed Redeemer hath given us to bear. We subscribe ourselves your real friends and well wishers,

" JEHU HOLLINGSWORTH,
" CHARLES DINGEE,
" THOMAS RUCKMAN.

" To William Henry, Esq.,
  " Michael Hubley, Esq.,
  " Charles Hall, Esq.
" Lancaster Jail, twelfth month 17th, 1778."

" These may certify whom it may concern, that I do hereby remit the fees to the within named, Jehu Hollingsworth, Charles Dingee, and Thomas Ruckman, respectively; and they are hereby and otherwise, pursuant to the within order, absolutely discharged from their confinement to go when and where they list. Witness my hand, the twelfth month 17th, 1778.

" ANDREW CUNNINGHAM,
" Jailor."

Under a later date of conference we find,—

" Thomas Ruckman (and probably the others also) was taken up by Joseph Miller, in Lancaster County, who tendered him the test of abjuration and fidelity to the States, so called; for refusing of which he was committed to Lancaster Jail, where he remained a close prisoner fifteen months and fifteen days; and was then released, by a repeal of the law, without paying prison fees or other demands."

"PHILADELPHIA, December 29th, 1778.

"In Council, ordered, That the fine of one hundred pounds adjudged by the Court of Quarter Sessions of the Peace for the County of Lancaster, to be paid by Joshua Bennett,—he having been convicted in the said court of having kept school, he not having taken the oath or affirmation of allegiance to the States according to law,—be remitted.

"Extracted from the minutes.

"T. MATLACK,
"Secretary."

"Whereas, Joshua Bennett was committed to my custody by judgment of the Court of Quarter Sessions, for a breach of law, in keeping school—not having taken the oath or affirmation of allegiance to the State of Pennsylvania,—until he paid a fine of one hundred pounds and costs of prosecution; and whereas, said fine is remitted, and I am ordered to enlarge said Bennett, I do therefore enlarge him without fees, pursuant to order. Witness my hand, this 23d day of the first month, 1779,

"ANDREW CUNNINGHAM,
"Jailor."

The want of success which attended their efforts to extort fines by means of imprisonment, soon satisfied them that they could not coerce the consciences of men whose chief dependence was upon God, and led to the speedy repeal of the law; a law which filled the prisons but left the coffers of government agents empty.

The laws which authorized the officers to distrain property whenever it could be found, were more successful, inasmuch as they left the peaceable and conscientious citizens without any alternative but to suffer, and were continued in force, to the

very great distress of Friends. The repeal of the law, "so far
as respected the persons," the imprisonment of Friends, appears
to have been more a necessity than a virtue. Little could be
gained by imprisoning men, when neither the fines nor jail-fees
could be collected.

CHAPTER XXV.

WAR.

THE upright and pacific policy pursued by William Penn and
his followers, in administering the Governments of New Jersey
and Pennsylvania, for a long time preserved them from hostile
collisions with the Indian natives; indeed, if such a policy had
been generally adopted and continued, collisions would never
have occurred. But a different, a war policy, was adopted in
some of the neighboring colonies, which soon involved them in
hostilities with the Indians, and the Quaker Colonies were
called upon, both by their sisters and by the home government, to
assist in their defence. This they could not do otherwise than
by interposing their friendly influence with the Indians, which
was freely done.

About the middle of the last century, when the war between
England and France was carried into their American Colonies,
causing what has been called the Canadian and Indian War,
each belligerent endeavored to turn the tomahawk of the savage
against the other, and with so much success as to cause much
cruelty and suffering in the frontier settlements. Friends
could not take part in the warlike measures of the day, but by
continuing their friendly intercourse and pacific influence with
the Indians, they were enabled to do more to repress their
hostile incursions than they could possibly have done by a
resort to physical force. Yet in those times of unbridled
passion and lawless violence, they were deemed by some as the
secret allies of the Indians, enemies of their country, and
threatened with a general massacre.

The governing power had passed into other hands before the struggle for independence commenced. Opposed to violence of every kind, Friends could not resort to physical force, either to set up, pull down, or reorganize any government; for, says Jesus Christ, " My kingdom is not of this world, else would my servants fight.'' They saw and deeply deplored the home policy towards the colonies; but their dependence was on God, and not on man. They believed, that if they continued to abide in a patient dependence upon him, that he would, in due time, dispose the hearts of the rulers to do them justice. Their principles were uncompromising; their path straight and narrow; they could do no consistent act, either to oppose the one party or to assist the other. But men who were accustomed to depend upon physical force for the redress of grievances, could hardly be expected to appreciate the motives, or to respect the conscientious scruples of the non-resisting followers of Christ, in the peaceable government of his kingdom. Hence, it is not strange that Friends were subjected to severe sufferings, for maintaining their peaceable testimony. But, how inconsistent is the conduct of men with the professions which they make to the world! Perhaps very few professors of the Christian name will admit a doubt of the coming of the millennium, foretold by the prophet Isaiah, when the peaceable kingdom of the Prince of Peace shall extend from sea to sea, and from the rivers to the ends of the earth; yet, when a very numerous and respectable religious society,—Friends,—have come to this desirable point, and have already realized the millennium in their own experience, these same professors and believers in its coming, resort to persecution, pains, and penalties, to compel them to abandon this high attainment.

The reliance of Friends upon the principles which they professed was sometimes put to trial. Thus, in 1688, the most alarming reports reached Philadelphia, that the Indians were assembled in great numbers at Naaman's Creek, for the purpose of making a general massacre of the English settlers. A messenger sent out returned with a confirmatory report, that the Indians, having a lame king, had taken the precaution to remove

him, together with their women and children, to some distant place
of safety.   The utmost panic prevailed except among Friends.
Caleb Pusey, a member of council from Chester County, volun-
teered " to go to the place, provided they would name five others
to accompany him, without weapons; which being soon agreed
on, they rode to the place; but instead of meeting five hundred
warriors, they found the old king quietly lying with his lame
foot along on the ground, and his head at ease on a kind of pil-
low, the women at work in the field, and the children playing
together."—(Praud I, 337.)

Again, in 1706, Governor Evans, not properly appreciating
the motives, and perhaps doubting the sincerity of the opposition of Friends to all warlike measures, and having been
foiled, through their influence, in his attempts to establish a
militia, determined upon a disingenuous ruse, to test their faith
in pacific principles, and to drive them from their position, by
concerting "a scheme to raise and carry on a false alarm, in
order most effectually to terrify the inhabitants, by a sudden
surprise, and thereby oblige them to have recourse to arms for
their defence."

"Robert French acted at Newcastle, by sending up a messenger to the Governor at Philadelphia, in the greatest haste
and consternation, to acquaint him that a number of vessels
were then actually in the river, and as high up as a place which
he named.   Upon this news immediately, the Governor acted
his part, and by his emissaries made it fly through the city;
while himself, with a drawn sword in his hand, on horseback,
rode through the streets in seeming great commotion, and a
behavior adapted to the nature of the occasion; commanded
and entreated people of all ranks to be properly assisting on
the emergency," &c.

After describing the great confusion which the alarm occasioned, the historian continues: "As to the Quakers, it is said
the principal part of them were attending their religious meeting, as usual, on that day of the week, even in the midst of the
confusion; and, as if they were aware of the design, in general
behaved themselves so far consistently, that only four persons

who had any pretence to be accounted of that Society, appeared under arms at the place of rendezvous."—(Praud, I, 470, &c.)

"'It being our meeting-day (observes Logan), and although the time and tide that was to bring them up, it did not prevent the meeting; nor did the surprise put many of our Friends into those military companies.' And Isaac Norris avers, that 'not a Friend of any note but behaved as becomes our profession.' "—(Janney's Life of Penn, 505.)

"When they (the people) saw how grossly they had been imposed upon, many of them so highly resented the usage, that the authors and promoters thereof were now obliged to consult their own safety from the fury of an enraged populace."—(Praud, I, 471.)

1739.—"Advised, that Friends be vigilant in keeping up the peaceable principles professed by us as a people, and in no manner to join with such as may be for making warlike preparations, offensive or defensive; but on all occasions to demean themselves in a Christian and peaceable manner, thereby to demonstrate to the world that our practices, when put to the trial, correspond with our principles."—(Yearly Meeting.)

1746.—"As it hath pleased the Lord, by the breaking forth of the light of his Gospel, and the shedding abroad of his Holy Spirit, to gather us to be a people, and to unite us in love not only one to another, but to the whole creation of God, by subjecting us to the government of his Son, the Prince of Peace, it behooves us to show our obedience to his example and precepts, who hath commanded us to love our enemies, and to do good even to them that hate us. Therefore we entreat all that profess themselves members of our Society, to be faithful to that ancient testimony, borne by us ever since we were a people, against bearing arms and fighting; that, by a conduct agreeable to our profession, we may demonstrate ourselves to be real followers of the Messiah, the peaceable Saviour, of whose government and peace there shall be no end."—(Yearly Meeting.)

We have now passed the "golden age" of Pennsylvania, a period of more than seventy years. Clarkson remarks: "While William Penn's principles prevailed, or the Quakers had the principal share in the government, there was no spot on the globe where, number for number, there was so much virtue, or so much true happiness, as among the inhabitants of Pennsylvania." Duponceau, after giving an eloquent picture of what Pennsylvania was, adds : "Not that her citizens were entirely free from the passions of human nature, for they were men, and not angels; but it is certain that no country on earth ever exhibited such a scene of happiness, innocence, and peace, as was witnessed here during the first century of our social existence." But the scene now changed. The defeat of General Braddock and the destruction of his army took place in 1755.

"The degree of excitement it caused in Pennsylvania was most intense. It was the first time that the territory of William Penn had been stained by the blood of the battle-field ; and now that the desolation of war had actually entered the province, the cry for means of defence became loud and overwhelming. Quaker principles were denounced as visionary and absurd ; and taking advantage of this state of things, the war party, at the election which followed in 1756, carried twenty-four out of the thirty-six representatives which composed the Assembly. From this date Pennsylvania ceased to be governed in accordance with the principles of the Society of Friends."—(Bowden's History of Friends, II, 160.)

A few extracts will show the exercises of Friends in those excited times.

1755.—"In an humble sense of Divine goodness, and the gracious continuance of God's love to his people, we tenderly salute you, and are at this time therein engaged in mind, that all of us who profess the truth, as held forth and published by our worthy predecessors in this latter age of the world, may keep near that life which is the light of men, and be strengthened to hold fast the profession of our faith without wavering; that our trust may not be in man, but in the Lord alone, who ruleth in the army of heaven, and in the kingdoms of men; before whom the earth is as the dust of the balance, and her inhabitants as grasshoppers."

"And as we, through the gracious dealings of the Lord our God, have had experience of that work which is carried on, not by earthly might nor power, but ' by my Spirit, saith the Lord of Hosts;' by which operation that spiritual kingdom is set up, which is to subdue and break in pieces all kingdoms that oppose it, and shall stand forever. In a deep sense thereof, and of the safety, stability and peace there is in it, we are desirous that all who profess the Truth may be inwardly acquainted with it, and thereby be qualified to conduct in all parts of our life as becomes our peaceable profession. And we trust that, as there is a faithful continuance to depend wholly upon the Almighty arm, from one generation to another, the peaceable kingdom will be gradually extended from sea to sea, and from the rivers to the ends of the earth, to the completion of those prophecies already begun—'that nation shall not lift up sword against nation, nor learn war any more.' "

"And now, dear Friends, with respect to the commotions and stirrings of the earth, at this time near us, we are desirous that none of us may be moved thereat, but repose ourselves in the munition of that Rock that all these shakings shall not move,—even the knowledge and feeling of the eternal power of God, keeping us subjectly given up to his Heavenly will; and feel it daily to mortify that which remains in any of us, which is of this world; for the worldly part in any, is the changeable part,—and that is up and down, full and empty, joyful and sorrowful, as things go well or ill in this world. For, as the Truth is one, and many are made partakers of its spirit, so the world is but one, and many are made the partakers of the spirit of it; and so many as do partake of it, so many will be straitened and perplexed with it. But they who are single to the Truth, waiting daily to feel the life and virtue of it in their hearts, these shall rejoice in the midst of adversity,

and have to experience, with the prophet, that, although 'the
fig-tree shall not blossom, neither shall the fruit be in the vine;
the labor of the olive shall fail, and the fields shall yield no
meat; the flocks shall be cut off from the fold, and there shall
be no herd in the stalls; yet will they rejoice in the Lord, and
joy in the God of their salvation.' "—(Yearly Meeting.)

1759.—" If we carefully consider the peaceable measures
pursued in the first settlement of the land, and that freedom
from the desolations of war which for a long time we enjoyed,
we shall find ourselves under strong obligations to the Almighty, who, when the earth is so generally polluted with
wickedness, gave us being in a part so signally favored with
tranquillity and plenty; and in which the glad tidings of the
Gospel of Christ are so freely published, that we may justly
say, with the Psalmist, ' What shall be rendered unto the Lord
for all his benefits?' "

" The dealings of God with mankind in a national capacity,
as recorded in Holy Writ, do sufficiently evidence the truth of
that saying, ' It is righteousness which exalteth a nation;'
and though he doth not at all times suddenly execute his
judgments on a sinful people in this life, yet we see, by many
instances, that where men follow lying vanities, they forsake
their own mercies; and as a proud, selfish spirit prevails and
spreads among a people, so partial judgment, oppression, discord, envy, and confusion increase, and provinces and kingdoms are made to drink the cup of adversity, as a reward of
their own doings. Thus the inspired prophet, reasoning with
the degenerate Jews, saith,—' Thine own wickedness shall
correct thee, and thy backslidings shall reprove thee; know,
therefore, that it is an evil thing and bitter, that thou hast
forsaken the Lord thy God; and that my fear is not in thee,
saith the Lord of Hosts.' . . . . Let us, then, awfully regard
these beginnings of his sore judgments, and with abasement
and humiliation return to him whom we have offended."—
(Yearly Meeting.)

The skeptic may boldly deny any interference of Providence

with the ways of men, but he can hardly doubt that the just, equitable, and Christian treatment of the Indians by Friends had the effect, either directly to mollify their savage nature, and dispose them to kindness and enduring friendship, or indirectly, through the influence of Divine grace upon their hearts, to afford protection and support to those who are willing to walk in the way of truth. Be this as it may, the fact ought never to be lost sight of, that, under all the wrongs and cruelties inflicted upon this unhappy people, and however much they might have been instigated by French emissaries to avenge their wrongs, the persons and the property of Friends were, throughout this period of conflict, respected and protected by them. Whatever instrumentality God, in His infinite wisdom, may see meet to employ, the conclusion is obvious, that He has so inseparably connected cause and effect, that neither individuals nor communities can transgress the divine law of righteousness without incurring the penalties which belong to their violation.

1775.—" Having taken under our weighty consideration the sorrowful accounts given of the public deviation of many professors of the Truth among us, from our ancient testimony against war, and being favored in this, our deliberation, on this affecting subject, with the calming influence of that love which desires and seeks for their convincement and restoration, in order that our union and fellowship may be preserved, and a faithful testimony maintained to the excellency of the Gospel dispensation, which breathes peace on earth and good-will to men, it is our united concern and desire that faithful Friends, in their respective meetings, may speedily and earnestly labor in the strength of this love for the reclaiming of those who have thus deviated; and, where it is necessary, that Quarterly Meetings should appoint suitable Friends to join their assistance in the performance of this weighty service; and, where such brotherly labor is so slighted and disregarded, that, by persisting in this violation, they manifest that they are not convinced of our Christian principles, or are actuated by a spirit and temper in opposition thereto, it is our duty to testify our disunion with them.

"And, as many Friends have expressed that a religious objection is raised in their minds against receiving or paying certain bills of credit, issued expressly for the purpose of carrying on the war, apprehending that it is a duty required of them to guard carefully against contributing thereto in any manner, we therefore fervently desire that such who are not convinced that it is their duty to refuse those bills, may be watchful over their own spirits, and abide in true love and charity, so that no expressions or conduct, tending to the oppression of tender consciences, may appear among us. And we likewise affectionately exhort those who have this religious scruple, that they do not admit or indulge any censure in their minds against their brethren who have not the same ; carefully manifesting, by the whole tenor of their conduct, that nothing is done through strife and contention, but that they act from a clear conviction of Truth in their own minds ; showing forth, by their meekness, humility, and patient suffering, that they are followers of the Prince of Peace."—(Yearly Meeting.)

1775.—" Several Friends, of a committee appointed by our last Quarterly Meeting, to assist Monthly Meetings, in treating with such as have acted as committee-men, or joined with the present commotions and tumults, and deviated from the testimony of faithful Friends, being here, this meeting appoints Josiah Bunting, John Horne, and John Humphreys, to join the Overseers in treating with such, agreeably to Discipline."—(Darby Monthly Meeting.)

1777.—" A concern being expressed, that a meeting of free conference might be held in each Particular Meeting of Friends, selected from others, for the information, cautioning, and strengthening of each other, in these times of commotion, and for our preservation through the many trials, and from the many difficulties which now abound, and are likely to increase. . . . . The following Friends are appointed a committee to sit therein, and make report of the service to next meeting, viz. : William Jones, George Dillwyn, Peter Worrall, John Hoskins,

Daniel Smith, Joseph Buzby, Aaron Wills, Moses Wills, David Ridgway, Cornell Stephenson, Thomas Enock, Isaac Bunting, John Harvey, and Joseph Ellison."—(Burlington Monthly Meeting.)

1777.—"At Kennet Monthly Meeting, held the 18th of the ninth month, 1777 [only seven days after the battle of Brandy-wine], a concern arising in this meeting for the distressed inhabitants among us who have suffered by the armies; therefore it is recommended to Friends in general to encourage benevolence and charity, by distributing of their substance to such as they may think are in want ; and Joshua Way, James Bennet, Amos Harvey, Thomas Carlton, Jr., Caleb Pearce, Thomas Gibson, Thomas Chandler, Jr., John Marshall, and James Wilson, are particularly appointed to inspect and endeavor to relieve such as are in distress, either from want of victuals, clothes, or other necessaries."—(Kennet Monthly Meeting.)

The same day the following paper of acknowledgment was presented to the meeting.

1777.—"Notwithstanding I have had a right of membership among the people called Quakers, but not enough regarding the principle of Truth in my own heart, have so far erred as to join with military preparations so far as to make wheels for cannon carriages, after being advised to the contrary, it being inconsistent with the principles professed by me ; for which error I am heartily sorry, and do condemn the same, and desire Friends to continue me under their care, hoping for the future to be more careful.

"18th of ninth month, 1777.

"A—— S——."

(Kennet Monthly Meeting.)

1777.—"The committee to extend relief to the sufferers from the army which recently passed through this neighborhood, reported, that the sufferings of many have been great, but that none appear to be in want of the necessaries of life, except one in the verge of New Garden Preparative Meeting, which is referred to the care thereof; and that they generally appear to bear their sufferings with a good degree of cheerfulness."—(New Garden Monthly Meeting.)

1777.—"A weighty concern attending this meeting on the account of the deviations of many of our members in bearing a faithful testimony against military service, by actually paying their fines, contrary to the established rules of the Society; to remedy such conduct in future, it is agreed to have a meeting for conference at Evesham on third-day next, at the tenth hour, at which time it is requested that all the members of Society should attend."—(Evesham Monthly Meeting.)

1778.—"Dear Friends,—Whereas I have paid a fine imposed on me for not appearing in a militant order with Andrew Tranburg and company, for which act of so doing I have received considerable condemnation, and am sensible that it is not consistent with a Christian life to do so; therefore, for the clearing of Truth and my own conscience, I thus give my testimony against that misstep, and hope for the future to keep nearer the spirit of Truth, that leads, and not astray.

"I am your friend,

"I—— H——."

(Wilmington Monthly Meeting.)

1778.—"We find in several different quarters a religious scruple hath appeared and increases among Friends, against the payment of taxes, imposed for the purpose of carrying on the present war; they being deeply concerned and engaged faithfully to maintain our Christian testimony against joining with or supporting the spirit of wars and fightings, which hath remarkably tended to unite us in a deep sympathy with the seed of life in their hearts.

"And feeling a sincere desire for the advancement of the kingdom of the Prince of Peace, in such a gradual progress as may be consistent with his Divine will; we earnestly recommend to all the members of our religious Society, that in singleness of heart we may be truly exercised in giving due attention to the dictates of unerring Grace, and strictly careful not to stifle or suppress the secret monitions thereof in our own minds. And that all may be closely excited to watchfulness and care to avoid complying with the injunctions and requisitions made for the purpose of carrying on war, which may produce uneasiness to themselves and tend to increase the sufferings of their brethren; which we apprehend will be the most effectual means of advancing our Christian testimony in purity, and preserving us in a conduct consistent with the holy principles we profess. And we shall experience fervent love and concord to prevail among us, which will enable us to seek and promote the edification one of another, in that faith which worketh by love, freed from every censure inconsistent therewith."—(Yearly Meeting.)

1779.—"We are desirous and earnestly recommend, that Friends in every quarter be encouraged to attend to their tender scruples against contributing to the promotion of war, by grinding of grain, feeding of cattle, or selling their property for the use of the army, or other such warlike purposes.

"And that, in Christian love and tenderness, advice should be extended to such who have deviated or are in danger of deviating from the testimony of Truth in these respects, in order that a united concern and labor may be manifested for the advancement of the peaceable kingdom, and our preservation in that bond of brotherly love which cements and unites the true followers of Christ."—(Yearly Meeting.)

The following is properly a case of suffering, but it so clearly illustrates the pernicious influences of the spirit and practice of war as to claim a place here. The effect of a military life is to eradicate from the mind of the soldier that sacred regard for human life which the Creator has placed in every breast; a token whereof was set upon the brow of Cain, lest human passions should impel men to violate the Divine law by avenging the blood of Abel. The narrative was furnished by a relative,—the venerable John Watson, of Doylestown:—

"Thomas Watson was a worthy, exemplary Friend and thrifty farmer of Buckingham, Bucks County, Pennsylvania. During the winter of 1779–80, several detachments of the

American army encamped for some days in the vicinity, producing a scarcity of hay. J—— N——, who kept a tavern at Centreville, applied to Thomas to purchase a stack of hay, which he had designed to distribute among his less fortunate neighbors. He declined to sell, and told J—— that it would be opened such a day, and if he would come he should have a share of it. J—— still insisted: Do you expect to get so much? naming a sum. Thomas said, No; the hay was not worth so much. Do you expect so much? and so much? till he found about what Thomas thought it was worth. He then tendered him that amount; which was refused. But the man still persisted. At length (said Thomas) a conviction came over me that I ought to bear my testimony against such money. I turned and told him that as it was made for the express purpose of carrying on war, I had never been free to take it, and could not do so now; but, if he would come when the stack was opened, he should have a share of the hay without any money at all. That was enough. J—— immediately went and informed General William Alexander, sometimes called Lord Sterling (who was at Newtown with a detachment of troops), that a rich old Quaker in Buckingham had a stack of hay to sell, but would not let him have it, because he had nothing but paper money to pay for it. It was not to be endured that a stubborn Quaker should plead religious scruples for refusing the currency of Congress, because it was issued to carry on the conflict in which they were then engaged.

"An order was issued to arrest the refractory Quaker, and a file of men sent to execute it. He was carried to Newtown, closely imprisoned, tried by a court martial, found guilty of refusing to take Continental money, and sentenced to be stripped and ironed, and on the next afternoon to be publicly hanged. Strenuous efforts were made for his release, but apparently without success. His nephew, Dr. John Watson, visited the family of Henry Wynkoop on the occasion. A young invalid officer lay on the floor wrapped in his blanket, and heard the conversation. At length, he raised upon his elbow and said, 'Young man, you may as well go home and make yourself contented, for you may depend upon it, your uncle will be hanged.' The nephew replied, 'I hope not; I do not think that the hanging of so good and useful a man, and one so well esteemed in his neighborhood, will be approved of, or do good to the cause of the people.' 'If your uncle is the man you describe, he is the less likely to escape. His death will strike more terror than the death of a dozen of a different character. Lord Sterling has long been determined to make an example. An opportunity is now offered, and he most certainly will not let it pass. His Excellency (meaning General Washington) has always stood between such men and the fate they deserve; but he is now too far off to be reached before the sentence will be carried into execution. You may go home, and rest assured your uncle will be hanged.'

"But the wife of the prisoner had a warm friend in the landlady of the inn at Newtown; and when was woman's kindness ever invoked for the relief of suffering, or woman's tact required in vain? She was advised not to apply in person for the release of her husband. The landlady had learned Lord Sterling's fondness for the creaturely comforts of life: and knew that wine had the effect to soften the severity of his temper. To take advantage of this disposition, she invited him to a sumptuous dinner. He did full justice to the delicacies of the table, and willingly partook of the generous old wine, which had been reserved for special occasions. As the wine warmed the General's good-nature and disposed him to kindlier feelings, she cautiously introduced the case of the condemned; pitied his condition, cold, and in irons; regarded his treatment as needlessly severe; and at length requested that his fetters might be removed and his clothes restored to him. He could not resist this appeal of his hostess; and a note was sent to the guard in answer to her request.

"The good woman continued her entreaties, and still plied the wine; when, at the proper moment, the wife was introduced. She fell on her knees before him, burst into a flood of tears, and told him who she was, and, with all the earnestness, feeling, and eloquence of a loving wife pleading for the

20

one she loved best on earth, begged him to spare her husband's life. Her entreaties were of a nature hard to be withstood. He remained some time silent; then, raising her to her feet, he said, 'Madam, you have conquered. I must relent at the tears and supplications of so noble and so good a woman as you. Your husband is saved.' He immediately wrote a pardon for the prisoner, and ordered his discharge. The happy pair now returned to their homes rejoicing.''

1790.—'' That part of the proposed militia law which offers exemption to such persons as conscientiously refuse to serve in the militia, upon condition of paying two dollars yearly towards defraying the expenses of civil government, coming under solid and deliberate consideration, it appears to be the united sense and judgment of this meeting, that no Friend can pay such fine or tax, consistent with our religious testimony and principle, it being a fine in lieu of personal services.''—(Yearly Meeting Extracts.)

Under the phrenzied excitement produced by the struggle for independence, cruel and oppressive laws were made, whereby Friends suffered much in their persons and estates; which sufferings were greatly aggravated by the unrestrained conduct of unprincipled and avaricious collectors. But when the excitement had passed by, the Legislature saw that Friends had nevertheless maintained their position without wavering; that the sufferings to which they had been subjected were as needless as they were cruel; and that where men place their whole dependence upon God, legal pains and penalties can never force them to violate their consciences, by doing any act which they believe is contrary to his will. It is not strange that legislators so circumstanced should relent; and such was probably the origin of the above militia law. Its framers must, however, have had an imperfect idea of the grounds of Friends' conscientious scruples, or they would have perceived that they could no more pay the fine, than render the personal service which the law required: the special appropriation of the money did not in any degree lessen the objection to its payment.

1805.—" It is the sense and judgment of this meeting, that it is inconsistent with our religious testimony and principles, for any Friend to pay a fine or tax levied on them on account of their refusal to serve in the militia, although such fine or imposition may be applied towards defraying the expenses of civil government; and where deviations in this respect occur, tender dealing and advice should be extended to the party, in order to their convincement and restoration ; and where they continue so regardless of the sense and judgment of the body, that the labor of their friends proves ineffectual, Monthly Meetings should proceed to testify against them."—(Yearly Meeting.)

CHAPTER XXVI.

SPIRITUOUS LIQUORS.

THE custom of using some sort of intoxicating liquors seems to have spread its baneful influence almost wherever man has placed his habitation.

While all deplore the obvious and melancholy effects of drunkenness, how few have traced the evil to its proper source,—a perversion of our family and social habits. While all can see the downward course of their neighbors, as they sink into this debasing habit, how few perceive that they themselves are pursuing the same downward path to destruction. It may not seem strange that one whose infancy has been cradled, whose childhood has been instructed, and whose manhood has been passed in the filthy styes of intemperance, should be thus insensate ; but that rational and reflecting men, of cultivated minds, who acknowledge the general obligations of a moral and religious life, should so far deviate from their accustomed modes of thinking and of acting, as to fall into this degrading habit, is an anomaly which is difficult to explain.

The pernicious effects resulting from the sale of spirituous liquors to the Indians, very early attracted the attention and required the exertions of both civil and religious society to abate the evil. But so long as it was made an article of commerce, and very extensively used by the whites, all their efforts to withhold it from the Indians were vain.

1679.—"It was desired that Friends would consider the matter, as touching the selling of rum unto the Indians, [whether it] be lawful at all for Friends professing Truth to be concerned in it."—(Burlington Monthly Meeting.)

1685.—"This meeting doth unanimously agree, and give as their judgment, that it is not consistent with the honor of Truth, for any that make profession thereof, to sell rum or other strong liquors to the Indians, because they use them not to moderation, but to excess and drunkenness."—(Yearly Meeting.)

1686.—"To all people that doth know or may hear of my being ensnared, or overtaken in drink, and are concerned thereat,—which was true, to my shame and great trouble, which none knows but the Lord alone; which causes me utterly to deny the practice, or any other which may bring dishonor to God and cause his Truth to be evil spoken of, which, I can truly say, was a great cause of my trouble at this time. And to as many as are or may be in the like condition, my heart's desire to the Lord is, that he may do for them as he hath done for my soul; and, also, that they may humble themselves under his smiting hand, and not fly his righteous judgments, which are not pleasant, but grievous through sin. Nothing else, but love and good will to all.

"Your loving friend,

"N—— L——."

(Concord Monthly Meeting.)

1687, third month.—"Whereas, it is offensive to see the great disorders that are among the Indians, by reason of the rum that is sold unto them, and that Friends may keep clear of selling them any, or to any that are Indian traders, it is agreed that Thomas Janney and William Yardley do speak with W—— B——, and caution him thereof."

Fourth month.—" Whereas, at last meeting, two Friends were appointed to speak to W—— B—— about selling rum to such as sell it to the Indians; [they] do say they have spoke with him; and his answer is, that it is not against the law, neither doth he know that it is any evil; however, if Friends desire him not to do it, he will for the future forbear it. It is the unanimous judgment of this meeting, that it is a wrong thing to sell rum to the Indians, either directly or indirectly, or sell rum to any person that the person so selling it believes it to be disposed of to the Indians; because we know and are satisfied that they know not—viz., the Indians—how to use it in moderation, but most commonly to the abuse of themselves and others. Agreed, that Lyonel Britain do speak to W—— B—— again, and acquaint him that it is the desire of Friends he would be very careful and wary how he doth dispose of rum to such as sell it to the Indians."—(Falls Monthly Meeting.)

W—— B—— was an eminent minister and member of Falls Monthly Meeting, which was long held at his house, and frequently chosen to the Assembly and Provincial Council. He was probably the only merchant in that vicinity who imported and sold rum. The coincidence in the language in this and the following minute, renders it probable that Falls Monthly Meeting carried the concern up to the Yearly Meeting.

1687, sixth month.—" The practice of selling rum, or other strong liquors, to the Indians, either directly or indirectly, or exchanging rum or other strong liquors for any goods or merchandise with them, considering the abuse they make of it, is a thing contrary to the mind of the Lord, and a great grief and burden to his people, and a great reflection and dishonor to the Truth, so far as any professing it are concerned; and,

for the more effectual preventing this evil practice, as aforesaid, we advise that this our testimony be entered in every
Monthly Meeting book, and every Friend belonging to said
meeting to subscribe the same."—(Yearly Meeting.)

Middletown Monthly Meeting has a minute of this kind,
signed by forty-nine members. Perhaps the earliest instance
of a temperance pledge on record.

1703.—" This Meeting desires W—— B—— to supply what
W—— P—— stands in need of, it being some molasses and
some rum."—(Falls Monthly Meeting.)

This was the same W. B. whom that Monthly Meeting had
prohibited selling liquors to the Indians some sixteen years
before. It was inconsistent; for when we reflect that the practice of drinking strong liquors was then almost universally
tolerated, we need not resort to the supposition, that the *rum*
was needed to prepare spirits of camphor, or to bathe a rheu-
matic limb.

1706.—" Advised that none accustom themselves to vain and
idle company, sipping and tippling of drams and strong drink,
in inns or elsewhere. For though such as use that evil practice may not suddenly be so far prevailed upon as to be drunk
to the greatest degree, yet they often inflame themselves
thereby, so as to become like ground fitted for the greatest
transgressions. And some that have had the example of virtuous parents have, from such beginnings in corners, arrived
to a shameless excess, to the ruin of themselves and their wives
and families, and the scandal of the holy name whereby they
have been called."—(Yearly Meeting.)

1711.—" This Meeting is concerned to take care to prevent
the bringing of drink near our meeting-house, in the time of
our Yearly Meeting, and therefore does advise that some
Friends of this Shore be appointed to address the government
for the prevention and suppressing the said evil practice, with

the evil consequences attending it."—(Thirdhaven Yearly Meeting.)

1719.—"Advised, that such be dealt with as sell, barter, or exchange, either directly or indirectly, to the Indians, rum, brandy, or other strong liquors, it being contrary to the care Friends always had since the settlement of these countries, that they might not contribute to the abuse and hurt these poor people receive for drinking thereof, being generally incapable of using moderation therein."—(Yearly Meeting.)

1721.—"Inasmuch as peoples being hurt and disguised by strong drink seems to be a prevailing evil, therefore, where any among us are overtaken therewith, they should be early admonished, and dealt with as disorderly persons. And it becomes the concern of this meeting to advise and caution all of our profession carefully to watch against this evil, when it begins to prevail upon them in a general manner, or more particularly, at occasional times of taking it; the frequent use whereof, especially drams, being a dangerous inlet, the repetition and increase of them insensibly stealing upon the unwary, by wantonness in the young, and the false and deceitful heat it seems to supply the aged with; so that by long habit, when the true warmth of nature becomes thereby weakened and supplanted, the stomach seems to crave these strong spirits, even to supply what they have destroyed."—(Yearly Meeting.)

These correct and very important conclusions, drawn from the suffering and experience of centuries, have been claimed as their own discoveries by some modern temperance men.

1724.—"The Friends appointed to attend the Quarterly Meeting, have produced to this meeting a copy of the Quarterly Meeting's minute, whereby we find it was the sense of the Quarterly Meeting, that no Friends in unity with us, who shall make sales, do suffer any rum or other strong liquor to be made use of, either directly or indirectly, by the crier or any other person in that behalf, to give the bidders, to provoke or encourage them to advance the price of the goods so exposed to sale."—(Middletown Monthly Meeting.)

1726.—"It having been observed, that a pernicious custom has prevailed upon the people; of giving rum and other strong liquors, to excite such as bid at vendues, and provoke them at every bidding to advance the price, which, besides the injustice of the artifice, is very scandalous, and leads to great intemperance and disorder; therefore, it is the unanimous sense of this meeting to caution Friends against the same; and if any under our profession do fall into this evil practice, or do by any means encourage the same (by giving or taking drams or strong liquor at vendues, or other noisy revelling gatherings), they should be speedily dealt withal as disorderly persons."—(Yearly Meeting.)

The Quarterly Meeting appears to have taken the initiatory step in this case, which was speedily followed by the Yearly Meeting, in order to discourage the practice. It is satisfactory to find almost the same language in the preamble to the law of Pennsylvania to prevent this pernicious custom, showing clearly from whence it was derived. "Forasmuch as a pernicious custom hath prevailed in many places of giving rum and other strong liquors, to excite such as bid at vendues to advance the price, which, besides the injustice of the artifice, leads to great intemperance and disorders," &c.—(Preamble, 1751.)

1727.—"R—— McK——, a member of this meeting, was overtaken with liquor about the middle of the last third month. He hath drawn up a paper condemning the same."—(New Garden Monthly Meeting.)

1736.—"This meeting repeats the caution of last year against the frequent use of drams or other strong drink in families and elsewhere, and particularly to be cautious of giving them to children, and thereby accustom them to the habit of drinking strong liquors."—(Yearly Meeting.)

The caution not to give drams to children will not avail, so long as they see their parents use them and give them to others, as a token of their friendship and hospitality. Such an exhibition only whets their appetite and renders them more solicitous for its indulgence. Nor does it in any degree lessen their desire to be told that such things are not good for children. The great mistake is, that children observe more closely and reason more correctly than most people imagine; hence the attempts to mislead and deceive them being discovered, produces a bad effect upon their tender minds. A consistent example is all important in the management of the young in this, as in every other case.

1737.—"We tenderly caution all Friends constantly to watch against the indecent and pernicious use of strong drinks, which sometimes prevails unexpectedly; and as we cannot but observe with grief and sorrow the frequent instances of its destructive effects, not only to men's persons and estates, but also to the ruin of their children and families, we fervently pray that all Friends may be careful not to give way to the gratifying an inordinate appetite for any kind of drams or other spirituous liquors."—(Yearly Meeting.)

1738.—"It was moved to this meeting, and accordingly recommended to the several Quarterly and Monthly Meetings to caution Friends that they be exceeding careful against the too frequent use of spirituous liquors,—it being remarked to be a pernicious and growing evil,—and to direct the Overseers to deal with such persons as may drink to excess, though they may not drink to such a degree as to disguise themselves.

"The proposal of Philadelphia Quarterly Meeting, respecting the great number of public-houses, being considered, it is recommended to such of the Friends of the Quarterly and Monthly Meetings belonging to this meeting, as are magistrates, that they use their endeavors to lessen the number of persons recommended for that service; and that Friends be careful not to sign petitions to recommend any but such as are proper persons, or where there is a real necessity."—(Yearly Meeting.)

There is instruction in these records. Friends are acknowledged to have been the pioneers in the temperance reformation; but they had more than their own long-established social habits to contend with,—the inveterate customs of the age were against them, while every neighborhood was provided with small distilleries for the manufacture of family products; hence we may learn how difficult it was for them to attain to the true temperance standard—total abstinence.

As few persons will candidly deny the immoral tendency of the sale of intoxicating drinks, or plead for the necessity of places where they shall be sold, the latter advice seems to cover the whole ground.

1743.—"Second query: Do Friends keep clear of excess, either in drinking drams or other strong drink?"—(Yearly Meeting.)

This general inquiry was all the Society could make at this early period, when the queries were first addressed to the subordinate meetings.

1750.—"That part of our Discipline which relates to the practice of giving of drams and other strong liquors at vendues, being now considered and spoken to pretty freely, it is the sense of this meeting, that the minute on this subject contained in the General Epistle from the Yearly Meeting, 1726, should be received and enforced by the respective Monthly Meetings; and that such persons who transgress the same, should be dealt with as disorderly persons; and, if they persist in justifying their conduct, and refuse to give satisfaction for the same, they ought to be testified against."—(Yearly Meeting.)

The advancement of the testimony required a corresponding change in the query. Thus in

1755.—"Are Friends careful to avoid the excessive use of

spirituous liquors, the unnecessary frequenting of taverns and places of diversion, and to keep to true moderation and temperance, on the account of births, marriages, burials, and all other occasions?"—(Yearly Meeting.)

1777.—"This meeting is engaged to exhort and admonish Friends to use great caution in that of distilling, or encouraging distillation, or using distilled liquors of any kind; and, in regard to the practice of destroying grain, by distilling spirits out of it, it is the sense and judgment of this meeting, that that practice ought to be wholly discouraged and disused among Friends, and that Friends ought not to sell their grain for that purpose, nor to use or partake of liquors made out of grain.

"Considering the difficulty and snares, both to our young people and others, which are attendant on that of keeping houses of public entertainment, beer-houses, and dram-shops, whereby the reputation of Truth has greatly suffered, and, in some places, the children and families of persons concerned herein have been brought into disgrace and loss, both spiritually and temporally, it is the united sense and judgment of this meeting, that Friends ought not to give way to the desire of outward gain arising from such employments, but to keep themselves clear thereof, by attending to the pointings of pure wisdom."—(Yearly Meeting.)

It was, perhaps, unfortunate for the progress of the cause, that the distinction was ever drawn between liquors made from grain and other products. I do not perceive its force, while it does seem to have had the effect of fixing the attention of Friends upon one kind of distilled liquors, and also of withdrawing it from all others, as well as from fermented drinks, which are more insinuating, and therefore more likely to create a morbid appetite, and form the incipient habit of intemperance.

Many of the Monthly Meetings, after reciting the above advices, recorded the results, some of which follow.

1777.—"Jacob Wright, Lewis Pennock, and David Moore,

are appointed to join the committee of the Quarterly Meeting in that service, within the verge of this meeting."—(New Garden Monthly Meeting.)

1777.—" Which coming solidly under consideration, the meeting appoints John Millhouse, Vincent Bonsall, Garret Blackford, John Yarnall, and Joseph Chambers, to take the necessary care therein, agreeably to the directions of the Yearly Meeting."—(Wilmington Monthly Meeting.)

1777.—"Several of the committee appointed by our last Quarterly Meeting in order to visit Friends, for reducing into practice the advice contained in the extracts relating to the distilling and use of spirituous liquors, now being here, . . . was appointed to join them in that service."—(Darby Monthly Meeting.)

1778.—"Friends appear united in desiring that Friends may be clear of those practices, and in order that they may be preserved from the evil thereof, and that we may be enabled to make a suitable report to the next meeting," a committee was appointed.—(Burlington Monthly Meeting.)

1778.—" The committee respecting public-house keeping, spirituous liquors, &c., now report, they have lately visited such of our members as are concerned therein, and that some of them don't yet decline the practice; a hint whereof is directed to be sent to the Quarterly Meeting."—(New Garden Monthly Meeting.)

1778.—" No grain sold for distilling, no liquor distilled out of grain used among Friends that we know of.

" Two taverns kept by men whose wives are members.

"Where spirituous liquors have been used by Friends among their workmen, we believe they have been used sparingly."—(Wilmington Monthly Meeting.)

1779.—"The Friends continued to discourage the distillation of spirits out of grain, &c., reported, there did not appear to be any of the members of this meeting concerned in distilling spirits, nor but one Friend concerned in selling spirituous liquors, at this time, whose husband keeps a public-house."—(Darby Monthly Meeting.)

1779.—"We find an increasing concern on the minds of many Friends, to discourage the unnecessary use of spirituous liquors on all occasions. Notwithstanding, we have sorrowfully to observe that some among us have been too liberal therewith, in the time of the late harvest. We know of none concerned in distilling from grain ; no taverner, except one woman Friend, whose case is under care."—(Concord Monthly Meeting.)

The following conditions of John Pemberton's lease to Gifford Dally, for the "Old London Coffee-house," at the corner of Market and Front Streets, show how careful he was to obviate the demoralizing tendencies of such a place.

1780.—"Said Dally covenants and agrees and promises, that he will exert his endeavors as a Christian to preserve decency and order in said house, and to discourage the profanation of the sacred name of God Almighty, by cursing, swearing, &c., and that the house on the first-day of the week shall always be kept closed from public use, that so regard and reverence may be manifested for retirement and the worship of God." "That under a penalty of £100, he will not allow any person or persons to use, play at, or divert themselves with, cards, dice, backgammon, or any other unlawful game."— (Watson's Annals, p. 340.)

It is due to the memory of John Pemberton to add, that he was not satisfied even with this, and soon after sold the premises for a store and private dwelling, "a thing which Mr. Pemberton said he much preferred."—(Ibid.)

1781.—"The care of Friends is enjoined to be continued to discourage the distillation of spirits from grain, or using spirits so distilled ; also the unnecessary use of other spirituous liquors, or the distillation of them ; likewise the keeping houses for public entertainment where such liquors are sold, by any of our members, the concern and labor of friends having been useful. The late minutes in relation thereto are again

recommended to the notice of Friends, in order to fulfil the
advices therein contained, particularly that in the minute of
this meeting in the year 1777 ; it being the judgment of the
meeting that no member of our religious Society should be
found in those practices."—(Yearly Meeting.)

At a period prior to 1783, perhaps as early as 1777, the
query was modified so as to read,—

" Are Friends careful to discourage the unnecessary distillation or use of spirituous liquors, frequenting taverns and places
of diversion, &c."—(See New Garden Monthly Meeting, 1783.)

1788.—" The evil effects of the use of spirituous liquors,
in the manner they are commonly used at the ensuing season
of gathering the produce of the earth, was weightily spread
before this meeting, with desires that Friends in their respective Monthly Meetings may be afresh encouraged and strengthened to bear a testimony, by example, as well as precept,
against the so frequent use of this baneful evil.

" Copied from the minutes of Chester Quarterly Meeting,
held at Wilmington, 12th of fifth month, 1788, by

"JOSHUA SHARPLESS,
" Clerk."
(Wilmington Monthly Meeting.)

1788.—" To the Yearly Meeting now sitting:—The committee appointed to take under consideration the very interesting
subject relating to spirituous liquors, have had a free open
conference on the occasion, in company with our friends from
Maryland ; and after hearing the sentiments of divers brethren,
not of our number, and inspecting the minutes of this meeting
in years past, find that there is an increasing concern harmoniously prevailing for the advancement of our testimony against
the practice of trading in, and making use of, an article which
is attended with obvious pernicious effects on the morals and
health of the people in general ; and therefore agreed to propose that it be recommended, in the most earnest, tender manner, to our Quarterly and Monthly Meetings, to manifest a due
interested regard and attention to the judgment and pressing
exhortations of the collective body of Friends, as expressed in

the minutes of the Yearly Meeting in 1777, and the subsequent advices to this time, as well as the renewed exercise which has attended the minds of the Friends now assembled, for the preservation of our fellow-members from the temptation of partaking in the gain of unrighteousness.

"And for the effecting of this desirable purpose, we think it expedient that the Quarterly and Monthly Meetings be excited and enjoined early to appoint committees, unitedly to proceed in visiting and treating with our members, individually, who are concerned in importing spirituous liquors from the West India Islands, or other places, either on their own account or as agents for others; and those who purchase and retail such liquors in greater or less quantities; as also those members who are concerned in the distillation of these liquors from grain, or other produce, either in their own families, or encouraging or promoting it in others.

"And we apprehend it is expedient to recommend and advise those who make use of spirituous liquors in their families, in a medicinal way, that they be careful to keep within the bounds of true moderation in the use of them for such a purpose; and that our members in general refrain from the practice of using them in the time of harvest, or otherwise.

"Hoping that the brotherly labor with all who continue in the practices here recited, may be effectual to convince them of the impropriety of their conduct, and the benefit of Christian fellowship, we much desire that the committees who may be appointed on the service now proposed, would be religiously engaged to perform it with diligence and care, under the influence of true love and affection; and that clear and explicit accounts be sent of the success of their endeavors, and the state of their members in general, in the respects before mentioned, in the reports to this meeting next year.

"Submitted to the further consideration of the Yearly Meeting, and signed on behalf of the committee, by

"JOSEPH PENROSE,
"JOHN EVANS,
"MARK MILLER.

"PHILADELPHIA, 4th of tenth month, 1788."

1788.—"Most of the committee appointed by last Quarterly Meeting attended here, and in order that the concern of the body may be more extensively spread, and the good purposes therein designed effected, this meeting appoints Samuel Pennock, David Graves, John Marshall, Samuel Harlan, Thomas Chandler, Samuel Nicholls, William Harvey, George Passmore, and Robert Lamborn, to take the subject-matter relative to spirituous liquors under their solid consideration, and proceed therein as they in the wisdom of truth may be enabled."—(Kennet Monthly Meeting.)

1789.—"Endeavors have been used to collect Friends generally at the several meeting-houses, where the concern of the body was publicly read, in the presence of men and women Friends. And labor has been extended to some where it has appeared necessary," &c.—(Kennet Monthly Meeting.)

1789.—"There are two Friends who are concerned in retailing distilled spirituous liquors (one of whom proposes shortly declining the practice), a few who keep stills (though latterly have done very little at distilling), and a few who have taken of their produce to be distilled; most of whom a committee out of our number have taken opportunities with. Most of the visited appear disposed to take the subject under close consideration," &c.—(Concord Monthly Meeting.)

1790.—"There is an increasing concern among Friends to discourage the unnecessary use of distilled spirituous liquors; and we do not find any in the practice of distilling, retailing, or importing them."—(Thirdhaven Monthly Meeting.)

1792.—"I, the subscriber, was so unguarded some time ago as to drink cider in public company, to my hurt, and to the reproach of the profession I make. For which conduct I have been favored to feel sorrow, and do hope, with Divine assistance, to be more watchful in future. I desire Friends to continue me under their care as my future conduct may deserve.

"W—— Mc——."
(New Garden Monthly Meeting.)

1794.—" To the Yearly Meeting, now sitting :—

" We, the committee appointed to take into consideration the subject of distilled spirituous liquors, having several times met and weightily deliberated thereon, as also examined former minutes of the Yearly Meeting on the subject, agree to report, that it is our united sense and judgment, it would be expedient for the Yearly Meeting to recommend to the Quarterly and Monthly Meetings to continue their care in a strict observance of the advices handed down by minutes of 1777 and 1778; and if any should reject the labor and advice of their Friends, by continuing in the practice of importing of, or vending, spirituous liquors, either on their own account or as agents for others, or distil or retail such liquors, or sell or grind grain for the use of distillation, that such should not be employed in any service in the Church, nor their contributions be received for the use thereof. . . . And we further propose, that if any should distil spirits out of grain, or retail such liquors, that Monthly Meetings should deal with them as other offenders; and, if they cannot be prevailed upon to desist from such a practice, be at liberty to declare their disunity with them.

" Signed, on behalf of the committee, the 3d of the tenth month, 1794.

" NATHAN COOPER,
" BENJAMIN LINTON."
(Yearly Meeting.)

1796.—" The committee appointed by our last Quarterly Meeting, in order to encourage and strengthen the members of our religious Society, in the different Monthly Meetings, to an upright faithfulness in our testimony against the use of distilled spirituous liquors, being now present, and having produced several minutes of our Yearly Meeting on the subject in years past, which being read in the audience of men and women Friends, and, after divers pertinent observations being feelingly expressed on the occasion, this meeting thinks best to appoint a committee to take the subject-matter religiously under their care, and to afford such advice and counsel as they may be enabled, to those of our members as are or may be in danger of wounding themselves or the testimony, on these accounts. Therefore, Caleb Kirk, Stephen Logue, Thomas Carleton, William Lamborn, John Marshall, and Caleb Sharpless, are nominated to the service."—(Kennet Monthly Meeting.)

1798.—"We, the committee in the case of distilled spirituous liquors, report, that there has been four of our number concerned in retailing, who have been visited; and one of them informed that he felt uneasy about it, and has declined the practice. The other three gave no encouragement of declining, though two of them have been often visited. No distillers among us that we know of; and we believe Friends in general have been clear of handing it out to their hands in the late harvest; though it appears there has been some small quantities made use of among the hands of a few, most of whom have been spoken to."—(Kennet Monthly Meeting.)

In the Book of Discipline, published in 1806, the query was further extended.

1806.—"Are Friends careful to discourage the unnecessary distillation or use of spirituous liquors, frequenting of taverns, &c. ?"—(Yearly Meeting.)

While I am willing to allow full credit to all co-laborers in the cause of temperance, and rejoice in their success, it is proper to say that Friends were the pioneers in this reformation. It is only to be regretted that they have not been more unitedly concerned in carrying on so noble a work. One special cause of this apparent neglect may, however, be found in the fact that they have operated upon the mass: their disciplinary regulations were applicable to all the members, and must needs be governed by the progress of the Society collectively. Others have only operated upon individuals (however numerous they may have been), and they could at any time enjoin total abstinence, or require a temperance pledge, let the numbers be many or few.

Formerly, the distillation of spirits was a family employment, the use of them as a drink was everywhere common; hence, the excessive use was of frequent occurrence. Indeed, it was found so difficult for a man to follow the exact line where sobriety ends and intemperance begins, that a slight departure from it was considered a venial error, and was soon forgotten.

But the evils of intemperance are not solitary,—they are legion. An attentive observer cannot fail to discover that a large proportion of the transgressions of former times, sprang from that prolific source of evil, the intoxicating bowl; among these, quarrelling and gross immoralities were exceedingly common.

By steadily pursuing the even tenor of their way, it is probable that Friends, as a class, are still in advance of any other religious association in regard to temperance.

1832.—"Monthly Meetings ought to take an early opportunity tenderly to treat with such of our members as are concerned either in the importation, distillation, or sale of spirituous liquors; and if, after faithful, patient labor to convince them of the awful, demoralizing effects of their conduct, and its inconsistency with the testimony of our religious Society, they cannot be prevailed upon to relinquish the business, the said meetings be at liberty to put the Discipline in practice against them."—(Yearly Meeting.)

The query was further altered to read thus, in

1839.—"Are Friends clear of the distillation or sale of spirituous liquors? and are they careful to discourage the use thereof as a drink, and from attending places of diversion, and the unnecessary frequenting taverns? and do they keep to true moderation and temperance on the account of marriages, burials, and other occasions?"—(Yearly Meeting.)

A CASE.

The causes of intemperance may be either social or physiological. In an age when intoxicating drinks were not only tolerated, but deemed almost an essential at the board of hospitality, when only their excessive use was censured, a discrimination between their use and abuse was required, often difficult to determine, until too late,—every man was deemed to be sober until he became drunken. By the continued social use, an appetite was soon formed for such drinks, which became difficult to control. The nervous systems of some persons are so constituted as seemingly to require, and apparently to be benefited by their use. But when the social and physiological causes co-operate, the subject of them requires not only deep sympathy and charitable indulgence, but constant aid, to shield him from the dangers which beset him.

Such, we apprehend, was the situation of A—— B—— (for so we shall call him), and such was the religious care of his friends, who snatched him as a brand from the burning, and restored him to usefulness in his family and in the Church. "Let him that thinketh he standeth, take heed lest he fall."

The account is condensed from the records of one of our Monthly Meetings, as meriting a place in this collection.

1742.—A—— B—— was allowed "liberty to sit with the ministers and elders in their meetings." He subsequently obtained certificates, in

1751.—"To visit some meetings of Friends in Maryland."

1752.—"To visit Friends on Long Island, and some parts of the Jerseys."

1756.—"To visit Friends at Maiden Creek."

1756.—"To visit the families of Friends in New York, and some on Long Island."

1757.—"To attend the Yearly Meeting at Choptank, Maryland."

1758.—"To attend the Yearly Meeting at West River. Maryland."

1759.—"To visit some meetings on the Western Shore, Maryland."

1762.—Without any complaint or dissatisfaction appearing on the record, or any apparent previous labor, A—— B—— now presents himself before the Monthly Meeting with the following paper :—

" To the Monthly Meeting of Friends, to be held, &c. :

" Whereas, I have for many years made profession of the Truth, but, for want of due attention to the dictates thereof, have unguardedly given way to drinking strong drink to excess, whereby I have brought great reproach upon our holy profession and grief to my friends, for which I am heartily sorry, and give this testimony against that evil; sincerely desiring that I may more and more experience a dwelling in that holy fear which is sufficient to preserve all; and it is my earnest breathing, that I may be reconciled to the Lord, His Church, and people, and witness our former unity to be restored; and that I may be enabled, through a circumspect and humble walking for the future, to effectually remove the reproach which my conduct hath occasioned.

"A—— B——."

1770.—We find A—— B—— again " recommended in the station of a minister, as heretofore." He subsequently obtained certificates, in

1771.—"To visit the Indians, and some Friends' meetings in West New Jersey."

1771.—"To attend some meetings on the Western Shore, Maryland."

1772.—"To attend the Yearly Meeting at West River," &c.

1773, seventh month.—"Our Preparative Meeting complains of A—— B—— for taking strong drink to excess. . . . are appointed to treat with him ; also to inquire how far his conduct has been reproachful," &c.

1773, ninth month.—"His conduct has been reproachful in several respects,—in taking too much strong drink several times, and still appearing in public ministry, both at home and abroad."

1773, eleventh month.—"Thinks there is rather encouragement for further labor."

1773, twelfth month.—"Appears to be under a considerable weight of suffering, on account of his transgressions; yet they consider him far short of that state of mind in which it would be proper for him to offer anything to this meeting by way of satisfaction."

1774, second month.—"He desired (by a friend) his case should still be continued."

1774, fourth month.—"This meeting, taking into consideration the situation of A—— B——'s standing upon record as a minister, concludes that he ought not to have the privilege of sitting in our Meetings of Ministers and Elders," &c.

1774, sixth month.—"He appeared here, and offered some lines by way of acknowledgment." "Best to leave it under consideration."

1774, seventh month.—"Another paper being produced somewhat different, and some straitness appearing, it is continued another month."

1774, eighth month.—"A—— B—— attended this meeting with a paper condemning his misconduct, ... which was read; and, after some alteration, was received. . . . . . is appointed to read it in a first-day meeting.

"'To Friends of ——— Monthly Meeting:

"'Whereas, I have made profession of the Truth, but, for want of keeping on my watch, have erred, by several times taking too much strong drink, also appearing in public as a minister soon after; for which reproachful conduct I am heartily sorry, and hereby take the shame to myself, and desire Friends to pass by my offences, and continue me under their care; hoping, through Divine help, to be more careful in future.

"'A—— B——.'"

1788.—"The recommendation of our Friend A—— B——, to the Quarterly Meeting of Ministers and Elders, as a minister approved by us, being again considered, and Women's Meeting concurring therewith, it is concluded to recommend him accordingly," &c.   He subsequently obtained certificates

1788.—" To visit some meetings on the Western Shore, Maryland."

1789.—" To visit Friends in New York and New England Governments."

1790.—" To attend meetings in Chester and Lancaster Counties."

1790.—" To visit Friends in Virginia, the Carolinas, and Georgia."

1791.—" To visit Friends in parts of Pennsylvania and New Jersey."

Some may entertain a doubt whether this Friend was sincere, and properly authorized to preach the Gospel. This may best be left to those who sat under his ministry. It was the practice of Friends, when ministers came from distant meetings, and their ministry was approved, to furnish them with return minutes to that effect. Subsequent to his third recommendation as a minister, he obtained and produced the following testimonials of this character to his Monthly Meeting, which are there minuted, and, for aught that appears, were satisfactory :—

1788.—From the " Quarterly Meeting at Baltimore."

1788.—   "   " Monthly Meeting at Indian Springs."

1789.—   "   " Yearly Meeting at Westbury, Long Island."

1789.—   "   " Yearly Meeting of Rhode Island."

1789.—   "   " Quarterly Meeting at New Bedford."

1789.—   "   " Quarterly Meeting at Oblong."

1789.—   "   " Monthly Meeting at Saratoga."

1790.—   "   " Quarterly Meeting of Salem, at Dover."

1791.—   "   " Yearly Meeting at Wainoak, in Virginia."

1791.—   "   " Quarterly Meeting at Center, N. C."

1791.—From the "Quarterly Meeting near Little River,
        N. C."
1791.—   "   "Quarterly Meeting of New Garden,
        N. C."

We have given this remarkable case by way of encouragement, both to the humble transgressor and to those whose
province it may be to labor for his recovery.

CHAPTER XXVII.

NEGROES AND SLAVERY.

WE apprehend the reader will approach this subject with
feelings of surprise that Friends should ever have become
slaveholders. The colonial history of our country explains,
but does not justify them in the practice. There have ever been
those in the Christian Church who held slavery to be incom-
patible with Christianity, as instituted by its Divine Author.
Thus the martyr Cyprian, who wrote sixteen hundred years
ago, declares, that "Both religion and humanity make it a
duty for us to work for the deliverance of the captive. They
[the slaves] are sanctuaries of Jesus Christ, who have fallen
into the hands of the infidel." The Puritan Fathers of the
Massachusetts colony took a bold stand, and sent back the first
cargo of Africans which reached their shores, declaring the
traffic "expressly contrary to the law of God and the law of
the country," and imposed the death penalty upon the further
infraction of it; while good old Roger Williams declared that
"no black mankind" should be held as slaves, or for life, in
the colony of Rhode Island; but that, "at the end of ten
years, the master should set them free, as the manner is with
English servants."
At the time of William Penn's arrival in his colony, and

for many years previous, both the English and Dutch were actively engaged in the African slave-trade, rendered doubly lucrative by the great demand for laborers in the colonies. By these means slavery had already been extensively introduced into the European settlements south of Rhode Island.

Moreover, the African slave-trade was now under the special patronage and protection of the British government, while William Penn was not invested with any power to interdict the importation of slaves within his territorial jurisdiction, as the subsequent history will show.

The practice was then common, for the settlers to purchase "redemptioners" as servants, and to hold them for a term sufficient to remunerate themselves for the price paid for bringing them from Europe. Viewing the destitute condition of those pauper immigrants, just off ship, after a tedious voyage, it was no doubt felt to be an act of Christian philanthropy, thus to give them an opportunity of working out their own freedom. And it is quite rational to suppose that Friends, seeing the much more wretched condition of the imported Africans, were sometimes prompted by the same benevolent feelings to purchase them. This supposition is strengthened by the well-known fact, that Friends, as a class, always used their bondmen with more humanity than most others, and early manifested a concern for the cultivation of their moral and religious faculties. Many of them, like Roger Williams, thought too, that after serving a few years, the negroes ought to have their freedom; but arbitrary power soon becomes avaricious, and the grasp grows tighter the longer it is held.

The Christian principles promulgated by George Fox and his coadjutors fully recognized the universal brotherhood of man, and his equal right to liberty, without regard to nation or color. Nor did they allow this recognition long to remain a mere inferential deduction; for in the year 1671, George Fox and several other Friends visited the Island of Barbadoes, where they first saw the practical working of negro slavery. George Fox says :—

1671.—"Respecting their negroes, I desired them to endeavor to train them up in the fear of God, as well those that were bought with their money, as those that were born in their families, that all might come to the knowledge of the Lord. And so with Joshua, every master of a family might say, As for me and my house, we will serve the Lord. I desired also that they would cause their overseers to deal mildly and gently with their negroes, and not use cruelty towards them, as the manner of some hath been and is; and that, after certain years of servitude, they should make them free."—(Fox's Works, II, 113.)

1675.—"And must not negroes feel and partake of the liberty of the Gospel, that they may be won by the Gospel? Is there no year of jubilee for them? Did not God make us all of one mould?" . . . . "Christ's command is, to do to others as we would have them do to us; and which of you would have the blacks, or others, to make you their slaves, without hope or expectation of freedom or liberty? Would not this be an aggravation upon your minds that would outbalance all other comforts? So make their condition your own; for a good conscience, void of offence, is of more worth than all the world; and truth must regulate all wrongs."—(William Edmondson's Address.)

Both George Fox, in 1671, and William Edmondson, in 1675, held negro meetings in Barbadoes, and were both complained of, that "making the negroes Christians would make them rebel."

1676.—"Recognizing the negroes as equal objects of our heavenly Father's regard with themselves, Friends were anxious to bring them to a knowledge of that glorious redemption which is in Christ Jesus our Lord, and invited them to their religious assemblies. But so opposed were the authorities to this attempt to impart religious truth to these poor oppressed people, that in Barbadoes they actually passed an act, in 1676, to prevent the people called Quakers from bringing negroes to their meetings,

&c. It was under this act that Ralph Fretwell and Richard Sutton, the former of whom had been one of the chief judges of the island, were severally fined in the sum of eight hundred pounds and three hundred pounds, for having negro meetings at their houses. In 1680, the Governor of Barbadoes interdicted Friends' meetings altogether; but his edict not being founded on any act or statute, was extra-judicial, and of no force."—(Bowden, II, 191.)

A company, called "The Free Society of Traders," was formed in England before William Penn sailed for his Colony, in 1682, of which he was a conspicuous member; one article of their association reads:

" If the Society should receive blacks for servants, they shall make them free at fourteen years' end, upon condition that they will give unto the Society's warehouse two-thirds of what they are capable of producing on such a parcel of land as shall be allotted to them by the Society, with stock and necessary tools. And if they will not accept of these terms, they shall be servants until they will accept of it."—[them.]—(Watson's Annals, p. 480.)

1684.—" William Dixon having a mind to sell a negro his freedom, desires this meeting's advice. This meeting refers him to the Yearly Meeting for advice."—(Third Haven Monthly Meeting.)

I believe there was then a law in Maryland against the liberation of slaves.

In 1683, a company of Friends arrived from Germany, and settled at Germantown.

" These unsophisticated vine-dressers and corn-growers, from the Palatinate of the Upper Rhine, the converts of the devoted William Ames, revolted at the idea of good men buying and selling human beings, heirs with themselves of immortality.

Faithful to their convictions, they very early bore an uncompromising testimony against the evil."—(Bowden.)

While those honest Germans seem to have had a special mission to the New World, the execution of it happily led them away from much suffering in their native land.

"While William Ames was in the Palatinate, in 1659, he became acquainted with the Baptists at Criesheim; and among those people he found such entrance, that some families, receiving the doctrines he preached, bore a public testimony for it there, and so continued until the settlement of Pennsylvania in America, when they unanimously went thither. Not, as it seemed, without a singular direction of Providence; for not long after a war ensued in Germany, where the Palatinate was altogether laid waste by the French, and thousands of people were bereft of their possessions and reduced to poverty."— (Sewell, I, 349.)

1688.—This is to the Monthly Meeting held at Richard Worrall's:—

"These are the reasons why we are against the traffic in man body, as followeth:—Is there any that would be done or handled in this manner, viz.: to be sold, or made a slave, for all the time of his life? How fearful and faint-hearted are many at sea, when they see a strange vessel, being afraid it should be a Turk, and they should be taken and sold for slaves in Turkey! Now what is this better than Turks do? Yea, rather it is worse for them which say that they are Christians, for we hear that most part of such negroes are brought hither against their will and consent, and that many of them are stolen. Now, though they are black, we cannot conceive that there is more liberty to have them slaves, as it is to have other white ones. There is a saying, that we shall do to all men like as we will be done ourselves, making no difference what generation, descent, or color they are. And those who steal and rob men, and those who buy or purchase them, are they not all alike? Here [in Pennsylvania] is liberty of conscience, which is right and reasonable; here, likewise, ought to be liberty of the body, except of evil-doers, which is another case. But to bring men hither, or to rob or sell them, against their wills, we stand against. In Europe there are many oppressed for conscience sake, and here are many oppressed who are of a dark color.

"And we know that men must not commit adultery;—some do commit adultery in others, separating wives from their husbands, and giving them to others; and some sell the children of these poor creatures to other men. Ah! do consider well this thing, you who do it, if you would be done at this manner, and if it is done according to Christianity. You surpass Holland and Germany in this thing. This makes an ill report in all those countries of Europe where they hear of;—that the Quakers do here handle men as they handle there the cattle; and, for that reason, some have no mind or inclination to come hither. And who shall maintain this your cause, and plead for it? Truly we cannot do so, except you shall inform us better hereof, viz., that Christians have liberty to practice these things. Pray, what thing in the world can be done worse towards us than if men should rob or steal us away, and sell us for slaves to strange countries, separating husbands from their wives and children. Being now this is not done in the manner we would be done at; therefore we contradict and are against this traffic in men body.

"And we who profess that it is not lawful to steal, must likewise avoid to purchase such things as are stolen; but rather help to stop this robbing and stealing, if possible. And such men ought to be delivered out of the hands of the robbers, and set free as in Europe. Then is Pennsylvania to have a good report. Instead, it hath now a bad one, for this sake, in other countries; especially, whereas the Europeans are desirous to know in what manner the Quakers do rule in this province; and most of them do look upon us with an envious eye. But, if this is done well, what shall we say is done evil?

"If once these slaves (which they say are so wicked and

stubborn men) should join themselves, fight for their freedom, and handle their masters and mistresses, as they did handle them before, will these masters and mistresses take the sword at hand and war against these poor slaves, as we are able to believe some will not refuse to do ?   Or, have these negroes not as much right to fight for their freedom as you have to keep them slaves ?

"Now, consider well these things, if it be good or bad. And, in case you find it good to handle these blacks in this manner, we desire, and require you hereby, lovingly, that you may inform us herein ; which, at this time, never was done, viz., that Christians have such a liberty to do so ; to the end that we shall be satisfied in this point, and satisfy likewise our good Friends and acquaintances in our native country, to whom it is a terror, or fearful thing, that men should be handled so in Pennsylvania.

"This is from our meeting at Germantown, held the 18th of the second month, 1688 ; to be delivered to the Monthly Meeting at Richard Worrall's.

" GARRET HENDRICKS,

" DERRICK UP DE GRAEFF,

" FRANCIS DANIELL PASTORIUS,

" ABRAHAM JUN DEN GRAEFF."

(Friend, 1844.)

1688.—"At our Monthly Meeting at Dublin [Richard Worrall's] the 30th of the second month, 1688.

"We having inspected the matter above mentioned and considered of it, we find it so weighty that we think it not expedient for us to meddle with it here; but do rather commit it to the consideration of the Quarterly Meeting, the tenor of it being nearly related to the Truth.

"Signed, on behalf of the Monthly Meeting,

" JOHN HART."

1688.—" This, above mentioned, was read in our Quarterly Meeting at Philadelphia the 4th of the fourth month, 1688, and was from thence recommended to the Yearly Meeting ; and the above said Derrick, and the others mentioned therein, to present the same to the above said meeting; it being a thing of too great weight for this meeting to determine.

"Signed, by order of the meeting,

"ANTHONY MORRIS."

1688.—"A paper was presented by some German Friends concerning the lawfulness and unlawfulness of buying and keeping negroes. It was adjudged not to be so proper for this meeting to give a positive judgment in the case, it having so general a relation to many other parts; and, therefore, at present they forbear it."—(Yearly Meeting.)

I cannot repress surprise that a Yearly Meeting, composed of Friends of high standing, should have shrunk from a bold and manly co-operation with those noble-hearted Germans; but, when I consider their faithfulness in other matters,—enduring reproach, persecution, imprisonment, expatriation, and even death, for the discharge of manifested duties,—it would be unreasonable to suppose that they were less faithful to their known duties in this particular.

Without daring more closely to scrutinize the ways of Providence, I am led to the conclusion that God, who has declared that he will teach his people himself, did not see meet to impose the burden of this testimony upon them, until, by the promulgation and acceptance of other long-neglected Christian truths, the minds of the people should be better prepared to receive it; and when they felt the burden to be laid upon them, they did not shrink from its support. Under this aspect of the case, I invite the reader's attention to the following brief narrative.

After a lapse of eight years, the following minute occurs:—

1696.—"Friends are advised not to encourage the bringing in any more negroes; and that such as have negroes be careful of them, bring them to meetings, have meetings with them in their families, and restrain them from loose and lewd living, as much as in them lies, and from rambling about on first-days and other days."—(Yearly Meeting.)

1700.—" Our dear friend and Governor having laid before this meeting a concern that hath laid upon his mind for some time, concerning the negroes and Indians: that Friends ought to be very careful in discharging a good conscience towards them in all respects, but more especially for the good of their souls; and that they might, as frequent as may be, come to meetings on first-days. Upon consideration whereof, this meeting concludes to appoint a meeting for the negroes, to be kept once a month, &c.; and that their masters give notice thereof in their families, and be present with them at the said meetings as frequent as may be."—(Philadelphia Monthly Meeting.)

"At the same time he introduced a bill into the Assembly ' For regulating Negroes in their Morals and Marriages;' also another, ' For their Trials and Punishments.' The former.was defeated by the jealousies then in the House. From the same causes (jealousies), an act of more security was substituted, in 1775, against the negroes, entitled, 'An Act for the Trial and Punishment of Negroes.' It inflicted lashes for petty offences, and death for crimes of magnitude. They were not allowed to carry a gun without license, or be whipped twenty-one lashes; nor to meet more than four together, lest they might form cabals and riots. They were to be whipped if found abroad after nine o'clock at night without a pass," &c.— (Watson's Annals, p. 431.)

Thus early, and in Pennsylvania, did the infliction of wrong upon the helpless and unoffending negro create feelings of insecurity for fear of retaliation; and the exercise of arbitrary power had so steeled the heart with cruelty, as to add outrage to wrong, and cause the infliction of severe punishments where there were no crimes.

William Penn, in common with many other Friends, was led to become a slaveholder; and it continues to be reiterated down to the present day, that he died in the possession of slaves. This may have been literally true, owing to some neglect of his legal representatives; but was substantially untrue, as has been repeatedly proved. Thus, before he took a final leave of the province, in 1701, he executed a will, in which he declared, "I give to my blacks their freedom, as is under my hand already; and to old Sam one hundred acres, to be his children's, after he and his wife are dead, forever." He prudently made assurance doubly sure, by repeating in his will what he had "already" done elsewhere; believing, with the wise man, that "if one prevail against him, two shall withstand him, and a threefold cord is not quickly broken." If his purposes failed, it was the fault of others. (See Janney's Life of Penn, p. 438.)

In the tobacco-growing districts of Maryland, slavery took deeper root, and Friends partook more largely of the evil.

1702.—"The last will of Alice Kennersly being read in this meeting, wherein she willed her negro woman Betty and her child to Daniel Cox, in consideration he should pay twenty shillings a year, for the full term of thirty years, to this meeting, for the paying of travelling Friends' ferriage in Dorchester County, or what other occasions Friends may see meet, when said negroes are delivered to D. Cox; therefore, this meeting advises D. Cox to be at our next meeting, to answer such questions as may be asked him concerning premises."—(Third-haven Monthly Meeting.)

Two years after, Joseph Kinnersly was appointed receiver of the above "for the service of Truth." A strange purpose to which to apply the unrighteous gain of oppression. But the good seed sown by the honest Germans in 1688, had begun to spring up in 1696, and now showed signs of producing fruit.

1705.—"As early as the year 1705, a duty was imposed on the importation of slaves, by the Provincial Assembly; this was renewed in 1710. In 1711, they struck at the root of the evil, by forbidding their introduction in future; but the Privy Council in England, scandalized by such liberal policy, in so new and so diminutive a community, whilst their own

22

policy was to cherish slavery in so many colonies, quashed the act in an instant. The Assembly, not daunted by such a repulse, again, in 1712, upon petition ' signed by many hands,' aimed at the same effect, by assessing the large sum of £20 a head. This was again cancelled by the same trans-Atlantic policy. When the petition for the £20 duty was presented, another was offered, in the name of William Southby, praying ' for the total abolition of slavery in Pennsylvania.' "—(Watson's Annals, p. 481.)

The Colonial Legislature was thus kept under the surveillance of the Home Government, and their philanthropic intentions frustrated. Not so, however, the Yearly Meeting, in its efforts to ameliorate the condition of the negro.

1711.—" The Quarterly Meeting of Chester declare their dissatisfaction with Friends buying and encouraging the bringing in of negroes, and desires the care of this meeting concerning it. . . . Advised, that Friends may be careful, according to a former minute of this meeting (1696), not to encourage the bringing in any more; and that all merchants and factors write to their correspondents to discourage them from sending any more."—(Yearly Meeting.)

1712.—" And now, dear Friends, we impart unto you a concern that hath rested on the minds of some of our brethren for many years, touching the importing and having negro slaves, and detaining them and their posterity as such, without any limitation or time of redemption from that condition. This matter was laid before this meeting many years ago, and the thing in some degree discouraged, as may appear by a minute of our Yearly Meeting, 1696 ; . . . . yet, notwithstanding, as our settlement increased, so other traders flocked in among us, over whom we had no Gospel authority; and such have increased and multiplied negroes among us, to the grief of divers Friends, whom we are willing to ease, if the way might open clear to the satisfaction of the general. And it being last Yearly Meeting again moved, and Friends being more concerned with negroes in divers other provinces and places than in these, we thought it rather too weighty to come to a conclusion therein. This meeting, therefore, desires your assistance, by way of counsel and advice therein; and that you would be pleased to take the matter into your weighty consideration (after having advised with Friends of the other American provinces), and give us your sense and advice therein."—(Yearly Meeting Epistle to London.)

As Friends in other colonies, Maryland, Virginia, &c., were more deeply implicated in the practice of slaveholding than those in Pennsylvania, the Yearly Meeting of London likewise felt it "rather too weighty" to come to a conclusion.

1713.—"You had better first have advised with other plantations, and so have stated the case conjunctly; for want whereof we shall say the less, until such time as it is more generally represented. Only this we think meet to impart to you as the sense of the Yearly Meeting, that the importing them from their native country by Friends is not a commendable nor allowable practice; and we hope Friends have been careful to avoid the same, remembering the command of our blessed Lord, 'Whatsoever ye would that men should do to you, do ye even so to them.'"—(London Yearly Meeting Epistle.)

1714.—"We kindly received your advice about negro slaves; and we are one with you, that the multiplying of them may be of dangerous consequence; and therefore a law was made in Pennsylvania, laying a duty of twenty pounds on every one imported there; which law the Queen was pleased to disannul."—(Yearly Meeting Epistle to London.)

1715.—"To be any ways concerned in bringing negroes from their native country, and selling them for slaves, is a trade not fit for one professing Truth to be concerned in."—(London Epistle.)

1715.—"I must entreat you to send me no more negroes for sale, for our people don't care to buy. They are generally against any coming into the country. Few people care to buy them, except for those who live in other provinces."—(J. Dickinson, Watson's Annals, p. 482.)

1715.—"If any Friends are concerned in the importation of negroes, let them be dealt with and advised to avoid that practice, according to the sense of former meetings in that behalf; and that all Friends who have or keep negroes, do use and treat them with humanity and a Christian spirit; and that all do forbear judging or reflecting on one another, either in public or private, concerning the detaining or keeping them servants."—(Yearly Meeting.)

Chester and Newark Monthly Meetings had sent to Chester Quarter their "dissatisfaction with Friends being concerned in importing and buying of negroes;" but neither the Quarterly nor the Yearly Meeting appeared prepared to embrace the intended advance.

The following year, Chester Quarter again brought the subject up; urging that "the buying and selling gave great encouragement to the bringing of them in; and that no Friends be found in the practice of buying any that shall be imported hereafter."

Although this was no more than a recognition of the axiom that the market makes the traffic, yet Friends of Chester were again disappointed.

1716.—"As to the proposal from Chester Meeting about negroes, there being no more in it than was proposed to last Yearly Meeting, this meeting cannot see any better conclusion than what was the judgment of the last meeting, and therefore do confirm the same. And yet in condescension to such Friends as are straitened in their minds against the holding them, it is desired that Friends do, as much as may be, avoid buying such negroes as shall hereafter be brought in, rather than offend any Friends that are against it. Yet this is only caution and not censure."—(Yearly Meeting.)

After this decision of the Yearly Meeting, Bowden says,

"No further notice of the subject appears on its minutes for
the space of ten years." But we find in

1719.—" Advised, that none among us be concerned in the
fetching or importing negro slaves from their own country or
elsewhere; and that all Friends who have any of them, do
treat them with humanity and in a Christian manner, and, as
much as in them lies, make them acquainted with the principles
of Truth, and inculcate morality in them."—(Yearly Meeting.)

It appears that Indian slaves were sometimes brought from
Carolina for sale. The making them slaves was so repug-
nant to the policy which Friends ever pursued towards the
Indians, that in the year 1719, the Yearly Meeting recommended

1719.—" To avoid giving them (the Indians) occasion of
discontent, it is advised that Friends do not buy or sell Indian
slaves."—(Yearly Meeting.)

Friends of Chester Quarter, ever true to their purpose, again
appealed to the Yearly Meeting, saying:—

1729.—" Inasmuch as we are restricted by a rule of Discipline from being concerned in fetching or importing negro
slaves from their own country, whether it is not as reasonable
that we should be restricted from buying them when imported?"
—(Chester Quarterly Meeting.)
1730.—" Friends of this meeting, resuming the consideration
of the proposition of Chester Meeting, relating to the purchasing of such negroes as may hereafter be imported, and having
reviewed and considered the former minutes relating thereto,
and having maturely deliberated thereon, are now of opinion
that Friends ought to be very cautious of making any such
purchases for the future, it being disagreeable to the sense of
this meeting. And this meeting recommends it to the care of
the several Monthly Meetings, to see that such who may be, or

are likely to be, found in that practice, may be admonished and
cautioned how they offend herein."—(Yearly Meeting.)

These advices were repeated every succeeding year, except
one, until 1743, and Quarterly Meetings enjoined to report
their attention thereto. In the year last named, the following
Query, with others, was addressed to the subordinate meetings.

1743.—"Do Friends observe the former advices of our
Yearly Meeting, not to encourage the importation of negroes,
nor to buy them after imported?"—(See Queries.)

About this period I find Ralph Sandiford,* Benjamin Lay,
Anthony Benezet, and John Woolman, co-laborers in the cause
of humanity.

But it was not until 1754 that the latter published his "Considerations on the Keeping of Negroes."

In that year the Yearly Meeting issued the following epistle
to its members, supposed to have emanated from the pen of
Benezet, and affording satisfactory evidence of progress in the
minds of Friends.

1754.—"Dear Friends: It hath frequently been the concern of our Yearly Meeting to testify their uneasiness and
disunity with the importation and purchasing of negroes and
other slaves, and to direct the Overseers of the several Monthly
Meetings to advise and deal with such as engage therein. And
it hath likewise been the continued care of many weighty
Friends, to press those that bear our name to guard as much
as possible against being in any respect concerned in promoting the bondage of such unhappy people. Yet, as we have with
sorrow to observe that the number is of late increased among

---

* "Kalm, the Swedish traveller, speaks of the then only free negroes in
Philadelphia, in 1748, as having been manumitted by a Quaker master;
probably referring to Ralph Sandiford, who freed all his in the year 1733,
and probably presented to us the first instance of the kind known in our
annals."—(Watson's Annals, p. 484.)

us, we have thought proper to make our advice and judgment more public, that none may plead ignorance of our principles therein; and also again earnestly exhort all to avoid in any manner encouraging the practice of making slaves of our fellow-creatures.

"Now, dear Friends, if we continually bear in mind the royal law of doing to others as we would be done by, we shall never think of bereaving our fellow-creatures of that valuable blessing liberty, nor endure to grow rich by their bondage. To live in ease and plenty by the toil of those whom violence and cruelty have put in our power, is neither consistent with Christianity nor common justice, and we have good reason to believe draws down the displeasure of Heaven; it being a melancholy but true reflection, that where slave-keeping prevails, pure religion and sobriety declines, as it evidently tends to harden the heart and render the soul less susceptible of that holy spirit of love, meekness, and charity, which is the peculiar character of a true Christian.

"How then can we, who have been concerned to publish the Gospel of universal love and peace among mankind, be so inconsistent with ourselves as to purchase such who are prisoners of war, and thereby encourage this unchristian practice; and more especially as many of those poor creatures are stolen away, parents from children, and children from parents, and others, who were in good circumstances in their native country, inhumanly torn from what they esteemed a happy situation, and compelled to toil in a state of slavery, too often extremely cruel? What dreadful scenes of murder and cruelty those barbarous ravages must occasion in these unhappy people's country, are too obvious to mention. Let us make their case our own, and consider what we should think, and how we should feel, were we in their circumstances. Remember our blessed Redeemer's positive command, 'to do unto others as we would have them do unto us;' and that 'with what measure we mete, it shall be measured to us again.' And we entreat you to examine whether the purchase of a negro, either born here or imported, does not contribute to a further importation,

and consequently to the upholding of all the evils above mentioned, and promoting man-stealing, the only theft which, by
the Mosaic law, was punished with death? 'He that stealeth
a man and selleth him, or if he be found in his hand, he shall
surely be put to death.'

"The characteristic and badge of a true Christian is love
and good works; our Saviour's whole life on earth was one
continued exercise of them. 'Love one another (says he) as I
have loved you.' How can we be said to love our brethren,
who bring, or for selfish ends keep them in bondage? Do we
act consistent with this noble principle, who lay such heavy
burdens on our fellow-creatures? Do we consider that they
are called, and sincerely desire that they may become heirs
with us in glory, and rejoice in the liberty of the sons of God,
whilst we are withholding from them the common liberty of
mankind? Or can the Spirit of God, by which we have always
professed to be led, be the author of those oppressive measures?
or do we not thereby manifest that temporal interest hath more
influence on our conduct herein, than the dictates of that merciful, holy, and unerring guide?

"And we likewise earnestly recommend to all who have
slaves, to be careful to come up in the performance of their
duty towards them, and to be particularly watchful over their
own hearts; it being by sorrowful experience remarkable, that
custom, and a familiarity with evil of any kind, hath a tendency to bias the judgment and deprave the mind.

"And it is obvious, that the future welfare of these poor
slaves who are now in bondage is generally too much disregarded
by those who keep them. If their daily task of labor be but fulfilled, little else perhaps is thought of. Nay, even that which
in others would be looked upon with horror and detestation, is
little regarded in them by their masters, such as the frequent
separation of husbands from wives and wives from husbands,
whereby they are tempted to break their marriage covenants
and live in adultery, in direct opposition to the laws both of
God and man, although we believe that Christ died for all men,
without respect of persons. How fearful then ought we to be

of engaging in what hath so natural a tendency to lessen our humanity, and of suffering ourselves to be inured to the exercise of hard and cruel measures, lest thereby we in any degree lose our tender and feeling sense of the miseries of our fellow-creatures, and become worse than those who have not believed?

"And, dear Friends, you who by inheritance have slaves born in your families, we beseech you to consider them as souls committed to your trust, whom the Lord will require at your hands, and who, as well as you, are made partakers of the Spirit of Grace, and called to be heirs of salvation. And let it be your constant care to watch over them for good, instructing them in the fear of God and the knowledge of the Gospel of Christ, that they may answer the end of their creation, and God be honored and glorified by them as well as by us; and so train them up, that if you should come to behold their unhappy situation in the same light which many worthy men who are at rest have done, and many of your brethren now do, and should think it your duty to set them free, they may be the more capable of making a proper use of their liberty.

"Finally, brethren, we entreat you in the bowels of Gospel love, seriously to weigh the cause of detaining them in bondage. If it be for your own private gain, or any other motive than their good, it is much to be feared that the love of God, and the influence of the Holy Spirit, is not the prevailing principle in you, and that your hearts are not sufficiently redeemed from the world, which that you with ourselves may come more and more to witness, through the cleansing virtue of the Holy Spirit of Jesus Christ, is our earnest desire."— (Yearly Meeting.)

1755.—"The consideration of the inconsistency of the practice of being concerned in importing or buying slaves with our Christian principles, being weightily revived, and impressed by very suitable advice and caution given on the occasion, it is the sense and judgment of this meeting, that where any transgress this rule of our Discipline, the overseers ought speedily to inform the Monthly Meeting of such transgressors, in order that the meeting may proceed to treat further with them, as they may be directed in the wisdom of Truth."—(Yearly Meeting.)

On a revision of the queries this year, the following was adopted in place of the one already given :—

1755.—"Are Friends clear of importing or buying negroes? and do they use those well which they are possessed of by inheritance, or otherwise, endeavoring to train them up in the principles of the Christian religion?"—(Yearly Meeting.)

1757.—" All clear of importing negroes or purchasing them for term of life; several have been purchased for a term of years. They are generally well fed and clothed; some are taught to read and taken to meetings; but others are taken little care of in those respects."—(Burlington Monthly Meeting.)

1758.—" There appears a unanimous concern prevailing, to put a stop to the increase of the practice of importing, buying, selling, or keeping slaves for term of life. . . . This meeting very earnestly and affectionately entreats Friends, individually, to consider seriously the present circumstances of this and the adjacent provinces, which, by the permission of Divine Providence, have been visited by the desolating calamities of war and bloodshed, so that many of our fellow-subjects are now suffering in captivity; and fervently desire that, excluding temporal considerations or views of self-interest, we may manifest an humbling sense of these judgments, and, in thankfulness for the peculiar favor extended and continued to our Friends and brethren in profession, none of whom, as we have yet heard, have been slain or carried into captivity, would steadily observe the injunction of our Lord and Master, ' to do unto others as we would they should do unto us;' which, it now appears to this meeting, would induce such Friends to set them at liberty, making a Christian provision for them, according to age, &c.

" And, in order that Friends may generally be excited to the practice of this advice, some Friends here now signified to the meeting their being so fully devoted to endeavor to render it effectual, that they are willing to visit and treat with all such Friends who have any slaves. The meeting therefore approves of John Woolman, John Churchman, John Scarborough, John Sykes, and Daniel Stanton undertaking that service ; and desires some elders or other faithful Friends in each quarter to accompany and assist them therein. And that they may proceed in the wisdom of Truth, and thereby be qualified to administer such advice as may be suitable to the circumstances of those they visit, and most effectual towards obtaining that purity which it is evidently our duty to press after.

" And if, after the sense and judgment of this meeting now given against every branch of this practice, any professing with us should persist to vindicate it, and be concerned in importing, selling, or purchasing slaves, the respective Monthly Meetings to which they belong should manifest their disunion with such persons, by refusing to permit them to sit in Meetings for Discipline, or to be employed in the affairs of Truth, or to receive from them any contributions towards the relief of the poor, or other services of the meeting."—(Yearly Meeting.)

Much exercise and labor continued to be bestowed from year to year, both by the Yearly Meeting and its subordinate branches, which we cannot find room to notice.

1762.—" The Friends appointed to visit such who are possessed of negro slaves, reported that they proceeded therein as they found a qualification for the service ; and, finding the concern to spread among many brethren, they now apprehend themselves released from the appointment, and request to be discharged."—(Yearly Meeting.)

1770.—" Friends having been favored with a time of much calmness and brotherly tenderness towards each other, it appears to be the solid sense and judgment of this meeting that, in future, Friends be careful to avoid appointing such Friends to the station of elders as are in possession of negro slaves, and do not appear to have a testimony in their hearts against the practice of slave-keeping."—(Thirdhaven Yearly Meeting.)

1773.—" The clerk was directed to transcribe the following paragraph from the London Epistle, to sign it on behalf of this meeting, and to communicate it to one or more members of the Upper and Lower Houses of Assembly, viz. :—

" ' Dear Friends: It is a matter of satisfaction to us that one of your neighboring colonies hath lately applied to government for aid to suppress the importation of negro slaves, as injurious to her commercial interests. When commercial considerations coincide with humanity, there is good ground to expect a reformation respecting this long complained of violation of the laws of nature,—this custom, founded on oppression, which arguments drawn from the remotest antiquity can never justify. If you reflect that negroes have the same natural rights with yourselves, and that they stand in the same relation to the Supreme Being that you do,—the consideration of your duty as Christians, and the feelings of your minds as men, we hope, will induce you to concur with a sister colony in endeavoring to abolish a custom, which is one continued violation of the laws of justice and of the principles of our holy religion.' "—(Thirdhaven Yearly Meeting.)

1774.—" Agreeably to appointment, we have weightily considered the sorrowful subject committed to us, and many brethren having an opportunity of freely communicating their sentiments thereon, after a solid conference, find there is a painful exercise attending the minds of Friends, and a general concern prevailing, that our Christian testimony may be more extensively held forth against the unrighteous practice of enslaving our fellow-creatures; to promote which, it is our sense and judgment, that such professors among us, who are or shall be concerned in importing, selling, or purchasing, or shall give away or transfer any negro or other slave, with or without any other consideration than to clear their estate of any future incumbrance, or in such manner as that their bondage shall be continued beyond the time limited by law or custom for white persons, and such members who accept of such gifts or assignments, ought to be speedily treated with in the spirit of true love and wisdom, and the iniquity of their conduct laid before them; and if, after this Christian labor, they cannot be brought to such a sense of their injustice as to do everything which the Monthly Meeting shall judge to be reasonable and necessary for the restoring such slave to his or her natural and just right to liberty, and condemn their deviation from the law of right- eousness and equity, to the satisfaction of the said meeting, that such members be testified against as other transgressors are, by the rules of our Discipline, for other immoral, unjust, and reproachful conduct.

"And, having deliberately weighed and considered that many slaves are possessed and detained in bondage by divers members of our religious Society, towards whom labor has been extended, but being apprehensive that a Christian duty hath not been so fully discharged to them as their various circum- stances appear to require, we think it expedient that the Quar- terly Meetings should be earnestly advised and enjoined to unite with their Monthly Meetings in a speedy and close labor with such members; and where it shall appear that any, from views of temporal gain, cannot be prevailed with to release from captivity such slaves as shall be found suitable for liberty, but detain them in bondage, without such reasons as shall be sufficient and satisfactory, the cases of such should be brought forward to the next Yearly Meeting for consideration, and such further direction as may be judged necessary; and, in the mean time, we think such persons ought not to be employed in the service of Truth.

"And having grounds to conclude that there are some breth- ren who have these poor creatures under their care, and are desirous to be wisely directed in restoring them to liberty, Friends who may be appointed by Quarterly and Monthly Meetings on the service now proposed, are earnestly desired to give their weighty and solid attention for the assistance of such who are thus honestly and religiously concerned for their own relief and the essential benefit of the negro.

"And in families where there are young ones, or others of

suitable age, that they excite the masters, or those who have
them, to give them sufficient instruction and learning, in order
to qualify them for the liberty intended; and that they be
instructed by themselves, or placed out to such masters and
mistresses who will be careful of their religious education, to
serve for such time, and no longer, as is prescribed by law and
custom, for white people."—(Yearly Meeting.)

The same minute advises against the hiring of slaves, and
serving as executors or administrators to estates where there
are slaves to be disposed of.

1776.—"Under the calming influence of pure love, we do
with great unanimity give it as our sense and judgment, that
Quarterly and Monthly Meetings should still speedily unite in
further close labor with all such as are slaveholders, and have
any right of membership among us; and where any members
continue to reject the advice of their brethren, and refuse to
execute proper instruments of writing, for releasing from a state
of slavery such as are in their power, or on whom they have
any claim, whether arrived at full age or in their minority, and
no hope of the continuance of Friends' labor being profitable
to them, that Monthly Meetings, after having discharged a
Christian duty to such, testify their disunity with them.

"It is recommended that the manumissions already executed,
and such as may hereafter be executed for slaves set at liberty,
should be carefully recorded in a book provided for that purpose, in each Monthly Meeting."—(Yearly Meeting.)

1776.—"The committee on the subject of negroes, &c., now
report, ...   That a considerable number have freely
manumitted their negroes by deeds duly executed, to take effect
immediately, or when they come to a proper age, in the mean
time engaging to take care of their education. And several
show a good disposition to do the like; so that the number who
hold back, and neglect taking the advice of Friends, are com-
paratively small, which gives us an encouraging hope that a
continuance of labor, in the meekness and life of truth, as

ability may be afforded, will in time clear us of holding any of that oppressed people as slaves," &c.—(Burlington Monthly Meeting.)

In this year the Yearly Meeting again made an alteration in the query, to suit the advanced condition of the testimony embraced by it.

1776.—"Are Friends clear of importing, purchasing, disposing of, or holding mankind as slaves; and do they use those well who are set free, and are necessarily under their care, and not in circumstances, through nonage, or incapacity to minister to their own necessities? Are they careful to educate and encourage them in a religious and virtuous life?"—(Yearly Meeting.)

1777.—"Our testimony against slavery appears to grow and afford encouragement; as by accounts brought to this meeting, seventy manumissions have been handed in to the several Monthly Meetings, to be recorded, since last year."—(Thirdhaven Yearly Meeting.)

The Monthly Meeting of Thirdhaven records several manumissions in the years 1777 and 1778,—thus:

S. & M. Roland, . . .	2
Sarah Register, . . .	2
Magdalen Kemp, . . .	2
John Kemp, ...	2
Samuel Harwood, . . .	6
S. Register, ...	3
James Turner, . . .	1
John Jenkinson, . . .	2
Elizabeth Powell, . . .	4
D. Wilson, ...	2
Solomon Neal, . . .	1
James Berry, ...	9—36

and Aaron Parrott and Peter Webb were disowned for refusing to manumit their slaves.—(See Record.)

1778.—"It is recommended to Friends in their several Quarterly and Monthly Meetings, seriously to consider the circumstances of these poor people, and the obligations we are under to discharge our religious duty to them; which, being disinterestedly pursued, will lead the professors of Truth to advise and assist them on all occasions, particularly in promoting their instruction in the principles of the Christian religion, and the pious education of their children; and also to advise them in respect to their engagements in worldly concerns, as occasion offers. And it is desired that Friends of judgment and experience may be nominated for this necessary service; it being the solid sense of this meeting, that we of the present generation are under strong obligations to manifest our concern and care for the offspring of those people, who, by their labor, have greatly contributed towards the cultivation of several of these colonies, under the affecting disadvantages of enduring a hard bondage; and many among us are enjoying the benefit of their toil."—(Yearly Meeting.)

1778.—" Our ancient Friend Joshua Johnson, having lately deposited a sum of money in the hands of Robert Johnson and John Chambers, in trust, for the benefit of the heirs of Sampson, a negro who served him in a state of bondage for several years after he arrived at the age of twenty-one years, for which service a considerable part of the said sum is intended as a compensation,—and as the instrument of writing, executed by the said Joshua Johnson and the said trustees respecting the same, directs that the application thereof is to be with the consent of three or more Friends of this meeting,—Benjamin Mason, Daniel Thompson, and Joshua Pusey, are appointed for that service."—(New Garden Monthly Meeting.)

1779.—" Thomas Wood mentioned to this meeting, that he has felt uneasiness of mind for some time past, concerning the situation of a negro man who was some years ago possessed by his father, and was by him set free, on condition of laying up a small sum yearly, which has arose to a considerable sum, and is now mostly under the care of the said Thomas; which, together with the negro's services after he was twenty-one

years of age, causes the uneasiness. On consideration of the
case, Thomas Woodward, Thomas Millhouse, William Miller,
Ellis Pusey, and John Sharpless, were appointed to advise and
assist in the case, as may appear best for him,—the negro's
benefit,—and the reputation of our religious Society."

Report: . . . "Having carefully inquired into the circumstances, do find that William Wood did, about sixteen years
ago, set free from a state of slavery the said negro, named
Cæsar, on consideration that he would behave himself indus-
triously and honestly, and also that he would lay up or deposit
in his, or some safe hand, the sum of three pounds yearly, that
in case he should be sick or lame, he might not be chargeable
to his said master's estate; and, in consequence of said condition, the said Cæsar has laid up forty-two pounds, which
appears to us to be his just property; and all the heirs of
William Wood who are arrived at full age (except one, who
resides in Virginia) cheerfully agreed to let him have it. But
as the said Cæsar informed us that he had no present necessity or use for the money, he agreed to have it deposited in
the hands of Joshua Pusey, and proposed to advise with him on
any occasion of applying it; with which this meeting is well
satisfied.

"It also further appears that the said Cæsar served his
said master, in the capacity of a slave, more than ten years
after he was twenty-one years of age; and upon a careful inquiry we find that he was tenderly used during the said time,
and nursed in the small-pox, which he had very heavy, and
was long before he recovered; so that we have reason to believe
that it took at least one year to defray the expenses thereof.

"These things the said Cæsar fully acknowledges, and
further informs, that his said master allowed him sundry privileges during said term, whereby he made for himself at least
five pounds a year, besides being well clothed and accommo-
dated. After considering the circumstances of this case, we
are unanimously of the mind that the further sum of five pounds
a year, for the nine years he was in usual health, ought yet to
be allowed him out of said estate, which the heirs, now present

and of age, also agree to.   And it is agreed, with Cæsar's free consent, to be deposited with the other sum.

"Signed on behalf of the committee,

"THOMAS WOODWARD."

(New Garden Monthly Meeting.)

1779.—"Whereas Thomas Williamson, in order to obtain the freedom of a negro woman named Hagar (which he some years ago sold for a slave), did enter bail to the court for thirty pounds, to be paid in case she should become a public charge ; and as there now appears to be sixty pounds of wages due to the woman, he now proposes to keep thirty pounds of the money in his hands, as allowed by the Quarterly Meeting's committee, which this meeting agrees to, in order to secure his bail, if occasion requires it ; and if he hath no occasion to apply it to the use intended in her lifetime, he agrees to pay the said thirty pounds, at her death, to her children, if then living, or the survivors of them : otherwise as she may see cause to dispose of it.   And the remaining thirty-three pounds, the said Thomas agrees to pay to such Friends as the meeting shall appoint to receive it, for the use of said negro woman.   Which proposal, if he comply with, this meeting concludes to accept as full satisfaction in respect to that affair."—(Concord Monthly Meeting.)

Cases analogous to these were not unfrequent in the Monthly Meetings.   The latter case was in the Monthly and Quarterly Meeting for many months before it was thus disposed of.

The following report will illustrate the care and concern of Friends, as recommended by the Yearly Meeting in 1778, relative to the free and liberated negroes.

1779.—"We, the committee of men and women appointed to visit the free negroes as recommended by our last Yearly Meeting, report, that we, in company with part of the Quarterly Meeting's committee appointed for the like purpose, have in our measure pretty closely attended to the service, in visiting all those people within the verge of our meeting (except three

or four single persons, whose circumstances are fully adequate
to their necessities, and they escaped our visit for want of opportunity), and in most places administered such counsel and
advice as we were enabled to communicate, which opportunities
generally afforded us satisfaction; and respecting their temporal circumstances, we have assisted them where we thought
necessary, inspected and settled their accounts, according to the
contract between them and their employers, wherein we
endeavored to do strict justice, and likewise administered
advice therein when necessary. Also, agreeably to the advice
of the Monthly Meeting, we have closely recommended to some
who have large families of children, the necessity of placing
them out, not only for the easement of the parents, but benefit
of themselves, by obtaining a suitable and necessary education.
There appears to be one that requires Friends' assistance in
that respect, the parents being aged and not well able to spare
her, and not of ability to discharge that duty themselves. We
likewise find them, in a general way, able to support themselves
with the necessaries of life, except one woman with two small
children and her husband a slave."—(New Garden Monthly
Meeting.)

The Quarterly Meeting on the Western Shore, reported to
the Yearly Meeting for Maryland, in 1779, that they have received manumissions for fifty-three negroes within the past year.
—(Thirdhaven Yearly Meeting.)

Yet it is a melancholy fact, that very many members residing on the Western Shore suffered themselves to be disowned,
rather than part with their slaves. Few or no Friends now
live in that section of the State of Maryland. The principles
professed and so nobly practised by Friends, are utterly incom-
patible with the practice of slaveholding; they cannot long
subsist together without one or the other gaining the ascendency.
This conclusion is fully sustained by the history of the American Colonies.

The memorable year of 1780 found Friends nearly, if not
entirely clear of slaveholding; while a strong feeling opposed

to the practice pervaded the State, and led the Legislature
to declare :—

1780.—"It is not for us to inquire why, in the creation of
mankind, the inhabitants of the several parts of the earth were
distinguished by a difference in feature or complexion. It is
sufficient to know that all are the work of an Almighty hand.
We find, in the distribution of the human species, that the
most fertile as well as the most barren parts of the earth are
inhabited by men of complexion different from ours, and from
each other ; from whence we may reasonably, as well as religiously infer, that He who placed them in their various situa-
tions hath extended equally his care and protection to all, and
that it becometh not us to counteract His mercies."

1787.—"Recommended to the watchful attention of the
Meeting for Sufferings in particular, and to Friends individually, that no opportunity be lost of urging to those in
power the moral and Christian necessity of suppressing the
cruel traffic in those afflicted people ; and manifesting to the
world the religious ground of our Christian testimony against
this public wickedness."—(Yearly Meeting.)

1790.—"The request of Abington Quarterly Meeting for
the sense of this meeting, whether it is not a breach of our
testimony for a Friend to make a purchase of a slave, and then
manumit him or her, and by agreement take an indenture or
other obligation of servitude, until the purchase-money is paid;
coming under consideration, it appears to be the sense of this
meeting, that such purchase and agreement is contrary to our
testimony against slavery."—(Yearly Meeting.)

Some may call this in question. Considerations of individual benevolence may lead to a different conclusion ; where,
for instance, a slave must be sold, either into interminable
bondage, or where he can thus work out his future freedom.
The choice seems easy. But, when viewed in its general bearing, is not such a purchaser accessory to two wrongs? First,
he pays the assumed owner for that which did not properly

belong to him, thereby encouraging him to pursue the wrong practice further; and, second, he renders himself responsible for the enslavement of the man. The master is changed; the slave is called an apprentice; but his slavery is continued for the stipulated term. The comforts of the individual may be increased; but is not the condition of countless thousands made worse, and their chains more securely riveted?

Ever faithful to the monitions of Divine grace in their own hearts, a Woolman, a Lay, a Benezet, an Evans, and a Hicks, with many others, were not slow to perceive that those who trafficked in and used the produce of the slaves' unrequited labor, were lending their aid to continue the oppression and injustice of slavery; and therefore felt themselves restrained from such traffic and such use. The support of this testimony will yet rest with greater weight upon the faithful members of our religious Society; and the blessing which has attended their past labors, affords an encouraging promise of success in those which are to come. In the year 1837, the Yearly Meeting so far recognized this concern as to recommend its members—

1837.—"To embrace every right opening to maintain and exalt our righteous testimony against slavery. And, where any of our members feel any religious scruples as to the use of the products of slave labor, that they faithfully attend thereto."—(Yearly Meeting.)

1854.—"Our testimony against slavery was impressively brought into view, and Friends were encouraged to increased fidelity in its maintenance. This portentous evil was felt to be like a dark cloud hanging over our beloved country, and we were admonished to seek for Divine aid and guidance in all our efforts in relation thereto. We were reminded that some of the earliest and most efficient laborers in this field of service felt themselves restrained from the use of the produce of slave-labor; and Friends were encouraged to attend to their conscientious scruples in this particular, at the same time bearing in mind that the progress of light is gradual, and hence, we should ever cherish that charity which thinketh no evil, which suffereth long and is kind."—(Yearly Meeting Extracts.)

There is deep instruction in the foregoing narrative. The unfolding of Divine Truth in the mind is a gradual work, dependent upon the degree of obedience rendered to its manifestations; for it will ever remain to be a truth, that they who are faithful in a little shall be made rulers over more. The progress of associated bodies is, however, retarded by causes which do not exist in individual cases. Religious society is necessarily constituted of heterogeneous materials. There are many gifts, but the same spirit; many states of religious experience; many degrees of obedience; while some may altogether refuse to walk in the light with which they have been furnished. The feeble will lag behind and require a helping hand; the doubting will wait for clearer manifestations; the perverse will refuse to move forward. Hence the adage, "heavy bodies move slow," is applicable to them. Yet herein is the beauty and the excellency of religious association. The strong and the confident are willing to wait for, to encourage and assist, the weak, the timid, and the desponding; casting off only those who wholly refuse their proffered assistance. This is beautifully exemplified in the instance before us. It required nearly a century for the Society to eradicate actual slaveholding from its borders. Yet, by long, patient, unremitted labors, and a full reliance upon the blessing of Heaven upon their exertions, the great end was accomplished; while the unity and harmony of the body were preserved, and very few of its members cut off.

Much yet remains to be done, in order effectually to wash our hands from participation in the guilt of slavery. But if it was so difficult for our forefathers to experience an anointing of their eyes, with the eyesalve of the kingdom, so that they could clearly perceive the sinfulness of slaveholding, let us profit by what they suffered, and earnestly seek to have our own vision so purified that we may more easily discern the duty which still rests upon us in this matter. And may the glorious beams of the sun of righteousness penetrate deeper and deeper into the dark recesses of our selfish nature, until we become cleansed from all the contaminations of slavery, and redeemed from every gratification whereby it is encouraged and sustained.

CHAPTER XXVIII.

PRIESTS' RATES—TITHES.

THE great object of William Penn, in settling his American Colony, was to establish and maintain religious and civil liberty among the people; and he was so far successful, as effectually to prevent a church establishment in Pennsylvania. Some of the neighboring colonies were less fortunate. Friends who lived on the Eastern Shore of Maryland, now embraced within the scope of this retrospect, often suffered from this cause, and require a brief notice.

1696.—"William Richardson gives account, and produces receipts, for 1228 pounds of tobacco, taken from him by execution, on account of the priests."—(Yearly Meeting at Third-haven.)

Similar records of that and the next year, show that there was in like manner taken from—

Richard Harrison,	.	.	1261 lbs.
Samuel Thomas, .	.	.	894 "
William Mears, .	.	.	290 "
William Harris, .	.	.	250 "
Robert Gover, .	.	.	560 "
William Richards,	.	.	604 "
George Regstone,	.	.	270 "
Richard Galway,	.	.	160 "

—— 4289 lbs.

Add for Wm. Richardson, as above, 1228 "

—— 6517 lbs.

Those nine Friends would thence have suffered an average annual distraint of 362 lbs. of tobacco. However low the nominal price of tobacco might have been, the high price of money in those days must have rendered this a very onerous tax for preaching, which they did not hear, and could not acknowledge.

1701.—"This meeting having understood that some called Friends receive tobacco that is executed for the priests; and therefore this meeting advises, that for the future, all Friends take due care that they receive no such tobacco."—(Yearly Meeting at Thirdhaven.)

Tobacco being the staple production of that part of the country, was not only most likely to be obtained as tithe, but had even become, in a measure, the circulating medium in business transactions. But their tobacco was not alone subject to execution for tithes, their persons were also liable to the same process.

1738.—"It was proposed from Cecil Monthly Meeting to this meeting, whether a Friend taken in execution for priests' rates, so called, and through the tenderness of the sheriff discharged, may, without breach of our testimony against this antichristian yoke of tithes, pay the officer's fees? It is the sense of this meeting that Friends can no more pay the sheriff, or officer's fees, than the county per poll or priests' dues, so called, it issuing from the same ground and foundation."—(Yearly Meeting at Thirdhaven.)

Nearly related to the payment of priests' rates, is that of acknowledging a man-made and mere educational ministry; for, saith the Apostle, "If any man speak, let him speak as the oracles of God; if any man minister, let him do it as of the ability which God giveth." Friends believe that this "ability" cannot be conferred by mere education, nor in the will of man, now, any more than in the apostolic age, and that without it, all ministrations must be dry and empty forms.

1731.—" Friends of this Monthly Meeting desire the advice of the Quarterly Meeting, concerning such Friends among us who, by going to burials, or otherwise, among those who are not of our Society, do join with them in prayer, by taking off their hats, who, after having been dealt with, refuse to give satisfaction."—(Abington Monthly Meeting.)

CHAPTER XXIX.

GAMES—LOTTERIES—DIVERSIONS.

1705.—"Whereas, T—— H——, at our last meeting, did acknowledge that he was drawn into error by evil company, to play at cards, to the dishonor of Truth; whereupon he brought to this meeting a paper of condemnation, to clear Truth of the same; which was accepted."—(Falls Monthly Meeting.)

1716.—"Advised, that care be taken to prevent Friends' children, and all professing Truth, from going to or being any way concerned in plays, games, lotteries, music, and dancing."—(Yearly Meeting.)

1719.—"Advised, that such be dealt with as run races, either on horseback or on foot, lay wagers, or use any gaming or needless and vain sports and pastimes; for our time swiftly passeth away, and our pleasure and delight ought to be in the law of the Lord."—(Yearly Meeting.)

1725.—" N—— H—— hath given in a paper condemning himself for his playing at cards; which paper the meeting receives, and orders him to read the said paper in the place where he was playing, in the presence of Benjamin Fredd and William Halliday; . . . and he is desired to forbear coming to meetings of business until Friends are better satisfied with him as to conversation and sincerity to Truth."—(New Garden Monthly Meeting.)

The card-playing was in a public-house.

1729.—"Nottingham Preparative Meeting acquaints this meeting that R—— K——, son of A—— K——, was wrestling for a wager, which he seems to evade; so this meeting appoints," &c.—(New Garden Monthly Meeting.)

1735.—"In answer to that part of the report from Chester Quarterly Meeting relating to lotteries, this meeting is of opinion that Friends should be careful not to engage in anything of that kind."—(Yearly Meeting.)

The sagacity of William Penn very early led him to interdict all theatrical exhibitions within his Province, "as tending to looseness and immorality." But in the year

1749, "The Recorder of the City reported to the Common Council that certain persons had lately taken upon them to act plays in the city, &c., which, it was to be feared, would be attended with very mischievous effects,—such as the encouragement of idleness, and drawing great sums of money from weak and inconsiderate persons, who are apt to be fond of such kind of entertainment, though the performance be ever so mean and contemptible; whereupon the Board unanimously requested the magistrates to take the most effectual means for suppressing this disorder, by sending for the actors and binding them for their good behavior."—(Watson's Annals, p. 408.)

1754.—"The Common Council, not then under the control of Friends, gave the actors license 'to act a few plays,' provided 'nothing indecent or immoral was offered.' "—(Bowden, II, p. 287.)

1759.—"They then came in the month of July to a theatre, prepared in the year before, at the southwest corner of Vernon and South Streets, called the Theatre on Society Hill. It was there placed, on the south side of the city bounds, so as to be out of the reach of city control."—(Watson, p. 409.)

1762.—Complaint was made against "W—— T——, Jr., for misconduct, such as accompanying fiddlers and dancers." —(Concord Monthly Meeting.)

1763.—Complaint made against "R—— L——, for neglect-

ing to attend meetings and frequenting a dancing-school."—
(Wilmington Monthly Meeting.)

1773.—" It being observed that a number of lotteries have
been set up for some time past, and desire of gain in this way
being contrary to our religious profession and unjustifiable;
and, from some of the accounts now received, there is cause to
apprehend that some professing with us have been drawn to
countenance and encourage this unjust and dishonorable practice, Monthly Meetings are desired to labor to maintain our
testimony against it, by advising and admonishing any who
may be in danger of being ensnared by such temptations; and
where any persist either to promote or encourage such means
of obtaining unjust gain, that they endeavor to bring them to
a due sense of their error; but if they cannot prevail with
them to acknowledge and condemn it, the testimony of Truth
should be maintained against them."—(Yearly Meeting.)

1778.—Complaint was made against " E—— S—— and
S—— S——, for deviating from plainness in dress and language, and frequenting places of music and dancing, and
joining therein themselves."—(Wilmington Monthly Meeting.)

1784.—In a remonstrance which Friends presented to the
General Assembly this year, they say:—

" We are informed that a company of stage-players have
lately, in a petition to the House, prayed your patronage, by
a repeal of the law against their pernicious entertainments.
. . . . That we may not be wanting in so obvious a duty to
our families, to our fellow-citizens, and to you in whom so
important a trust is reposed, we take the liberty to represent
our alarming apprehensions of the imminent danger attending,
and the unhappy effects there is reason to dread from, your
compliance with the prayer of the said petition; whereby the
sanction of legislative authority may be given to that torrent
of vice and irreligion, which abundant experience evinces to be
the invariable attendant of those delusive diversions. . . . We
are earnestly solicitous that you would seriously and impartially examine the reasons which operated with your predecessors to enact the law in question, and duly and wisely inquire

what just cause can have arisen, from a variation of circumstances, to induce its repeal. . . . .

"Distinguished as you are by your station, as delegated
guardians of the public welfare, we fervently desire you may
be so favored with the spirit of sound wisdom as clearly to
discern, and firmly to adhere to, the essential interests of the
people, as founded in, and inseparably dependent on true
religion."

The law was probably repealed, notwithstanding this cogent
remonstrance, for in 1793 the theatre in Chestnut Street was
erected.

If the theatrical amusements of that day were so objectionable, what shall we say of those of modern date. The
modest and the virtuous may attend them, but they must soon
lose both their modesty and virtue, or abandon the practice.
Notwithstanding these, their principal support is from a different
class. Disguise the fact as we may, the comedy is low buf-
foonery, without rationality; the tragedy is love and murder
in their most repulsive forms, without any redeeming quality:
they are both incentives to licentiousness. While they stimu-
late, they also teach the foul arts of the seducer, and lead their
votaries down to the grog-shop, and often the brothel, both of
which stand near with open doors to receive them.

CHAPTER XXX.

SORCERY.

1695.—"Whereas this meeting being acquainted (see Concord Monthly Meeting Record for ninth month, 1695) that some
persons under the profession of Truth, and belonging to this
meeting, who, professing the art of astrology, have undertaken
thereby to give answers and astrological judgments concerning

persons and things, tending to the dishonor of God and the reproach of Truth, and the great hurt both of themselves and those
who so come to inquire of them : And whereas it is reported,
that some professing Truth among us seem too much inclined
to use rhabdomancy, or consulting with a staff, and such like
things ; all which have brought a weighty exercise and concern upon this meeting, as well because of the reproach
already brought upon the Truth thereby ; as also to prevent,
as much as in us lies, its being further reproached by any
among us that may attempt to follow the like practices for
time to come :

"Now, therefore, being met together in the fear of the Lord,
to consider not only the affairs of Truth in the general, but
also that it may be kept clear of all scandal and reproach by
all that profess it in the particular ; as also, to recover, if possible, any who, for want of diligence and watchfulness therein,
have not only brought reproach thereto, but have also hurt
their own souls, darkened their own understandings, hindered
themselves as to their inward exercise and spiritual travel
towards the land of rest and peace ; which, as we all come in
a measure to be possessed of, shall feel great satisfaction and
sweet content in our condition, as God by his good hand of
providence shall be pleased to order it. Whether we have
much of this world or not ; whether we get of it or not ;
whether we lose or not lose, every one being in his place,
using his or her honest and Christian endeavors ; we shall be
content with the success of our labors without such unlawful
looking of what the event of this or that or the other thing
may be ; by running to inquire of the astrologers, magicians,
soothsayers, star-gazers, or monthly prognosticators, which of
old could not tell their own events (neither can they at this
day). For we read, that when God pronounced his judgments.
against Babylon and Chaldea, how the prophet in the zeal of
the Lord called upon such men in a contemptuous manner,
saying, ' Evil hath come upon thee, thou shalt not know from
where it riseth.' ' And,' said he, ' let now the astrologers and
star-gazers, and monthly prognosticators stand up and save

thee from these things that shall come upon thee.' 'Behold,' said he, 'they shall be as stubble, they shall not deliver themselves,' &c.

"And further, we may read how the Lord strictly commanded His people, saying, 'There shall not be found among you any that useth divination, or an observer of times, or an enchanter, or a witch, or a charmer, or a consulter of familiar spirits, or a wizard, or a necromancer; for all that do these things are an abomination to the Lord.' So that, upon the whole, we do declare against all the aforesaid or any such like practices; and do exhort all, not only to forbear practising any of those things themselves, but also that they discountenance the practice thereof in all those whomsoever it doth appear; and, forasmuch as we understand that those among us that incline to those things are chiefly some youths, who, being unacquainted with the enemy's mysterious workings and devices, whereby he allures their minds to seek and aspire after such knowledge, which, when they have attained all they can, is at best but uncertain and failable, as they themselves confess, and therefore is but knowledge falsely so called; we do, therefore, in the fear of God, caution, warn, and exhort all parents, who, if at any time they see, or otherwise understand, their children do practice, or are inclined to practice any of those things, that speedily thereupon they use their utmost endeavors, not only like Eli of old, to forewarn them, but also to restrain them. And further, it is the sincere and Christian advice of this meeting that, when any among us have been found acting in any of those things, that Friends of the particular Monthly Meeting where such dwell, do use their utmost endeavors, in the way and order of the Gospel practised among us, to bring such person or persons to a sense of their wrong practices therein; and that they do, for the clearing of Truth, and also for the good of their own souls, condemn what they have already done as to these things; and that, for time to come, they lay them aside, and practise them no more.

"And also, that they bring in all books that relate to those things to the Monthly Meeting they belong to, to be disposed of as Friends shall think fit; and, if any shall refuse to comply with such their wholesome and Christian advice, that then the Friends of the said respective Monthly Meetings do give testimony against them; and so Truth will stand over them, and Friends will be clear.

"Let this be read in all Monthly Meetings, and at all such First-Day Meetings where and as often as the Friends of the respective Monthly Meetings do see service for it."—(Concord Quarterly Meeting.)

I have not found that the Yearly Meeting had issued any disciplinary advice relating to this matter; hence the Quarterly Meeting felt constrained to take action in the premises. It was not until twenty-eight years after that the following minute was issued:—

1723.—"It is the sense and judgment of this meeting that, if any professing Truth, shall apply to such person or persons as, by color of any art or skill whatsoever, do or shall pretend knowledge to discover things hiddenly transacted, or tell where things lost or stolen may be found; or if any, under our profession, do or pretend to any such act or skill, we do hereby, in just abhorrence of such doings, direct that the offenders be speedily dealt with and brought under censure."—(Yearly Meeting.)

1738.—"J—— T—— offered an acknowledgment for his disorderly marriage; 'and for going to a man to be informed concerning my horse. I can truly say I had no desire he should make use of any bad art in that affair; and, if he could not tell me anything by his learning in an honest way, to go no further. Likewise was ignorant of Friends' rules in that affair; but, being since better informed, hope, for the future, not to fall into the like again.' "—(Concord Monthly Meeting.)

This was another case wherein the want of learning was not the only deficiency to be lamented.

CHAPTER XXXI.

THOSE who are familiar with the cruel sufferings which early Friends endured in England, even unto death, because they could not conscientiously render the homage of taking off the hat to those who arrogated to themselves the right to demand it, can properly appreciate the sagacity and foresight of William Penn in providing against the like occurrences in Pennsylvania. This was done in a code of laws prepared in England, and enacted by the first Assembly, which was called at the house of Robert Wade, in Upland (now Chester), soon after the landing of the proprietor at that place, in 1682.

In the year 1720, Governor Keith instituted a Court of Chancery, he being Chancellor by virtue of his office. In this new position he seems to have forgotten the law above referred to.

1725.—"At this court, in which Sir William Keith was President, John Kinsey, who was a Quaker and a lawyer of eminence, who was afterwards Chief Justice of Pennsylvania, was, in the year 1725, obliged, in the way of his business, to attend; where, appearing with his hat on his head, according to the usual manner of that people, the President ordered it to be taken off, which was accordingly done."—(Praud, II, 197.)

This arbitrary proceeding called forth

"The humble address of the people called Quakers, by appointment of their Quarterly Meeting, held in Philadelphia, for the city and county, 2d of second month, 1725:—

"'May it please the Governor: Having maturely considered the inconveniences and hardships which, we are apprehensive, all those of our community may be laid under who shall be obliged or required to attend the respective courts of judicature

in this province, if they may not be admitted without first
having their hats taken off from their heads by an officer, as
we understand was the case of our friend John Kinsey, when
the Governor was pleased to command his to be taken off, before
he could be admitted to speak in a case depending in a Court
of Chancery, after that he had declared that he could not, for
conscience, comply with the Governor's order to himself to the
same purpose; which, being altogether new and unprecedented
in this province, was the more surprising to the spectators,
and, as we conceive (however slight some may account it), has
a tendency to the subversion of our religious liberties.

" ' This province, with the powers of government, was granted
by King Charles the Second to our proprietor, who, at the time
of the said grant, was known to dissent from the national way
of worship in divers points, and particularly in that of outward
behavior, of refusing to pay unto man the honors that he, with
all others of the same profession, believe only to be due to the
Supreme Being; and they have, on all occasions, supported
their testimony, so far as to be frequently subjected to the
insults of such as required that homage.

" ' That the principal part of those who accompanied our
said proprietor in his first settlement of this colony, with others
of the same profession, who have since retired into it, justly
conceived that, by virtue of said powers granted to our proprietor, they should have a free and unquestioned right to the
exercise of their religious principles, and their persuasion in
the aforementioned points and all others, by which they were
distinguished from those of all other professions. And it seems
not unreasonable to conceive an indulgence intended by the
Crown, in graciously leaving the government to him and them
in such manner as may best suit their circumstances; which
appears to have been an early care in the first legislators, by
several acts, as that of Liberty of Conscience, and more particularly by a law of the province, passed in the thirteenth year
of King William, Chapter xcii, now in force. It is provided,
' That in all courts, all persons, of all persuasions, may freely
appear in their own way, and according to their own manner.

24

and there personally plead their own cause, or, if unable, by
their friends;' which provision appears to be directly intended
to guard against all exceptions to any person appearing in their
own way, as our friend at the aforesaid court.

" 'Now, though no people can be more ready and willing, in
all things essential, to pay all due regard to superiors, and
honor the courts of justice, and those who administer them,
yet, in such points as interfere with our conscientious persuasion, we have openly and firmly borne our testimony in all
countries and places where our lots have fallen.

" 'We must, therefore, crave leave to hope, from the reasons
here humbly offered, that the Governor, when he fully considers
them, will be of opinion with us, that we may justly and
modestly claim it as a right, that we and our friends should,
at all times, be excused in the government from any compli-
ances against our conscientious persuasions; and humbly request that he would, in future, account it so to us, thy assured.
well-wishing friends.

" ' Signed by appointment of the said meeting,

"'JOHN GOODSON,　　　　"'RICHARD HILL,
"'ROWLAND ELLIS,　　　 "'RICHARD HAYES,
"'REECE THOMAS,　　　　"'MORRIS MORRIS,
"'SAMUEL PRESTON,　　　"'ANTHONY MORRIS,
"'WILLIAM HUDSON,　　　"'EVAN EVANS.'"

" 'On consideration had of the humble address presented,
this day read in open court, from the Quarterly Meeting of
the people called Quakers, for the city and county of Philadelphia; it is ordered, that the address be filed with the Register,
and that it be made a standing rule of the Court of Chancery
for the Province of Pennsylvania, for all time to come, that
any practitioner of the law, or other officer or person, whatsoever,
professing himself to be one of the people called Quakers, may,
and shall be admitted, if they so think fit, to speak or otherwise officiate or apply themselves decently unto the said Court,
without being obliged to observe the usual ceremony of uncov-
ering their heads, by having their hats taken off.　And such

privilege, hereby ordered and granted to the people called Quakers, shall at no time hereafter be understood or interpreted as any contempt or neglect of said Court; and shall be taken only as an act of conscientious liberty, of right appertaining to the religious persuasion of the said people, and agreeable to their practice in all civil affairs of life.

"' By Sir WILLIAM KEITH,

"' *Chancellor.*' "

Much credit is due to Governor Keith for thus respecting the rights of conscience and promptly responding to the remonstrance of Friends. It is, moreover, a keen rebuke upon those of our profession who manifest their inconsistency by taking off their hats upon such occasions. The following story conveys a moral :—

"The Governor of Virginia wanted a cooper to mend his wine-casks, and some told him there was a workman near, but he was a Quaker. He said, if he was a workman, he made no matter what he professed. So the Quaker, such as he was, was sent for, and came with his hat under his arm. The Governor was somewhat at a stand to see the man come in after that manner, and asked if he was the cooper he had sent for ? He said, 'Yes.' 'Well,' said the Governor, 'are you not a Quaker?' 'Yes,' replied the man, 'I am so called, but I have not been faithful.' He then asked how long he had been called a Quaker? The poor man said, about twenty years. 'Alas for you, poor man,' said the Governor, 'I am sorry for you.'"—(John Richardson's Journal, p. 148.)

1800.—"Reported from the Preparative Meeting, that John Mears, in acting as a justice of the peace (with other misdemeanors), hath so far deviated from the testimony Truth led our predecessors to bear against formal compliments and ceremonies, as to command a man to put off his hat when he came before him."—(Catawissa Monthly Meeting.)

It would be well for Quakers who have not been faithful, to consider how often they are exposed to the rebuke of the Governor of Virginia, "Alas for you, poor man, I am sorry for you."

CHAPTER XXXII.

SUFFERINGS.

1706.—"It was ordered by this meeting, that there should be persons appointed out of each Particular Meeting belonging to this meeting, to speak to every Friend belonging to their respective meetings, to bring in an account to the next Monthly Meeting, of the goods strained from them for refusing to pay to the upholding of the militia."—(Burlington Monthly Meeting.)

1709.—"It being moved at this meeting, that all Friends within the limits thereof, from their several Quarterly Meetings, bring in an account of all Friends' sufferings, that have been or may happen among them, for the testimony of Truth, that it may be done yearly. Unto which the meeting agrees, and recommends the care thereof to the several Quarterly Meetings."—(Yearly Meeting.)

It has already been mentioned that the Canadian and Indian War, which took place about the middle of the last century, did much to create a military feeling among the people, and, from a mistaken view of the relations which Friends continued to maintain with the Indians, subjected them to much unmerited suspicion and censure.

The difficulties referred to were only the prelude to greater. The political commotions tending to the war of the Revolution soon began, with the multiform evils which followed in their train.

In the fifth month, 1777, the Western Quarterly Meeting, which was then composed of Kennet, New Garden, Nottingham, Bradford, Sadsbury, Deer Creek, and Duck Creek Monthly Meetings, issued the following minute of advice to its constituent branches.

1777.—"Under consideration of the present prospect of the sufferings of Friends for the testimony of Truth against wars and fightings, it is apprehended it may be of service, and therefore we recommend it to each Monthly Meeting, to appoint a number of suitable Friends, to have under their care and consideration suffering cases within the compass of the meetings they belong to, and be ready (if there is occasion) to advise or assist their brethren under sufferings or difficulty, on account of their faithfulness in maintaining the testimony of Truth. And such committees are desired to keep regular minutes of their proceedings, and also endeavor to preserve and transmit a faithful account of all such sufferings, agreeably to the advice of the Yearly Meeting."—(Western Quarterly Meeting.)

1777.—"Which being considered, Isaac Jackson, Thomas Millhouse, Daniel Thompson, William Swayne, Joel Bailey, and Joshua Pusey were appointed for that service."—(New Garden Monthly Meeting.)

The minutes of the committee just named are now before me, with many of the vouchers for the statements which they contain, up to the early part of the year 1782. Each of the other Monthly Meetings made a similar appointment. It is probable that a simultaneous action was taken by the Quarterly and Monthly Meetings throughout the Yearly Meeting, for in the ninth month of the following year, 1778, that body issued the following minute :—

1778.—"We think it expedient to recommend to the committees appointed in the several Monthly Meetings to assist in suffering cases, pursuant to the advice of the Yearly Meeting, with other faithful Friends, speedily to appoint a solid meeting or meetings of conference with each other in the several quarters in which the grounds of our principles on this head may be opened, and our objections to complying with those laws fully explained, and a united concern maintained to strengthen each other in the way of Truth and righteousness :

and to warn and caution, in the spirit of love and meekness, those who may be in danger of deviating."—(Yearly Meeting.)

Pursuant to this advice, the committees of the seven Monthly Meetings, and a large committee of the Quarterly Meeting, agreed to meet and hold a conference, as recommended, once a month.

The minutes of this conference from second month, 1779, up to fifth month, 1787, a period of more than eight years, are also before me.

From these authentic and interesting documents much curious and valuable matter may be gleaned.

While the records preserved by the committees of the several Monthly Meetings furnish the details of individual suffering, those of the conference afford a more summary account of the whole within the wider sphere of its operations. Special attention is invited to the means employed to make the officers of government acquainted with the true position which Friends occupied in that perilous period.

The following accounts of seizures of the property of Friends on account of military demands, are taken from the Minutes of the Committee on Sufferings of New Garden Monthly Meeting:—

1777.—"A person, called Captain William Crispin, and three other men with him, came from Philadelphia, in order to procure blankets for the soldiers, and took from Friends as follows, viz.:

"From	Jonathan Lindley,	1	coverlet,	.	.	£1	10s. 0d.
"	Joseph Moore,	1	blanket,	.	.	0	12 0
"	David Moore,	1	"	.	.	0	15 0
"	Jacob Halliday,	1	"	.	.	1	0 0
"	John Jackson,	1	"	.	.	0	17 6
"	Thomas Millhouse,	1	"	.	.	0	15 0
"	Isaac Jackson,	2	"	.	.	1	13 0
"	William Miller,	2	"	.	.	1	4 0
"	George Mason,	1	"	.	.	0	14 0

From Francis Lamborn,	1 blanket,	.	.	£0 14s.	0d.
" Jacob Wood,	1 "	.	.	0 15	0
" Thomas Wood,	1 "	.	.	0 15	0
" Stephen Cook,	2 "	.	.	1 10	0
" David Harlan,	1 "	.	.	0 7	6
" Francis Wilkinson,	1 "	.	.	0 15	0
" Joshua Pusey,	2 "	.	.	0 15	0
	18			£24 12	0

"They also took from Joshua Sharpless one blanket, worth 10s., and left money with his son, a lad; but Joshua afterwards sent the money to them.

"They also took from John Elliot one blanket, worth 15s., and through persuasion, he took pay for it; but some time after, being uneasy in his mind, he returned the money.

"The aforesaid men also got one blanket from Thomas Hutton (his wife consenting thereto), worth 7s. 6d., and left money; but Thomas, being uneasy, returned the pay.

"And Benjamin Hutton let them have two blankets, worth £1 10s.; and James Pyle one blanket, worth £1; but they both grew uneasy in mind, and returned the money.

"The same men also came to the house of Joseph Hobson, he being from home, and took two blankets; in which his wife Elizabeth stood faithful, refusing pay for them."

"The old Assembly of the Province of Pennsylvania, having passed a resolve imposing a fine on such of the inhabitants as should not attend on certain days to learn the military exercise; on which account, in the eighth and ninth months, 1777, John Hindman, accompanied by several armed men, took from Friends in London Grove Township as follows, viz.:

"From Joseph Moore, a saddle and great coat,	£5 17s. 0d.		
" Jacob Halliday, wearing apparel.			
" Richard Flower, horse and bridle, .	.	24 00	0
" John Jackson, blankets,	.	2 10	0
" Thomas Millhouse, blankets, .	.	2 10	0
" Samuel Sharp, two coverlets, one blanket,	4 10	0
" Joseph Taylor, side-saddle, bridle, boots,	8 00	0

"From Moses Starr, hat, silk handkerchief, . £1 10s. 0d.
" David Moore, mare, ... 25 00 0
" James Lindley, buckskins, . . . 5 10 0
" John Cain, two hats, one blanket, . . 2 10 0
" John Pusey, coverlet, pair of sheets, . 1 15 0
" Ephraim Wilson, ten yards of linen, . 1 10 0
" Francis Wilkinson, coverlet and pair sheets, 2 15 0
" William Allen, coverlet and pair sheets, 2 12 6
" Thomas Wilkinson, coverlet, blanket, sheet, 2 13 4
" Stephen Cook, cash, &c. (acc't refused), 7 00 2
" Joshua Pusey, coverlet and sheet, . . 1 16 0
" Thomas Wood, horse and blind-bridle, . 20 3 9
" Josiah Lamborn, coverlet, pair blankets, 3 00 0
" George Passmore, money o×t of pocket-
        book, ... 3 10 0
N.B. We have since understood this was Con-
gress money, and, therefore, not to be taken ac-
count of.*
" From Samuel Jackson, riding-coat and blanket, 3 10 0
" Joseph Richardson, coverlet, blanket, sheet, 2 15 0
" Thomas Lamborn, " two " " 3 16 0
" Henry Hayes, quilt, • " " 3 15 0
" Francis Lamborn, coverlet and sheet, 1 10 0
" William Chandler, coverlet and blanket, 2 10 0
" Jacob Wood, a horse, ... 20 00 0

                              £163   7s. 3d.

1778.—"In the beginning of the year 1777, the new Assembly passed an act entitled, 'An Act to Regulate the Militia
of the Commonwealth of Pennsylvania;' directing that all the
men between the ages of eighteen and fifty-three, should be
enrolled as soldiers, and go out to war by turns, two months
at a time ; and if any one should refuse to go or send a man

---

* This account is crossed in the manner I have given it, and the N.B.
is an interlineation. The "Congress money," so called, was expressly for
the purposes of the war, and, as such, conscientious Friends could not consistently use it. Hence it was rejected from the account.

in his stead, it was enacted that certain officers should hire a
substitute in his room, and seize upon his effects to pay said
substitute ; on which account was taken from Friends as follows, viz. :—

James Dunn, and several men with him, took—

From Joshua Baily, a colt, worth	£20	0s.	0d.
" Thomas Passmore, a colt, worth	20	0	0
" Isaac Baily, a colt, "	20	0	0
" Aaron Baker, horse, "	15	0	0

—— McClelland and others, took—

From John Passmore, mare, bridle, &c.,	31	1	0

Thomas Irwin took—

From Ellis Pusey, colt and two heifers,	26	0	0

Henry McClelland, and others, took—

From George Harlan, two mares and blanket,	30	16	0

Samuel McClelland, George Copeland, James
McCarlin, and others, with muskets and other
arms, took—

From Joseph Pyle, a horse, bridle, &c.,	19	5	0
" Thomas Jackson, mare and blanket,	31	5	0
" Caleb Jackson, two cows, ten sheep, &c.,	19	0	0
" Caleb Hurford, horse and bridle,	30	0	0
" Caleb Johnson, mare and blanket,	28	15	0
" John Jackson, Jr., yoke of oxen, two cows, &c.,	24	12	0
" Caleb Swayne, young mare,	30	0	0
" Jonathan Chalfant, watch and blanket,	9	0	0
" " " for a balance, bull,	5	0	0
" Edward Hoin, mare and bridle,	30	4	0

1778.—"Robert McGomery, by orders from
Thomas Strawbridge, took—

From James Way, a horse and mare,	37	0	0
" Thomas Millhouse, colt and bridle,	20	0	0
" Thomas Wood, a mare,	16	0	0
" Jacob Wood, a horse,	22	0	0
" John Wickersham, a mare,	20	0	0
" George Passmore, a mare,	23	0	0
" Lewis Pusey, a horse,	28	0	0

From John Pusey, a mare,	£30	0s. 0d.
" Joshua Pusey, a mare,	24	0 0
" Francis Lamborn, a horse,	12	0 0
" Thomas Lamborn, a mare,	25	0 0
" Josiah Lamborn, horse and 20 bus. corn,	12	0 0
" Joseph Richardson, mare,	25	0 0
" Stephen Cook, mare and colt,	18	0 0
" Samuel Jackson, two horses, gear, &c.,	36	5 0
" Francis Wilkinson, mare,	20	0 0
" Samuel Sharp, yoke of oxen,	28	0 0
" Richard Flower, horse, wagon, &c.,	32	0 0
" Rumford Dawes, mare,	20	0 0
" William Allen, 40 bushels wheat, 6s.,	12	0 0
" Jacob Halliday, mare,	15	0 0

By an order from Andrew Boyd, John Sharp took—

From Joshua Edwards, a horse and bridle,	15	5 0

And by orders from said Boyd, James Dunn took—

From Joel Baily, mare and cow,	32	0 0
" David Windle, mare,	28	0 0
" Samuel Swayne, horse and three cattle,	29	0 0
" Caleb Pennock, horse,	25	0 0
" William Windle, two cows and three cattle,	18	0 0
" Caleb Johnson (a balance), two cows,	15	0 0
" Isaac Pyle, one heifer and eight sheep,	11	0 0
" William Baily, twenty-one yards linen,	2	12 6
" Elisha Baily, cart, and watch,	11	0 0

And by an order from said Boyd, was taken by
  Francis Ruth—

From Isaac Woodraw, mare and bridle,	28	0 0
" Caleb Pusey, young mare,	26	0 0
And for a fine for Moses Windle, six young cattle,	22	0 0
From Aaron Baker, Jr., feather-bed,	6	0 0
" Joseph Pyle, three cows,	19	10 0
" Jeremiah Barnard, one fat steer, being for a fine charged on his nephew of the same name,	9	11 0

£1130   8s. 6d.

"N.B.—The demands on account of the above were from about £22 to about £50; but it was difficult for Friends to ascertain them exactly;—the persons who collected them, in several instances demanding considerable more from the same person at one time than another, for the same fine. And, though the value here set down to the effects taken, may appear lower than the demand, they being here valued at moderate prices, as they might have sold for several years ago. But goods being now got to an extravagant price, occasioned by the very large quantities and small credit of paper currency issued for carrying on the present war, it is likely these mostly sold for as much as the demand; and some, as we have been informed, for much more."

1779.—"A concern being revived that our brethren in profession may be preserved from complying with the payment of taxes, or other requisitions for the support of war, it is agreed that the members of this committee may, in each branch of the meeting, divide into suitable companies, and visit all belonging to our Monthly Meeting, whom they apprehend to be in any danger of being taken in these snares, in order for their encouragement to faithfulness."

Having completed the extracts from the minutes of New Garden Monthly Meeting's Committee on Sufferings, it will be necessary to go back a little, to commence with those of the Conference of Committees, already mentioned. The first minute in our possession is,—

1779.—"At a Meeting for Conference, held the 1st of second month, 1779, present fifteen Friends appointed by the Quarterly Meeting, and thirty-two by the Monthly Meetings; also our friend Thomas Carleton.

"The Friends appointed to visit some officers or persons concerned in levying fines, &c., have all attended to the service, and produced a report, viz. :—

"Agreeable with the intention of our appointment, we have conferred together, and, dividing into several companies, proceeded to visit Robert Smith, called sheriff and lieutenant of the county; Andrew Boyd and Robert Wilson, sub-lieutenants; John Evans, one of the judges; Evan Evans and John Hammons, magistrates,—all in this county; and, in the county of Newcastle, Evan Reese and James Black, magistrates; and James Boggs, collector; and had opportunity of laying before them the reasons and grounds of our refusal to comply with several requisitions, made for the support of, or that have near connection with, war; and to open our principles, and the consistency thereof with the doctrines of the Gospel, as set forth in the New Testament and pointed out by the prophets, and the inconsistency of Christians oppressing one another for conscience sake.

"They generally appeared friendly, and to receive our visit kindly, some of them particularly so; and most of them acknowledged that the prophecies concerning the disuse of carnal weapons, pointed to the Gospel dispensation, and was much to be desired.

"We had good satisfaction in the performance of this service, believing truth owned it, and that there is encouragement for Friends to use further endeavors of this kind. Signed, on behalf of the committee, by—

"THOMAS PIMM."

"The committee is continued to the service, and Abraham Gibbons, William Downing, Joseph England, Elisha Brown, and Jacob Starr, added."

"And, as there are collectors in many townships or hundreds, now employed to collect taxes that are for the support of or that have near connection with war, it is desired that the committees in suffering cases, in each Monthly Meeting, would take this matter under their solid consideration, and if way should open, visit those collectors, and lay before them the reasons why we cannot comply with demands of such a nature."

Third month, 1779.—"Several of us, since last meeting, have visited Sketchly Morton and Daniel Lloyd, commissioners in this county, in which opportunities, way opened for their

information, agreeably to our report to last meeting. We had
good satisfaction in visiting them, and have reason to hope it
may be of some service to the visited. They manifested, by
their conduct and disposition, some regard to, and sense of, our
visit, and expressed satisfaction therewith."

" Our friends, Thomas Lightfoot, Joshua Baldwin, William
Marshall, and Samuel Trimble, attended this meeting by
appointment, from the committee in suffering cases belonging to
Chester Quarter, in order to confer with us in the above concern,
who are desired to join with said committee in considering of
the concern."

" The committee is continued, and Joseph Husbands, William
Cole, Jr., and John Cowgill, added, to use further endeavors as
way may open."

Fourth month, 1779.—" Several of us have been engaged,
since last meeting, in the service we were appointed to, and
have visited, in Newcastle County, George Evans, called
lieutenant of the county; George Craighead, magistrate; John
Strawbridge, sheriff of Cecil County, Maryland; and in Chester
County, Lewis Gronaw, lieutenant; William Evans, James
Moore, Robert Smith, and Philip Scott, magistrates; and had
full and satisfactory opportunities with most of them, . . .
which all of them, except two, seemed to receive kindly," &c.

As the service appeared to be nearly gone through, the committee was now released, yet special committees were appointed,
from time to time, as occasion required. In this way were
subsequently visited, Thomas Clarke, commissioner; Moses
Erwins, Patrick Ewin, Patterson Bell, magistrates; —— ——?
sheriff of Hartford County, Maryland; John Marshall, sub-
lieutenant; Daniel Mackey, sheriff; and Andrew Boyd, commissioner.

Eighth month, 1779.—" Present, fifteen Friends appointed
by the Quarterly Meeting, and forty-one by the Monthly
Meetings."

"A concern having often arisen in this committee, and [being]

livingly reviewed at this time, that Friends might exert themselves in laboring to have their brethren convinced of the
pernicious consequences of continuing to circulate the Continental currency, so called, it being calculated to promote
measures repugnant to the peaceable principles we profess to be
led by, and having [as we believe] greatly increased our sufferings, and brought dimness over many, by continuing in the use
thereof; it is therefore agreed to mention it to the Quarterly
Meeting for consideration."

Friends had strong reasons for objecting to the use of this
Continental money.

The creation by law of a circulating medium of fictitious
value, for the purpose of a gradual depreciation, cannot be
reconciled with truth and justice, however necessity may seem
to require it. To say to the people you shall pass this paper
for a certain nominal value to-day, but only at a less value to-
morrow, and still less the day following, till it becomes entirely
valueless, is a repudiation of a contract,—a refusal to pay a debt
by the Government. As a substitute for taxation, its operation
is extremely unequal, and therefore to the same degree unjust.
Viewed in this light, it was strictly a requisition for carrying
on the war, which Friends could not consistently pay.

First month, 1780.—"Mention being now made that David
Mackey (called high-sheriff of this county) is likely to be
instrumental in distressing Friends for conscientiously refusing
to serve as assessors, or collectors of the taxes for military
uses; in order that the nature of such unrighteous proceedings
may be weightily laid before him, a freedom arose at this time
to appoint Abraham Gibbons, Jacob Lindley, Richard Barnard,
Benjamin Mason, and Thomas Millhouse, to endeavor to discharge a Christian duty to him, and labor according to ability
given, to convince him of the inconsistency of such conduct
with the Gospel spirit."

For four consecutive months the committee made report that

"they have endeavored to comply therewith, but have not succeeded." But in the—

Sixth month, 1780.—"They had a full and solid opportunity
with him, and endeavored to lay before him the inconsistency
of his conduct in the execution of his office, with the spirit of
Christianity, and to open the nature and consistency of our
principles with the peaceable kingdom of Christ."

"Friends from Nottingham inform that a number of their
members are summoned to appear at a court at Cecil. In order
that the testimony of Truth may not suffer thereby, William
Swayne, Joseph Husbands, John Truman, John Way, Amos
Davis, William Mode, and Joseph Richardson, are appointed
to attend, with the committee of that Monthly Meeting, in a
solid opportunity with those Friends, and to give them such
advice (or otherwise assist them) as best wisdom may direct."

The precise character of the summons does not appear from
the record, but was probably some illegal or irregular process
issued to coerce or intimidate Friends to a compliance with
military requisitions.

"They mostly attended, and gave such advice as they were
then favored with, which appeared to be well received.

"As there appears some deficiency in collecting suffering
cases, the sense of Friends being expressed thereon, it appears
to be the mind of this meeting, that the committees, or some
of them, in taking accounts, should visit each family, in order
to inspect into the nature of their sufferings, and to excite
them to faithfulness therein."

1780.—"Joshua Pusey, Jacob Lindley, Joseph Richardson,
and Thomas Millhouse, are appointed to visit William Whiteside, who hath been active in taking Friends' property for demands of taxes for purposes of war, and inform him of the
grounds of our refusal; and, as they may be enabled, lay the
weight of the testimony upon him." They reported, "That
three of them had a full opportunity, and were enabled to open
matters to him, to the ease of their own minds."

Ninth month, 1781.—" It appearing that great spoil and havoc have been made of Friends' goods by extravagant seizures, and a prospect that sufferings may increase, whereby great distress may, in all probability, be the portion of many families, a concern now arose that we may be clear of the blood of those who execute such unrighteous laws and proceedings, and also that we may manifest a due regard to our suffering brethren; wherefore it is left with Friends of the Monthly Meetings committees, if way opens to them, to visit the collectors, in order to obtain of them a regular account of the seizures and sales of Friends' goods, the better to enable us to convince them of their wrong proceedings.* And the following

---

* Accordingly, New Garden's committee minuted the following, viz.:—

" Friends having reason to believe that several of those who are employed as collectors have, in many instances, distressed Friends farther than the law required, it is thought best, that we may be able to have a clear account of their proceedings, in order, if necessary, to lay them before their employers, that some Friends do visit them, and, on behalf of our friends, request a particular account of the demands, seizures, and sales of Friends' goods."

From the minutes which have been preserved, it appears that

Joshua Pusey, Thomas Wood, Joseph Moore, Jacob Halliday, and Thomas Millhouse,	were appointed to visit	William Thompson, Francis Williamson, and James Williamson.
William Swayne, Joel Baily,	to visit	Joseph Lucky, Ezekiel Bowen.
Isaac Jackson, Daniel Thompson,	to visit	William Whiteside.
Henry Chalfant, Isaac Pyle, Jeremiah Barnard,	to visit	David Mackey.
Joseph Moore, Joseph Richardson,	to visit	John Hindman.
Joseph Moore, Thomas Wood, Jeremiah Barnard,	to visit	Robert Nethery.

From the reports, it appears that William Whiteside promptly refused to comply with their request.

Friends are named to take the subject of visiting the commissioners, or others under authority, under their weighty consideration, and to proceed therein as best wisdom may direct."

This concern led to much arduous and faithful labor, by appointments both from the Conference and the Monthly Meetings committees. A few extracts may suffice.

Reported to Conference:—"We proceeded to Lancaster, and had a seasonable opportunity with Samuel Boyd, lately chosen commissioner, who appeared sensible of the unequal burdens and great oppression laid on Friends and some others, and, we apprehend, was disposed to be moderate in the execution of his office, and expressed a desire that our case might be stated and laid before the Assembly.

"Then proceeded to visit John Hopkins, called sub-lieutenant, and endeavored to lay the iniquity of his conduct upon him. He felt to us dark and unfeeling, yet heard us with a degree of patience. We left him much silenced. Proceeded to John Slaymakers, a commissioner, with whom we had a solid, favored sitting, and believe he was reached with a sense of Friends' distresses, and expressed uneasiness with his office, because of the difficulties it subjected him to. Through this visit we were supported with a degree of Divine strength and innocent boldness, to bear our testimony to the raising of the standard of the Prince of Peace.

"The Friends appointed to visit Joseph Strawbridge report, they have attended thereto, and three of them had a full opportunity with him to a good degree of satisfaction."

12th month, 1781.—"A consideration being now opened concerning the tendency of the oppressive laws now in force in

Francis Williamson, James Williamson, Joseph Lucky, Ezekiel Bowen, and David Mackey, all gave promise, but afterwards refused.

William Thompson presented a full account.

Concerning Robert Nethery and John Hindman, the record is not complete. The latter had promised to comply.

our country, and a desire prevailing, as at a preceding meet-
ing, that the nature and iniquity thereof might be laid before
those in legislative power, and considerable time being spent in
Friends solidly expressing their sentiments thereon; intima-
tion also being given that the Meeting for Sufferings, desire that
Friends might send up such materials as appear suitable on
the occasion; therefore, Thomas Millhouse, Joshua Pusey,
George Churchman, William Downing, William Lamborn,
James Bennet, Amos Davis, Isaac Coates, Nathan Cope,
Benjamin Hough, Joshua Brown, William Harvey, Jacob
Lindley, William Swayne, James Jackson, Joseph Brinton,
Thomas Fisher, Thomas Baldwin, and Benjamin Mason, are
appointed to meet together and confer thereon, and, as way
opens, prepare and present to that meeting what appears best;
and the committees of Monthly Meetings to furnish them with
cases or sufferings of Friends for that purpose."

" Who now report, that seven of them attended (the Meeting
for Sufferings) with the essay, which was revised, and with
Friends' attention and concern, approved by that meeting.
And said Friends were encouraged by them to present the
representation to the Assembly; where it was read, during
which there appeared an increasing solemnity among the members of that House, and was by them agreed to be further considered.

" Which appears satisfactory to this meeting, and is as
follows :

" To the General Assembly of Pennsylvania :—

" Some observations offered to the serious consideration of
those in legislative authority, by a number of the inhabitants
of Lancaster County and the western part of Chester County,
on behalf of themselves and many other peaceable sufferers,
who are restrained, by a principle of tender conscience, from
joining or contributing towards the support of warlike measures,
lest they should offend him who is the Supreme Lord of
conscience and dread of nations.

" Also, a representation, offered from a sense of duty, con-

cerning the cruel havoc and spoil of the property of many industrious people under some late laws.

"The people called Quakers, ever since they became a
religious Society, under every power, in every nation, island,
and province, where they have lived, have, as a body, been
men of peace. Nor can they act inconsistent with this character while they live up to their · principles, founded on the
doctrine and precepts of the Prince of Peace, our Lord and
Saviour, and his apostles and followers. These teach us not
to resist evil, to do violence to no man, to love our enemies, to
follow peace with all men, to seek the good of all, and to have
no fellowship with the unfruitful works of darkness. These
peaceable fruits are produced by taking heed to the manifestations of the Spirit or Grace of God, which hath appeared
unto all men, teaching and assisting those who believe in and
observe it, to live soberly, righteously, and godly, in this present world ;. to deny pride, envy, strife, with all ungodliness
and the world's lusts, from whence contention about worldly
matters, wars, and fightings proceed. This doctrine we believe
ought to have great weight with all Christians, being expressly
taught and clearly held forth in the New Testament, as absolutely needful to be observed, which we may find was also
taught and maintained by Christians of the first three hundred
years after Christ.

"Therefore, why should Christian rulers of this age seek to
suppress it, by laying grievous burdens on those who apprehend they are called, and in duty to the Almighty believe
themselves religiously bound to maintain it ? Or why should
any think it strange if this peaceable doctrine should spread
more, and even rise higher in these latter days than for many
ages past, seeing many prophecies in Scripture give us encouragement and sufficient grounds to believe that it will rise
and spread.

"And although individuals may have fallen short, yet we as
a religious body have endeavored to maintain this testimony,
through all the changes in power which have happened since
we were a people. Neither have the difficulties we have been

subjected to in these latter days of contest lessened our con-
stancy herein, nor our zeal for the advancement of this peaceable doctrine and testimony, however we may be misrepresented
by some as being obstinate, or having party views to promote.

"Now we think it necessary to inform you, that being lately
met together (near fifty persons) to consider of the circumstances of our suffering brethren, we were sensibly affected
with the accounts of increasing sufferings, which have been
remarkably felt, especially in these parts, for our adherence to
the peaceable principles before mentioned, whereby many
respectable families are, and others likely to be, much deprived
of the means of procuring the necessaries of life ; by having
their grain, horses, cattle, sheep, household goods, &c., in an
extraordinary manner wrested from them, for demands of fines
and taxes imposed by late laws, which, for the reasons aforesaid, they are conscientiously restrained from complying with.
And feeling near sympathy for all sufferers on these accounts,
and much good-will towards those who are or have been the
instruments thereof, we are concerned to lay before you, who
are in legislative authority, a representation of some striking
circumstances, which we apprehend demands your serious
attention.

" Visits having been paid by some of us in a friendly manner, to divers officers concerned in the executive part, who we
find shelter themselves under the laws now in force; and at
the same time some of them express a sense of the injustice
and unequal burdens thereby imposed. And as it is righteousness alone that exalteth a nation, oppression on those who are
under religious restraints being displeasing to the Lord, and
thereby of dangerous consequence to the well-being of any
country, ought much to be feared by those in authority, lest
they draw down his displeasure. We doubt not, but if you
seriously weigh the following propositions and representation
of matters of fact herewith presented, and bring things to
trial, by that unerring standard whereunto, sooner or later,
we shall all be brought, you may be favored to see and judge
aright.

"First. Whether laws imposing fines on those who, in obedience to the doctrine of Christ, are restrained from mustering to learn warlike exercise, or from marching out in a warlike manner, and giving liberty to hard-hearted men, officers and others, whereby the property of honest, industrious persons, at a rate double, treble, or sometimes manifold more in value than the sums demanded, are, without mercy, torn away from the proper owners, can be safely approbated and continued by a legislative body composed of members professing faith in Jesus Christ, who blessed the peacemakers, the meek, and the merciful, and at whose tribunal righteousness only will meet with approbation?

"Second. Whether laws imposing heavy taxes, which are often very unequally laid, and doubled, or in a higher proportion, on those who are religiously restrained from taking a test, or giving in returns of their estates upon affirmation, and who cannot join with or contribute towards the support of war, should continue, or can be countenanced by Christian legislators, where they pay a proper regard to equity in the sight of the Almighty, who will plead the cause of the oppressed, and render to all men, in every station, a reward according to their works?

"Third. Whether guilt is not likely to be increased on that country where laws are enforced requiring the unusual imposition of oaths, rendering such solemnities cheap and trifling, whereby weak and earthly-minded persons may be brought under temptation to swear falsely, or to make false returns to save themselves from high taxation; and their innocent neighbors, who cannot swear at all, because Christ hath forbidden it, nor take an affirmation to countenance taxation for warlike purposes, are brought under the penalties of unjust and exaggerated levies, whereby their property is rent from them, often as it were by wholesale; allowing room for collectors to become purchasers themselves of their neighbor's goods greatly under value, whilst men who would choose to act in moderation, care not to take upon them such offices under those laws?

"Other things respecting the laws above hinted at, and their
effects, might be mentioned, concerning the insolent conduct of
collectors and others under them; some of whom have rifled
houses, broken doors, &c., while sufficient property was to be had
without such measures. Likewise the bringing in pistols, and
other warlike weapons, in an imperious, hostile manner among
peaceable, tender women and innocent children, while their
husbands and fathers were absent. And this, with much other
unchristian conduct and severity, all done under color of exe-
cuting the laws, which we incline not to enlarge upon, committing our cause to the Lord, the righteous Judge; humbly
believing that where his fear prevails, equity will take place,
unrighteous laws and unequal burdens cease, and the attention of those in authority be principally given to things which
are for the promotion of peace on earth and the proper execution
of justice, for the punishment of evil-doers, and the praise of
them that do well.

"A specimen of the sufferings of Friends in parts of Chester
and Lancaster Counties in the cases following named: not
chosen as the most oppressive, but briefly to represent the
general devastation of property for non-compliance with
requisitions appertaining to war, since the beginning of last
year.

"From Samuel Cope, three horse-creatures, a
yoke of oxen, seven other cattle, fifteen sheep,
nine swine, seventy-five bushels of wheat,
twenty of corn, ten yards fine linen, a ton of
hay, &c. £126 8 6

From Abiah Taylor, six horse-creatures, nine
cattle, sixteen sheep, two swine, a feather-bed,
two casks of flour, one hundred and twenty-
five bushels wheat, and seventy of corn, rye,
and buckwheat, ... 234 1 6

From John Hoopes, Jr., four horse-creatures, a
yoke of oxen, seventeen other cattle, thirty
sheep, six swine, a watch, five sides of leather,
&c. 233 15 0

From Moses Coates, two horse-creatures, nine
cattle, four sheep, cash £5, and four and a
half cwt. of iron, ... £98 11 0
From Benjamin Hutton, a horse, nine cattle,
thirty and a half bushels corn, and bed clothing, ... 66 16 9
From William Dixon, four horse-creatures, and
six bushels of wheat, ... 101 19 0
From Thomas Millhouse, a large yoke of oxen,
ten other cattle, a mare, four sheep, eighteen
bushels oats, wearing apparel, &c. . . 96 18 0
From John Pusey, three horse-creatures, fourteen cattle, and bed clothing, . . . 100 2 6
From Moses Brinton, twenty-one cattle, fifty-
two bushels wheat, ten of rye, and seven and
a half tons of hay, ... 122 9 0
From Andrew Moore, one horse, twelve cattle,
a wagon, and other farming utensils, and
household furniture, ... 76 8 6
From John Webster, Jr., two cows, thirteen
sheep, a hog, a case of drawers, a hearse, a
cart, &c. 26 15 0
 He being a tradesman in low circumstances,
holding no land.
From Isaiah Brown, one cow, six bushels of corn
one hundred and twenty pounds of bacon, a
stack of hay, smith's bellows, &c. . . 21 6 0
 He holding about forty acres of land, and in
low circumstances.
From John Ferree, four horse-creatures, thirteen
cattle, seven and a half bushels of wheat,
twenty of clean rye, one stack of do., forty
bushels of corn, two stacks of oats, and one
of hay, ... 187 7 0
"Within one of our Monthly Meetings alone hath been
taken, since the year 1777, exclusive of the late large tax
and divers preceding demands, not yet taken account of by

us, from about one hundred and twenty families, property to
the amount of £6108 19s. 11d., rated at such prices as the
several articles would have generally sold for eight or ten
years ago, without having regard to the fluctuating prices of
later years. For instance, wheat not exceeding 6s. 6d. per
bushel, in our valuation, and other things in proportion.

"Divers of those recited are farmers having families of
small children, who live on poorish land, and, in prosperous
times, just lived reputably above want; but are, with many
others, so reduced by the conduct of collectors, under the
sanction of law, as to have no cow left, and some but one
horse, some no sheep, and greatly stripped of other utensils,
clothing, &c.

"And many of us, before we were acquainted with such
usage, had purchased plantations to live on, for which we run
considerably in debt, expecting, through the blessing of Providence on our industry, to have paid for them in a few years;
which is now rendered impracticable, by having the means
taken from us, even to a considerably greater amount than our
plantations would have rented for. Thus are an industrious
and very considerable part of the community made a spoil of,
and many likely to suffer for the necessaries of life, if a stop
is not put to such proceedings; which, in the end, certainly
will greatly affect the public, as well as themselves; for it is
not the acquisition of large tracts of uncultivated land, but the
produce of the industrious, raised by cultivation, which sup-
ports the community at large.

"Signed, on behalf and by appointment of the committee
aforesaid, the 18th of twelfth month, 1781, by

"Joshua Brown,	"Benjamin Mason,
"William Swayne,	"Joshua Pusey,
"Richard Barnard,	"Isaac Coates,
"Amos Davis,	"Samuel Cope."
"William Lamborn,	

"And as the Friends who attended the Assembly were given
to understand that they would probably be called upon to
answer to some particulars in the representation; therefore,

in order that the said Friends may be in readiness to make suitable reply, Enoch Wickersham, James Bennet, John Jackson, Thomas Wood, Hezekiah Rowles, Joseph Edmundson, Isaac Coates, Thomas Baldwin, Robert Moore, and William Downing, are appointed to endeavor to procure well-attested accounts of the particulars alluded to therein."

"The Friends continued to attend the committee of the Assembly, called a Committee on Grievances, now report: We, being notified, attended at Philadelphia, and endeavored to have an opportunity with them, though only eight waited to hear us; with whom we had a pretty full opportunity, which was in a good degree satisfactory, and left with them such further proofs of the oppressive usage mentioned in the Representation, as to us appeared necessary."

Eleventh month, 1782.—"Friends from Kennet now mention that some persons, under the present authority, have orders to require an account of the losses which the inhabitants sustained by the British army; which being considered, and a desire prevailing that all our members may be preserved from being caught in any snare, to the wounding of their minds and the reproach of our testimony, the Monthly Meetings' committees are desired to warn and caution such as they apprehend may be in danger."

Eighth month, 1785.—"Friends from Bradford mention, that of late, duplicates have been sent to a number of their members, in order to impose the office of collector of the public taxes on them, with heavy fines threatened for non-compliance therewith; the principal part of which taxes many Friends conscientiously refuse to pay, it being raised to defray the expenses of war.

"And some Friends appointed by Concord Monthly Meeting in suffering cases, also attended here with a minute, setting forth that divers of their members, residing in the township of Bradford, are subjected to the like trial; and, for refusal, are called upon to appear before the commissioners, to give reasons for their conduct therein.

"Which case, coming solidly under consideration, as a

matter that nearly affects our peaceable testimony, and deep
suffering likely to be the consequence if put in execution, it is the
sense of this meeting that some Friends be appointed, to unite
with those to whom the duplicates have been offered, to endeavor weightily to lay before those men the grounds of our
Christian testimony, and the reasons why we are conscientiously
bound to refuse a compliance therewith: wherefore, William
Harvey, Joshua Pusey, Jacob Lindley, and Benjamin Mason,
are nominated for that purpose." Who reported, "That
three of them attended to the service, and, in company with
the said Friends, had a solid opportunity with those men, and
were enabled to give such reasons as appeared to have weight
with them. They behaved respectfully to us, and appeared
moderately disposed."

Second month, 1786.—"A subject was opened by Friends
of New Garden Monthly Meeting, respecting the conduct of
Robert Smith, (called) lieutenant of the county, in collecting
or proposing to collect fines which have already been collected,
and also fines for not marching as soldiers in the year 1781,—in
which case it appears that the officers had countermanding
orders previous to the day proposed for marching. And understanding that the Executive Council of this Government, on
complaint against the said Smith, have ordered a suspension
of his proceedings until the last second-day in this month, when
he and those who have complained are to have a hearing before
them; and as we believe his, or the conduct of those he has
employed, has been rigorous and very oppressive, and what he
has in prospect unjust; and also as a door is now opened,
wherein Friends have a prospect, not only of laying the weight
of their sufferings before that body of men, but also of advancing our Christian testimony: therefore, Friends of each
Monthly Meeting are desired speedily to endeavor to collect all
such materials as are likely to answer the end proposed; and the
following Friends are appointed to select out what may be
suitable to lay before the Council, and attend therewith, viz.:
Enoch Wickersham, Moses Pennock, Jonathan Dutton, William Harvey, John Parker, Isaac Jackson, Jacob Lindley, John

Jones, Francis Wilkinson, Joseph Richardson, Caleb Swayne, Thomas Richards, Benjamin Mason, Benjamin Hough, Edward Churchman, Thomas Baldwin, Richard Barnard, Isaac Coates, and William Iddings."

1787.—" This being the last Meeting for Conference, being dissolved by the Quarterly Meeting (at their own suggestion), after near ten years' exercise for the preservation one of another in a line of conduct that would be most conducive to the advancement of our Christian testimony; and the promotion of the increase of the government of the Prince of Peace, which we believe will, in the Lord's time, abolish all the machinations of war, swallow up all wrath, and spread from the rising of the sun to the going down of the same."

In tracing this hasty sketch of the interesting labors of the Meeting for Conference, I have preferred not to break the connection, by inserting the reports of cases of suffering from the committees of the several Monthly Meetings. Those reports, after being carefully examined, corrected, and approved by the Conference, were sent to the Quarterly Meeting, and thence, through the Meeting for Sufferings, to the Yearly Meeting.

Before giving a tabular summary of said reports, I will copy a minute of Conference, and the Monthly Meeting's report upon which it is predicated, that the reader may understand the kind of material of which the summary is composed.

1782.—" At a Meeting for Conference, held at New Garden, the 2d of ninth month, 1782.

" Thomas Millhouse, on behalf of the committee appointed at last meeting, reports: That they all attended to the service, and revised and produced (according to directions) the two lists mentioned at last meeting; also one brought from Kennet and one from Sadsbury. A general account of the latter is as follows:

" From Friends of Sadsbury Monthly Meeting, for refusing to pay fines and taxes, chiefly for war purposes, was taken by George McIlvane, Thomas Kenny, Hugh Cunningham,

Alexander White, John Ross, William Steele, John Crow, Thomas Davis, William Boggs, John Powel, James Johnson, John Brisbane, Abraham Kenny, Martin Hewey, Benjamin Vernor, and others,—horses, cattle, sheep, grain, flour, hay, farming utensils, household furniture, wearing apparel, provisions, &c., amounting to £1135 18s. 7d."

"An account of the sufferings of Friends belonging to Sadsbury Monthly Meeting, occasioned by the present war:

JOHN FERREE'S ACCOUNT.

1779,	1st mo. 20.—Light-horsemen took 20 cwt. good hay,	£3	0	0
"	John McCabe, light-horse officer, took 23 bushels of oats,	2	17	6
"	3d mo. 25.—George McIlvane, constable, took for tax, 16 bushels corn,	3	4	0
1780,	7th mo. 15.—Thomas Kenny, constable, took for tax, a horse,	23	0	0
	Also one bull and one cow,	8	10	0
"	9th mo. 9.—Alexander White took for militia service, 7½ bushels wheat,	2	5	0
1781,	5th mo. 5.—Thomas Kenny, constable, took for tax 40 bushels corn,	8	0	0
"	8th month.—Said Kenny and Jacob Fouts took a man,	30	0	0
"	9th mo. 3.—Hugh Cunningham, subsheriff, by order of John Hopkins, sub-lieutenant, for a demand of £33 hard, and £3 State money, for militia fines, took 2 horses,	42	0	0

Five milk cows, and other
cattle, . . . £40 0 0
One stack of rye, com-
puted 35 bushels, and
20 bushels of clean rye, 11 0 0
One stack of oats, com-
puted 70 bushels, . 7 0 0
One stack of good hay,
computed 3 tons, . 7 10 0
1782, 1st mo. 19.—Jacob Touts sold for tax,
19 cwt. 1 qr. of flour, . 17 6 6
And 27 bushels of wheat, 8 2 0
———————
£213 15 0

JOHN M'DONALD'S ACCOUNT.

1780, 12th mo. 15.—John Ross and Joseph
Walker took for tax, one
cow, ... 5 0 0
"   3d mo. 15.—William Steele, sub-lieutenant, took for muster
fines, one great-coat, 4
yards linen, one twilled
sheet, and pair of pin-
cers, ... 2 17 6
1781, 9th mo. 7.—Said Steele took for muster fines, one sow and 4
shoats, 7 delf-plates, one
pot, one pair tongs and
a cutting-box, . . 2 10 0
———————
£ 10 7 6

JOHN TRUMAN'S ACCOUNT.

1780, 11th month.—Taken by one Pinker-
ton, $2\frac{3}{4}$ bus. wheat, per
tax, ... £0 16 6

1781, By John Crow and Thomas Davis, 3 cattle, . .	£11 10	0
" 4th mo. 9.—By do. 21 bus. wheat, for fines and tax, . .	6 6	0
" 8th mo. 27.—By William Boggs and John Daniel, for tax, 2 cattle,	7 0	0
" 10th mo. 10.—By John Crow and Joseph Evans, 2 cattle, per tax and fines, . . .	7 0	0
" 12th mo. 3.—By Davis and Boggs, 9 cattle and 11 sheep, per tax and fines, . .	42 0	0
1782, 1st month.—By do. 50 bus. corn and 20 cwt. good hay, per tax and fines, . .	12 0	0
" " By do. 20 cwt. good hay, and 32 bus. wheat, per tax and fines, . .	12 12	0
" 2d mo. 13.—By John Daniels, 8½ bus. corn, per tax and fines,	1 14	0
" " 22.—By Davis and Boggs, 45 bus. wheat, per tax and fines, . . .	13 10	0
" " " By George Boyd, 13 bus. wheat, for militia fine, .	3 18	0
	£117 6	6

WILLIAM TRUMAN'S ACCOUNT.

1781, 8th mo.—Taken by John Powell, one cow, ...	£4 0	0
" 11th mo.—By do. 1 colt, 4 head of cattle, and 16 cwt. of hay, . .	21 4	0
	£25 4	0

ISAAC TAYLOR'S ACCOUNT.

1781, 8th mo.—James Johnson, collector of tax, took one large bull and steer, used for draught. Said cattle were bought and turned home by John Hastings; and about the 13th of the tenth month, said Hastings took, in place thereof, without any direction or knowledge of the owner, 22 bus. of wheat, . £6 15 0

JAMES MOORE'S ACCOUNT.

1781, 3d mo. 21.—John Ross took for tax, 26 bus. wheat, . . . £7 16 0

" " One cow and bell, and two blankets, . . . 5 7 6

" 9th mo. 28.—Taken by Stephen Heard, for a demand of tax, 40 bus. wheat and 1 horse, 24 0 0

£37 3 6

JOHN SMITH (HEIRS OF).

1781, 1st mo. 12.—Taken by Samuel Henry, for muster fines, 1 heifer and 2 sheep, . . £4 10 0

" 6th mo. 25.—By do. for militia and muster fines, 4 loads of good hay and a steer, . . 17 0 0

" 12th mo. 7.—By John Brisbane, collector of taxes, 12 bus. wheat, threshed, and supposed 110 bus. in the sheaf; also 6 bus. of rye, threshed, and 100 in the sheaf, . . 53 16 10

One cow with calf, and 3 steers, . . .	£17	0	0
	£92	61	0

ABRAHAM GIBBON'S ACCOUNT.

1780, 12th mo. 21.—By Abraham Henry, for muster fines, 7 bus. corn in the ear, . . .	£1	4	6
1781, 11th mo. 12.—Said Henry took, for militia fines, 2 heifers,	9	0	0
" " Also 2 fat hogs, and 15 bus. corn, . . .	6	12	6
" " And one load timothy hay,	3	0	0
1782, 11th mo. 21.—By Benjamin Vernor, collector for taxes, 146 bus. wheat and 4 of rye, .	44	12	0
" 4th mo. 23.—Said Vernor, for taxes, 56 bus. wheat, . . .	16	16	0
	£81	5	0

JOSEPH DICKINSON'S ACCOUNT.

1781, 1st mo. 8.—Taken by James Johnson, collector, for a demand of tax, £8, 4 cattle, . . .	£14	0	0

JOHN MOORE'S ACCOUNT.

1781, 1st mo. 3.—John Pennel took, for fines, 1 fat bullock, . . .	£8	0	0
" " And 1 cow, and ox-chain, .	5	4	0
	£13	4	0

JAMES SMITH, SEN.'S ACCOUNT.

1781, 8th mo. 28.—John Slater took, for tax, 2 steers and 5 sheep, .	£12	0	0

1781, 12th mo. 24.—Samuel Henry, for muster
fines, hay computed at
50 cwt.,   .   .   .   £7 10 00

                                                    £19 10 00

MOSES BRINTON'S ACCOUNT.

1780, 12th mo. 8.—Martin Henry, sold for
muster fines, supposed
to be 30 cwt. of hay, .   4 10 00
1781, 4th month.—By Benjamin Vernor, for
taxes, 24 bus. of wheat
and 10 of rye, 4 cattle,
and about 6 tons of hay,   43 7 00
"   8th mo. 24.—Martin Huey, for fines, 9
tons of hay, 2 steers and
2 sheep,   .   .   .   31 00 00
"   11th mo. 21.—Said Huey, for fines, 80
bus. of rye, unthreshed,   14 13 4
And 20 bus. of threshed
rye, ...   4 00 00
Also, 3 loads of hay, 12
bus. corn, and one
large fat hog   .   .   15 9 6
1782, 1st mo. 21.—Benjamin Vernor, collector, 221½ bus. wheat, .   66 9 00

                                                    £179 8 10

ROBERT MOORE'S ACCOUNT.

1781, 3d. mo. 15.—William Steele, sub-lieutenant and Hugh Cun-
ningham, took for muster
fines, one silver dollar, .   00 7 6
"   "   21.—John Ross, collector, took
one young horse and a
bridle,   .   .   .   30 3 00

1781, 9th month.—Said Steele and Cunningham, sub-sheriff, for mi-
litia fines, 4 milk cows,
2 young cattle, and a
Dutch fan, . . . £23 15 00
Also, 67 dozens of wheat
in the sheaf, supposed
54 bush., and 54 dozens
rye in the sheaf, sup-
posed 45 bush., . . 25 4 00
                              ―――――――
                              £79 9 6

ANDREW (SON OF LYDIA) MOORE'S ACCOUNT.

1780, 11th mo. 17.—John Crow and Thomas
Davis took a colt, . 10 00 00
1781, 6th mo. 25.—Said Crow and William
Irwin took 5½ yds. of
cloth, and 3 ewes with
their lambs, for tax and
muster fines, . . 4 1 6
1782, 1st mo. 14.—Thomas Davis, 9 cattle and
1 cow, . . . 23 00 00
And 10 flour casks, . . 1 00 00
                              ―――――――
                              £38 1 6

JOSEPH GEST'S ACCOUNT.

1781, 3d mo. 16.—William Steele and Hugh
Cunningham took in
money, for muster fine, 1 10 00
Said money was got by
picking a lock.
"   "   21.—John Ross, a quantity of
bees-wax, a flitch of
bacon, 6 lbs. of hackled
flax, near 6 yds. of linen,
a smoothing iron, a pair

of saddle-bags, pair of
steelyards, a calfskin,
and one bag, . . £6 17 5
1781, 9th mo. 28.—Stephen Heard, collector,
for tax, a wagon, . 10 00 00
1782, 1st mo. 31.—Stephen Heard, 6 head of
cattle and 2 sheep, . 25 00 00
———————
£43 7 5

BENJAMIN HOAR'S ACCOUNT.

1781, 8th mo. 31.—James Johnson, collector,
took for tax, 4 cattle, £9 00 00

ANDREW MOORE, SEN.'S ACCOUNT.

1781, 3d mo. 15.—William Steele and Hugh
Cunningham took, for
muster fines, 7 yds. of
linen, ... 1 1 00
"   4th mo.   2.—John Ross, collector, took
for tax, a wagon, a pew-
ter dish, and 6 plates, . 11 00 00
Also, chains and back-
band, one table and one
kettle, . . . 3 2 0
"   9th mo.   6.—Said Steele and Cunningham, for fines, a Dutch
fan, milk cow, 5 young
cattle, 2 loads of hay, 11
sheep, a horse and bridle, 44 1 6
———————
£59 4 6
For a demand of £22 4s.

JOHN MOORE MILLER'S ACCOUNT.

1780, 11th mo. 14.—John Crow and Thomas Davis, collectors of taxes, 3 cattle, . .	£9	0 0
1781, 3d mo., 4.—Said Crow took one mare,	27	0 0
	£36	0 0

GEORGE COOPER'S ACCOUNT.

1781, 1st mo. 3.—William Steel and John Pennel took, for fines, a horse, . . .	10	0 0
Horse gears, swingle-trees, and a bag, .	1	9 0
1781, 1st mo. 5.—A watch, . . .	7	10 0
10th mo. 12.—John Ross, collector, took, for tax, one saddle, a pair of spatter-dashes, 1 chair, 1 candlestick,	3	0 6
Stephen Heard took, for tax, 2 saddles, . .	4	15 0
1782, 2d mo. 8.—He also took one heifer, Dutch fan, . . .	6	10 0
1 sleigh, 3 hogs, 2 good collars, . . .	4	15 0
4 sheep, one cart-bed and shafts, well ironed,	4	0 0
	£41	19 6

JOHN COOPE'S ACCOUNT.

1781, 10th mo. 30.—William Cowen, collector of militia fines, forced open several locks near the middle of the night, and took, in gold and silver, . . .	£18	0 0

Amount, £1135   8   7

" Read in Sadsbury Monthly Meeting, held the 17th of the seventh month, 1782, and signed on behalf of the same, by

" ISAAC TAYLOR."

The above is a fair specimen of the materials from which the following summary is constructed, and shows the practical working of cruel and unjust laws, when administered by more cruel and unjust men.

A Summary of Sufferings, as reported to the Conference by the Committees of the several Monthly Meetings, during a period of eight years.

N. B.—Some committees were not prompt in reporting; hence the dates prefixed can only indicate the time when the reports were received. The sums have been reduced from pounds to dollars, as nearly as could be done in round numbers.

Year.	Kennet M. M.	New Garden M. M.	Notting-ham M. M.	Brad-ford M. M.	Sads-bury M M.	Deer Creek M. M.	Duck Creek M. M.	Total.
1779	1552	1394	509	1984		139	314	5892
1780	770	2301	563	1704		213	229	5780
1781	3768	*9130	1291	2560	2419		681	19,849
1782	3471	6472	1085	3685	3029	514		18,256
1783	1157	2944		1373				5474
1784		1936			1261			3197
1785	600	944	379	853			4242	7018
1786	594	837		1772				3203
	$ 11,912	25,958	3827	13,931	6709	866	5466	68,669

Through all this fiery dispensation, Friends continued to place their dependence upon the Divine Arm, believing that if they abode patiently under their sufferings, it would be overruled for good in the councils of Eternal Wisdom.   In

* " Friends from the Monthly Meetings which produced the above accounts, gave some account of the situation of their members, respecting their testimony against military requisitions; from which it appears that a good degree of faithfulness is maintained by much the greater number, though some weakness and some failures were found."—(Minute of Conference.)

laboring with the legislative and executive authorities, in order
to influence them to juster and more lenient measures, they
believed, with Solomon, that though they should cast their bread
upon the waters, it would be found after many days:—so it
appears to have been found in the measure alluded to in the
following extract:—

1789.—"This meeting being informed that the Commissioners within the Province have the power invested in them,
by the late Assembly, to inspect, consider, and determine all
cases respecting military fines imposed before the year 1788,
and have advertised in order to meet and hold an appeal for
all that might think themselves aggrieved thereby; and this
meeting—taking the subject-matter into consideration, believing that Truth's testimony may be affected thereby—appoints
James Bennet, James Jackson, Samuel Nicholls, Christopher
Hollingsworth, Samuel Harlan, Jonathan Graves, Thomas
Chandler, William Harvey, Enoch Wickersham, and Robert
Lamborn, to attend thereto, as they may be enabled."—(Kennet Monthly Meeting.)

The following act of Assembly, which is referred to in the
above minute, was unmistakably passed in consequence of the
cogent appeals which were made by Friends for the meliora-
tion of their condition.

"An Act to establish a Board of Appeal within the several
    Counties of this State, and to grant Exonerations in cases
    of Militia Fines. Passed March 27th, 1789.

" Whereas, it hath been represented that gross abuses have
been committed in the levying and collecting of militia fines,
whereby many individuals, as well as families, have been
greatly aggrieved and oppressed; and as such abuses may
still be continued, unless better provision than now subsists be
made for the hearing of appeals and granting exonerations,—

" Sect. 2. Be it therefore enacted, and it is hereby enacted
by the Representatives of the freemen of Pennsylvania in

General Assembly met, and by the authority of the same, that within each of the counties of this State, there shall be constituted and established, and there is hereby constituted and established, a Board, consisting of the Commissioners of the several counties in this State, who, or any two of them, shall have power to receive all appeals from persons charged in the several counties with militia fines, who may consider themselves aggrieved thereby; and also to receive the applications of such persons so charged, who may pray relief on account of peculiar hardships or inability; and the said Board shall have full power and authority to determine on such appeals and applications, and to give relief and grant exonerations, according to their judgment and discretion, and as justice and humanity may require; and shall also give certificates of such relief or exonerations, which shall be available to the appellants against the payment of the amounts to the collecting officers."

Sorrowful must be the condition of any people where the laws afford neither personal protection nor security for the possession of property, but where the mansion of the opulent, the domicil of the artizan, and the cottage of the laborer, may be entered at any hour and rifled of its choicest contents; where even the bed beneath him, the coat he wears, the provisions in store for his subsistence, the tools of his trade, and the means of tilling his land, may be rudely torn from him. Such was the situation of Friends at this period. Their peaceable, non-resisting principles, no doubt, gave greater license to unprincipled plunderers; but by yielding obedience to the manifested will of the Divine Master, they were wonderfully sustained; and though often despoiled of much of this world's goods, they were marvellously blessed in basket and in store, affording a singular contrast with the condition of those who had been their persecutors. They could indeed say with the Psalmist, "I have been young, and now am old; yet have I not seen the righteous forsaken, nor his seed begging bread."

Placing their dependence for protection on the arm of Omnipotent Power, they believed it their duty patiently to suffer whatever afflictions might be permitted to come upon them, until that arm should be extended for their deliverance; which they have often signally experienced, and have great cause to be thankful for.

The sufferings which Friends have endured for the maintenance of religious liberty and the rights of conscience, have long been matter of history;—a history little read, and still less understood.

People do not sufficiently estimate the price which has been paid for the civil and religious liberty which they enjoy. It must be conceded that Friends have contributed very largely of their substance, by their personal sufferings, and even with their lives, to the attainment of this important end. If George Fox had not asserted religious liberty and the rights of conscience to be paramount to all human laws; if innocent women had not been scourged at the cart-tail through the streets of Boston; if Laurence Southwick and his sons had not suffered their ears to be cut off; if William Robinson, Marmaduke Stephenson, William Ledra, and Mary Dyer, had not sealed their testimony for the Truth with their blood on Boston Common; and if William Penn had not published his frame of government of Pennsylvania, we have little reason to suppose that Thomas Jefferson would ever have written the celebrated Declaration of Independence.

It may even be worthy of serious consideration, how far the result of the struggle for American Independence was achieved by the arms of the warrior, and how far by the humble dependence and hopeful looking unto God for preservation, by those who could in nowise seek to obtain it by force, but whose constant prayer was, "Spare thy people, O Lord, and give not thine heritage to reproach."

It is impossible for us at this distance of time to appreciate the degree of intolerance and sectarian bigotry which prevailed among the Puritan fathers of the Massachusetts Colony. "Not only the Episcopalians (says Bowden), but Roger Williams and his party, as well as the Antinomians and the Baptists, had severally suffered themselves to be driven as exiles from the country. The antichristian legislation of the ruling sect had triumphed over all opposition, and it was not until it joined issue with Quakerism, that it had to contend with principles more potent than its own. On the Society of Friends devolved the noble work of contending successfully against the exclusive principles of sectarian legislation in New England, and of ecclesiastical tyranny in North America."

But it should be remembered, that it was not the people of New England who so cruelly imprisoned, and whipped and hanged the holy messengers of God's love, whom he was pleased to send among them. The civil authorities, urged on by their ecclesiastical leaders, did this. The popular feeling was outraged by their inhumanity, and in many instances restrained their murderous intentions.

CHAPTER XXXIII.

CONCLUSION.

In bringing this retrospective view of a large and interesting portion of the religious Society of Friends to a conclusion, it would be instructive to compare the present with the past, and from thence to deduce the prospective future. Many circumstances, however, render such a comparison difficult and uncertain.

1. The constitution of the Society has greatly changed. *Then*, it was largely composed of new converts, who had been brought under deep conviction, and who were urged by the strong impulse of religious duty to maintain and promulgate the Christian principles which they had espoused. *Now*, it is mainly composed of birthright members, a considerable portion

of whom, while they belong to the household of faith, have never embraced, from conviction, its principles and testimonies. They are Friends by education and habit, rather than from any strong pervading sense of religious duty.

2. The internal regulations of the Society have changed. *Then*, none but the elder, the religiously concerned, the sober-minded, those whose life and conversation were conformable to the principles which they professed, were permitted to attend Meetings for Discipline. *Now*, all the members are admitted to equal privileges in such meetings.

3. The external relations of the Society have changed. *Then*, Friends were a despised and rejected people, cruelly persecuted, and in a measure cut off from social communion with the surrounding world. *Now*, they daily mingle with, and are courted by those who once despised and persecuted them. *Then*, the Christian advices which were issued, and the disciplinary rules which were enacted, were indicative of the state of that privileged class only who then attended the meetings of business. *Now*, the young and inexperienced, and those who have never submitted to the regulating influence of the cross of Christ, attend our Meetings of Discipline, and partake in their deliberations.

There is hardly another equally large body of people in existence, who could thus assemble day after day, to deliberate upon its own concerns, without any acknowledged visible head or moderator, and preserve so much order and decorum as a Yearly Meeting of Friends. How is this accomplished? Simply by obedience to the command of Jesus Christ to his disciples, and through them to all succeeding generations: "Tarry ye in the city of Jerusalem, until ye be endued with power from on high." This is the only power which can subdue the boisterous passions and control the selfish feelings of man's nature. It is the ark of our testimony, the anchor of our hopes, the foundation of our faith, the rock of our salvation, and will lead all those who rely upon it for direction and safety, in the way of holiness, of which it is declared, that " Wayfaring men, though fools, shall not err therein."

It has been shown that the past and present states of our religious Society exhibit different views, and therefore lead to uncertain conclusions. We compare the lives and sentiments of a select few of the former with the masses of the latter. To avoid the error which this would lead to, we must turn to the criminal records of Society, to the proceedings of Monthly Meetings in the treatment of offenders, and by their reflected light inquire what disorders then prevailed, before we can judge of the moral and religious condition of the members, in a collective capacity. This is the most reliable means we possess, and, if I am not greatly mistaken, will lead to the conclusion that the existing condition of the Society is far in advance of what it was three half centuries ago. This is especially true, as regards the observance of the moral obligations and restraints.

The practice of holding slaves, and the habitual use of intoxicating drinks, were then prevalent. The possession of arbitrary power in the one case, and the intemperance inseparable from the other, in connection with the low standard of moral and social order then generally prevalent, must have introduced many disorders into the Society. Hence we find drunkenness, quarrelling, and fighting, and even the grosser immoralities, to have been of frequent occurrence, and which compare unfavorably even with the more refined sensualities of modern times.

The constitution of the religious Society of Friends, like that of the civil Government under which we live, is republican, and we must ever remember that virtue and intelligence can alone preserve either, upon this basis. If our Society adheres to that vital and fundamental principle which first gathered it, it will go on to extend the sphere of its usefulness and to enlarge its borders; if not, it will sooner or later sink into merited oblivion, to be succeeded by such other organizations, which God in his infinite wisdom may see meet to raise up as a means of carrying on his work in the earth.

I will close with the admonitory and encouraging language of the Evangelist:

"To the angel of the church that is in Philadelphia, write:

These things saith He that is holy, He that is true, He that hath the key of David, He that openeth and no man can shut, and shutteth and no man can open. I know thy works. Behold I have set before thee an open door, and no man can shut it; for thou hast a little strength, and hast kept my word, and hast not denied my name. Behold I will make them of the synagogue of Satan, which say they are Jews and are not, but do lie. Behold I will make them come and worship before thy feet, and to know that I have loved thee. Because thou hast kept the word of my patience, I also will keep thee from the hour of temptation, which shall come upon all the world, to try them that dwell upon the earth. Behold I come quickly. Hold fast that which thou hast, that no man take thy crown. Him that overcometh will I make a pillar in the temple of my God, and he shall go no more out; and I will write upon him the name of my God, and the name of the city of my God, which is New Jerusalem, which cometh down out of heaven from my God; and I will write upon him my new name."

APPENDIX.

THE NICHOLITES.

THE similarity in sentiment and practice, between this interesting people and Friends, their close proximity and social intercourse, and especially their ultimate assimilation and union, renders an extended notice of the rise and progress of the Nicholites, proper in this connection; but, after much inquiry, I have been able to obtain only a very few authentic records to aid in the construction of their history. Most of the information within my reach is of a traditionary character. In only a very few instances have I been able to determine dates.

A hundred years ago there lived in Kent County, Delaware, a young man named Joseph Nichols. Though uneducated, he very early evinced a mind of considerable activity and strength, alike potent for good or for evil. The natural vivacity of his disposition, a peculiar talent for affording amusement, in common parlance, for making fun, was well-nigh proving the ruin of himself and many of his jovial companions. On first-days, and other times of leisure, his company was much sought after by many of his cotemporaries, and their time wasted with trifling and frivolous amusements. This continued for a season, until God, in his mercy, saw fit to overrule it for good.

Joseph Nichols was sometimes met in a narrow way, and made to feel that he was born for a higher and nobler purpose than he had yet fulfilled, and that he ought, with all sobriety, to seek more rational and enduring pleasures than those which he had been pursuing. The exercise of his genius had given him an almost unlimited control over his companions, and qualified him to become their leader. Hence, when they assembled, he now began to turn their thoughts to subjects more in unison with his own changed feelings. Sometimes he would propose the reading of a passage from the Scriptures, at others he would lead them into serious and rational discourse.

Having yet more experienced the operation of the spirit of truth to open his understanding, and to lead him in the path wherein he should walk, he was gradually brought to see with clearness the line of duty which was marked out for him to pursue, and that his own peace of mind required that he should yield an unreserved obedience thereto, regardless of the opinions and the customs of others.

Joseph Nichols's juvenile companions appear not to have forsaken him in his more serious moments; but as he became more circumspect in life and conversation, they became so too. In conduct and appearance, he must now have contrasted strangely with his earlier years. He felt himself called upon to appear among them as a minister. His early reputation, but more the fervency of his zeal and his heart-searching appeals, soon occasioned his meetings to be largely attended; many became convinced, and very early embraced his views, and conformed their lives to the principles which he inculcated.

He taught his followers that all the passions and propensities of man's nature which, by indulgence, would lead to anything but good-will to our fellow-men, and which would prompt to a manner of living which would not come up to the golden rule of doing to others as we would have them do unto us, should be subdued; that everything which had a tendency to exalt the creature, or was at variance with the principle which he had laid down, must be regulated thereby, and be brought into subjection thereto. A strict adherence to these views, led him and his followers into great singularities, which less scrupulous and conscientious persons might think bordered on extravagancies.

As a sect, they soon acquired the name of Nicholites, from their leader; but in the records which we have seen, they style themselves " Friends, or New Quakers." As they were brought more and more into obedience to their acknowledged leader and director, Christ, they were successively led to bear a firm and unwavering testimony against war and all warlike measures, profane and even judicial swearing, the holding of their fellow-men in bondage, and against all superfluity and extravagance in dress, furniture, and address, and against a man-made and hireling ministry. In maintaining these testimonies, they sometimes suffered persecution, distraints of property, and imprisonment.

Among the sufferers was William Dawson, who endured a long imprisonment for his testimony against a hireling ministry; which, as is usual in such cases, tended to promote inquiry and to advance the cause of Truth.

William Dawson and James Harris were also among the foremost to set an example of justice to those of the African race whom they held in bondage, by setting them free,—alike regardless of the discouragements thrown in their way by the laws and by those who administered them:—being an act of conscientious duty, they did not hesitate to perform it. This humane testimony soon spread, and became incorporated in their discipline, so that even to hire a slave was made a disownable offence. James Horney even refused to partake of the hospitality of slaveholders, being unwilling to participate in using the produce obtained by their unrequited labor.

Forbidden by their principles to acknowledge a man-made ministry under any circumstances, they could not consistently consummate their marriages before a priest, although required so to do by the laws. They, therefore, applied for and obtained an act of toleration from the State of Maryland, allowing the "Nicholites or New Quakers" to marry among themselves, and also allowing them to take an affirmation instead of an oath.

The mind is often led by unseen influences, and in a way contrary to its inclinations. Tradition tells of some of their females who, on becoming convinced of the Truth, felt that it would be right for them to dispense with their personal ornaments, but whose husbands were unwilling to allow them to do so. Unable to prevail upon them to wear what they felt to be forbidden to them, their husbands at length accompanied them to their meeting, hoping there to turn their plainness into

ridicule; but, so far from effecting their purpose, these men
themselves became convinced of the same Truth as their wives
had been, and united with them in the support of it.

Joseph Nichols, the founder of this little band of "Friends,"
—for such was the appellation they familiarly gave themselves,—
did not live to complete the organization of his Church. He
was a man who adorned his profession by a consistent life, in
all sincerity practising the Christian virtues which he taught,
and thereby rendering his whole conduct a becoming example
to his flock. To the poor, he was kind and generous almost
to a fault. It is reported of him, that he once took off his coat
and gave it to a poor slave who came to meeting without one:
thus literally and practically fulfilling the injunction, "He
that hath two coats, let him impart to him that hath none."
It is further stated, that he divided the last toll-dish of grain
with a poor man who came to his mill for bread. Though removed from his labors at an early period, yet he had sown the
seed of life in ground prepared by the great Husbandman of
Souls, and it grew and flourished.

As the Society of Nicholites became organized, and their
numbers increased, grounds were purchased and meeting-
houses erected at Northwest Fork, Centre, and Tuckahoe
Neck, all in Caroline County, Maryland, where they principally resided. Meetings were regularly held in these houses
on first-days and in the middle of the week; where it was
their practice to sit down and wait in silence for the Divine
principle to strengthen and direct their spirits,—without which
they did not believe that any religious service could be performed, which would be acceptable to Him whom they professed to worship.

They also held Meetings for Discipline once a month (much
after the manner of Friends); but, as they had no higher
organization than those meetings, they do not appear to have
established a detailed system of Discipline; leaving each
meeting to determine its own proceedings. We however find
among the scanty records before us, the subjoined interesting
paper, which may contain all the written Discipline which they
possessed:—

" On the first day of the first month, 1793, the following was considered and adopted for Rules of Meeting among us of the Society of People called Nicholites, or New Quakers, viz.:—

" 1. That all marriage certificates be recorded; births and deaths also.

" 2. Any member joining in marriage with one that is not a member of our Society, do thereby forfeit their right among Friends; or allowing such marriage in their house, do also forfeit their right among Friends.

" 3. Any member attending such marriages, shall be called to give a reason for their conduct in that respect.

" 4. Any member intending to marry, shall first inform the Elders of the meeting to which they belong, and if no objection, then the same to be minuted, that a necessary inquiry may be made of the clearness of the parties from others, and consent of parents, or any other necessary inquiry may be made; and if nothing to the contrary appears by the next Monthly Meeting, the parties to be left to their liberty, to twice publish their intentions, and if no objection comes forward they may consummate their marriage, according to the good order practised among Friends.

" 5. Two or three Friends of good repute, to be chosen as Overseers of each Monthly Meeting, and to render an account of their service and duties to the said meeting whensoever called thereto.

" 6. Those that neglect to attend meetings for worship and discipline at the hour appointed, or fall asleep, or frequently go in and out, or otherwise disturb the meeting, let them be cautioned privately, and then, if need be, reprove them publicly, and if they cannot be reclaimed by Christian endeavors of their friends, to be disowned.

"7. Any Friend moving from the limits of one meeting to another, they shall procure a certificate from the meeting to which they belonged, that they may be received as they are.

" 8. When any Friend of the ministry proposes to travel in that service, they should first acquaint the Monthly Meeting where they belong, in order for their brotherly advice from the meeting.

" 9. The members of the meeting only, have a right to sit in

27

meetings for business, except on application and an admittance by the said meeting.

"10. Any Friend having anything to offer in meetings of business, should stand up, the better to preserve the good order of one speaking at a time.

"11. Any person holding a slave, is not to be admitted to be a member.

"12. No member shall go to law with a member, except some urgent necessity; nor with others until first endeavoring, by easy terms, offering to have the same settled by others."

These rules are recorded in a book containing a record of about sixty marriage certificates, occurring from 1766 to 1800, which opens with the following minute :—

"Agreed by a meeting of Friends, assembled together on the fifth day of the twelfth month, Anno Domini, 1774, 'to consider of some things relating to the general benefit of the Church of Christ.'

"The aforesaid assembly did then agree to hold their Monthly Meeting at the house of James Harris, the first and second day of the first week in every month, viz. :—

"The first day for the worship of God; the second day to consider of such business as may concern us, as touching our religious Society. The aforesaid assembly did then conclude, by the consent and approbation of many more brethren, that Friends should carefully collect their marriage certificates, and bring them to the said meeting, in order to have them entered upon record.

"Signed in behalf of the Society by us,

"WILLIAM DAWSON,	"WILLIAM WARREN,
"WILLIAM BATCHLOR,	"JAMES ANDERSON,
"WILLIAM HARRIS,	"RICHARD ACCLES,
"THOMAS STANTON,	"JOHN RICHARDSON,
"NOBLE COVEY,	"JAMES HORNEY,
"ROBERT BISHOP,	"JOSHUA CHILCUTT,
"JAMES HARRIS,	"WILLIAM BERRY,
"ANN ANDERSON,	"MARY HARRIS,
"ANN ACCLES."	

In a second book, containing a record of near four hundred births, is a minute precisely similar to the foregoing, except that the words "children's ages" are substituted for "marriage certificates."

Up to the year 1778, marriages appear to have been consummated "in a public congregation of people," at a Friend's house; whether at the time and place of holding their monthly or other regular meetings does not appear. From the period last named, they were mostly accomplished at Friends' meeting-house in Caroline County;" and not till 1785 do we find, "at Friends' meeting-house in Northwest Fork." In 1784, mention is made the same way, of the meeting-houses at Centre, and at Tuckahoe Neck.

From all which, I conclude that they held one Monthly Meeting (and that at Northwest Fork, after 1778), until, by the increase and spread of their members, two other meeting-houses were built, and Monthly Meetings established therein, about 1784.

At this period their Monthly Meetings usually held three days. First, on seventh-day was held a meeting of the ministers and elders in the morning, then a public meeting, and after that their Society concerns were transacted, select, the men and women sitting together. On first-day, and also on second-day following, public meetings were held, at which there were often supposed to be near one thousand people." Their manner of conducting business in their Monthly Meetings was much the same as that of Friends;—such as reading and answering queries, receiving members, ordering marriages, and treating with offenders.

Certificate of marriage :

"These may certify all whom it may concern, that Jacob Wright and Rhoda Harris, both single persons, of Caroline County, and State of Maryland, having first publicly made known their intentions of marriage, and no lawful objection being made, they, the said Jacob Wright and Rhoda Harris,

did, on the fifth day of the twelfth month, seventeen hundred
and eighty-nine, in a public congregation at Friends' meeting-
house in the county aforesaid, acknowledge their marriage engagements, one to the other,—the man taking the woman to be
his lawful wedded wife, the woman taking the man to be her
lawful wedded husband ; in consequence of which, the woman
hereafter assumes the sirname of the man. In testimony of
which we, the subscribers, being present, have hereunto subscribed our names, the day and year aforesaid.

" JACOB WRIGHT,
" RHODA WRIGHT."

(And fourteen witnesses.)

The above is the common form. I will insert another, not
so much, however, for its novelty, as because it is characteristic of the simplicity, integrity, and impartiality of this
people :—

"Be it remembered, and hereby certified, that Isaac Linager
did, on the 16th day of the fourth month, Anno Domini 1769,
in the presence of a public congregation of people at the
house of Mary Caldwell, after our manner, take a certain
woman to wife, named Rosanna (who was formerly held as a
slave by Daniel Adams, of Dorchester County, in Maryland,
deceased, which said Adams did, in his lifetime, discharge the
said Rosanna from her slavery and bondage). In consequence
of which, the said woman hereafter assumes the name of the
man. In testimony whereof, we, the subscribers, being present,
have hereunto subscribed our names.

" ISAAC LINAGER,
her
" ROSANNA ✕ LINAGER."
mark

(And thirteen witnesses.)

It may not be improper to add in this place the signatures

to another certificate, in 1775, tending to exhibit the low state
of school instruction among them :—

NOBLE COVEY,

her

MARY ✕ COVEY,

mark

his

JOSHUA ✕ CRAMER,   DANIEL SULLIVAN,

mark

his

JOSEPH ✕ OSTEN,   ISAAC CHARLES,

mark

his   his

THOMAS ✕ WILLIS,   WILLIAM ✕ BATCHELDER,

mark   mark

his   his

WILLIAM ✕ BERRY,   ELIJAH ✕ RUSSELL,

mark   mark

JAMES HARRIS,   WILLIAM HARRIS,

her

JAMES HORNEY,   RHODA ✕ COVEY.

mark

It may be that an all-wise Providence sometimes sees proper
to lead those who are called to be reformers, into extremes, in
order that the folly of their opposites may be made more manifest
thereby. Be this as it may, the strong contrast is often exhibited in that manner. So with the Nicholites. Their zeal
for plainness was so great as not to allow them the pleasure
of cultivating flowers, merely for ornament; nor to wear striped,
nor flowered, nor colored stuffs in their garments, not even the
wool from black sheep. They seem to have imbibed a horror
for color. Hence their clothing was generally of the natural
white of wool, flax, and cotton, even to the exclusion of black
shoes. This cherished aversion to color was doubtless believed
by them to be a testimony for Truth, and they will receive
the reward due to their faithfulness; yet it is dangerous to
depend too much upon the outside observance of forms and
ceremonies, and thereby fail to realize the substance of true
religion in the soul.

I will close this narrative with a brief history of the conclusion of this interesting, but ephemeral sect, and its amalgamation with Friends.

The great similarity which existed between Friends and the Nicholites, in regard to religious doctrines, disciplinary regulations, and social customs, was obvious to all, and to none more than themselves. They were, indeed, a unit in the great and fundamental principle of their faith,—the manifestation of the spirit which is given to every man,—hence it is not strange that they should instinctively incline to each other; and such was the fact.

James Harris, a worthy and influential minister among them, was deeply interested and labored for years to effect a union with Friends. The proposition was repeatedly considered in their meetings, but still there were some who could not unite. The number of the latter having become small, they proposed that such as were prepared to join with Friends had better do so, which might prove a benefit to those who remained, by leading them into a closer examination of their own situation. A minute was accordingly made, and a committee appointed to lay their application for admission before Friends, as follows:—

" To the Members of Thirdhaven Monthly Meeting, to be held the 12th of the tenth month, 1797 :

"We, the people called Nicholites, herein present to your view and serious consideration the names of those that incline to unite with you in membership [here follow one hundred and six names].

" Given forth from Centre Monthly Meeting of the people called Nicholites, held the 30th day of the ninth month, 1797.

" SETH HILL EVITTS,

"*Clerk.*"

The foregoing minute has been published as official, but it does not seem to convey the wishes of the applicants very clearly, and may not be a correct copy, especially as I find a different one on a loose sheet in one of the record books, which seems to be official; I give it also, and regret not having full copies from the records of Thirdhaven Monthly Meeting:—

"To the Friends and Members of Thirdhaven Meeting:

"Whereas, a part, and perhaps the greater part, of the people in session, called Nicholites, have had a concern, at sundry times, to be united with the people called Quakers, believing it might be a benefit to us, and, we trust, no hurt to them, and perhaps more generally useful to others; and under this apprehension and prospect of good being done, we have believed it to be our duty to inform you of the desire we have to be one with you, truly united to the Head of [the] True Church, and one to another; so have proceeded to enrol the names of those who desire the unity proposed should be brought about. The next larger number is those that see not their way into the matter, but are not inclined to oppose it. We have also sent forward the names of those that have a birthright only who unite with the matter.

"Given forth from Centre Monthly Meeting, held the 5th of the eighth month, 1797, and signed on behalf of the same, by

"SETH HILL EVITTS,
"*Clerk.*"

Then follow the three lists mentioned above.

First, one of eighty names, "all of which is agreed to the aforesaid proposal." Next, one of twenty names, marked "neuter;" and one of twelve names, marked "nominal."

The first list is headed by James Harris.

The foregoing paper was laid before Marshy Creek Preparative Meeting by two of their number, and forwarded thence to the Monthly Meeting of Thirdhaven, as directed.

"Which paper and names being read in the Monthly Meeting, and some time spent in the consideration thereof, the meeting agreed on appointing a committee to take an opportunity with them in a collective capacity, and treat the matter with them as way may open, as to the grounds of their request, and report of their situation and state of unity in regard thereof to our next meeting, viz. : James Fairbanks, William Atkinson, Tristram Needles, Levin Wright, John Bowers, James Edmundson, John Register, Solomon Neal, Joseph Neal, Samuel Troth, William Needles, Robert Moore, and Batchelor Cheever."

The committee visited them in their meetings, and reported to the next Monthly Meeting, when the case was referred to the Quarterly Meeting for its advice. That meeting recommended that they should be visited individually or by families, which appears to have been done. The committee reported in favor of receiving the larger number of the applicants, who, with their children, amounted to about four hundred. Many of those who were not accepted expressed their willingness to be left for the present.

Here was a voluntary and harmonious division of a religious society, as rare as it is instructive. The sequel will show that there was no feeling of animosity, no criminations and recriminations, no contest about property, which so often occur to the great disgrace of religious society.

A separation was arranged, but they were not yet ready to carry it into effect. There appears to have been some troublesome and unruly spirits among them, who were under dealing at the time, and those who were to remain, began to apprehend that their greatly reduced numbers might not have sufficient religious weight to finish that service properly, and requested their seceding brethren to stay with them and lend them the aid of their spirits till this work was accomplished, which was cheerfully granted.

Those who had thus voluntarily relinquished their right of membership with their former brethren, in order to join Friends, supposed that they had forfeited all claim to a further use and occupancy of their meeting-houses ; but their brethren thought otherwise, and desired that they would continue to meet together as heretofore, in their meetings for worship, only that Friends should change the times of holding their Meetings for Discipline, so as to avoid interference. This was cheerfully complied with. Oh! the happy feeling, "Let there be no strife, I pray thee, between me and thee, and between my herdmen and thy herdmen, for we be brethren."

In 1800, Friends established a Monthly Meeting at Northwest Fork; and as the fear of the remaining Nicholites, respecting the deterioration of their brethren who joined with Friends, had not been realized, the most of them soon after followed their example, and were received into Northwest Fork Monthly Meeting. It appears, however, that those living at Northwest Fork Meeting made earlier application than those living at the Centre Meeting, as the following minutes show. Of the transfer of Tuckahoe Neck we have no account.

"We, the people called Nicholites or New Quakers, do hereby constitute and appoint James Wright and William Williams, to sell and make over all our right and title of, in, and unto, our meeting-house at Northwest Fork, called Northwest Fork Meeting-house, to any of the people called Quakers, on such conditions that they will repay them their money they raised toward building the said meeting-house, if required, and on such terms as our Friends aforesaid and they may agree.

"Given forth from our Northwest Fork Monthly Meeting, held the seventeenth day of the eighth month, 1799. And signed in and on behalf of the same, by

"ELIJAH CREMEEN,
"Clerk.

"And make a return to the next Monthly Meeting at Centre Meeting-house, of their care and conduct in this matter. And the return is, they have sold it and made over all our right and title thereof."

A similar minute is recorded, appointing Azal Stevens and Beauchamp Starron, for the like purpose (except that there is no provision for the payment of any money), for Centre Monthly Meeting, dated the 31st of the twelfth month, 1803, and signed by the same Friend as clerk.

By this transfer of property the title only was changed, the use thereof remained the same, and so continues to the present time.

Happy would it be if other kindred sects would profit by this example,—cease from their bickerings and animosities, and unite in promoting the spread of the Redeemer's kingdom in the earth.

INDEX.

www.ingramcontent.com/pod-product-compliance
Lightning Source LLC
Chambersburg PA
CBHW031820270326
41932CB00008B/488